SHADOWS ON THE GREEN

Golf's Scandals, Tragedies, Triumphs, and Offbeat Tales

Lyle Slovick

SHADOWS ON THE GREEN: *Golf's Scandals, Tragedies, Triumphs, and Offbeat Tales*

Published by Lulu Press, Inc.
627 Davis Drive, Suite 300, Morrisville, NC 27560
www.lulu.com

Printed in the United States of America

For dear Isis,
my former professors Art Martinson, Phil Nordquist, Dick Jobst,
James O. Horton, and Edward D. Berkowitz.
And with everlasting love, to the memory of my mother and father,
Helen and Bud Slovick, and my sisters Lynda and Dena.

Contents

Preface

My dear late mother used to say that life belongs to the living, but I also think it's useful at times to consider those who came before. This is a book about the amazing lives of people who happened to play golf. Not the "great" men and women of the game known to all, but those who reside in the shadows of our collective memory.

Most people live life without much genuine consideration for history, which they see as abstract – a subject taught in school and never to be remembered beyond one's teenage years. But it *is* people. We are all a part of it, whether we know it or not, whether we like it or not. For me, my interest in history began in grade school, listening to my teacher read to us from Laura Ingalls Wilder's *Little House* books. The vibrant pictures Wilder painted in my mind allowed me to feel the cold wind whipping snow in my face during a prairie blizzard and hear the unnerving howls of wolves in the woods.

It was at Cannon Beach, Oregon where my love of history really came to the fore, as I used to vividly imagine how it must have been for Lewis and Clark when they reached the Pacific Ocean almost two-hundred years earlier. My mom and dad had friends who owned a vacation cabin there, and I remember the anticipation of going to the beach for Memorial Day and Labor Day weekends. I remember coming over the coast range mountains on Highway 26 and seeing that majestic blue ocean stretched before us, the setting sun reflecting an orange glow off a shimmering expanse of water. It stirred the soul. This must have been what Lewis and Clark felt, I thought, as I was filled with the sincere excitement of visiting such a beautiful place in God's creation.

Golf courses are also wonderful places, and when I'm on one that's pleasing to me I feel at peace, as if the land knows I'm there and is watching over me. The green grass and the trees are comforting. Charles Blair Macdonald, who helped bring the game to the United States and designed the Chicago Golf Club in 1892, wrote about its pleasures:

> Wandering over the links, inhaling and enjoying the
> fresh air of the country, the senses are awakened,
> and all alert, one takes pleasure in the landscape,
> watching the varied shades of sunlight and shadow,

which become gentle features of the game, until with sunset, happily tired, he is primed to enjoy a good dinner and a restful evening. No game gives a player's better nature a wider scope, and herein is its charm.[1]

The first real golf ball I ever hit full force was a five-iron off the first tee of a nice little par-3 course in Battleground, Washington on a drizzly warm day in September of 1973. The course isn't there any longer, replaced by a shopping center, but the memory holds fast in my mind. I remember that first shot – it was a decent one, landing just to the right of the green 110 yards away. The grass on the greens was so velvety, so pure, and the fir trees lining the fairways were so pretty – the aesthetic just blanketed me in beauty.

I guess because the game was so foreign to me, every aspect had its own thrill. I remember that first tee shot, I recall the first bunker shot I ever hit. I remember my first birdie. Conversely, I don't remember the first basketball I shot, or the first football I threw, or my first hit in baseball. What has made the difference? I don't know. Like a wonderful love affair, I've never tried to understand it all, but rather accept the game's ups and downs and remain faithful to it, unconditionally.

Jimmie DeVoe, a great African American professional and teacher featured in this book once said that golf is a romantic game, because you can really fall in love with it: "You hit a good shot and you go home and in the middle of the night you wake up and you think about it. Golf is like a lover – you can't get it off your mind. I guess you could call it unrequited love, because you never possess it."[2]

The confluence of my love of golf and history therefore motivates me. But why this book, now? In an earlier career I worked at George Washington University as an archivist in the Gelman Library. I used to tell people I was surrounded by dead people every day, since I assisted researchers using papers and documents created by people who had long since passed away. When you're an archivist or special collections librarian you get to know the people whose work is entrusted to you.

I organized the papers of many men and women, and felt a responsibility to maintain and protect them; to be a good steward. I also found some wonderful stories that I felt should be told. My boss was able to create an online encyclopedia of the university's history and we each wrote articles for it, making bits and pieces available to researchers. I was a believer in making collections available even if they weren't fully processed (organized), not being content to just keep them neat and orderly and in their place. What's the point of history if you aren't curious about it and don't explore it?

For example, we had wonderful diaries kept by a school boy, George Coffin, who later attended the university, with first-hand accounts of life in Washington, DC during the Civil War. I published an article on him in *Washington History* magazine, bringing Coffin out of dusty archival boxes stored for years on climate-controlled shelves and into the light of day.

When you hold his diaries in your hands, feel the rough texture of the thick paper, and read the words written in brown oxidized iron gall ink, you feel transported back in time. Among other things, Coffin describes the aftermath of Lincoln's assassination and attending the trial of the conspirators. He later became a cartoonist for the *Washington Post*, and many of his cartoons have appeared in numerous books and documentaries over the years.

Likewise, the lives of other people who attended the university or taught there – J. Edgar Hoover, Jacqueline Kennedy Onassis, Red Auerbach, Edward Teller, and Dr. Walter Freeman, among others – made their way to the PBS *American Experience* series, ESPN, the History Channel, and NPR Radio, along with many other outlets. Their lives still have meaning years after their deaths, and I see golf history in the same way. Over the past couple of years I kept thinking about all the "hidden" stories in golf's history that have never been told, or if so, generally lack substance. I wanted to say, "Hey, there is more to the story, and here it is" – as I did in my first book.

My choices are driven by my historical interests, which are particular to each individual, as historian Carl Becker makes clear. After hitting that first 5-iron in 1973, the following spring I began reading instructional books, as well as those on golf history. One day I was in my junior high school library and found a book that had a photo of Old Tom Morris from the 1890s, standing in a bunker with a club in his hands. He peered out from behind his bushy beard, and was wearing a heavy jacket and trousers. "They played golf that long ago?" I remember thinking. So began my interest in the game's past and the people who played it.

People may think that 50 or 100 years is a long time ago, but consider this: if we wake up on a Sunday morning at 7 a.m. – and if every hour represents 50 years – by 11:23 p.m. on Monday we will have gone from the birth of Christ to today. So time is relative, but stories of the human condition can be timeless.

Over the past 40-plus years I have seen how the same stories seem to be told over and over again, some better than others. It's human nature, like the stories our parents or grandparents retold many times, never varying from the narrative and rarely adding anything new. They become stale. Myth and misinformation are part of golf, as they are in everything in life, and usually do no harm, but the truth is many times more intriguing.

Over time I've come across various people and events that I found compelling, and wanted to know more about them. The more I kept looking at them, the more I felt they deserved – like George Coffin – to be brought from the shadows and into the light. There is something there worthy of our attention, and it would be a pity for them to languish in the musty pages of old books, manuscripts, magazines, and newspapers.

I strive to be as accurate as possible in presenting the facts, realizing what we call history is imperfect knowledge (or memory) of past events, since we can never revive them and observe them directly. We may accept as a fact that an event once occurred, but it has slipped away forever. All that is left to us is "some material trace" of that event, as Carl Becker told us, and we concede that history is relative, "always changing in response to the increase or refinement of knowledge."[3] So what I write here is my best attempt to refine our knowledge of what was, understanding there are surely a few nuggets I failed to uncover in my research, which took me to various libraries and archives in this country and Scotland.

I poured over numerous manuscript collections, as well as hundreds of books, newspaper and magazine articles, and think I have added some new insight into my subjects. I could keep digging, but am consoled by the profound words of Professor Richard Stott at a faculty talk while I was working at GWU: "There comes a time when you just need to finish the book, otherwise you'll keep writing forever."

Historian Frederick Jackson Turner once said that history is "ever becoming, never completed," and I hope this book contributes to that "becoming."[4] If you don't learn anything new and compelling, I haven't done my job. Happy reading.

Introduction: "History is Ever Allusive and Likes to Stay Hidden"

Golf. A good walk spoiled, as Mark Twain famously described it. Flog spelled backwards, noted one observer of irony. A sissy sport for dudes and the effete. A rich, white man's game. Those who don't understand its charms would probably agree with these descriptors, and provide a few more of their own. Casual observers tend to think of golf as a genteel, somewhat boring game, short on drama. However, that misses the point. At its core, like anything else in this world, the game is tied to people and the lives they lead.

The subjects of this book all shared golf as a common thread, and their lives were intertwined with the game. But the stories of what they did with those lives, good and bad, offer insights into our own human nature. In these tumultuous, fractured political and social times, we may think the problems we face are unique to our generation, but as Harry Truman was fond of saying, "The only thing new under the sun is the history we don't know." Like life itself, golf is full of scandals, trials, tragedies, and triumphs.

Most of us live quiet lives that nobody outside our family and friends know anything about. We live, we die, and when we're gone, the memory of who we were quickly fades away. This is natural and understandable. Perhaps a few artifacts are left behind – a scrapbook, a memento or two, a few photos and letters – to freeze time and remind those who knew us that we once were. Even famous people fade from the memory over time, which is a shame when their lives can teach us much. It's these forgotten or never told stories that I am interested in.

As part of my research, I visited the historic Green-Wood Cemetery in Brooklyn, New York, where 600,000 people have been interred since 1838. Among the imposing mausoleums and impressive obelisks are also headstones so weather-worn that you can't read the names on them, and others that have been knocked over by storms or vandals, or are missing. You see that in any cemetery, unfortunately, but each of these graves represents a life, a human soul, and it's a shame to see their final resting places marred or neglected. It's analogous to the people in my book; I don't want them to be forgotten or abandoned. I want to honor the memory of real people and pay tribute to their legacy. I believe it is proper and fitting to do so.

Frederick Jackson Turner, the famous historian, wrote in 1891 that the aim of history is "to know the elements of the present by understanding what came into the present from the past. For the present is simply the developing past, the past the undeveloped present."[1] Many people long for the "good old days" that don't exist anymore. They want to bring back the past for the sake of the past, while the historian strives to show the present by revealing its origins in the past.

Golf has a history stretching back 500 years that can inform our present, and the darker sides of human nature – drug and alcohol abuse, hedonism, mental illness, suicide, racism, and murder – have all spilled into it. I find these stories worthy of examination not only because they fall outside the stereotype of golf as a straight-laced game on a higher moral plane than others, but more importantly, because they are fascinating.

Not all is gloom, doom, and cautionary tales of woe in this book. On the brighter, hopeful side, it also reveals the better angels of our natures, showing us people who overcame the most trying personal and family circumstances, as well as physical disabilities and the challenges of old age. The stories of their strength of character and perseverance provide life lessons we can all learn from.

Finally, golf has had its own collection of oddball characters and misfits, and weird, head-shaking events, which illustrate the lighter side of the game. These varied and divergent stories – the sad and pathetic, the inspiring and uplifting, the odd and quirky – have all contributed to golf's long-memory, and provide you, the reader, with something original and evocative.

When Tiger Woods won his fourth Masters Tournament in April of 2019, capping arguably the most improbable comeback in golf history, it was an emotional moment celebrated by all who follow golf. Forgotten was the scandal in 2009 that sent his life reeling into a maelstrom of relentless tabloid and social media scrutiny. His victory was seen by 18 million viewers on television, and one-hundred years from now his life and career will most likely be remembered in the same way Old Tom Morris's is. But what about those people time has forgotten? Don't their lives merit our consideration?

On a personal level, remembering can be painful for us, but it can also expand our minds and trigger deep feelings we once felt long ago that have lain dormant within us. This is what history does; it's a conduit to the past and provides an expansion of our minds and sentiments. The past allows us to feel not only for ourselves, but for others. In these times when we are seemingly losing our compassion, it's important to realize that others have had greater challenges than we face. I thank you, the reader, for taking the time to broaden your own perspective not only on the game and its history, but on human nature itself.

Historian Carl Becker believed that our effort to understand the past is an effort to understand ourselves. I discovered him as a graduate student in 1991, and he seemed to me a kindred spirit. We are all historians, he contended, as we remember the past in our own lives. What if we woke up tomorrow and had no memory of anything? For Becker, "The result is that I don't know who I am, where I am, where to go, or what to do."[2] We would be lost souls, with a present unintelligible and a future meaningless.

We are connected to everything by history, and the historian has to "devote himself to what interests him in the past, to emphasize those aspects of the past which he deems important. Undoubtedly one historian will differ from another in this respect." The subjects in this book are here because I deem them important, and I offer my own interpretation of their lives. "But by no possibility," affirms Becker, "can the historian make affirmations describing all of the facts – all of the acts, thoughts, emotions of all of the persons who contributed to the actual event in its entirety."[3]

History is thus allusive, and we can never know much about anything in the past, but rather just a little slice of what was. Just walk into a library or bookstore, scan all the books on the shelves, and you realize how much is out there that can never be read, that can never be known. There is good stuff there, and a lot of drivel, and the challenge is to have the doggedness to find the former. If persistence wins out, and we dig deep enough and look in the right places – not everything in life can be "Googled," and wisdom isn't found on Twitter – we can come closer to the truth. This book therefore aspires to bring you substance, not fluff.

The people, the events, the facts, according to Carl Becker, "do not say anything, do not impose any meaning. It is the historian who speaks, who imposes a meaning."[4] *Shadows on the Green* is not a scholarly work per se, but I do attempt to frame many of the stories within the larger context of the times to which they belonged, illustrating the stubbornness of human nature. This book fills a void by bringing you stories of people and events "hidden" in plain sight in golf's past, which represent a mix of mostly brand-new material and new interpretations of previously told stories. The lives of these people were not so different from Tiger Woods's. As Eleanor Roosevelt once said, no person is wholly good or bad. We all struggle with the same angels and demons in this world, and can learn from the problems and challenges these people faced.

Some of the subjects in this book, unlike Woods, sadly found no redemption in this life. Part 1 shows, among other things, that the scourge of drug and alcohol abuse is nothing new. I was introduced to Nathaniel Moore while doing consultant work at the United States Golf Association (USGA), and thought he was just another rich boy gone wrong. But when I looked closer, I found a man who had played golf with Harry Vardon, and was an Olympic champion in 1904. But he was also a morphine addict who died ignominiously in a Chicago brothel. I knew that Cyril Walker, the 1924 U.S. Open champion, was a hopeless alcoholic who died homeless, but didn't realize the extent to which his friends tried to help him, giving him every chance to rehabilitate himself, only to be scorned and alienated to the point of no return.

Eben Byers was a name I recalled from early research on Bobby Jones; he and Jones played a match in the 1916 U.S. Amateur that featured much profanity-laced club throwing by the 14-year-old Jones and the 36-year-old Byers, the winner in 1906. But I didn't realize the gruesome nature of his death in 1932, the victim of a supposed patent medicine elixir. It poisoned him with radium and ate away the bones in his jaw and head, bringing about an agonizing end.

I learned of the horrible murder of Marion Miley at the hands of career criminals a few years ago while doing research for my first book and wanted to learn more about her life, not only her death. Beyond scandals and pathetic endings, the book shares stories of perseverance in the face of adversity. Part 2 deals with triumphs and inspirations, such as John Shippen, the first African American to play in the U.S. Open in 1896, who faced not only discrimination from society, but rejection from his family, who looked down on his chosen profession and his wandering ways. I have always been drawn to underdogs, and began studying African American history in my late-20s. When I got my Master's degree in history, I wrote my thesis on Nannie Helen Burroughs, a black civil rights activist who established a training school for young black women in Washington, DC in 1909. This gave me a basic understanding of that area of our nation's history.

I have known about John Shippen for years, but it was only while doing research on him in connection with the 2018 U.S. Open's return to Shinnecock Hills, his old course, that new material was uncovered. I found evidence in the Library of Congress that challenges the myth that he took an 11 in the final round of the 1896 U.S. Open which ruined his chance at victory.

At the Smithsonian's Anacostia Community Museum Archives and Howard University archives I also found valuable information regarding his family, which I find as compelling as his golf career. His father committed suicide. One of his sisters had a Ph.D. and was an English professor, highly unusual for an African American woman in the first half of the twentieth century. His brother Cyrus was a Yale graduate and also a teacher (at the famous Dunbar High School in Washington, DC), and was influential in getting one of his students, Edward Brooke, to enter public life. Brooke would go on to be elected to the U.S. Senate in 1966, becoming the first African American to serve in that body since Reconstruction. These are all things I wanted people to know about, not just his golf career.

Racism was a fact of life for Shippen, as it was for others who followed him, who faced fierce opposition from a white society not wanting black people to play the game at all, especially at the highest levels. Robert "Pat" Ball was a great golfer in the 1920s and '30s who played in events sponsored by the United Golfers Association, founded in 1925. Ball was one of only two African Americans entered in the 1928

U.S. Public Links, conducted by the USGA, but he and his fellow-competitor, Elmer Stout, were both disqualified, allegedly for cheating. The institutional racism affecting this decision is evident in correspondence from the USGA, which I first came across in 2013 while doing consultant work there.

Jimmie DeVoe partnered briefly with John Shippen to organize tournaments for black players in the New York area. He later relocated to the Los Angeles area and became the first African American to compete in the Los Angeles Open in 1944. DeVoe became a respected teacher; among his pupils were Joe Louis, Jackie Robinson, and Althea Gibson, the great tennis champion and first black women to play on the Ladies Professional Golf Association (LPGA) Tour in 1963. DeVoe was also the first African American to gain membership in the PGA of America after it repealed its "Caucasian clause" in 1961, which had prevented minorities from joining. At age 74, he was the oldest member to be elected to the Association, but he remained young at heart, winning senior tournaments into his late 80s.

Lucious Batemen, like DeVoe, began as a caddie in the early 1900s. Born in Mississippi, he moved to California after World War II and became a teacher at an Oakland driving range. He played in many local tournaments, but the color of his skin precluded him from competing at the highest levels. Like DeVoe, he also loved teaching kids, and did it free of charge for many years. Among his pupils were a number of PGA Tour members, including Tony Lema, who won the 1964 British Open. Lema contended that if not for Bateman, many kids would have been in jail instead of on the fairways.

Maggie Hathaway began as a singer and dancer in Hollywood, and then became a civil rights activist. She established the Beverly Hills chapter of the NAACP in 1962, and later led picket lines against several segregated Los Angeles golf courses, forcing them to admit blacks. Author James Dodson thinks she should be called the Rosa Parks of golf in this country.

DeVoe, Bateman, and Hathaway were all introduced to me when I lived in Washington, DC and was researching African Americans in golf at the Martin Luther King, Jr. Memorial Library. They kept stirring in my mind, especially when I organized the papers of the African American Golf History Archive at the USGA as a volunteer in 2013.

Part 2 of the book also discusses the lives of physically challenged players, long before the era of inclusion and the Americans with Disabilities Act. This became a real interest of mine after undergoing back surgery in 2006 that has left me with permanent discomfort. I can still play golf, but the swing will never be the same, and I personally find inspiration from these folks.

People like Thomas McAuliffe, who lost both arms in an accident as a boy, yet played the game and was able to shoot in the 90s. Charles Boswell lost his eyesight in World War II, but took up golf and won the National Blind Golf Championship 16 times. Jimmy Nichols lost his right arm in an automobile accident, yet was good enough to be a PGA professional. Mike Reeder, who lost both legs in the Vietnam War, shot a 79 at St Andrews, the home of golf, from a wheelchair. The story of Skip Alexander, who was a PGA Tour winner and Ryder Cup member, is the prime focus of this chapter on physically challenged players. He was the lone survivor of a plane crash in 1950 that left him with burns over 70 percent of his body. His son Buddy was gracious enough to talk with me about his father's life and offer new insights that add to this compelling story.

Senior golfers also offer inspiration. As I have grown older, I have gained greater appreciation for their considerable spirit. As Sherwin Nutland writes in *The Art of Aging*, "Whatever else aging may represent to us, it is first and foremost a state of mind."[5] Chuck Kocsis was a great amateur player who broke his back in a car accident when he was 35, but recovered and continued to play the game with great success. He won six Michigan Amateurs, was the NCAA champion in 1936, runner-up in the 1956 U.S. Amateur, and a Walker Cup team member in 1938, 1949, and 1957. At the age of age 89, he shot 72 for eighteen holes.

Kocsis was a great player that very few people know about. Other seniors include everyday golfers like Jean McCabe, 79, who suffered from chronic pulmonary disease, but kept playing two or three times a week even with an oxygen tank at her side. Elsie McLean, who made a hole-in-one at the age of 102, said "If you want to keep playing golf, you've got to enjoy yourself, quit complaining about your aches and pains and stay away from doctors." George "Dad" Miller, 97, spoke for many when he said, "You don't get old playing golf, you get old when you stop playing."[6]

Part 3 reveals how the evolution of two famous golf courses, Pebble Beach and the Old Course at St Andrews, were influenced by two families. The winner of the first U.S. Women's Amateur in 1895, Lucy Barnes Brown, impacted the evolution of Pebble Beach – her granddaughter owned the piece of property which Jack Nicklaus used to build the new fifth hole in 1998. I knew very little about Brown until January of 2019, when I was doing research on Pebble Beach and found a reference to her granddaughter, whose father was a former Congressman and Franklin Roosevelt's roommate when they were students at Harvard University. This led me to do some detective work, and with the help of Harvard, I was able to locate the great-granddaughter of Lucy Barnes Brown and talk to her about her family and its legacy at Pebble Beach.

The business activities of the Dempster family breeding rabbits threatened to destroy the Old Course at St Andrews in 1801, a story I was introduced to over 20 years ago and was able to delve into deeply when I visited the University of St Andrews Special Collections Division for the first time in 2012. Within the dusty 220-year-old correspondence of the James Cheape Papers and the Records of the Burgh of St Andrews, some going back 300 years, I found wonderful primary documents to add depth to the story.

Part 3 also tells stories of sexism, and the struggles of women in golf. This includes Babe Didrikson Zaharias's career from the 1930s to the 1950s, who was seen as being too masculine, a perception that put into question for years not only her femininity, but her sexuality. In 1935 she was suspended from the USGA from amateur competitions for playing professional sports earlier, but many saw this action as being driven by class differences, as she was a poor girl trying to dominate a rich person's game. Zaharias was featured in my first book, but I have found new correspondence at the USGA, as well as other sources, that sheds new light related to these issues.

Decades later Jan Stephenson was used by the LPGA to explicitly sell sex appeal to attract male fans in the 1970s and '80s. She and another pretty young player, Laura Baugh, were both used in this way. The campaign expanded to feature LPGA players modeling clothes and bathing suits in an annual installment of *Golf Magazine* for more than 15 years beginning in 1976. *Golf Digest* magazine also contributed to this, conducting a "Most Beautiful Golfer" contest for over 30 years. I remember well the furor Stephenson caused when she posed in a bathtub full of golf balls in the mid-1980s, and also how announcers on TV used to refer to the players as "snappy dressers" and "pretty gals."

On the rank and file level, women golfers continued to deal with prejudices and limited course availability that began in the early 1900s up to the 1990s. In the early years of golf in this country, many felt women had no business on the course. According to one writer, "They can neither stand still nor stop chattering," adding that golf "is too serious a thing to be interrupted by frivolity." An article from 1936 quoted a club caddie as saying women golfers were "avoided on general principle."[7] When I began playing golf in the 1970s, this feeling was still prevalent. My own prejudices were put to rest while in college, when I played with a young woman who was as good, or better, than as I was.

Women had to deal with sexism and paternalism, and women of color had the added burden of racism. This is touched on briefly through the experiences of Ann Gregory, Althea Gibson, and Renee Powell. For example, in one Florida tournament, Powell, the second African American to play on the LPGA Tour, had her life threatened by a man who wrote a letter telling her that if she wanted to live, she better leave town. Unfortunately, we are still struggling with issues of race today, and probably will be for decades to come. It is therefore important to never forget the oppression that came before.

The final section of Part 3 includes shorter anecdotes meant to both entertain and inform. These include USGA President Bill Campbell offering Ben Hogan a special exemption to play in the 1983 U.S. Open at the age of 70, and Luke Ross, who caddied for Bobby Jones, remembering the first time he met his idol at the 1920 U.S. Open. Not to be forgotten is "Rockin' Rollen" Stewart, a "groupie" fan who was seen on TV almost weekly in the early 1980s, wearing a rainbow afro-wig and a shirt with "John 3:16" emblazoned on it. Nor Craig Wood and Vic Ghezzi, who heard Orson Welles's "The War of the Worlds" radio broadcast in 1938 while driving from a tournament and believed it was real.

This book offers something new and different, and digs into the real stories of what happened in the past. Most golf books focus on how to play the game better, and biographies tend to focus on the "great" men and women of the game, not the people in the margins. I like to look at those who haven't had much of a voice. While in graduate school, I wrote, "Since history is dead without somebody to affirm it, the duty of the historian is to write about it and keep it alive in the minds of men and women." This I attempt to do, to both add to the considerable literature devoted to the history of golf, and also provide the reader with a greater appreciation of the past.

Chapter 1: Nathaniel Ford Moore – "From Gold Medal to Golden Syringe"

"He was handsome, pretty almost, with fine, elegant features; only his ears, protruding like teacup handles, marred the symmetry of his face."[1] So wrote Karen Abbott in describing Nathaniel Ford Moore for her book on the seedier side of Chicago, *Sin in the Second City*. A photo of him printed at the time of his death reveals cold and distant eyes staring out from a mournful, joyless, face. Looking at him, one wonders what distressing pressures, urges, fears and insecurities drove him to the drug addiction that hastened his death at the age of 25.

Born January 31, 1884, Nathaniel Moore was the only son of James Hobart Moore, who was a friend of financier of J.P. Morgan. The elder Moore and his brother William were active in the formation of the U.S. Steel Corporation. James also had controlling interests in the National Biscuit Company (forerunner to Nabisco), Continental Can, Diamond Match Company and the Chicago, Rock Island & Pacific Railroad, and provided his family with all the luxuries that great wealth allowed.[2]

Affluence is both an antiseptic and a liberator, especially so in the Gilded Age that Moore was born into. It kept the rich safe for the most part from the dangers of living among the wretched masses, of being infected with diseases such as tuberculosis and typhoid fever. It also freed them to live wherever they chose – not in crowded vermin infested squalor, sleeping three or four to a bed, but in sparkling, opulent mansions. With the influx of immigrants from Europe in the late nineteenth century, urban populations swelled. By 1890, Chicago's foreign-born inhabitants, drawn to the city by the demand for unskilled and semiskilled laborers, almost equaled the entire city population in 1880.[3]

Poor workers lived in dirty tenements, and had to struggle through life in a hostile environment. The wealthy didn't have to scrounge city dumps, as the poor did, searching for wood to heat their stoves and anything else of practical use. The rich didn't have to use communal toilets reeking of urine and excrement. They could afford indoor plumbing and had the luxury of bathing regularly. They could buy

21

proper wholesome food, instead of having to settle for stale bread, rancid meat, and half-rotten vegetables. Their physical growth wouldn't be stunted from poor nutrition. They could go to good schools. They could see doctors when they fell ill and dentists when their teeth needed attention.

Money meant they didn't have to toil in sweatshops rolling cigars or making garments. Whole families might work together in their own crowded apartments. Said one doctor, "The pay these tenement folk receive is extremely dear; the price they pay is the stunted bodies and dwarfed minds of their little children." James Moore and his son would never have to worry about working 12-hour days in the stifling heat of one of Chicago's meatpacking plants so nauseatingly described in Upton Sinclair's *The Jungle*. They'd never be crippled; or worse, lose their lives in an accident there. If a man fell into "one of the rendering tanks and had been made into pure leaf lard and peerless fertilizer," that was just part of the job.[4] Great wealth can also be a curse for those who lack the discipline and wisdom to use it for good – but whereas every poor person dreams of being rich, I doubt any rich person wishes he or she could be poor. I'm sure Nathaniel Moore didn't.

As a young boy "Nat," as he was called, enjoyed sports, and being free from the daily work lower class children had to attend to inside and outside the home, he had time for golf. He began playing the rich man's game at the Lake Geneva Country Club in Wisconsin, near one of the family's summer homes. Golf, in its embryonic stages in the United States, was confined mostly to the privileged elite who formed country clubs, which themselves seemed to run counter to the keystone American ideal of equality. The Moores were certainly associated with this country club set. According to James Mayo, author of *The American Country Club: Its Origins and Development*, golf "appealed to the aesthetic tastes of club members," and the "early country club landscape physically articulated a limited liability sense of community."[5]

Upper class practitioners of "conspicuous consumption" – a term Thorstein Veblen coined in his 1899 book *The Theory of the Leisure Class* – spent money, it was argued, to satisfy no other need than to impress others and build personal prestige. Their pursuit of various leisure activities symbolized the freedom wealth provided them. As golf grew in the 1890s, it afforded members of the leisure class an alternative to more expensive sports such as yachting, polo, hunting, racing, and shooting – all sports which separated and distinguished the wealthy from the lower classes.[6]

Golf came to the United States with Scottish and English immigrants as early as the 1700s, but didn't take hold until the 1880s. At that time it was, as H.L. Fitzpatrick wrote in *Outing* magazine, "a sport restricted to the richer classes in this country," with the next challenge being to establish "village links, virtually free, throughout the length and breadth of the land." Once the game broadened "from a class pursuit," Fitzpatrick contended, "it will never die out."[7] Democratization, however, would have to wait.

"It is debatable whether America's sporting life was ever truly democratic," writes Donald J. Mrozek in *Sport and American Mentality, 1880-1910*. He maintains "it is certain that democracy of nearly any description had no place in the world of the very rich. Using their sports as badges of social status, the ultra-rich generally confined themselves to pursuits whose cost put them out of reach of ordinary Americans."[8]

Author and member of New York society Price Collier asserted that the rich "began playing golf at a time when business was dull, when money was dear, and when people were talking of hard times…Men were glad to take up with some less extravagant form of amusement." Three years into a recovery from the Panic of 1893, Collier would hypothesize in 1900 that the country had by then become prosperous enough to choose its leisure pursuits, arguing that it could never have happened in 1860 or 1870. "Sport follows surplus. Money, in its last analysis, is merely leisure; leisure is choice, and choice is time…We in the United States have reached a condition of prosperity when we can choose – when we are not forced to hammer and shovel and shoot to keep ourselves sheltered and fed." Golf therefore offered "a very agreeable, wholesome, and suitable way of spending our surplus of time and energy."[9]

Boston and New York's wealthiest families ensconced themselves in Newport, Rhode Island each summer and took over the town, many playing the new game. A boom in country clubs in the eastern states began in 1894 and 1895, when at least 50 clubs laid out courses, spurred on by the short-term influence of Scottish-Americans and Scottish immigrants who taught the game.[10]

Golf quickly replaced hunting, horses, and cricket as the principal country club leisure, "in part because foursomes offered a comfortable atmosphere for socializing and for consummating business deals." As one New Jersey newspaper declared, the "victims of acute golf mania are to be avoided by all who are not in touch with the passing vogue," but the golf bug stuck and held faithful followers in its grasp.[11]

The game had its own primitive charms. "No one who has wielded a club can forget," declared *The Gentlewoman's Book of Sports* in 1892, "the feeling of pleasure and pardonable self-satisfaction which was experienced by the sight of the clean-hit ball soaring into a wall of azure, a tiny, white speck in the far distance."[12]

Theodore Arnold Haultain discussed the tactile lure of the course, each with its own personality and varied terrain, in his book *The Mystery of Golf*. Speaking of the delights of the game in 1910, he described the varied elements that stimulate our senses:

> The great breeze that greets you on the hill, the whiffs of air – pungent, penetrating – that come through green things growing, the hot smell of pines at noon, the wet smell of fallen leaves in autumn, the damp and heavy air of the valley at eve, the lungs full of oxygen, the sense of freedom on a great expanse, the exhilaration, the vastness, the buoyancy, the exaltation.[13]

It is a game that is different because the ball must wait for us. It isn't baseball or tennis where a ball comes towards us that we have to react to in a split second. The golf ball just lies there passively, sometimes seeming to taunt us. It's up to us to make it go. "There is no hurry," wrote John Low in *Concerning Golf*, rather "we fix our own time, we give ourselves every chance of success." It is this deliberate quality of the game which "makes it so testing to the nerves; for the very slowness which gives us opportunity for calculation draws our nerves out to the highest tension...." A year after the formation of the United States Golf Association (USGA) in 1894, *The New York Times* noted that "it is not at all improbable that each succeeding year will exceed the other in the excellence of its golf and enthusiasm for the sport."[14]

Golf offered an outlet for those who wished to get into the sporting arena, and the game grew. It would struggle against the stubborn prejudice that viewed it as a sissy sport for dudes and the effete. Jerome Travers, a great amateur champion of the early 20th century, when looking back at "the stormy path of this game in its early days here, and all the fun that was poked at it, and the actual indignities its supporters sometimes had to endure, it seems to me that it is the only sport that has grown and flourished in the face of ridicule."[15]

Yet it did flourish. By 1900 there were 1,040 golf clubs in the country. New York led the way with 165, Massachusetts 157, Pennsylvania 75, and New Jersey had 63. Illinois, Nathaniel Moore's home state, had 57 by then.[16] He had a gift for the game, and in 1900 the *Chicago Tribune* reported that the 16-year-old Moore won a small tournament in Williams Bay, Wisconsin, beating 19-year-old Walter Egan in the final at the Lake Geneva Country Club. While the eastern elite went each summer to Newport, many Chicagoans like the Moores went to Lake Geneva, which became a popular spot after the great fire of 1871.[17]

Walter Egan was a formidable opponent for Moore to beat, as he would go on to win the Western Amateur in 1903 and finish runner-up in the 1901 U.S. Amateur to the great Walter Travis. Two and a half years older than Moore, Egan's parents also had had a summer home at Lake Geneva, where on this lovely lakeside Walter enjoyed playing all outdoor sports. His father had retired from business when Walter was eleven, and had learned, while on a tour of Europe with his family three years later, that friends were building a golf course at the lake and made him a founding member. When they returned home in June 1896, the Lake Geneva Country Club opened and Walter and his father began to play.

Walter took lessons from James Conicher, the Scottish professional the club hired, and in 1897 took up the game in earnest. He spent the winter of 1897-98 abroad, in Cannes, where he "profited by the very capable instruction" of Bernard Nicholls, the professional there. When he returned home he was ready to compete in tournaments. "So you can see we were really hooked," Egan wrote in 1967, "and we soon had lots of company, for the game was gaining many enthusiastic recruits all over the country." He would enter Harvard in 1901 and play on the golf team there, a member of the privileged class playing a privileged game, and like Nat Moore, living a life as foreign to the average American as if they were members of royalty.[18]

Walter's cousin Henry (H.) Chandler Egan, who was Nat's age, visited Lake Geneva in the summer of 1898 and fell for the game as well. The Egans would compete against Nat Moore as teenagers and had "many a close rub on the links" in tournaments at Exmoor and Onwenstsia in Chicago, where Moore was also a member. Two weeks before losing to Moore in the 1900 Williams Bay tournament, Walter Egan teamed with Arnie E. Tollifson to defeat Harry Vardon on the final hole of a 36-hole match played at the 5,658 yards Lake Geneva course during Vardon's famous American tour.[19]

Harry shot a course record 72 on the second eighteen, which meant his opponents played an amazing game to beat him. "Egan made some fine plays and saved the game several times," reported the *Chicago Tribune*. The day before the match, Vardon had played an informal match, shooting a 36 for nine holes playing with Moore's father and two other members. After lunch he played nine more holes with Nat, William Holabird, Jr., and another player, shooting a lackluster 41. Holabird would tie for 37th in the U.S. Open that October at the Chicago Golf Club.

Vardon astonished the crowd with some 240-yard drives (about 340 yards today), but "his putting at times was indifferent," according to the *Tribune*, and he was defeated 2 down. "The tenth and eighteenth holes were lost to Moore, a new star in the golfing sky." Walter Egan had played the course in the morning, shooting a 78, which tied the course record before Vardon broke it the same day. The *Lake Geneva Herald* reported that Vardon was later a guest at the home of James Moore, and one wonders what conversations Nat might have had with Vardon about golf and life.[20]

Vardon had sat through many dinners like this since achieving fame, surrounded by deferential servants quietly serving food on the finest china, and drinking his host's most expensive wine. The home's round-arched fireplace and immense glazed mahogany bookcases were impressive to the eye. Vardon may have gazed at Nat, his mustache camouflaging the slight smirk on his lips as he lit his pipe and sucked on it. *Do you have the foggiest notion of how lucky you are to have all this? Bloody hell!* Money allows the freedom of lifestyle choices the poor cannot conjure in their wildest dreams.

Harry had come a long way from his own harsh youth, when as a 12-year-old he was hired out as a servant to help earn money for the family. He spent 60 hours a week working on a local dairy farm, rising at dawn from a cold bed, working until sunset, and caddying about twice a week at the Royal Jersey Golf Club. After two years of that he became the servant for a wealthy doctor, working for him 14 hours a day for three years.[21] Harry exhaled a haze of smoke, recalling those hard days. *Could you have done that little man?* Nat, for his part, may have had dreams of becoming a great player like Vardon, wondering if he really was "a new star in the golfing sky," living in blissful oblivion, surrounded by the luxuries that pampered him.

Two years later, in 1902, Moore played in the U.S. Amateur in Golf, Illinois, shooting an 88 to qualify for match play (defending champion Walter Travis was the medalist with a 79.) Moore played well in his first round match over the 6,266-yard Glen View course, beating J.P. Thorp, a professor at Harvard, 3 and 1, but was defeated in the second round by Walter Egan. Later that fall, he reached the semi-finals in the Western Amateur only to lose to Egan again, 1 down.[22] The Western, begun in 1899, has been a prestigious tournament over the years, with past champions including Chick Evans, Francis Ouimet, Jack Nicklaus, Phil Mickelson, and Tiger Woods.

In July 1903, at the Western Open in Milwaukee, the second-oldest championship in this country after the U.S. Open, Moore tied for 13th with Willie Smith, winner of the 1899 U.S. Open. This suggests that he had the talent to compete with the best golfers in the country. Smith's brother Alex won over a rain-soaked 6,050-yard course with a score of 318. Alex beat Laurie Auchterlonie by two shots and Willie Anderson by five. Anderson had won the U.S. Open at Baltusrol a month earlier, and Auchterlonie had won it the year before. Alex would himself capture the first of two U.S. Open trophies three years later. Moore indeed was keeping elite company.

Nat had finished ahead of Louis James, the 1902 U.S. Amateur champion, H. Chandler Egan, and his old nemesis Walter Egan, in a strong field that included other top players such as Fred McLeod, and Gilbert Nichols. Nat had been in good form coming into the event. The *Lake Geneva Herald* reported a couple weeks earlier that Nat was "playing a stronger game than last year and he was then considered one of the best."[23]

The following year, 1904, Moore played in his only U.S. Open at Glen View, missing the cut. Willie Anderson won the third of his four Opens there, while H. Chandler Egan finished tied for 20th, and Walter Egan 46th (last among those who made the cut.) That September, the third iteration of the modern Olympic Games was held in St. Louis, and golf was played over the picturesque and hilly 6,203-yard Glen Echo Country Club course, designed by 1896 U.S. Open champion James Foulis. A club spokesman said the "greens are large, natural hazards are in plenty, and artificial hazards have been arranged, so that the crack player can show his superiority over a poor one."[24]

Eighty-three golfers entered the tournament and seventy-five started. Moore shot 87-90 to qualify for match play, one of six Chicagoans to make the finals. He was defeated by H. Chandler Egan 7 and 6, who had just won the U.S. Amateur a couple of weeks earlier, and who would lose the Olympic championship to George Lyon. Egan would blame his 3 and 2 defeat as the result of being "overgolfed," but said, "I deserved to lose. The golf played by Mr. Lyon was superior to mine." Egan was also unnerved by his own wildness off the tee, and having his older opponent consistently outdrive him, which was also a surprise to the 1,000 spectators who braved pouring rain in the morning round to see the finish.[25]

Not surprisingly, opinions of the event's significance differed depending on which side of the Atlantic they came from. "While the event was far from representative of the world's best talent and hence could not with any justice be called a real world's championship," noted the U.S. based *Golf* magazine, "the presence of National Champion Chandler Egan, and Ex-Champion George S. Lyon, of Canada, with many others who hold or have held divisional titles and club championships gave the event rank as a good starter for the future line of Olympic golf events."[26]

The U.K.'s *Golf Illustrated* observed, rightly so, that calling it a "World Championship" without a single English or Scottish player in the field was trite hyperbole. Describing it as such, "or any other high-sounding title which rings sweetly in American ears" was wrong, since "a grandiose title cannot, per se, give prestige to a meeting." The author of the article didn't know if the Royal and Ancient Club of St Andrews, the governing body of golf outside the United States and Mexico, had been consulted, but concluded it wouldn't have approved of external bodies "trying to muscle in on their 'territory....'"[27]

This is accurate, as in 1913, when the R&A was asked if it would support the inclusion of golf in the next Games and work to support such a movement, meeting minutes record it unanimously approved the recommendation of the Green Committee "that the Club should refuse to have anything to do with the inclusion of golf in the Programme of the Olympic Games." Notwithstanding such sentiments, the 1904 individual winner George Lyon cherished receiving one of the finest "trophies ever given in a golf tournament; I also got a very pretty gold medal."[28] Like Old Tom Morris and Horace Rawlins, winners respectively of the first British and U.S. Opens, beating fields of eight and fourteen players respectively, Lyon's name would remain in the record books, even if the competition was lacking. Nobody could take that away from him, no more than they could deny Morris and Rawlins their laurels.

In addition to the individual competition, there was also an Olympic team championship held the week before. "Each member of the winning team will be awarded a medal," announced *The Golfer's Magazine*, "and the team a special silver cup."[29] The $500 trophy, like that which Lyon won, was taken home by the team of the Western Golf Association, captained by H. Chandler Egan. Egan was born in Highland Park, Illinois, and played his first game of golf at the age of 12 at Lake Geneva, where his family also summered. As a student at Harvard, Egan won the Intercollegiate Championship and the first of four Western Amateurs in 1902. A proven winner, he led his team to victory.

Nathaniel Ford Moore.

Nathaniel Moore, 1904.

Ten players made up each of the three teams, all of whom played 36 holes of stroke play, with the lowest total score winning. Egan had the best scores for his winning team, which was "made up entirely of young Chicago players," as follows: H. Chandler and Walter E. Egan, Clement E. Smoot, and Edward M. "Ned" Cummins (all from Exmoor); Mason E. Phelps, Robert E. Hunter and Kenneth P. Edwards (Midlothian); Daniel E. "Ned" Sawyer (Wheaton); Warren K. Wood (Homewood); and Nathaniel F. Moore (Lake Geneva.) By virtue of this team event, small as it was, Moore became an Olympic champion, if only a devalued one. "And so a novel venture came to an inglorious end," recorded *Golf Illustrated*, "unnoticed and, no doubt, unlamented."[30] Moore's achievement, as well as that of his teammates, was virtually forgotten.

At the end of the year, newspapers reported that Moore was ready to take a job and "had decided to adopt railroading as an occupation." The time had come for the 20-year-old to turn his attention to a career, and naturally he chose to follow in his father's footsteps, although it was more symbolic than substantial. "He will be given a subordinate position in the operating department and is to be shown no favors, but to be allowed to carve out his own career." There was just one problem – Nat Moore didn't like to work.

The next year, 1905, found him engaged to be married. The circumstances behind it suggest the impulsive nature of the man. Nat was touring the east in his new fangled two-seater automobile, a sure symbol of wealth, as it cost more than the average worker made in a year. At the end of May, he was in Hot Springs, Virginia, chugging slowly along the dirt road when he came upon another such machine. Passing it, he saw through his driving goggles one of its passengers, a "graceful vision with dark eyes and the most delicately perfect features."[31] He glanced back, hungry for another look, only to have her face hidden behind a cloud of swirling dust kicked up by his vehicle. *She is too delightful to leave behind*, he thought, and slowed down to let her car pass by. He accelerated to catch up with it again, pulling alongside for a few seconds, gazing at the girl. *That's mama sitting beside her*, he observed. *She doesn't look like such a dragon.*

When they arrived at their hotel, he stopped behind them. The young woman turned and smiled at him as she exited the car gracefully. Her figure was as alluring as her face, and after removing the scarf from her head, she shook her hair in a coquettish manner while turning back to him briefly, teasingly, before proceeding inside with her party. Moore, fully smitten, brushed the dust off his jacket, ran his hands through his hair, and quickened his step to the dining room, bribing the waiter to be seated at her table. This hypnotizing beauty was Helen Fargo of New York, the 18-year-old daughter of the founder of the Wells-Fargo Company, William C. Fargo. She would recount the meeting in a letter to her cousin Grace Fargo. "Really he is the most startling boy. Are they all so sudden out West, I wonder? But I rather like it." They spent the rest of the day together, dancing that night.[32]

The next few days were a blur for both, and they were well aware of Mrs. Fargo's natural misgivings. "Do you think this irrepressible boy minded mama's glacial glances?" she wrote to Grace.

31

"Not a bit." He took Helen and her mother for rides in the country and on the fourth day spirited Helen away for some private time. "We were gone only about 15 minutes – and I returned engaged to a man I had met only four days before."

This news did not sit well with her mother, to say the least. "She said Mr. Moore appeared to be a gentleman," recounted Helen, "but what did we know about him except that he was from a good family?" The Fargos soon returned to their country home Ardsley-on-the-Hudson in New York, but before leaving, Moore asked if he could meet her there. "I said 'yes' real quick, before mama could catch her breath." He arrived at her doorstep the day after their return, and stayed for awhile, getting to know the family. She overheard her mother asking her father, "What do we know about the character and habits of this stranger?"[33] Mr. Fargo would then offer a bold suggestion: Nat and Helen should take a trip together.

As her father William contended, all the "innate traits of a man come out in the discomfort of travel." His wife suggested Nat meet them in Europe. "He did meet us in Paris," noted Helen, "and mamma was most watchful." Once there he bought a new car and they toured with her mother, an aunt, and her cousin Preston Fargo. It was through "Paris to Dijon and through the funny old French towns of Aix le Bains and Geneva that he won mama." Two weeks of travel revealed only the most gentlemanly behavior from Moore, convincing Mrs. Fargo that he was indeed worthy of her daughter. Moore presented his fiancée with a string of pearls worth $80,000, and they were married November 8, 1905.[34]

Before the wedding, Nathaniel's father pulled his checkbook from his desk, and after a moment of thought, wrote in an amount – two-hundred and fifty thousand dollars. "This is the second big check Mr. Moore has given his son within a comparatively short time," reported the press. The year before his father gave him a check for $100,000; these total gifts of $350,000 equate to about $10 million today.[35] With money like that, why would Nat Moore ever want to work?

Young Nat's life became the epitome of "conspicuous consumption." The *Chicago Tribune* noted that the $100,000 check he received on his 21st birthday in 1905 had been waiting for him in an envelope left beside his plate when he came to the breakfast table to start his day at their Santa Barbara, California summer home. "He spent the money and thousands on top of it with a lavish hand," continued the *Tribune*, "and distributed it in all parts of the country from the Pacific coast to the Atlantic seaboard."[36]

A year after their marriage, the Chicago *Inter Ocean* reported that "Nathaniel Moore has a princely way of doing things," in describing a trip he and his wife took to visit his parents. They arrived by train, but the "next day he decided that he wished to return by motor car, and take a party of friends with him." Since all of his cars were at Lake Geneva or in New York, "he did the simplest thing possible – just bought one at a trifling expense of a few thousand dollars. Then, when at the end of the trip, he had no especial further use for the machine, he turned it over as a present to one of the party."

Shocking excess such as this was a way of life for Moore, along with an irresponsible nature. In March 1906 he spent several hours in a jail cell in Santa Barbara after being "charged with drunkenness and driving his automobile at a dangerous rate of speed through the streets." After being bailed out, he was in the paper again a few days later, but this time to announce he had won the club championship at Santa Barbara Country Club.[37] Life was just one big game for Nat Moore.

Moore's competitive golf days were mostly behind him. His last great foray was at the celebrated North and South Amateur at Pinehurst, North Carolina, in 1907, where he was trounced in the final by Allan Lard, 12 and 11. Lard, eighteen years Moore's senior, had also participated in the 1904 Olympics, and would successfully defend his North and South title in 1908. The year of his defeat to Lard, Moore gave a dinner for fifteen couples in New York City to celebrate his 23rd birthday. He described it as "just a jolly little affair," for him and his wife.

He called on some friends, who supplied him with ten theatrical men and ten chorus girls, then procured a string orchestra, and had a dinner followed by dancing at the famous Rector's restaurant. Attired in a "gorgeous purple dressing gown figured over with his initials," Moore arrived at 11 p.m. and presented party favors to his guests: gold and pearl necklaces with lockets in the form of "23" for the women and diamond cuff buttons inscribed "23" for the men. "We became so noisy the Rector people told us to calm down." Moore told a reporter. They adjourned to Churchill's for coffee and liqueurs, as the party went on until 5 a.m. the following morning. The *Chicago Tribune* reported that the dinner cost an estimated $20,000 (a mind-boggling $500,000 today, or in his era 40 times the annual wage of the average worker.)[38]

"NAT" MOORE GIVES $20,000 GOTHAM "SKIDOO" SUPPER

HOSTESS WHO ENTERTAINED $20,000 "SKIDOO" PARTY.

MRS. NATHANIEL F. MOORE

Young Chicagoan Observes His Twenty-Third Birthday—Chorus Girls Help Him— Favors Worth $1,000 Each.

Headline and photo from the Chicago *Inter Ocean* of Helen Fargo Moore, 1907.

At another party, Moore "amused" guests, "the feminine portion of whom were actresses," by having servants spread $20 gold pieces across a bed of ice, from which he snatched up a coin and dangled it before each woman's face. He would linger for a moment, a lascivious smile spreading across his face, before dropping the gold pieces down the front of the women's necks and into their welcoming cleavage.[39] After such indiscretions, Helen left Nat and returned to Chicago, although they would later reconcile.

Moore was a libertine, a seeker of pleasure and avarice. Honoré de Balzac wrote in 1834: "Pleasure is like certain drugs; to continue to obtain the same results one must double the dose, and death or brutalization is contained in the last one." His words could have been written for Nat Moore. According to the newspapers, the young millionaire had for several years been addicted to morphine, "excessive drinking, and unrestrained indulgence...."[40] He paid little attention to his marriage vows and displayed physical symptoms of his addiction. However, as is the case today, his wealth and status insulated him from the public knowing the real story.

In August 1909, Moore suffered from heat stroke while on vacation in Wisconsin. "Playing golf to excess and work over plans for buildings on two islands he had just purchased, led to over exposure to the sun," reported the Chicago *Inter Ocean*. This was followed in November by a "fainting spell" that lasted "four hours." Physicians who "attended him then said he had taken an overdose of some drug."[41]

These episodes, however, weren't enough to dissuade him from trying to convince others that he was still serious about being a businessman. He made an announcement in November "that he was tired of loafing and intended to go to work in the freight department of the Rock Island Railroad company to begin to learn the railroad business." As he told the press about his new $40 a month job [about $1,100 today] as a freight loader in Chicago's Rock Island yards: "I know it will mean getting up pretty early in the morning and a lot of other inconvenient things, but I'm ready to stand for all of them. Loafing makes one very tired, you know, and I'm going to try some hard work." His faux ambition was driven by a desire to emulate his successful cousins, Edward and Paul Moore. *The Brooklyn Daily Eagle* wrote that his "friends believed that he had abandoned his old life and that he would eventually be a big success."[42] It was never to be, as his life had been given over to addiction.

How Nat Moore was introduced to morphine we don't know. Most likely it had been prescribed by a doctor for some painful ailment and he got hooked. Perhaps he was predisposed to addiction, as science suggests roughly 10 percent of the population is. A healthy adult brain has a hundred billion neurons that connect at a quadrillion synapses. These neurons continually release chemical pulses that travel between receptors, and morphine releases dopamine into the body, which gives us the feeling of pleasure. Moore liked the feeling, and use lead to abuse.[43]

"Like no other particle on earth," writes Sam Quinones, *Dreamland: The True Tale of America's Opiate Epidemic*, "the morphine molecule seemed to possess heaven and hell." It allowed for modern surgery, saving and improving too many lives to count, but also stunted and ended many lives with addiction and overdose. While drugs do cause structural changes to the brain, the most pronounced changes are functional. The brain is hijacked, as drugs take over the receptors and bind to them. The connections are impaired, the brain becomes dysfunctional, and the addict can't escape. Their bodies crave the drug.[44]

Morphine induces a euphoric sensation that lessens emotional distress and lasts three to six hours after being injected. Dr. T. D. Crothers explained the effects in 1902: first a "dullness of the senses, and then obliteration of pain followed by serenity, comfort, and rest. Later a tendency to sleep, and, after a short period of unconsciousness, a quiet wakeful season follows."

Injecting the drug sends the entire dosage into the bloodstream at once, which not only raises the risk for a potentially fatal overdose from suppressed respiration rates, but also can lead more quickly to addiction. Even if Moore acknowledged he had a problem, in that era drug addiction was still seen by many as a sign of insanity rather than a disease, and his next stop might have been the insane asylum.[45]

Today, our country faces an opioids epidemic, just as it did in the late 19th century, a real example of the cyclical nature of history. Morphine, and other opiates such as heroin, trace their origins to a single plant – the opium poppy. German scientist Friedrich Sertürner first isolated morphine from opium in 1803. A very powerful painkiller, it is the active narcotic ingredient in opium, and in its pure form, is ten times stronger. Sertürner, later realizing the negative addictive qualities of the drug, said in 1810, "I consider it my duty to attract attention to the terrible effects of this new substance in order that calamity may be averted."[46]

Opium derivatives, including morphine, became widely used pain relievers, particularly in the United States during and after the Civil War. Prior to 1906, only nine states and territories had laws prohibiting the sale of morphine without a prescription, making it easy to procure. The Pure Food and Drug Act, enacted that year, banned foreign and interstate traffic in adulterated or mislabeled food and drug products, forcing drug manufacturers to disclose the contents of patent medicines and the amount of dangerous drugs they contained.[47]

Even so, it put no ceiling on the amount of drugs they could contain, nor did it require that active ingredients be placed on the label if the manufacturers sold the products in the same state in which they were produced (in which case they were subject to state rather than federal regulations). Patent medicine sales had skyrocketed in the previous half-century, going from $3.5 million in sales in 1859 to almost $75 million by the twentieth century. It was obvious that a demand was driving such an increase.[48]

In 1878, New York neurologist George Miller Beard coined the term "neurasthenia" to describe people whose "lack of nerve strength" made them susceptible to addiction. It reached its peak of popularity between the mid-1880s and the first decade of the twentieth century. Beard described it as a nervous condition affecting the upper class, caused by a combination of overwork and hereditary predisposition characterized primarily by mental and physical fatigue, insomnia, headache, inability to concentrate, phobias, and a variety of systemic irregularities.[49]

He explained that a person whose nervous system had become "enfeebled" by the demands of modern industrial society, all of which combined to heighten cerebral tension and make life particularly taxing, would naturally turn wherever he or she could for support. Thus, "anything that gives ease, sedation, oblivion, such as chloral, chloroform, opium or alcohol, may be resorted to at first as an incident, and finally as a habit." Not merely to overcome physical discomfort, but to obtain "the relief of exhaustion, deeper and more distressing than pain, do both men and women resort to the drug shop." In 1888, Dr. E. P. Thwing added to the theory by claiming that as cities were growing larger and massing people of increasingly diverse backgrounds, "evil influences become more potent to undermine the welfare of society."[50]

Whatever social or psychological influences may have affected him, Nathaniel Moore was a drunk and an addict, known to inject morphine into his arm with a solid-gold syringe. He also frequented prostitutes in Chicago's "Levee," bordered by 18th and 22nd Streets, and State and Armour (Federal), one of the nation's most infamous sex districts. The area contained a variety of "resorts" ranging from the most extravagant brothels to small houses of prostitution located in boardinghouses or the back rooms of saloons.[51]

There were around one thousand brothels in Chicago then, with five thousand full-time prostitutes, a "number that didn't account for the thousands of streetwalkers, part-timers, and girls who hustled on the side." The most elegant brothel was the Everleigh club, run by sisters Ada and Minna Everleigh, which opened in 1900. Located in a double brownstone at 2131-33 South Dearborn, its clientele included authors Theodore Dreiser, Ring Lardner, boxer Jack Johnson, and businessman Marshall Field, Jr. (until he was shot and killed there in 1905.)

The Everleigh Club "butterflies," as they were called, pocketed from $100 to $400 each week (about $3,000-$12,000 today), an unthinkable salary in other houses. "One $50 client is preferable to ten $5 ones," Minna Everleigh advised her courtesans. "Less wear and tear." A customer had to fork over $50 just to get in the place, and in an era when one could enjoy a three-course meal for fifty cents, dinner at the club's Pullman Palace Buffet could run $150.[52]

The other major brothel Moore frequented was Chez Shaw run by Victoria "Vic" Shaw, just down the street. As a 1949 *Chicago Tribune* article on Shaw described it: "As each era brought forth its weird assortment of hoodlums, politicians, reformers, and society playboys, Vic greeted them with open arms and champagne...." Among these society playboys was Nat Moore.

Moore began the night of January 8, 1910 at the Everleigh club, and after an evening of carousing left, not for home, but for a saloon on Wabash Avenue. "He drank several bottles of wine," reported the *Tribune*, and when it closed at 1 a.m. he went with the proprietor, "Big" Fitzgerald, a friend of Vic Shaw's, to her brothel. Once inside, still inebriated, three of her best girls swarmed around him. "I'm tired," he told housekeeper Hattie Harris, "and I want to go to bed and rest." He beckoned the three girls. "Come, talk to me until I get to sleep." Since morphine addiction causes impotence, Nat probably wasn't in shape to do much, even if he was sober. Harris said of Moore: "Nat was the biggest baby who ever visited this place. He seemed to care more about being petted and talked to than anything else. He was a spoiled child."[53]

Vic Shaw recounted that early in the morning of January 9, Moore sent for her and asked her to call a doctor. When he arrived, Moore "implored him to give him a dose of morphine. He met refusal with insistent demands, asserting he would die without it." Dr. M.F. Murray later testified that he gave Moore an injection of morphine and atropine. "Moore was extremely nervous when I attended him at 8 o'clock in the morning, but I did not think there was any danger of death."

Hattie Harris said that soon thereafter she heard Moore and the girls talking. He then called to her. "Hattie, you're tired and need rest," he said, "but before you go to sleep please bring me a cold glass of beer." She fetched the drink, "and before I left him the four were asleep." About 3 p.m., Nina Webster, one of the girls with him, checked on Moore and found him unresponsive. Frightened, she called Hattie. "His face was cold. I awakened the other girls and we called the police and sent for the doctor." But it was too late to do anything. Nat Moore was dead.[54]

Vic Shaw knew that Moore had been in the district ten days earlier and "was taken unconscious from a resort and revived only by strenuous efforts of the physicians and the application of strong stimulants." She had been worried that he might do the same in her place, and now, worse than that, he was dead. A sad event for sure, and very bad for business. "Vic and her cadets hastily conspired to plant his body in the Everleigh club furnace," recounted Norma Lee Browning in her series on Shaw in 1949. "One of the girls who used to work there tipped off her former employers. The Everleigh sisters marched right over to Vic's place and had it out. The body wasn't removed until after the police had arrived." Lieutenant Daniel Helleher arrived at the house after someone telephoned to say a man had died.[55]

Capitalist's Son Who Died in Resort.

Nathaniel Moore at the time of his death, 1910.

Being a well-known figure, the police sought to keep the death of young Moore, "particularly the place of his demise, from the public." This didn't sit well with the State's Attorney, who started an investigation to learn if there was anything criminal connected with Moore's death and also to discover why the police suppressed the facts for hours after the death was reported to them. The news of Moore's death was not released to the press until after midnight the next day, once the body was taken to Jordan's funeral parlor. From there, police officials and a representative of Jordan's went to Moore's residence at 1100 Lake Shore Drive to break the news to Mrs. Moore. "She swooned and has been under the care of physicians since," reported the press.

Permission was obtained to take the body to the residence, where a representative of Jordan's remained during the night. The widow made the odd request that "the body of her husband be wrapped in a purple robe after the postmortem examination," perhaps the same robe he wore at his famous 23rd birthday party. Moore's parents were at their winter home in Santa Barbara, California, and sent instructions that the body be placed in a vault in Oak Woods Cemetery awaiting their return.[56]

Newspapers reported that Moore's death would "cause the police to make wholesale raids in the district. The entire police detail of the South side is investigating the death of the young millionaire, but there were no marks of violence found on his body." The police at first believed a drug, "often used to keep liberal spenders awake in resorts, so that they would continue to buy drinks freely, may have been the cause of Moore's death." Moore was said to have given Shaw a check for $1,500 two weeks earlier, but police reported there was only $2.50 in his pockets. Shaw acknowledged that he had paid her money towards his bill, but said he wasn't robbed by the girls, and wasn't in the habit of carrying much cash.[57]

Initially, Shaw denied to the press that Moore had been at her house. "I knew Mr. Moore well. He was a fine fellow…He had not been at my house for over a month. Nobody was taken from my house today or any other time. Nobody has died in my house." When the facts became known to the public, she finally admitted the truth. The increased police scrutiny the death brought to her house made her philosophical. "I have been trying to get out of this business for a month. I want to lead a

40

better life." Her husband said the place had been cleared out. "There haven't been any girls around here for several days. Oh, maybe one or two, but they have all gone now."

An autopsy found no drugs in Moore's body, and the "verdict that he died of heart disease met the unanimous approval of three physicians and coroner Peter Hoffman." Hoffman said there was also no sign of violence. The examination of the internal organs did show that Moore "was in poor physical condition." Death was caused by acute dilation of the heart, endocarditis, persistent thymus, chronic interstitial nephritis, and chronic gastritis. People knew Moore had been in bad shape. Friend William Wygatt said Moore had suffered from fainting spells at times and that his physical condition was poor. Dr. M.H. Rosenberg told reporters he had attended to Moore at different times for a year and that he suffered from heart and kidney diseases. "I attended to him four weeks ago and at that time it was a surprise to me that he did not die."[58]

Moore's widow Helen was said "to have borne with her husband despite frequent ructions that threatened more than once to result in a divorce." Friends of Moore's from "both ends of the social scale contributed details and incidents to the case of a character unchronicled and as unusual as pitiful." The 1911 publication of *The Social Evil in Chicago*, a government report issued by the Vice Commission, prompted a flurry of reforms, including the closing of the Levee's most famous brothel, the exclusive Everleigh Club. Soon after, the U.S. state's attorney launched an attack on the Levee that resulted in it being shut down in 1912.[59] But it didn't put an end to the world's oldest profession, it only changed the locations where it operated. Nor did it do anything to end the use of drugs.

A year after Moore's death, *The New York Times* ran an article titled "Uncle Sam is the Worst Drug Fiend in the World." "The opium and morphine habits have become a national curse, and in some way they must certainly be checked, if we wish to maintain our high place among the nations of the world and any elevated standard of intelligence and morality among ourselves." It pointed out that the United States consumed more smoking opium per annum than six great European nations combined. "We are the greediest drug takers in the universe, and have begun to suffer from it, as, of course, was quite inevitable."

Morphine is still the precursor to all other opioids, including prescription narcotic painkillers which are being abused today. Dr. Harvey W. Wiley, a famous food-chemist in his time, claimed that people poisoned themselves with bad food, bad drink, and bad habits. He said in 1911, "It is true that alcohol is not the only drug to which the American people is addicted. We are, unfortunately, becoming a drug-cursed people. The habit of drug taking is increasing rapidly throughout our territory, more especially in our congested centers of population." He added, "We are a nation of extremists. We are extremists in our eating, our starving, smoking, drinking, playing, working."[60] Sadly, the same could be said today.

If Nat Moore was living today, perhaps he would have sought treatment for his addiction, and found a way out of his self-destructive lifestyle. In 1914 the Harrison Narcotic Act placed legal access to drugs more fully under the control of the medical profession and the federal government. An effort to ban narcotics completely from over-the-counter drugs failed, but top limits were decreed for opium, heroin, morphine, and cocaine.[61]

In 1915, more than two per cent of the people of the United States were addicted to the use of opium and cocaine, and fully 90 per cent of the opium imported was used for illegitimate purposes. As is the case today, a public health report at the time claimed that more addicts "have been created by the refilling of prescriptions than in any other way." Analyzing 213 cases of drug addiction studied by one researcher, the majority, 54.6 percent, became that way through physicians' prescriptions or treatment. It concluded that "from 90 to 95 percent of the persons habitually using narcotics do so entirely unnecessarily."

Twenty year earlier, Dr. M.J. Mattison, addressing the New York Academy of Medicine, warned colleagues that many "cases of the morphine habit could have been avoided had the family physician not given the drug in the first place." Another doctor described as "almost criminal" the practice of leaving morphine and syringes with patients, and instructing them on how to self-medicate whenever they felt pain, since dependency could occur after only three or four doses.[62]

Fast forward a century. In 1992, before the major push for opioids from pharmaceutical companies, doctors wrote 112 million opioid prescriptions. In 2016, that number had increased to 236 million after a peak of 282 million in 2014. Everyone knows opiates have painkilling benefits, and Purdue Pharma, the manufacturer of OxyContin, touted its safety. "If you take the medicine like it is prescribed," said Dr. J. David Haddox, the company's point man for the drug, "the risk of addiction when taking an opioid is one-half of one percent." Iatrogenic (or doctor-caused) addiction, Purdue said, was said to be "exquisitely rare." They were wrong. As evaluating pain became the "fifth vital sign," it was used not only for pain associated with stage-four cancer, but for people with moderate back injuries, wisdom-tooth surgery, and bronchitis.[63]

In 2015, the United States saw 52,404 deaths from drug overdoses, and 63 percent of drug deaths were tied to opioids. The cost of prescription opioid misuse in this country amounts to close to $80 billion a year. Although Purdue Pharma declared bankruptcy in 2019, the result of lawsuits filed against it by 36 states claiming deceptive marketing, the problem is pernicious, with no end in sight.[64]

Nat Moore's life ended long ago, and although morphine was not the direct cause of his death, it played a part in it. Perhaps he realized innately the seriousness of his other illnesses, and pursued a hedonistic life out of fear of what lay ahead. Today, medical technology might have helped his heart condition, and given him more years of life. But he had no reason to be hopeful if he sensed he was in trouble. Self-medicate and enjoy what time was left to him, he may have thought.

Like many failed lives, one could hate the sin but still love the sinner. Moore was a lavish spender and was known far better along Broadway in New York than in Chicago. According to one newspaper, he was one of the "most picturesque spenders of the gay White Way. Nothing was too good for Moore and his friends." He was generous with tips to bell boys, bartenders, and others "who rendered him slight services." A friend claimed that "Moore was the greatest hearted lad I ever knew. He loved friends and friendship more than anything else in the world. And the fact that he early formed a habit of entertaining them and himself along the easiest way brought his downfall. He was pampered from the moment he was big enough to think for himself....."[65] And perhaps it was this, being pampered and never forced to grow up, that proved his greatest handicap.

Life would go on, as it always does. His widow would marry again late in 1911, to Lemuel Hastings Arnold, a prominent New York attorney (he passed away in 1917.) Moore's father James died in 1916, and it was said that the death of his "beloved son" had "embittered the last years of his father's life." Nat's mother would find another husband in 1922 before divorcing him. Had he lived, Moore would have received one million dollars from his father's estate (about $23.5 million today.)[66]

Nat's old competitors Walter Egan and H. Chandler Egan continued playing golf. Walter moved to Monterey, California in retirement, and was a member of the Cypress Point Club. His cousin H. Chandler also moved to the West Coast (Oregon) and ran an apple orchard. He won the Pacific Northwest Amateur five times, played in the 1934 Walker Cup, and also designed golf courses. With Robert Hunter (Alister Mackenzie's design partner), Egan renovated the Pebble Beach Golf Links for the 1929 U.S. Amateur, in which he played and reached the semifinals.[67]

Bob Jones was beaten by Johnny Goodman in the first round of that U.S. Amateur, which put into motion his meeting Mackenzie, their subsequent discussions of golf course architecture, and the genesis of Augusta National and the Masters Tournament. Today we remember Egan and Jones as gentlemen of the game, and for the legacies they have left us. Nathaniel Moore, the poor little rich boy gone bad, left behind nothing but the detritus of a troubled life. He was an Olympic champion, as was Egan, and he played with the great Harry Vardon, as did Jones, but Nat Moore, unlike all of them, has sadly faded into the mist of memory.

Chapter 2: Eben Byers – "He Was Doing Alright Until his Jaw Fell Off"

On a glorious September day in 1931, Robert H. Winn, a lawyer for the Federal Trade Commission, along with some colleagues visited the stately mansion of Eben Byers in Long Island, New York. They were there to collect testimony from him relating to his use of a deadly patent medicine. "A more gruesome experience in a more gorgeous setting would be hard to imagine," observed Winn. "There we discovered him in a condition which beggars description." Winn continued:

> Young in years and mentally alert, he could hardly speak. His head was swathed in bandages. He had undergone two successive operations in which his whole upper jaw, excepting two front teeth, and most of his lower jaw had been removed. All the remaining bone tissue of his body was slowly disintegrating, and holes were actually forming in his skull.[1]

Everybody in the room, including Byers, realized they were talking to a dead man. How did this wealthy industrialist and former U.S. Amateur golf champion, whose money could buy him almost anything, end up like this? Six months later, at the age of 51, his suffering would end when he succumbed to radium poisoning. His death would elicit a nationwide response, not only from the medical profession, but also the federal government, resulting in countless future lives being saved.

Eben MacBurney Byers was born April 12, 1880 in Pittsburgh, the son of Alexander MacBurney Byers, who established the A.M. Byers Company in Pittsburgh in 1864. His company manufactured steel and wrought iron, and when other producers attempted to undersell him with cheaper materials, he vowed that he would produce quality wrought iron pipe "or bust." His company was responsible for innovations in iron production, and produced much of the pipe still in use in many Pittsburgh homes. It also sold pipe to golf courses for irrigation systems. "Byers pipe of genuine wrought iron has never been known to cause a serious failure after being buried in the ground for upwards of 30 years," boasted one advertisement of its durability.[2]

45

In February 1876, Byers and his brother Ebenezer acquired sole ownership of the company, but 18 years later their partnership ended in scandal. In August 1894, newspapers reported that A.M. Byers's sister-in-law was claiming that her husband had been kidnapped on A.M.'s orders for the purpose of forcing him to give up his interest in the company. The story is straight out of a soap opera.

Annie Hays came from one of the "oldest, wealthiest, most aristocratic and most influential" families in Western Pennsylvania. She was a member of the Daughters of the American Revolution and one of the recognized belles of the area, a true beauty when she married Ebenezer M. Byers 20 years earlier. He was handsome and charming then, and she was infatuated with him.

Her family, however, strongly opposed the marriage, "not only because they considered his family inferior but also on account of his habits." Like many men, he turned out to be a bad husband. He and his brother A.M. came from a family of poor farmers and he felt insecure on account of his wife's social superiority. According to Annie's friends, Ebenezer began to annoy her with "references to her 'blue blood,'" and would fill his house with "his sisters and brothers, who were uneducated people."[3]

Byers was also an alcoholic with a "jealous disposition" and "violent temper." He was reported to "be a regular Jekyll and Hyde. He could be pleasant and agreeable at times, and was well liked by his friends and acquaintances except when drinking." His drinking sprees would frequently incapacitate him for three to four weeks at a time, and his abuse of his wife was "often so terrible she had to flee to the houses of her neighbors, and from them she could not conceal the black and blue marks from his blows on her face and neck." Annie frequently called the police to the house seeking relief from her husband's outbursts, but when confronted Byers claimed he was innocent of any wrong doing, and instead insisted she and the servants were liars. Annie would kick him out of the house and he'd go to his brother A.M.'s or his sister's boarding house, sometimes remaining away for months. Both her and his health began to suffer.[4]

It was reported in the winter of 1892-93 that men from A.M.'s office would come by and induce her husband to drink. "She says they tried to persuade him to sign certain papers or go to the office and sign them," reported the *St. Louis Post Dispatch*. "Ebenezer refused to do either." One day she returned home and discovered her husband was gone. She claimed A.M.'s agents had forced Ebenezer to sign papers changing the firm's name and assigning his interest to A.M.

More disturbing, she charged that her husband had been kidnapped and placed in seclusion under the care of a doctor, Lewis W. Tallman (who was indeed later charged with kidnapping.) She hired a detective to locate Ebenezer, which took over a year, when he was finally discovered in Japan, "with his mind in a very bad state."[5]

When finally returned to the United States, Ebenezer Byers was committed to Kirbride's Insane Asylum in Philadelphia. "That his mind is unbalanced is unquestioned," asserted Superintendent John B. Chapin. His brother A.M. didn't deny that he wanted control of his brother's affairs, but he also added that Ebenezer had desired "to get away from his wife." A month later, in October 1894, it was reported that a guardian had been appointed for the "lunatic."[6]

A.M. Byers now had total control of the company, and his brother died the following year in the asylum. Annie Byers continued to maintain that her husband had been coerced, and had not been of sound mind when he signed away his interest in the company. In a pathetic twist of fate, she was also declared insane in 1899, but was later released and died in 1910. Eben Byers was 14 years old when this drama unfolded, and it must have been emotionally upsetting as well as an embarrassment for him and his family. His classmates at the St. Paul's School in Concord, New Hampshire would have probably known of the scandal.

Founded in 1856, it was a school for the elite. Graduates have included Robert Mueller, former director of the FBI and Special Counsel overseeing an investigation into allegations of Russian interference in the 2016 U.S. presidential election, Watergate Special Prosecutor Archibald Cox, banker J. P. Morgan, Jr., and John Jacob Astor IV, who died on the *Titanic*. Eben Byers was among rich kids in his privileged social class, as he would be later at Yale.[7]

Alexander Byers accepted his power as a given, as would his sons, and he was determined to hold on to it. This was an era when workers were at the mercy of their bosses, with 12-hour days, seven days a week being common. From the 1890s onward, union leaders in the steel industry pushed for reforms, but employers chose to keep the long day as the standard.

In reality, there was little concern for workers. As one steel mill worker explained in the late 1880s:

> They wipe a man out every little while. Sometimes a chain breaks, and a ladle tips over, and the iron explodes...Of course, if everything is working all smooth and a man watches out, why, all right! But you take it after they've been on duty twelve hours without sleep, and running like hell, everybody tired and loggy, and it's a different story.[8]

Andrew Carnegie was "kinder," as his workers only toiled six 12-hour days. "It sweats the life out of a man," said another worker. "I often drink two buckets of water during twelve hours; the sweat drips through my sleeves, and runs down my legs and fills my shoes."[9] Men like Alexander Byers and Andrew Carnegie built this country, at times ruthlessly, and for those injured in their mills, there was no workman's compensation; men were simply out of a job, and perhaps permanently crippled.

Nine months after Eben Byers's aunt was declared insane, his brother A.M., Jr. died in December 1899. The following year (coincidently on the same day it reported news of Harry Vardon winning the U.S. Open in Chicago), the *Pittsburgh Daily Post* announced the passing of A.M. Byers. He had suffered from heart disease, and it was said he never recovered from the shock of his son's death. Eben would never have to worry about money, as his father left behind an estate estimated between eight to twelve million dollars (around $230 to $355 million dollars today.) Byers's sons, Dallas, Eben, and John succeeded each other as the head of the company.[10]

After graduating from Yale in 1901, Eben began working in the A.M. Byers firm, as well as with the Girard Iron Company in Ohio, and served as the latter's president from 1904 to 1910. He was named president of A.M. Byers in 1909 upon the death of his brother Dallas, and held that post until 1925, when his younger brother J. Frederic took over (J. Frederic also served as president of the United States Golf Association from 1922 to 1923.) Eben Byers would later serve as the Chairman of the Board of A.M. Byers, as well as the boards of numerous banks.[11]

By 1912, according to the Bureau of Labor, 82 percent of all employees in blast furnaces worked seven days regularly, down from 97 percent in 1907. With World War I came a boom for steel and other industries, and the percentage of manufacturing employees working 12-hour shifts actually stood higher in 1919 than it had in 1911.

In 1919, before the Senate Committee on Education and Labor, John Fitzpatrick, chairman of the National Committee for Organizing Iron and Steel Workers, stated, "The home life of the entire family is destroyed where a 12-hour day obtains." The committee reported that the policy of working men 10 and 12 hours per day in the steel mills was "unwise and un-American…An 8-hour day with a living wage that will enable men to support their families and bring up their children according to the standards of American life ought to be a cardinal part of our industrial policy." The Federal government and public opinion supported a change, but it was slow in coming. Only when the industry saw that profits were not affected did the transition to the 8-hour day begin in the late 1920s.

Thousands of workers had more leisure time, as from 1922 to 1926 the average full-time hours worked in steel mills dropped from 72.3 to 59.8 and across all occupations stood at 54.4, down from 63.2 in 1922. "Reckon that's how I spend my time now – findin' out what's goin' on in the world," said one steelworker. Now when he came home from work he could play with his children and not simply eat his dinner and collapse into bed. He said he wouldn't go back to the long day "for anything in the world." It might have meant more money, but in his view, "The rest makes up for the money."[12]

Eben Byers probably wasn't overly concerned with his workers, as they were faceless creatures from a different social class, a different world. He was an industrialist by birth, but much preferred playing golf and entertaining women. He wasn't an imposing physical specimen, standing 5'4" – some compared him to a jockey – but was nice enough looking and did have a way with the ladies. At Yale, his suave demeanor and conquests at nearby girls schools earned him the nickname "Foxy Grandpa." Money and success can also be powerful aphrodisiacs.

On the golf course, he played a good enough game to team with future collegiate champion Charles Hitchcock, Jr. in an April 8, 1900 match against Harry Vardon at the New Haven (Connecticut) Country Club. Vardon, as mentioned in the previous chapter on Nathaniel Moore, was on his tour of the United States, and won the 18-hole match 1 up.[13] In July Byers played in the U.S. Amateur for the first time, during his summer break from Yale, only two months before his father's death.

Two years later, in 1902, he lost in the finals of that event to Louis James 4 and 2 over a water-logged course at the Glen View Club in Illinois. His swing technique brought mixed reviews.

> One man, who can be said to speak with authority, pronounced it the best he had ever seen in an amateur in this country, whilst others declared it was not at all attractive. Perhaps the charm of the style lay in its ease. The swing was short, slow, and deliberate, with a halt at the top. It seemed as if the ball would go a very short distance, but to everybody's astonishment Byers generally got as long a ball as any of his opponents. Such good results are seldom attained with such apparent ease.[14]

On his way to the finals Byers beat Walter Travis, one of the great amateurs of the day, who remarked that Byers's "game was simply unbeatable." But against James, after being two up in the morning round, his putting failed him. *The New York Times* reported that the match was played under the most "unfavorable conditions," as rain came down in torrents off and on. Despite the weather, a gallery of 1,600 (a third of them women), "probably the largest that ever witnessed a golf game in this country," followed the play. Byers disappointed numerous supporters who had bet money on him, but said "James defeated me fairly, and I have no excuses...He is a fast and plucky player. I was off on my putting, and should really have made a better showing."[15]

In 1903 he lost again in the finals, this time to Walter Travis, whose putting from three to ten feet was deadly. Two weeks later they both played in a special match against a team of Oxford and Cambridge golfers at the Ekwanok Club in Vermont. While Travis was defeated, Byers beat Norman. F. Hunter of Cambridge in the finals, 1 up.[16]

After being defeated in the early round in the 1904 and 1905

Eben Byers on the green, c.1906.

U.S. Amateurs, Byers broke through with a victory in 1906 at the now defunct 6,203-yard Englewood Golf Club in New Jersey, a Donald Ross design. Byers defeated George Lyon of Canada in a nip-and-tuck match (Lyon had won the golf competition at the 1904 St. Louis Olympics.) Lyon was a former cricketer and the "results he obtained from his absolutely unorthodox methods lessened the value in many minds of the teaching of the authorities," noted *Golf* magazine. Lyon dispatched the ball from the tee "with one clean, smashing hit delivered with sledge-hammer force and the full shots through the green were played in the same manner. But he got results."

Byers, for his part, was said to have iron play that had no superior, although that week he was suffering from a sprained wrist. "Mr. Byers's weak spot, perhaps, is his ability to miss short putts, but in this year's championship the failing was not conspicuous."[17] Byers gained a measure of revenge on Walter Travis from 1903, beating him in the semi-finals to make it to the championship match. Lyon had beaten defending champion H. Chandler Egan in an earlier round, the same man he beat for the Olympic gold medal.

Byers made a dramatic entrance for the final, arriving by automobile from Manhattan as Lyons was on the putting green getting in some last-minute practice. At 10:30 a.m. they teed off, and as the pair descended the hill toward the green, a multitude of golfing enthusiasts chased after them, intent on seeing every shot. The committee walked in front holding a rope stretching across the course, a precaution to prevent the too excitable in the gallery from crowding upon the players.

President Ransom H. Thomas of the USGA refereed the match. A.W. Tillinghast, future icon of golf course architecture, who spent his summers at Toronto, wanted to caddie for Lyon, but Lyon thought it "might change his luck to desert his regular boy." About 2,000 people came out to watch, and their numbers hindered play at times. Around 10,000 came out for the entire week's play, setting an attendance record. Top players even stayed to watch the final match. Jerome Travers, who would win the next two U.S. Amateurs and the 1915 U.S. Open, followed the afternoon round, as did Georgianna Bishop, 1904 U.S. Women's Amateur champion. Walter Travis followed the morning round before having to leave.[18]

Eben Byers (middle with bucket hat), and George Lyon (with the club), at the 1906 U.S. Amateur. USGA President R.H. Thomas on the far right.

"Every good stroke or clever bit of play was applauded with an impartiality which was keenly appreciated by the players," wrote the Chicago *Inter Ocean*. The crowd, however, was glad that the championship cup was not won by the Canadian. When Byers made his best putt of the day to par the 160-yard finishing hole and secure a 2 up victory, he was carried off the green by two competitors who went out in the early rounds. Archie Reid (son of John Reid, who helped bring golf to the United States in the 1880s) and Hugo Johnstone put him on their shoulders and "bore him up a steep bank at the home green to the clubhouse."[19]

One advantage Byers had was that of a good caddie, Jock Hutchison, who would go on to win the 1920 PGA Championship and the 1921 British Open. A newspaper asserted that the "combination of Byers' spirit, fine brassie and spoon shots, accurate putting, and Hutchinson's [sic] sound advice turned the trick at Englewood." William C. "Billy" Carnegie, a nephew of the famous Andrew Carnegie, had hired Jock's older brother Tom to give his family golf lessons at his winter estate on Cumberland Island, Georgia. But tragedy struck on December 11, 1900, when Tom was thrown from a horse and killed. After the death of his 21-year-old brother, Jock was asked by Carnegie to come over from St Andrews, Scotland and become his tutor and caddie. Jock later served at the Pittsburgh Golf Club and Allegheny Country Club in Pennsylvania, and while at the latter he "became 'Eb' Byers's personal coach and caddie."[20]

The Brooklyn Daily Eagle reported that the "only regrettable feature of the day was the employment of a professional caddie." Hutchison had also carried for Byers at the Metropolitan Amateur earlier that May, where Jerome Travers beat him in the finals 3 and 1. "On the face of things there was nothing objectionable about Hutchinson's [sic] work, but a most pernicious principle is involved. It offends no law, but as Travis said more than once, it is unsportsmanlike."[21]

That U.S. Amateur was the zenith of Byers's career. He would compete in nine more U.S. Amateurs, his best finish being in 1907, when he reached the semi-finals before losing to winner Jerome Travers. He also played in two British Amateurs (in 1904 and 1907) and missed the cut in his only U.S. Open in 1908.

In 1913 Byers played in two exhibition matches against Harry Vardon and Ted Ray on their tour of the U.S. that year. On August 26th, he partnered with Joe K. Bole at the Mayfield Club in Cleveland, as the two lost a 36-hole match 5 and 4. John D. Rockefeller was an interested spectator there. On September 25th, with 1910 U.S. Amateur champion William C. Fownes, Jr., another 36-hole match was played. The result was the same, as they were defeated 5 and 3 at Oakmont, outside of Pittsburgh.[22]

The last match he ever played in the U.S. Amateur was against Bobby Jones, who in 1916 was playing in his first national championship at Merion Cricket Club. Charles "Chick" Evans, the winner that year, would recall years later "scanning the course and seeing Bobby and Eben Byers engaged in a club-throwing exhibition."

Jones won that match 3 and 1, and used to joke later in life that he only won because Byers ran out of clubs first.[23] Eben tried to qualify for the U.S. Amateur three more times, the last in 1926, with no success. The Byers family helped found the Allegheny Country Club and the Rolling Rock Club in Pennsylvania, the former being Eben's home course.

Fred Brand, Jr., who served on the USGA's Executive Committee and whose father was brought from Carnoustie, Scotland by Byers in 1903 to be the head professional at Allegheny, used to caddie for Byers. From 1922 to 1926, Brand was paid $15 a week [about $220 today – pretty good pay for a 16-year-old kid] during the summertime, when he was out of school.

Eben Byers as a member of the Yale University golf team, 1899.

He would be at the club every day by 10 a.m., and if Byers didn't show up by three o'clock he was free to carry another member's bag. He said he had a wonderful relationship with Byers, and that he was a "perfectionist in every respect, and his caddie had to be on his toes at all times."

Brand also maintained that Byers contributed to the practice of matching clubs. Each year Burt Kilroy (who later headed MacGregor's clubmaking division and was the clubmaker for Brand's father) would make up eight complete sets. Byers would then go through all of them and pick out the clubs that worked best for him to make up his set. When he died, more than 1,200 clubs were found in his home. Byers had also "given away another 50 or so sets over the years."[24]

When Alexander Byers died, his sons kept the same tight reins on the company that he had, and retained a corps of managers familiar with the company's operations and inherent philosophy. As late as 1923, the Byers family held almost absolute control of the firm, and survived the Great Depression. Eben Byers continued to lead a life of privilege after the stock market crash, maintaining homes in Pittsburgh, New York, Rhode Island and South Carolina.

Eben Byers's swing, 1903. Note the high left heel and bent left arm on the backswing, the form of the day.

He had horse-racing stables in New York and England, and his entries appeared in many important races. He followed baseball with enthusiasm and had box seats at Forbes Field in Pittsburgh for many years. Byers also won numerous trophies for trap-shooting, a sport he took up in 1916, which supplemented his womanizing and frequent visits to Palm Beach, Florida.[25]

Life was good. Then, while returning from the annual Yale-Harvard football game in 1927, he fell hard from the upper berth of his Pullman car, and things began to change. Supposedly, the injury to his arm resulted from "some post-game revelry." For the next several weeks,

Byers complained of muscular aches and a run-down feeling that undermined both his athletic, and, it was rumored, sexual performance.

He went to see a Pittsburgh physiotherapist named Dr. Charles Clinton Moyer, who recommended he try Radithor, a patent medicine blend of radium and water. Its manufacturer, the Bailey Radium Laboratory in New Jersey, claimed it was a cure for dyspepsia, arthritis, high blood pressure, impotence and more than 150 other endocrinologic maladies. Byers began taking it in December 1927.[26] He didn't realize it at the time, but the day he emptied that first half-ounce bottle of the stuff down his throat, he was sentencing himself to death.

When Marie and Pierre Curie discovered radium in 1898, it caused great excitement within the scientific community, with claims of its power to cure a variety of ailments. Like DNA and stem cell research today, it was hoped that radium might have the potential to be a medical miracle. Marie Curie wrote that the luminous effect of radium, "seemed suspended in the darkness [and] stirred us with ever-new emotion and enchantment." The U.S. Surgeon General said it "reminds one of a mythological super-being."

The Curies initially thought it could selectively destroy cancerous cells and enhance the growth of healthy ones. It was thought that small doses taken internally – known as "mild radium therapy" – could revitalize damaged cells and tissue. Dr. Roger M. Macklis, an oncologist, studied the Byers case while at Harvard and helped frame the case in the context of his times. "Radium can indirectly cause increased production of red blood cells," he says, "and hence an invigorated feeling."[27]

"For the first few months after taking radium into the body," wrote Robley D. Evans in his early study on radium poisoning in 1933, "there is a sensation of well-being and general physical improvement. Soon, however, the deadly alpha ray bombardment of the blood producing centers begins to be felt, and death follows in a year or more, depending on the total quantity of radium fixed in the system. Protection of the public from these nostrums is mainly a matter of public health education and legislation."[28]

However, in the early 1900s, mild radium therapy quickly gained legitimate standing in the medical community. The *American Journal of*

Clinical Medicine claimed that "Radioactivity prevents insanity, rouses noble emotions, retards old age, and creates a splendid youthful joyous life." Other scientists proclaimed that radioactivity carried "electrical energy into the depths of the body and there subject[ed] the juices, protoplasm, and nuclei of the cells to an immediate bombardment by explosions of electrical atoms...causing the system to throw off waste products."[29]

Radithor was a "status drink." At $1 a bottle [about $15 today], only the well-to-do could easily afford it. It was marketed as a health drink by William J.A. Bailey. "Radioactiviy is one of the most remarkable agents in medical science," he claimed. "The discoveries relating to its action in the body have been so far-reaching that it is impossible to prophesy future developments. It is perpetual sunshine."[30]

Dr. Macklis began studying the Byers case in 1989, when he came across several empty bottles of Radithor in a medical antiques shop and bought one on a whim. Because of his medical training, he knew it was possible to make water temporarily radioactive by incubating it with radium.

> The radium gives off radon, a radioactive gas whose half-life is short. I assumed that the maker of the patent medicine had resorted to this very inexpensive process and that the Radithor's residual activity had decayed to insignificance long ago. I was wrong. Tests performed by my colleagues [in their gamma-ray spectroscopy unit] revealed that almost 70 years after it had been produced, the nearly empty bottle was still dangerously radioactive.[31]

Dr. Macklis asserts that Bailey "was a born con man" who peddled various miracle cures, especially for impotence, for years. Radithor was his big success, the result of years of laboratory research Bailey claimed, but actually it was just distilled water laced with one microcurie each of two isotopes of radium. He sold more than 400,000 bottles for $1 each – a 400% profit, says Dr. Macklis, adding: "He was the chief impresario in the radioactive patent medicine field."[32]

Whereas Eben Byers was born to wealth, William John Aloysius Bailey, four years older, grew up in a rough-and-tumble section of Boston. In spite of poor entrance exams, he was admitted to Harvard in 1903, although two years later financial difficulties forced him to drop out. He bounced around through various schemes for the next few years, and was arrested on mail order fraud charges in 1915, being found guilty with two others and sentenced to 30 days in jail. In 1918 he was fraudulently promoting a patent medicine for male impotence, in which the active ingredient was strychnine.

Radiation research was a natural draw for Bailey, says Macklis, "because it had become a glamour field in medicine." Claiming to be a Harvard graduate with a doctorate from the University of Vienna, he sought legitimacy for his views. In 1925 Bailey moved to East Orange, New Jersey and opened the Bailey Radium Laboratories, where he created his best money-maker, Radithor.[33]

Bailey was not alone in pushing radium products, as across the country advertisements in magazines were claiming that radium could restore vitality to the elderly, making "old men young." Radithor became the energy drink of the day. One aficionado wrote: "Sometimes I am halfway persuaded that I can feel the sparkles inside my anatomy." Radium shone "like a good deed in a naughty world." One could shop for radium jockstraps and lingerie, and radium-laced butter, milk, toothpaste, face creams, soap, and rouge.[34]

When Eben Byers went to see Dr. Moyer in 1927, he was looking for something to give him a pick-me-up. Radithor was it, and it was also used as an aphrodisiac. "Improved blood supply sent to the pelvic organs and tonic effect upon the nervous system generally result in a great improvement in the sex organs," touted a pamphlet entitled *Radithor, the New Weapon of Medical Science*, which was mailed to doctors in the mid-1920s.

Dr. Moyer, like many others, found willing subjects ready to open their wallets. It did not require a prescription, and Bailey sold it to physicians for $25 a case (30 half-ounce bottles with about $3.60 worth of radium in them); the public had to pay $30 a case (over $400 today.) Bailey made money, doctors like Charles Moyer made money, and people like Byers were destroyed.[35]

For the next two years, Byers gulped two or three bottles of Radithor a day. Initially, he found it a wonderful elixir. A cousin of his, Buckley Byers, Jr., remembered that Eben was once "so intoxicated by Radithor" that he played a multi-day golf marathon/competition with some friends, also under its influence.

> They went through the woods, down paved roads, and along the Ohio River from the Byers mansion in Pittsburgh to another family residence in Sewickley, 30 miles away. There was a big family quibble back then because Eben was hoarding the Radithor in the basement, the wine cellar, everywhere. He was filling both houses with train-car loads of the stuff.

So pleased was he with the results that he had cases of it sent to his friends, colleagues and female acquaintances. He even fed some of it to his racehorses. Like other ardent Radithor enthusiasts, Byers consumed vast quantities of it, drinking approximately 1,500 bottles, and probably accumulated a radiation dosage equivalent to thousands of X-rays.[36]

While the science of the day gave some measure of support to Byers's faith in radium water, regulatory agencies at the time were more focused on truth in advertising issues than in the harmful effects these products were having on people. The Federal Trade Commission (FTC), for instance, took action against makers of potions that lacked advertised levels of radioactivity, and initially paid little attention to other people whose health was suffering due to their exposure to radium – watch dial-painters.[37]

When the United States entered World War I, soldiers had trouble seeing their watches at night, which could have catastrophic consequences when needing to know what time to move in the field. Watch dial factories in Newark, New Jersey (the United States Radium Corporation) and Ottawa, Illinois (the Radium Dial Company) hired workers, mostly young women, to paint the dials with a greenish-white luminous paint, which went by the name "Undark." It contained miniscule bits of radium, the most valuable substance on earth, with a single gram selling for $120,000 in 1917 ($2.3 million today.)

Each woman added radium powder to water and a gum arabic adhesive to create the paint, and when mixed with zinc sulfide, the reaction created a brilliant glow. When a thin layer of this paint was applied to the watch dials, they glowed, making them easier to read at night on the Western Front. The dust, however, would waft in the factory air and settle down into the women's hair, covering their shoulders, faces, arms, and necks, making the girls gleam. "When I would go home at night," recalled Edna Bolz, "my clothing would shine in the dark." The young women would paint their lips, eyebrows, and even their teeth before going out at night. Then, upon returning home, and turning off the lights, they'd surprise their boyfriends and husbands by glowing in the dark.[38]

Their pay was roughly three times that of the average working girl, and the work was light. Without exception, the "radium girls" were told the paint was safe to handle, and virtually no precautions were taken to protect them. During the course of their work, to ensure that the paint did not get on parts other than the dial, the tips of their already fine brushes had to be constantly wetted with a cloth to keep them at a fine point. But quickly the cloth was discarded and the women moistened the tip with their lips. It was lip, dip, paint all day long.

Within a few years, it became evident that they had been lied to, as many began to suffer from radium poisoning – it affected their teeth, legs, hips and joints. One was Amelia "Mollie" Maggia, who had some teeth pulled in 1922, and developed ulcers in her mouth and gums. The doctors thought she had syphilis, but after investigating further, learned she had been poisoned by radium. She was in agonizing pain, and went back to her dentist. As he gently examined the bone in her mouth, he was horrified to have her jawbone break off in his fingers. He removed it by "merely putting his fingers in her mouth and lifting it out." Mollie would die a few months later, a "painful and terrible death," according to her sister.[39]

Radium deposits itself in the bones like calcium, and once there is in a position to produce peculiarly effective damage, since it bombards the bones like bullets from a machine gun. Eben Byers didn't know about Mollie – why would he? We are all oblivious to most things in the world, unless they are close to us and affect us directly. If he had known of her condition he probably would never have taken Radithor, but it was too late.

There were others. Grace Fryer's spine had been shattered by radium – it "eats bone as steadily and surely as fire burns wood," writes Kate Moore in *The Radium Girls* – and Grace had to wear a back brace in order to walk. Even with all this, there were those who spoke out publicly against attempts to link radium to the dial-painters' deaths. "It is a pity," said huckster William Bailey, "that the public [is being] turned against this splendid curative agency by unfounded statements."[40]

Katherine Schaub began having trouble with her teeth in 1924, and was also diagnosed with radium poisoning. She described the pain she experienced as comparable to "a dentist drilling on a live nerve hour after hour, day after day, month after month."[41] She would later be one of several who testified in a lawsuit against the United States Radium Corporation, whose five defendants each won a judgment of $10,000 in cash, a pension of $600 a year for life, and past and future medical expenses. Katherine died five years later, in 1933, a year after Eben Byers.

Shortly after the death of Schaub, Catherine Donahue, one of the dial-painters in Illinois, found herself too ill to go to church on Easter Sunday. A Catholic priest gave her communion at her home. A horrified friend recalled that as he was doing so, part of "her jawbone broke through the flesh and [came] out into her mouth." Donahue had to keep picking out pieces of jawbone from her mouth, which excreted a considerable discharge of pus and gave off a foul order. "I just remember her moaning, moaning," said her niece. "You know that she was in pain, but she didn't have the energy to scream." When she died at the age of 35, Catherine weighed less than 60 pounds.[42]

Many dial-painters experienced pain in their teeth and had abscesses in their mouths and lesions on their faces. Their limbs were also affected. Necrosis – the death of body tissue, occurring when too little blood flows to it – was present in many of them, brought about by the radiation poisoning. This would also affect Eben Byers.

By 1930, Byers began feeling the ill effects of Radithor. He was losing weight and complained of severe headaches, and pain in his jaw. He told his private physician that he had lost that "toned-up" feeling, only to be told that he just had a bad case of sinusitis. However, when his teeth began falling out, he became alarmed. A radiologist from New York, Dr. Joseph Steiner, was consulted and reviewed Byers's X-rays. He saw similarities with the bony lesions in Byers's jaw to those described in dial-painters who had recently died. Dr. Frederick B. Flynn, a radium expert from the Department of Industrial Medicine at Columbia University, was called for a consultation. He confirmed Steiner's suspicions. "Byers's body was slowly decomposing," wrote Dr. Roger Macklis, "the result of massive radium intoxication from the Radithor."[43]

Flynn didn't share his conclusions with the public, however, in part because others, including Byers's personal physician, refused to believe them. William Bailey's company had sent pamphlets via mass mailings to nearly every physician in the nation touting the use of Radithor, complete with convincing testimonials from doctors and patients alike.

Although the cases of the watch dial workers provided evidence that even small quantities of radioactive material could be devastating to health, the public was slow to take notice. The Food and Drug Administration (FDA) had issued warnings, but had no recourse to legal action. Therefore the Federal Trade Commission took over the investigation into Bailey's claims in 1928. On February 5, 1930, the agency filed an official complaint charging Bailey with false advertising regarding the efficacy and safety of his products.[44]

On September 10, 1931, with the commission's investigation well under way, Robert H. Winn went to Byers's residence to take his testimony, since he was now too ill to travel. His upper and lower jaw had been removed. Although his bone marrow and kidneys were failing, and a brain abscess had left him nearly mute, he was able to answer the questions posed to him. Byers was asked about his consumption of Radithor. "Well, I think I have not had it for about a year or two years," he responded, "and I took it for about two years before that – about four years ago, I would say." When did his physical problems begin? "Well, that was a year ago last January [1930] that it really got bad."[45]

Byers said that two years earlier, in December 1929, he "had a tooth pulled and it would not heal and kept getting pus out of it. That was the start of everything. I had an operation in Palm Beach in January of

62

the next year." Many doctors attended to him, and he said Dr. Frederick Flynn examined him with "an instrument, whatever they call it to detect the presence of radium in my system."[46]

On December 19, 1931, the FTC issued a cease-and-desist order enjoining the Bailey Radium Laboratories from continuing to market Radithor. The American Medical Association, which had allowed the internal use of radium to remain on its list of "New and Nonofficial Remedies" even after the discovery of the dial-painters' deaths, finally removed it as an accepted treatment. It was too late to do Byers any good. All he could do was wait. *My God, what did I do to myself?* His thoughts must have been similar to Katherine Schaub's, one of the "radium girls" who said, "I have to remain here [at home] and watch painful death approach. I am so lonely."[47]

There was no future for Byers, only the past. Painful ones of a family scandal, of the deaths of his brothers, of the first time he drank Radithor. Perhaps he let himself imagine those days on the golf course, of the orange and brown leaves swirling slowly down from a sentinel of trees surrounding the green on a crisp fall day, of the friends who joined in the reverie after his triumph at Englewood in 1906. It was only yesterday, and yet a thousand years ago. A profound sadness must have drained his spirit at the realization that there would be no tomorrows.

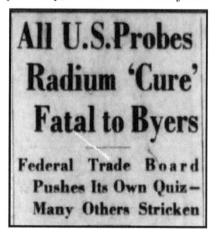

All U.S. Probes Radium 'Cure' Fatal to Byers

Federal Trade Board Pushes Its Own Quiz — Many Others Stricken

Brooklyn Daily Eagle **front page headline announcing the death of Byers, April 1, 1932.**

Eben Byers died from radium poisoning in the early morning of March 31, 1932 at Doctors' Hospital in New York City. *The New York Times* reported that he "had been a patient there from time to time during the last two years, and that he had been there continuously for the last month." Byers's death was forecast almost a month earlier by Chairman W.E. Humphrey of the Federal Trade

Commission. On March 10th he had said, "Medical science can hold out no hope for him; his is a slow, torturous, certain death."[48]

Byers's body had shriveled to 92 pounds, says Dr. Roger Macklis, and his once youthful face, set off by deep-set eyes and dark hair sculpted by pomade, had been disfigured by operations that removed his disintegrating jaw and part of his skull in an attempt to halt the destruction of bone. His brother in law J. Dennison Lyons said Byers "was in great pain during the last six months," adding a lie that he was "unaware that his life was in danger until about two weeks ago."[49]

News of Byers's death and the mysterious circumstances surrounding it made its way to his former colleagues on Wall Street almost immediately. A.M. Byers Company stock, already battered by the Great Depression, lost a third of its value in the week after his death. Friends and relatives, worried that he might have died from something contagious, reached out to Byers's doctors to ask what he died from. The day after his death, a criminal investigation was opened as his body was being prepared for autopsy.[50]

The autopsy was performed by Chief Medical Examiner Charles Norris and Assistant Medical Examiner Thomas A. Gonzales "after the Bureau of Vital Statistics had rejected the original death certificate ascribing death due to radium necrosis – a gangrenous condition – of the right jaw and neck." The death certificate signed by Dr. Norris listed radium poisoning, abscess of the brain, necrosis of the jaw, terminal bronchial pneumonia and secondary anemia as the causes of death. Dr. Norris stated that the death was accidental and added the annotation that Byers "drank radium water for the past two years."

Dr. Charles Moyer, the physician who prescribed the Radithor to Byers, was defiant, arguing that the death was not due to radium poisoning, but rather the combination of two ailments which had induced gout. "I believe that radium water has a definite place in the treatment of certain diseases," claimed Moyer, "and I prescribe it when I deem it necessary," adding that he had taken as much or more radium water as Byers and was still active and healthy.[51]

The autopsy confirmed that Byers's bones and organs were dangerously radioactive. The fact that his extracted teeth and remaining jawbone, placed on an X-ray film-plate overnight, produced a dramatic exposure pattern, was proof of this conclusion. "Distributed through his bones," noted *Time* magazine's report of the autopsy, "were 36 micrograms of radium. Ten micrograms is a fatal quantity." Dr. Macklis said in 1990, "He took enough radium to kill four people if he took it all at once. The mystery is how did Byers survive so long, feeling so good, and have such a super-lethal burden in his body?"[52]

The *Literary Digest* noted there was a "chill of apprehension over the country" after his death, and the FDA issued a warning against "radioactive" drugs because of serious injuries to users. *The Pittsburgh Press* reported April 1st that more than 100 patients who used Radithor had been afflicted with radium poisoning. "The deadly radium racket," declared the New York *Daily News*, "which in the last five years has poured thousands into the pockets of quack doctors and vendors of patent medicines and appliances," was under fire from Federal and city investigators on the heels of Dr. Norris's autopsy results. "In the Middle West and on the Pacific Coast, 200,000 persons are supposed to be using radioactive waters and apparatus for the infusion of radium energy."[53]

Dr. Harrison S. Maitland, medical examiner of Essex County, New Jersey, who had determined the source of the radium poisoning that affected dial-painters in Newark and Orange (New Jersey), was then called into the case by Dr. Norris. Health officials began investigating radium belts, radium coated chocolate bars, face salves, and other radium laced products. The news of Byers's death alarmed some members of the upper class, although New York City Mayor Jimmy Walker, an admitted radium water user, was hesitant to give it up, insisting that it "made him feel so good." There were also whispers in the Pittsburgh press about a lady friend of Byers's who had also died of a mysterious ailment. Some doctors stepped forward with evidence of other cases, and one went on a New York radio program and held the radioactive bones of one victim in front of a Geiger counter to demonstrate "the deadly sound of radium."[54]

With Byers's death, the FTC reopened its investigation, and the FDA began campaigning for more sweeping powers. Medical societies denounced patent medicine sales, and many voices called for radium control laws throughout this country and Europe. But it wasn't the end of flim-flam. In 1937, William Bailey was fined for selling "Kelpodine

Tablets," a concoction made of seaweed and kelp that "were fraudulently offered for the treatment of 82 specific diseases and 'other conditions.'"[55]

Bailey was never prosecuted for Byers's death, and he maintained his potion was safe. "I have drunk more radium water than any man alive, and I have never suffered any ill effects," he claimed. The Federal Trade Commission shut down his Radithor operation in late 1932, but Bailey continued with other radioactive scams. Hounded by the press and Newark public health officials, Bailey dropped from the limelight.

He died in 1949 from bladder cancer, and left an estate of only $4,175. Although he died of cancer, he never believed that small doses of radioactivity were harmful, and asserted that his health and spirits were excellent almost to the end. Nearly 20 years after Bailey's death, medical researchers exhumed his remains, finding them ravaged by radiation, and still "hot."[56]

Eben Byers is interred in a lead-lined coffin in the Byer Mausoleum, Section 13, Lot 67, of the Allegheny Cemetery in Pittsburgh. Robley D. Evans, who did the study on radium poisoning in 1933 as a young man, wrote in 1981 that the "precipitating event which put me on the path of exploring the biological effects of radiation was the heavily publicized death" of Byers in 1932. As part of a radium program at the Massachusetts Institute of Technology, he and a team exhumed Byers in 1965 to measure his total radium intake.[57] As with the remains in William Bailey, his were also "hot," and in another 1,600 years will have lost only half of their radioactivity.

It wasn't until 1938, when the Food, Drug, and Cosmetic Act was signed into law by President Franklin Roosevelt, that drugs such as radium water were outlawed as being dangerous to health even when used according to directions on the label. The deaths of Eben Byers and the "radium girls" were tragic, but they did set in motion measures that would protect future workers exposed to radioactive material in the nuclear age. After World War II, an official from the Atomic Energy Commission said, "If it hadn't been for those dial-painters, the [Manhattan] project's management could have reasonably rejected the extreme precautions that were urged on it and thousands of workers might well have been, and might still be, in great danger." The lessons learned from the experiences of these women had been, officials said, "invaluable."[58]

Eben Byers died a horrible, painful, lingering death brought about by his own vanity and desire to drink from a fountain of youth that didn't exist. He joined countless other victims who were not rich or famous, but who suffered just as much. All were victims of the scoundrels who sold them poisonous products, as well as a medical community that gave them a false sense of security, and failed to protect them until it was too late.

Chapter 3: Cyril Walker – "The Sad Tale of a Self-Destructive Man"

Golf professionals of the early 20th century were known for their fondness of drink – a wee dram, a stiff snort, a flask of hooch, a shot and a beer, liquid courage in a bottle – all would do, and did, frequently. George Bernard Shaw wrote that "alcohol is the anesthesia by which we endure the operation of life." It can destroy lives, however, and not even U.S. Open champions are immune to its addictive power. Fred Herd was notorious for having to offer a deposit before the USGA would present him with the trophy in 1898, so great was its fear he might pawn it to pay for booze. But he didn't lose his life to it, as did the winner in 1924.

Ben Hogan said Cyril Walker was derided as a "'cheese champion,' a rank outsider who came by the honor through sheer luck. These charges were not so." Although Hogan had never seen him play, he heard "from old-timers like Hagen and Sarazen that Walker had more than his share of 'moxie' that day."[1]

Walker was a dour fellow, irascible, acerbic, and sarcastic, yet in spite of these less than loveable qualities, he had friends who tried to help him when he fell on hard times. Sadly, as the years passed by, he exhausted their generosity and patience through incessant abuse, and lost many. Like Hogan, he carried a big chip on his shoulder, but when faced with adversity, he climbed into a bottle and couldn't escape. Certainly, Walker surprised the golfing world when he beat Bob Jones on a long and difficult Oakland Hills course to capture the 1924 U.S. Open. But he wasn't a hacker who never contended before or after. He was just a hard-luck case, with an abrasive personality that didn't endear him to friends or fans of the game.

"I believe I am the most unusual golf champion that ever lived," said Walker after his triumph. "Don't mistake me. I am not saying that I think myself the greatest of the champions of the links. Or the brainiest. Or the most mechanically perfect. No, unusual is the word." Born in Manchester, England on September 18, 1892, Walker struggled to thrive from the beginning, almost dying at the age of two after being scalded by a boiling pot of starch left on the stove. "I was long in the most critical condition, it being doubtful whether I would live or die. For two years I was, so to speak, 'on my back,' unable to take part in childhood pastimes." He was a sickly child but his life changed at the age of eleven when he was introduced to golf. He became a caddie and took to playing the game, which strengthened his health.[2]

Walker had planned on being a stock broker, but recalled sitting in an office all day "thinking of the beauties of the outdoor life I had enjoyed as a caddie," adding, "I loved the game and loved it dearly." He decided to change his path in life, and became an assistant professional at Trafford Park in Manchester. After shooting a 69 one day, the 18-year-old young man felt he had the talent to "battle with the great[s] of the land." Soon thereafter, Walker had a match with his boss, Thomas G. Renouf (who played in numerous British Opens, twice finishing fifth), and played horribly. When they finished Renouf told him matter-of-factly, "Ah, you'll never be able to play golf!" Walker claimed the "bitterness which this declaration aroused in me" persisted from that day forward. He had something to prove to the world, and wanted to leave Trafford Park.[3]

A friend helped him secure a position at history-laden Hoylake, home club of the legendary John Ball and Harold Hilton. It was there that Walker received some encouraging words from the great Jerome Travers when they met a couple of years later. Walker qualified for the 1913 British Open, although he withdrew after two rounds. He had met and played with some of the Americans and their "conduct and their conversation filled me with the belief that the United States was the land of opportunity." He asked Travers what it would take to make it as a professional there. Travers told him he could succeed if he was "willing to work hard and not get discouraged," and wrote him a letter of reference, which provided young Cyril with a much needed boost in confidence.[4]

"My family was against the proposition," Walker recalled years later, "but my mind was made up." He sailed for New York in 1914, "trusting to luck and Jerry Travers' recommendation, for I had no job in sight." He was able to get a job as an assistant pro in Connecticut, grateful that Travers' letter had done the work. By September he had met and married Elizabeth Wright, whom he called "Tet," with whom he would have a son, Donald.

Thus began his peripatetic life, as he later went to Indiana, where he won the 1916 Indiana Open, then to New Jersey, Minneapolis, then back to New Jersey again, where he settled at the Englewood Golf Club, site of the 1909 U.S. Open.

When the United States Golf Association cancelled the 1917 U.S. Open on account of World War I, it instead held the "Patriotic Open" (called the "Patriotic Tournament" in newspapers.) Played that June at the Whitemarsh Country Club, outside of Philadelphia, all entry fees and prize money went to the Red Cross. Jock Hutchison won with a score of 292, with Walker finishing 10th in a field that included Jim Barnes, Fred McLeod and Wilfrid Reid.

Walker could play. In 1921 he won the Pennsylvania Open, and reached the semifinals of the PGA Championship, won by Walter Hagen. He shot a course record 66 at Pinehurst in 1922, with an immaculate 29 on the front nine. Even though a small man, he was a long hitter. Jim Barnes, winner of multiple major championships, said Walker had strong wrists that allowed him to swing his light clubs "without great effort, and he sends the clubhead through at greater speed than anyone I ever saw." But he was notorious for his glacial pace of play, which was an irritant to fellow professionals and galleries alike.[5]

While playing a shot, Walker would sometimes walk 150 yards to the green and back to his ball, recalled a friend, picking up "imaginary pebbles, leaves and tiny piece of cut grass. Always with a snarl on his face, Walker would swing two or three clubs before selecting the one he intended to use." Then he would incessantly waggle the club – usually more than a dozen times – before finally pulling the trigger. O.B. Keeler recalled an instance at the Florida Open in 1922, when Cyril was playing the last round with fellow-competitors Gene Sarazen, Patrick "Paddy" Doyle, and George Kerrigan. "Paddy was looking on with an amused and philosophic air and Gene Sarazen, just then coming on his game for his greatest year, was fretting noticeably."[6]

Toward the end of a round that required three hours and twenty minutes – wouldn't it be wonderful if they could play that *fast* today – Walker was putting last, the others having holed out. "He lined up a four-footer with extreme care, and inspected the line microscopically. Then he lined it up again and took his stance." Then he stepped back, and lined it

71

up again. At this point, Sarazen "tossed his putter in the air and said 'Ha-Ha' not at all as if he was amused." Cyril made the putt and then turned to Sarazen: "You play your game and I'll play mine!" he said curtly. "If old age doesn't get you first," shot back Gene.[7]

One story goes that Jock Hutchison, 1921 British Open champion, who was known for his colorful sweaters, bought one with black and white checks about an inch square, and wore it when paired with Walker. As the two were waiting to tee off, Walker remarked in a joking manner, "Jock, it looks as if you intended to play checkers instead of golf from the appearance of that sweater." Hutchison told him that was exactly why he chose it. "I knew I would have plenty of time, so I donned this sweater to fill in with checkers between shots." That silenced Walker.[8]

In 1923 Walker finished second to Walter Hagen in the prestigious North and South Open. Newspapers reported that if not for his slight frame he "would stand right in Hagen's class as one of the earth's leading golfers." Walker had been plagued with health problems since he emigrated to the United States, and maintained that the climate had an unfavorable effect on him. "But, in addition, I was temperamentally unfitted and by habit opposed to the conditions I soon encountered as a professional at an American country club. The American custom of hurry was my undoing. The pressure of my business proved too much for me. Bolted lunches and crowded days undermined my health. In time I developed chronic intestinal inflammation."[9]

O.B. Keeler reported that it was this "severe stomach trouble which was keeping his nerves ragged, and this was the main reason for his painful slowness and preparation for each shot." Walker was competing at the highest levels. In the U.S. Open, he had finished 13th in 1921, and tied for 40th in 1922. After the 1923 U.S. Open, where he tied for 23rd, Walker said "it was decided that my tonsils were filling my system with poison. This diagnosis, followed by an operation, proved to be correct. I soon showed a great improvement." His operation took place six months before the 1924 championship. "By the time it rolled around I was in better condition than at any time since coming to the United States. But when I stepped on the scales just before the play began I tipped them at only 116 pounds."[10]

Walker recalled he "was increasingly conscious of a new tone in my playing which I had not noticed before. Rid of my old distress and worries, I was acquiring an efficiency I never had possessed. The ambitions and hopes of my more youthful days revived in me in full force." He was playing terrific golf, shooting many practice rounds at par or better, and felt ready by the time he arrived at Oakland Hills. The course, at 6,880 yards, was to that point the longest ever in the event's history, and as Walker said, "one of the most treacherous I ever played. The greens were particularly difficult."

Nevertheless, his stellar play continued, and after practice rounds of 72 and 73 his wife asked him how he liked the course. He replied, "I'm absolutely sure that I'm going to win this championship." He must have been convincing, for she jumped to her feet and told him, "I know you are!" Tied for the lead after three rounds with Bobby Jones, he went to the locker room, too keyed up to eat. There, players were telling him, "You've got to beat Jones," adding to the pressure, with many offering advice on just how to beat the best amateur – and best player – in the game. "What I wanted was not advice but quiet. I finally found it in a remote corner of the locker room."[11]

Cyril Walker putting in the 1924 U.S. Open at Oakland Hills.

With encouragement from his playing partner Leo Diegel, Walker went out for the final round in blustery conditions and played steady golf. Walker was as slow as ever, reported *The American Golfer*, taking minutes to hit every shot, "testing wind currents with a moistened finger; arguing with his caddie about what club to use; exchanging one weapon for another and then returning to his first choice." The crucial hole was the par-4 16th, where he "made the shot that clinched the title, the best play under the conditions I have ever executed." With a stiff wind in his face, he took a 2-iron from 175 yards and caught the ball perfectly. It shot off with a low, piercing draw, cleared the pond fronting the green, and finished five feet from the hole.[12]

Poor Diegel's cheerleading had given way to impatience by then, however. As Walker surveyed the putt from every conceivable angle, Diegel stretched himself out on the turf, "pillowed his head on his arm and told his caddie, 'Wake me up when it's all over – I can feel myself growing older.'" Even though it took Cyril forever to play, he showed "the sureness of his touch and his nerve control at this point," wrote Grantland Rice, by making the putt and basically closing the door on the championship.

Coming off the green, newspaper man Fred Kennedy told him that Jones had finished at 300 and Bill Mehlhorn at 301. Walker then parred the last two holes for a three shot victory. After finishing, he ran into Walter Hagen at the clubhouse door. "Well, well, well, Cyril. We've all got to respect you know." Bobby Jones praised the winner, saying "Any man who can shoot that last nine in par today deserves to be champion. My hat's off to Cyril Walker."[13]

It was the pinnacle of his career, as he would play in only three more U.S. Opens, finishing tied for 47th in 1925, tied for 55th in 1926, and missing the cut in 1933. Walter Hagen shellacked him 17 and 15 in the 72-hole unofficial "World Championship" played in Miami and Pensacola in February 1925. "At no time during the match was Walker able to find his real game," it was reported. "He was obviously nervous when he started against Hagen at Miami and never recovered." He would win the Princess Anne Country Club tournament in Virginia later that year by a shot over Gene Sarazen, and the Miami Four-Ball with partner Clarence Gamber in 1930, beating Sarazen and 1928 U.S. Open champion Johnny Farrell in semi-finals on their way to victory. "The little veteran threw his boundless energy and enthusiasm into the fight," noted *The American Golfer*, patting the long-hitting Gamber on the back and encouraging him along the way. There would be no more encouragement in Walker's life, as that was the end of his success on the golf course.[14]

Walker crossed the Atlantic in 1926 to play his second and last British Open, where he tied for 18th. Two weeks prior to the championship, he played for the American side in a match against British professionals at Wentworth, the forerunner of the Ryder Cup. It wasn't official because several players on the U.S. side, including Walker, were not native-born. Walker lost to Fred Robson in the singles matches, and

Cyril Walker (left) and Clarence Gamber, 1930.

lost his foursomes match as well, with Britain winning in a rout, 13½ to 1½.[15]

Walker's health was never good, and even during his victory over Jones in 1924, he suffered terribly from dysentery throughout the week. Afterwards, health problems continued. "'Drink a little brandy,' he was told. It will help.'" He drank more than a little because he found he liked it, and became one of the 10 to 15 percent of people who become alcoholics after trying it. For a man whose personality could rub people the wrong way to begin with, his drinking only exacerbated matters. Oblivious to his own failings, he needled other pros. Tommy Armour told him once, "For heaven's sake, Cyril, keep quiet and sober up." Walker responded indignantly, "Sir, I don't mind being told to be quiet, but my private life is my own."

Walter Hagen drove him back to town one night from a Chicago tournament and, as they passed a driving range, Walker hiccupped. "Stop here. All I need is a while to straighten out my swing and I'll be back at the top." He never got back on top, although he kept trying. Duke Hancock, a friend and fellow caddie, remembered Walker as being "confident and sarcastic. His sour actions cost him many a friend. His slow play caused most of the other players to shun him, even in the locker room." Hancock claimed that the only time Walker "showed any speed was when reaching for a drink, or grabbing for a pair of dice. He was an expert in both departments."[16]

After winning the U.S. Open, Walker paired with Bobby Cruickshank, who won 17 events on what we could then call the fledgling PGA Tour, and embarked on an exhibition tour. This endeavor, along with other deals, such as endorsing "Correct Golf Grips," and writing a syndicated newspaper column offering golf tips, were said to have earned Walker $150,000 (about $2 million today.) One newspaper account had him retiring in 1926, after quitting his post at Englewood at the end of 1925, but in the Great Depression he "lost most of the fortune he had sunk into a golf course in New Jersey." This was in reference to $45,000 he lost in a "sucker play he was drawn into" at the Saddle River Country Club, his last regular club professional job. He supervised the laying out and building of the Paramus, New Jersey course and clubhouse, and put "his own money into a venture that was doomed from the time the first mower went over the fairways."[17]

Walker wasn't afforded much respect. People "called him 'Handsome Cyril' because he wasn't." One newspaper headline described the jug-eared, snaggle-toothed Walker as a 115-pound "midget." He had trouble with galleries because of his slow play, and they could become abusive. Once, he rebuked a group of spectators who weren't quiet enough while he played, and was reprimanded by tournament officials.

The low point came when he was disqualified for delaying play in the rich $10,000 Los Angeles Open in February 1929. Two-time PGA champion Paul Runyan recounted that day in Al Barkow's wonderful book, *Getting' to the Dance Floor: An Oral History of American Golf.* Runyan had shared a taxi ride from the Hollywood Plaza Hotel to the Riviera Country Club with Walker, Tommy Armour, and Frank Walsh the morning of the second round. "Walker kept us enthralled all the way telling funny stories and singing," remembered Runyan. "He sang quite beautifully." Playing with eventual winner Macdonald Smith, the overflowing crowd began to agitate Walker. At one point he stepped off

76

the distance from his ball to the green 300 yards away, and then back again. He changed clubs, examined his lie and dawdled. Officials went out and told him to hurry up and make way for Smith.

At this point, Walker became abusive. "Who the hell are you? I'm an ex-U.S. Open champion." He said he came out "3,000 miles to play in their diddy-bump tournament," according to Runyan, and was defiant, saying "he'd play as slow as he damn well pleased." When Walker reached the ninth hole, the officials returned, this time with two policemen, and informed him he was disqualified. "The hell I am! I came here to play and I'm going to play." The two officers picked him up by the elbows, recalled Runyan, "and I can still see him being carried up the hill, kicking his legs like a banty – he was a small man. They threw him off and told him not to come back or he'd go to the pokey."[18] After that, tournament officials would often have Walker tee off last and play with only his caddie in order to save the rest of the field from his antics.

Over the next decade, Walker's fall was precipitous and unrelenting. In 1931 he was forced to withdraw from the New Jersey Open after being charged with assault and battery. John Pagano, a 15-year-old caddie at the Ridgewood Country Club, said he and a friend were walking the course that July when Walker approached them. Claiming they stole golf balls from the nearby Saddle River course, Pagano alleged Walker "struck him in the face five times with his fist and three times on the arms and legs with a golf club." Four days later the caddie dropped the charges, claiming it was a case of mistaken identity. He later maintained, however, that after he accused Walker, he was approached by Detective Jacob Cox of the Bergen County prosecutor's office and intimidated into withdrawing the charges. Walker's wife claimed her husband was home at the time of the alleged incident.[19]

In early 1933 Walker was replaced as professional at the Saddle River Country Club and later that year was arrested on a charge of malicious mischief. The police charged he ran his car against a large sign advertising the rival Orchard Hills Country Club on property adjoining the Saddle River Club. Walker denied the charges, and there was not enough evidence to bring an indictment.[20]

A year later, after spending the winter of 1934 in Florida, he returned to Saddle River. A newspaper reported that the southern climate had restored Walker's "rhythmic swing and perfect control of the shots that made him one of the most feared competitors" of the 1920s. He wouldn't say much about getting back into tournament action "except to grin and repeat 'The old swing is back. I never hit the ball better.'" He was engaging in delusional self-deception, as just a few weeks earlier he failed to break 80 while finishing dead last in the inaugural Masters Tournament, a whopping 50 strokes behind winner Horton Smith.

Two months later, broke and in need of cash, he decided to withdraw the last $40 from his bank account. However, he made the mistake of driving there while drunk, and was arrested. Appearing in court, Walker, "noted for his temperamental outbursts," according to the newspaper, asked for leniency after pleading guilty. "The best I can say is that I'm sorry, and that I won't do it anymore," he told the judge, claiming he had been unemployed for three years. Walker's driver's license was revoked for two years, and facing three months in jail if he couldn't pay the $262 fine (about $5,000 today), he found a friend who was able to do so.[21]

A newspaper article soon reported that Walker "recently said he would accept a job as assistant professional 'anywhere' because he needed work in order to live." He was given a position with a New York department store in its sporting goods department. "Just as it was in 1924, his future is in his own hands," wrote one reporter. "I hope the next ten years will prove kinder." Tragically, they didn't. This article appeared only a month before Macy McSwain filed a $100,000 lawsuit against Walker, seeking $50,000 for a breach of promise, and $50,000 for alleged seduction.

It was charged that Walker, then 41, met the 25-year-old McSwain at a Pinehurst Hotel, where she was employed, on February 24, 1934, and that two days later he proposed marriage to her. On March 27th she drove with him to Newark to be married, she said, only to find that Walker already had a wife. Walker posted an $8,000 bond to guarantee his appearance at the trial, but newspapers of the time give no further reports as to its disposition. His wife remained with him, as he continued his wandering ways in search of work.[22] Walker obviously had major problems with alcohol to toy with this young woman so, and disrespect his wife in such a blatant manner. He kept stumbling along, an increasingly lost soul, skipping around aimlessly from one place to another, trying to survive.

By early 1937, Walker was said to be "scraping out a living at a Hollywood, Florida driving range." Two months later he was back in New Jersey, working at a driving range in Union. A newspaper article made brief mention of him, noting "how far the mighty have fallen." In June it was reported that he found a new job as assistant pro to Bill Malcolm at Essex County Country Club. His pattern of short stints of work, interrupted by run-ins with the law, continued.[23]

Alcohol can also cause depression by inhibiting the neurological system that regulates moods. Walker may have felt cheery after a couple of drinks, but after the sixth, seventh, or eighth he could turn angry, fly out of control and then afterwards, feel depressed. The cycle would then repeat itself. According to the National Institute on Alcohol Abuse and Alcoholism, over 15 million adults in the United States have alcohol use disorder (AUD), and an estimated 88,000 people a year die of alcohol-related causes. AUD is defined as a "chronic relapsing brain disease characterized by an impaired ability to stop or control alcohol use despite adverse social, occupational, or health consequences."[24] Poor Cyril Walker's life sadly fit this description; his marriage was in shambles, he had few friends, he couldn't keep a job, and his health was poor.

Walker giving his son Donald a lesson, 1924.

In June 1938, Walker was arrested by a patrolman in New Jersey while walking on the shoulder of Route 4 in Paramus, drunk. He was found guilty of disorderly conduct and given a suspended sentence. Judge Walter McIntyre told Walker, "If you made good once, there is no reason that you can't make good again." But he couldn't make good, even though given countless chances.[25]

In 1940, George Jacobus, who had served as President of the PGA from 1933-1939, wrote a letter to Bob Jones, asking for advice on what to do about Walker. Jacobus was head professional at the Ridgewood Country Club in New Jersey, in close enough proximity to Walker to keep tabs on him. He said that he had been called at least 25 times by the owners of the Saddle River course to "straighten Cyril out and to get him out of difficulties which I would rather not mention here."

One time Jacobus arranged an exhibition match with Walter Hagen and two others, in which Walker was to make up the fourth. It was done for Walker's benefit, but he "had been on a tear," drinking and didn't show up, so Jacobus was called on to take his place. He wanted Jones to know what he and other pros had experienced in trying to help Walker. When they felt they couldn't keep giving him money, the PGA of America stepped in, sending Mrs. Walker a monthly check for more than a year. Jacobus told Jones it was not given to Walker directly "for obvious reasons. Cyril condemned me for this severity."[26]

In October 1939, another exhibition to help Walker was arranged at Crestmont Golf Club in West Orange, New Jersey, with Henry Picard and Byron Nelson playing Johnny Farrell and Jim Barnes. On the side they held an auction for several sets of clubs and golf balls, recalled Jacobus, "and the entire fund was used to send Cyril to Bill Brown's camp for treatment. He left the place. The boys have now reached the point where they feel that they have done everything possible for him."

William J. Brown, a former wrestler and boxer, and later New York State boxing commissioner, operated a health camp in Garrison, New York. "No more and no less than a professional gentleman's training camp," as one newspaper described it. Clients were up at 6 a.m. to do calisthenics, and took long hikes up "Damnation Hill" to help strengthen their bodies and clear their minds. "His patients as a rule are full of poisons which their overworked systems can't throw off. It's poison after all that kills us." Brown's doctrine was "to sweat the poisons out."[27] His system, unfortunately, didn't succeed in reforming Walker.

Concluding his letter to Jones, Jacobus said Jim Barnes had later given Walker a job that lasted but a few weeks before he walked off one day and disappeared. He asked Jones for any suggestions to help Walker, but admitted that "by and large the down-and-outers have only themselves to blame. They blew opportunities the average man would have given an arm to have had."[28] So was the pathetic case of Cyril Walker.

In 1940, newspapers around the country carried stories of the former U.S. Open champion caddying in Florida. "If you play the Miami Beach Country Club course you undoubtedly have seen him sitting on the caddie bench. Possibly he has even carried your bags. He's a wizened, shriveled Englishman, looking older than his 50 years – in the red turtle-neck sweater." Walker was paying 25 cents a night to live at a Salvation Army hospice. "I just roll along," he said. "A man has to keep trying, sir, but I wish I could get a job. Five years ago I could make $15 and $20 a day right off that first tee – could do it now if I wasn't sick."

Walker had hopes of going to Philadelphia, where he had a job offer from a man for whom he caddied in Miami. "I may have to hock my clothes to do it, but I'll get there." Estranged from his wife and son, who was employed at a Wall Street brokerage firm, he had come to Florida at the end of 1939 "for a fresh start on money he earned at a summer camp in upstate New York last year."[29] One might assume this was money earned from gambling while at Bill Brown's health camp before he took leave of it.

At the end of one interview, Walker found 35 cents in his pocket. "There's just enough to buy us a drink, if you'll have one with me. I never take anything but port wine myself." The reporter acknowledged the invitation, but said there was "the Salvation Army to consider. It would have been out a quarter and one distinguished guest that night." Philosopher William James, who struggled with his own demons and contemplated suicide many times in his life, believed, "The sway of alcohol over mankind is unquestionably due to its power to stimulate the mystical faculties of human nature, usually crushed to earth by the cold

81

facts and dry criticisms of the sober hour."[30] This aptly summarizes the later life of Cyril Walker.

Walker did move back north, and was hired as caddie master and assistant professional at the Blue Ridge Golf Club in Harrisburg, Pennsylvania for the 1940 season. "I have hit the top, and I've been at the bottom. I have played all over this country and I have won a share of the tournament prizes but I have never met any finer men than I have met here." But less than a month later he was gone, though the circumstances are unclear. "The board of governors of the club released him from his contract," reported a local paper. "His new position is with a club in Jackson Heights, Long Island, New York." It wasn't.[31]

The Boston Globe reported on Walker's life, suggesting "by cumulative degrees his course following the winning of the Open championship was retrogressive." Walker went from Pennsylvania back to New Jersey and the Terminal Driving Range in Hackensack. "During the past winter his fortunes hit a new low, and he caddied in Florida," reported the local paper. "Now he's back at his game again – teaching golf."[32]

Cyril Walker was still a proud man. "I am an American citizen and glad of it," he said in 1940, but he couldn't remain on the straight and narrow. In April 1942 he was sentenced to 60 days in jail in Hackensack, New Jersey, after pleading guilty to being "a disorderly person." By November he "was up on disorderly conduct charges for the umpteenth time again." He gave his address as "car number four, Buick parking station, Hackensack." Police Chief Frederick Ripperger told the court that Walker "frequently came 'home' after making whoopee with whiskey and got into the wrong 'house.'" Ripperger added, "This has got to be stopped...Nobody'll make a complaint against him because they feel sorry for him." For his part, Walker recounted his life adventures in court, and the bitter Saddle River experience which "led him to the pitfall of alcohol...."[33]

In 1944, his wife Elizabeth was granted a divorce after almost 30 years of marriage, charging that he deserted her on May 6, 1936. The only time she ever saw her husband, she told the court, was when he came around asking for money. Walker was said to be caddying at

Phelps Manor Country Club in New Jersey at the time. The next month he was arrested again for being drunk and disorderly.[34]

In the summer of 1944, he was found caddying at a Red Cross tournament in New York. It was a "moral victory for Walker," wrote one newspaper, because he had been turned down once "when the powers of the Professional Golfers Association ruled against his serving as a caddie – because it would be a knockdown for golf to have a former top-notcher on display in a menial role." This referred to the Miami Open of a few years earlier, when Walker asked his old friend Bobby Cruickshank if he could caddie for him. In response, Cruickshank, saying nothing, reached into his pocket, pulled out a few bills and discreetly handed them to Walker. A reporter asked Bobby if a caddie job had been discussed. "Yes, but no former National Open champion is going to pack my bag."[35]

Poor Cyril kept moving, a troubled man who could find no peace. A year later he was back in Miami, arrested for sleeping in Bayfront Park. He was released after telling Detective Lt. C.W. Potterton that he had been working as a porter at the Royal Palm club, a teen-age dance and amusement center. But when the place changed management, he was left without a job. Inasmuch as Walker had $3 in his pocket, and said he had a prospective job as porter in a bar, Potterton ordered his release.[36]

Walker wandered a few more years, tired and worn out. In 1948, he was back in New Jersey, working as a dishwasher. One August evening, with no place to sleep, he went to the local jail and asked Sergeant Ralph Pinot if he could lodge in a cell for the night. Go ahead, Pinot said. The following morning, August 6th, when Sergeant Daniel Bebus went to awaken Walker, he found him sitting in a chair, dead. It was later discovered that he had been walking around with plural pneumonia. A little more than a month shy of his 56th birthday, Cyril Walker's tempestuous life was over.[37] One wonders what thoughts passed through his mind that final night. Perhaps, mercifully, he closed his eyes after staring listlessly through the bars of that sterile cell, and allowed memories to carry him back to the beautiful green fairways of Oakland Hills and the vibrant day in 1924 he called the greatest of his life.

Upon reading of his death, O.B. Keeler recalled the roar of the crowd at that final hole of the U.S. Open, when Walker "canned that short little putt and took his bow as champion." But he also sadly remembered seeing him years later in the gallery at the International Four-Ball tournament in Miami, a "pathetic, skinny, ragged little figure, back of the home green."[38] Poor Cyril.

Ben Hogan wrote at the time of Walker's death that he had developed a persecution complex. "He faded into obscurity, despite anything friends could do to help him," adding it was difficult "to help a man who refused to help himself." Walker had overcome much to become a champion, but then lost everything to alcohol – his wife and son, his friends, his career, and ultimately his life, in a maelstrom of self-destruction. "Perhaps," as Hogan suggested, "his life was always foredoomed to tragedy." Walker was buried in a Potter's field, broken and alone. "He was a queer genius who did not understand this world and it did not understand him," claimed golf writer H.B. Martin.[39] We can only hope that poor Cyril's spirit rose up and found peace somewhere on the other side of this life.

Cyril Walker, 1925.

Chapter 4:   Marion Miley – "She Was Killed for $140"

Marion Ego Miley was an attractive, bright young woman with a competitive spirit that made her one of the best amateur players in the country, but 1941 had not been one of her best years. Hampered by a nagging thumb injury, she experienced another disappointment at the U.S. Women's Amateur at The Country Club in Brookline, Massachusetts. After winning her first two matches, she was sent home in the third round by publishing heiress Sylva Federman Leichner, losing on the 20th hole. Marion was still young, just 27-years-old, and surely had many more chances in the future.

She returned home to Kentucky and licked her wounds while helping out her mother, who managed clubhouse operations at the Lexington Country Club. Two weeks later, Marion went to play cards with friends, and returning home late that Saturday night, quietly glided up the stairs, careful not to wake her mother, asleep in her room down the hall. Getting under the covers of a warm bed, the scent of the freshly washed sheets made her feel secure. Laying her head on the pillow and drifting off to sleep, she may have wondered if 1942 would be the year she'd bring home the Women's Amateur trophy. She couldn't have imagined the terror which would engulf her and her mother in a few short hours. Tragically, this was to be the last day of her life.

Marion Miley was born in Philadelphia on March 14, 1914, the daughter of a golf professional who was good enough to play in the 1919 U.S. Open, shooting 90-86 to miss the cut the year Walter Hagen won his second Open. Fred Miley moved the family to Florida in the 1920s, one of many professionals to head south during the land boom there, which saw the construction of many new courses. Marion grew up in Fort Pierce, a few miles north of Palm Beach, and was introduced to golf when she was 12.

In that era, the "only 'nice' sports for girls and women were croquet, swimming, tennis, and golf," said Elizabeth "Betty" Hicks, winner of the 1941 U.S. Women's Amateur. With the proviso, she added, that the "competition did not reach a level of ferocity, accompanied by the stricture that the women played only for the joy of the sport and never for the money."[40] This ethos ran deep in the culture until the 1960s.

In 1929, Fred accepted a job as head pro at Lexington Country Club, founded in 1901 and designed by Tom Bendelow. Fred's wife Elsie, who emigrated from Germany in 1892 and became a citizen in 1912, served as the club's manager. They lived in a two-bedroom apartment on the clubhouse's second floor.

Very few could afford to play golf in those Depression years, as between 1929 and 1933 average family income dropped 40%, and in the 1930s the average family had $20-25 (about $375 to $475 today) to feed, clothe, and house itself each month. Like the other great amateurs of that time, Marion had the means to play an elitist game. Fred kept his hand in the game as well, playing in the 1930 Miami Four-Ball, when he and his partner Bob Tinder were beat in the first round by 1924 U.S. Open champion Cyril Walker and Clarence Gamber.[41]

Under her father's guidance, Marion's game took shape, aided by her natural athleticism. "Nobody knows the will power and strength of Marion as I do," said Fred, claiming she could take on any man weighing 135 pounds and wrestle him to the ground in two minutes. She was a long hitter, able to outdrive the great Patty Berg by 15 yards or more. At the Augusta Invitational one year, Miley startled Babe Didrikson, her closet competition, by winning the driving contest. Spotty putting seemed to be Miley's only nemesis.[42]

Both father and daughter admitted that Marion wasn't much for domestic chores. "I'm just not cut out for domesticity," she said. "I don't like it and I'm no good at it, so I don't see why I shouldn't stick to things I can do well and enjoy." Golf was just one thing she excelled at, as she was also a good tennis player and swimmer, a fine horsewoman, and a first-rate bridge player. She also loved reading and music. Marion was a striking woman, tall and slender with flashing brown eyes, a beautiful smile, and chestnut-colored hair in a stylish bob cut.

She was popular with her fellow players and fans alike, and very dedicated to her father. Helen Dettweiler, a top amateur and later one of the original founders of the Ladies Professional Golf Association, was a good friend of Miley's and used to travel with her frequently. She claimed Marion and her father were very close, more like siblings than father and daughter.[43]

As Marion would say, "All I am in golf I owe to my father." Following high school she enrolled in Florida State College for Women in Tallahassee (now Florida State University), with a physical education major and a minor in music. She also expressed a desire to study medicine, but soon golf became more important than anything else. She won the first of her six Kentucky Women's Amateurs in 1931, at age 17. In the next seven years she won it again five of the six times she entered, by scores that were uber-dominating; three times she won the final match by 10 and 9, and once by 16 and 14. After her sophomore year in college, she dropped out and focused all her attention on the game.[44]

In 1933 she qualified for the U.S. Women's Amateur for the first time, going out in the first round. There was no professional tournament circuit for women in the 1930s (the Women's Professional Golf Association would not be formed until 1944), so the aim was to win the major tournaments, and with success earn a spot on the Curtis Cup team. This biennial competition between teams from the United States and Great Britain and Ireland, began in 1932 and was a goal of every amateur player.

The big tournaments coveted by players then were the Women's Metropolitan Amateur (established in 1900); Western Women's Amateur (1901); North and South Women's Amateur (1903); Eastern Women's Amateur (1906); Women's Southern Amateur (1911); Trans-Mississippi (later the Trans-National – 1927.) Of course, the biggest prize was the U.S. Women's Amateur (1895.) Another big event was the Western Derby (a stroke-play event), and nearly a dozen tournaments in Florida during the winter offered a competitive tune-up for the season. In January 1934, Marion drove south to give it a go, travelling with a black cat she named Stormy Weather. As she would say, "I don't like to play unless there's something big at stake."[45]

Founded in 1918 with the Palm Beach Championship, the Florida tour drew the top players. Marion made her debut with some three dozen top players, and when the circuit ended, they headed north to Augusta, Georgia for the invitational tournament there, the forerunner of The Titleholders, another major event.

She endured a grueling final against Jean Bauer in the 1934 Riviera Championship in Miami. Their match went 36 holes, then 17 extra holes, and Marion won 2 and 1. "Old timers around golf courses were trying to hark back to a women's tournament final that lasted as long as this" wrote *The Miami News*, "but they could remember no 53-hole matches on the book." She played well the rest of the winter but lost 1 down to Jean Bauer that April in the Augusta Invitational final.[46]

Maureen Orcutt was a key to the tour's press coverage. She was one of the best amateur players in the country, making it to the finals of the U.S. Women's Amateur in 1927 and 1936, and also won the Women's Metropolitan Amateur three times in the 1920s. Orcutt could still play, beating Miley 5 and 4 in the 1934 Florida Women's Golf Championship, the same tournament where Miley "provided a surprise," according to the *Chicago Tribune*, by beating former U.S. Women's Amateur champion Helen Hicks in the semifinals. As an indication of the popularity of the game, that final match with Orcutt drew more than 5,000 spectators.[47]

Orcutt was also a prominent journalist, covering golf at the time for the *New York World*, and later *The New York Times*. She had a long career, playing into her late 80s, and would win two U.S. Senior Women's Amateur championships. Orcutt brought the players to the public on the sports pages, As the late Rhonda Glenn wrote:

> Almost equally talented, they were a cross-section of American life. One tournament might be won by a society woman, such as the stately Grace Amory, or a business executive's daughter such as dynamic little Patty Berg or the graceful Betty Jameson. The next might be won by the gifted Babe Didrikson, daughter of a carpenter, or even Marion Miley, daughter of a club professional. They all made good copy.

Glenna Collett Vare was in a class by herself. A six-time U.S. Women's Amateur champion between 1922 and 1935, she was fiercely competitive. Others included Jean Bauer, Betty Hicks, Virginia Van Wie, Charlotte Glutting, Kathryn Hemphill, Dot Kirby and Peggy Chandler. As a teenager Collett met former U.S. Open champion Alex Smith, and after spending a short while with her, he realized what he was dealing with. "The kid is good, and if I can't make a champion out of her I'm a disgrace to the Smith family." Smith gave her lessons twice a week for three years. "He strengthened my driving to such an extent that when I was 18 – standing 5 feet 6 inches and weighing 128 pounds – I drove a ball off the tee for a measured distance of 307 yards, the longest drive ever made by a woman golfer." She lifted her left heel high off the ground on the backswing, like Jack Nicklaus, and Smith was always reminding her to plant it first on the downswing.[48]

Vare used her power to dominate, but her swing was solid. "She had learned from the boys," her son Ned would explain, "how to be purely athletic, without a trace of self-consciousness. And with an aggressive nature well-hidden by a beautiful face and figure, she attacked the ball and the course with startling force." She taught a new power game. *The American Golfer* wrote of how she went after the ball "with a grim determination and wallops it hard, and if she gets into a bad place, why she wastes no time worrying or thinking of consequences, but just keeps her mind on the ball, goes after it and wallops it hard again."[49]

Marion Miley was also a power player known for her booming drives, and quickly gained a national reputation. In 1934 she was selected as an alternate to the Curtis Cup team when Helen Hicks turned professional. Winner of the 1931 U.S. Women's Amateur, a 16-year old Sam Snead caddied for Hicks in her first attempt in 1928. She earned a spot on the 1932 Curtis Cup team and two years later L.B. Icely of Wilson Sporting Goods, seeing she was a natural performer with a warm smile and vivacious personality, signed her to do exhibitions and promote her own line of golf clubs. Hicks's popularity moved Wilson to sign Opal Hill in 1938 and Helen Dettweiler in 1939 (who would become a Women Airforce Service Pilot in World War II), to travel the country promoting and selling clubs. As for the 1934 Curtis Cup, Marion didn't hit a shot in the 6½ to 2½ U.S. victory. At the U.S. Women's Amateur that year she won her first match but was put out in the second round.[50]

The 1935 season was even more fruitful. Marion won three straight Florida tournaments that winter, including the Augusta Women's Invitational in March. That summer she earned her first titles of national importance, winning the Western Derby and the Women's Western Amateur, beating a 17-year-old newcomer named Patty Berg in both. In June, Miley won the Women's Trans-Mississippi, overpowering Berg again, 9 and 7. The Associated Press tagged Miley's day as "one of the finest performances in a women's golf tournament."[51]

At the end of the year, entertainers Bing Crosby, Joan Bennett and W.C. Fields went to the Baja Peninsula and watched Miley win the Mexican Women's Amateur. Crosby was a dedicated golfer, and when he met Marion promised to call her for a game. This was heady stuff, but her self-confident bearing and impressive game would woo fans throughout her life. She told reporters she wanted to get her college degree someday, but added, "I wouldn't give up these past few years of travelling around and meeting all sorts of people. I don't think much else than golf could have given me that enjoyment."

Marion Miley, 1941.

She also enjoyed playing for her fans. Helen Dettweiler said she had seen her stop and "interrupt her concentration on a difficult shot, just to answer someone in the gallery who had spoken to her. She was always friendly with people in the galleries."[52] But Miley couldn't crack the higher tiers of the U.S. Women's Amateur. She won two matches in 1935 before bowing out, but would have good chances at the title in each of the next three years.

In 1936, Marion won twice on the Florida tour and defended her Trans-Mississippi title, making the Curtis Cup team once again as an alternate. She was not played by Captain Glenna Collett Vare when the teams met at Gleneagles in Scotland, but the press fell in love with the vivacious 22-year-old Miley, and her 18-year-old teammate Patty Berg, the youngest members of the team. The matches ended in a 4½ to 4½ tie.

Marion and the other players stayed to play in the Ladies British Open Amateur at Southport, England. No American had ever won the event to that point, but Miley came close. While the other players were victims of the wind and weather, Miley survived to do battle with seven

Englishwomen for the trophy. Marion won her quarterfinal encounter against Elsie Corlett, but was defeated 3 and 1 by Bridget Newell. It was reported that she "stubbornly declined to alibi her loss," although she didn't like the British seeding system. Newell lost to Pamela Barton in the final match.[53]

Barton kept up her good play at the U.S. Women's Amateur that September, defeating Marion in the semifinals 3 and 1, on her way to a victory over Maureen Orcutt in the finals. Like Miley, Barton didn't live to the age of 30. A member of the Women's Auxiliary Air Force in World War II, she died in a plane crash in 1943.

In 1937, Miley began the year by winning the Augusta Women's Invitational at the Forest Hills course, beating Babe Didrikson 6 and 4. The Louisville *Courier-Journal* reported that "a shivering gallery of approximately 1,000" braved the weather to watch the match. "Miss Didrikson's lack of tournament experience," it noted, "the result of few opportunities for such competition, showed up under the pressure of the final."[54] Didrikson had been banned by the USGA in 1935 from competing in amateur events (which is detailed later in Chapter 11) and was able to play in Augusta because it was an invitational open to professionals and amateurs.

Marion took the Women's Western Amateur for second time in three years by defeating Betty Jameson by 7 and 6 at the Town & Country Club in St. Paul. She also captured the Western Derby for the third consecutive year with a record score for 72-holes of 309 (beating the previous record by 11 shots.) At the 1937 U.S. Amateur, Miley won her first two matches before being beaten by Opal Hill, who would turn professional in 1938 and was one of the original founders of the Ladies Professional Golfers Association in 1950.[55]

In 1938 Miley won her first Women's Southern Amateur championship in Birmingham, Alabama. She "staged one of the most gallant rallies in the history of southern golf" to beat Estelle Lawson Page, the reigning U.S. Women's Amateur, on the 37th hole. "It was a whirlwind finish for a record crowd of 3,000 spectators," reported *The Atlanta Constitution*, "who followed every inch of the way ah-ing and oh-ing as every shot was fired." Page had been 6 holes up with 13 to play before Marion staged her comeback, making birdies on the 35th and 36th holes to square the match and winning it on the first extra hole. Page lost despite being one under par for the 37 holes, showing how well Miley played. Fellow competitor Dorothy "Dot" Kirby noted that Marion "has the type of game that is consistent and as she proved today can stand up to pressure."[56]

Marion won her sixth Kentucky State Women's Amateur that year, pummeling her opponent by 10 and 9, the same margin as the year before. But in that year's U.S. Women's Amateur, she would lose again in the semifinals to eventual winner Patty Berg, who beat her in a tight match, 2 up. It was the closest Miley would get to the crown jewel of women's amateur golf. She made the 1938 Curtis Cup team and finally got a chance to play, winning a point in two matches in the close 5½ to 3½ U.S. victory, the last matches to be played before the war.

In May of 1939, displaying masterful pitching and putting, Miley defended her Women's Southern Amateur title by defeating Peggy Chandler 2 and 1 at Ponte Vedra Beach, Florida.[57] She made the quarterfinals of the U.S. Women's Amateur that year, losing 1 down to Betty Jameson, who would beat Dorothy Kirby in the finals.

Marion had been competing on the amateur circuit for five years, and being accustomed to the country club environment she grew up in, moved with ease among these imposing social circles. She had hundreds of friends, and thanks to a stint working in a department store, dressed beautifully, wearing crisp blouses and skirts hemmed at mid-calf on the golf course. Marion was pretty, but sportswriters also wrote of her not playing a "feminine game" since she hit the ball farther than most average male amateurs. One sportswriter called her "mannish," and others used the same term to describe her clothes.

Miley played in more than 100 charity exhibitions, gave speeches and was wined and dined by entertainers and politicians. She was intelligent, and took advantage of her newfound celebrity. As Patty Berg said, "Marion had a great many friends. Her friends were very close, not only in golf circles, but elsewhere." She did enjoy male company and one "result of her fondness for the opposite sex" was that her mother accompanied her to tournaments in the 1941 season.[58]

Miley's diaries reflect her hobnobbing with the rich and famous. From September 30, 1940, commenting on a trip to California: "Played golf with Delores Hope, Ruby Keeler and Peggy Rutledge. Met Clark Gable, met Hedy Lamar. Dinner at Hope's – cocktails at Ruby's." Hope was the wife of the famous entertainer Bob Hope, Keeler was a famous actress, and Rutledge another top amateur player.[59] Marion was a young woman enjoying a life most people couldn't imagine.

Standard Oil of Kentucky hired her as an ambassador of sorts, taking advantage of her vivaciousness and fame as a golfer. She travelled the country distributing courtesy cards at filling stations and reporting on their operations. Marjorie Hoagland wrote in *The Courier-Journal* that Miley was doing a little pioneering by breaking into a field reserved for men, working "for an old-line firm only recently converted to the thought of women in their advertising offices."

Marion had taken the initiative, contacting the vice president of the firm and asking for a job. She wasn't hired due to her ability to hit a golf ball, she maintained, but because she "was the best bet for the promotional job at hand." Hoagland described Miley as a "svelte figure tastefully dressed in dark sports clothes," well within the "modern business girl tradition…Her voice is low and well-modulated; she speaks quickly and without hesitation."[60] She took the job seriously, and didn't just collect a paycheck.

Miley's diaries from 1940 to 1941 reveal a very active life. In addition to her golf, she records everyday events: shopping, going to the movies, the roller derby, the hairdresser, church, the dog and horse races, and fishing. She also mentions dating (including Cincinnati Reds pitcher Paul Derringer), dining, cocktail parties, and dancing. Some of her interactions with fellow competitors and friends are also recorded: Helen Dettweiler, Betty Hicks, Patty Berg, Louise Suggs, Clara Callender, and Grace Amory being among those mentioned.

Also prominent, mentioned dozens of times, are references to her work for Standard Oil; of going to the office, inspecting stations, and writing reports. "January 1, 1940 – Here's hoping the next five years can top the last – they're starting with a lot of work to say the least. Up all night, worked on reports all day." From May 1, 1940: "got up at 4:30 a.m. to go to Birmingham, got there at 3 p.m. and went to the office only to be told to go on to Mobile, stopped for the night at Montgomery." On

January 9, 1941: "All day it rained, so all day checked stations – 25 of them."[61]

The job allowed her to make a living while playing golf along the way. A diary entry from January 20, 1941 illustrates the point. "Quiet day – went to all the stations on the beach then to the office and then back to the house. Practiced with the clubs that came today." Later that spring, on a swing through Texas, she was pulled over for speeding. She was adamant that she wasn't guilty when she appeared before the judge. He told her she could either pay the $25 fine or go to jail. "I'll rot here before I pay the fine!" she said righteously. After four or five hours of stubborn defiance during which she calmly read a book in her cell, the judge let her go.[62]

While in Georgia for the Augusta Women's Invitational, she attended the 1940 Masters Tournament, going with Dot Kirby and Kathryn Hemphill to see Jimmy Demaret win. The following year she spent more than a week in the area, attending practice rounds and the tournament proper. For round one she noted on April 3, "Went over to the National to see the men play – Craig Wood low with 66." Wood ended up winning, and on April 10th Miley recorded that she played the course with three friends and shot an 83.

In 1940, Allan Trout, correspondent for the Louisville *Courier-Journal*, interviewed Miley and asked about her future. She flashed a smile and said she wanted to become the best woman golfer in the world. She had beaten the best in the game – Helen Hicks, Betty Hicks, Betty Jameson, Babe Didrikson Zaharias, Louise Suggs, and Patty Berg among them, so she had reason to believe in her future.[63]

Had she been born 75 years later, she would surely have become a multi-millionaire playing golf, between on-course winnings and endorsement deals. But in her day there was no women's professional tour. Helen Dettweiler told reporters in 1940 that she was interested in organizing a women's professional association. At that time, she was one of only about a dozen women pros in the country – hard to believe today – and they only had about seven or eight tournaments a year. "I think we could make a go of a national organization and that it could successfully handle a National Open tourney." With such an organization and tournament, she was confident top amateurs would turn professional, confident there was a future that could pay them for their efforts.

"Right now the Women's Western Open is the biggest tournament for women pros," said Dettweiler. "If some of the amateur stars like Marion Miley, Jean Bauer, Betty Jameson, and Elizabeth Hicks would promise to compete in our national open, I think it not only would be a success but the biggest women's tournament in the country." She was prophetic, but it would be more than a generation for real monetary rewards to come. Betty Hicks, collaborating with Hope Seignious, founded the Women's Professional Golf Association (WPGA) in November 1944.[64] The LPGA followed in 1950, and in 2020 there are 33 official events, with the women playing for a Tour-record $75.1 million in total prize money. It would behoove this generation of professionals to give thanks to pioneers such as Dettweiler and Miley and others who came before. We all stand on the shoulders of those who paved the way for us.

1941 was not such a great year for Marion on the course, as she suffered from recurring tendinitis in her thumb. She had been fortunate not to have any serious injuries, although she did have to have her appendix taken out in October of 1937. A diary entry from January 18, 1941 had her at the driving range all morning before going to the horse races, where she won $12.85. Hellen Dettweiler remembered that Marion, her father, and the whole family, enjoyed going to the horse races.[65]

The next month Miley tied for first with Jean Bauer in an invitational event in the Bahamas. Her diary from February 21, 1941, recorded this: "Had to tee off at 8 a.m. – shot a 36-38 to catch Bauer – so we tied with 232s – Met H.R.H. Edward, Duke of Windsor and Wally [Wallace Simpson]. To the beach – dinner and to the night clubs." Miley said that when she played golf, she gave it everything she had, but at the end of a round, she tried to forget about it. She attempted to do the same thing in the business world, believing that some business women had "handicapped themselves in the past by their inability to forget struggles once they are over."

On the course, Marion's thumb ailment had hampered her swing for a couple of years and professional Tommy Armour had suggested swing changes. On her trip to the Masters in 1940, she had met Armour, who offered to help her if she'd come to Chicago and see him at Medinah, where he was teaching. So far, the results had been disappointing.[66]

She went to the U.S. Women's Amateur on September 8th. She won her first two matches, and even wrote a newspaper column of her experiences, but came home early after a stinging third round defeat in which she hit her tee shot out of bounds on the final hole. The winner of the event, 20-year-old Betty Hicks, received the ornate Cox Cup that September 13th on the clubhouse porch.[67]

Since women weren't allowed in the clubhouse, the porch was as close as she would get to the inner sanctum of this venerable club. Hicks would later speak of "this grossly, undemocratic, alleged National Championship" when referencing the experience, language illustrative of the struggles women faced in the male dominated world of the time. Miley would have traded places with Hicks in a heartbeat, and been happy to stand on that undemocratic porch with the trophy in her hands. Earlier that year Hicks had called Miley "the toughest opponent I ever played."[68]

Disappointed, Marion spent her time at home going over a new contract with Standard Oil and helping her mother prepare for a dance to be held at the club on Saturday, September 27th. On the night of the dance, she spent the evening at the home of Mrs. Howard Isaacs, playing bridge with her and two friends, who drove her home around midnight. Mike Rowady recalled the band had just stopped playing for the night. Marion came in as he and a friend were standing by the stairs leading up to the apartment. She saw them and stopped to say hello, shaking their hands before going up. The next morning, Rowady recalled almost 75 years later, he "read in the Lexington Herald that she'd been murdered."[69]

In early 1940, Mrs. Miley had hired Raymond "Skeeter" Baxter as a groundskeeper, who was the same age of Marion. The sleepy-eyed Baxter, who had just finished a year's probation for buying stolen property, was a drinker and smoked marijuana daily. He spent weekends at the club as night watchman, sleeping in the caddie shed. Fred had taken a more lucrative job at Maketewah Country Club in Cincinnati in 1937 and thought this would provide some added security.[70]

Baxter told his friend Tom Penney that the kind of dance to be held at the country club could take in $5,000 to $10,000. The scar-faced Penney, a 31-year old former carpenter and metal worker, had served prison terms for auto theft and armed robbery (having shot two men), and was out on parole. He delivered beer to the club as an employee of the Lexington brewery, and knew the layout of the place. Seeing an easy score, and had asked Bud Tomlinson, a service station attendant and Tom Lundsford, a tavern employee, to join him in the scheme the day before but they refused. Penney did get an old prison mate and Louisville nightclub owner, Robert H. Anderson, 35, to join him for a break-in. Anderson had served time in the Federal Penitentiary in Atlanta on a prohibition charge and in Kentucky for robbery. Penney had once asked him for a job at his nightclub. *The Cincinnati Enquirer* reported that the decision to carry out the robbery that night was made while the three "sat in a roadhouse drinking beer" only a few hours before in Louisville.[71]

A little after 2 a.m. they arrived at the club. Baxter had opened a window in the basement for them to enter. They turned off the electrical breakers, stopping the clock at 2:25. Then they cut the telephone lines, and not finding any dance receipts on the ground floor, went upstairs. The door to the apartment was locked, and hearing snoring, they returned to the kitchen to find something to bash the door in with. At this point Baxter was waiting outside as a lookout, and Anderson went to the car and got two guns he had there, giving one to Penney.[72]

Anderson broke out the panel in the apartment door and entered with Penney behind him. The noise awakened Elsie, who ran into the hall, where one of the men hit her with a flatiron wrapped in a Turkish towel that sent her reeling across the bed. They shouted, "Where's the money?" Marion, hearing the ruckus, rose from her bed with a rush of adrenalin and came running to her mother's defense, lunging at Penney and knocking him down. Penney later testified that there "was a bunch of screaming and scuffling before I got in and as soon as I got in, something hit me on the chin and I got knocked down." *The Courier-Journal* reported that Miley "knocked him down with her first, then wrapped a powerful arm around his neck." Penney said, "I hit at the person with the gun in my hand and it went off and then the shooting started." As he struggled to get up he fired the gun toward the floor. "I don't know how many times I shot or how many times Anderson shot. Then everything got quiet ...."[73]

Mrs. Miley had been shot three times, twice in the stomach and once in the left thigh. Penney said, "I could see the woman on the bed, but I didn't know she was shot. I knew someone was hurt, though, because there was blood on my hands and shoes." The men demanded again to know where the money was. Elsie pointed weakly to the middle drawer of the chest-of-drawers, where they found a cloth bag containing coins and a paper one with bills. They had no idea that it was just a fraction of what they thought would be rich proceeds from the dance, since most club members had their expenses charged to their accounts that night instead of paying in cash.[74]

The men grabbed the bags and scurried out, stepping over the negligee-clad body of Marion, lying in the hall. She fought the intruders fiercely, as skin, blood and hair were found under her fingernails. Her father and friends acknowledged that Marion had "unusual strength for a woman," and one former male acquaintance expressed the opinion that she "could hold her own with any average 160-pound man." Furniture and lamps were knocked about violently in the fight, as Marion struggled valiantly, but she was overpowered. Driven to her knees, she lunged at Anderson, biting his leg hard enough to break the skin. His anger further aroused, he shot her in the back, taking her face first to the cold floor. A second bullet to the back of her head killed her instantly.[75]

J.A. Watson, owner of a farm bordering the golf course, came forward later to say he heard six shots fired about 2:30 a.m. the night of the murders. The first three, he said, came in rapid succession and the next three followed about 90 seconds later. An hour later, he "heard a piercing cry from the direction of the club driveway."[76] One might surmise the scream came from the injured Elsie Miley as she discovered the dead body of her daughter.

With the phone cut off, Elsie somehow staggered down the stairs and crawled and walked almost a quarter mile across the way to the Ben-Mar Sanitarium. Intermittent ringing of the front door awakened J.M. Giles, manager of the health resort at 4:15 a.m. An ambulance was called, and while he and his staff administered first aid, Elsie recounted the story as best she could before being rushed to St. Joseph Hospital. Surgery was performed and four blood transfusions were given to her, but she remained unconscious, lapsing into a coma at 7 a.m. Her husband Fred was called and hurried home from Cincinnati, learning about the death of his daughter from a newspaper headline that morning.[77]

Death certificate of Marion Miley, 1941.

Chief of Police Austin B. Price received a call telling him of a murder, and when county patrolmen Virgil Mann and John Doyle arrived, they found Marion lying face down in a pool of blood. Harry Miller witnessed the scene that morning. His father was called in to help with the case and asked Harry if he'd like to go to the club with him, even though he was a young boy. "And they were showing us various things up the stairs," Miller recalled, "when they identified something as Marion Miley's brains, and with that it just turned my stomach completely and I ran down the steps, went outside and threw up." Coroner J. Hervey Kerr reported that Marion had numerous bruises and wounds to the head and body; there was also blood on her hands and knuckles.[78]

99

Initially, there were few clues to go on: an ice pick, screw driver, several strands of light brown hair, six automatic pistol shells (from a .32 caliber gun) and five slugs, and two buttons from a man's coat. Police also found 15 fingerprints, some blood stained, found on envelopes in the apartment. These were all turned over to the FBI. It was two days before they had a clue as to the perpetrators. Hugh Cramer, 17, a delivery boy for the *Lexington Herald*, came forward to say he saw an unfamiliar blue and gray Buick sedan at 3:40 a.m. parked by the clubhouse when he delivered the morning paper. The car belonged to Bob Anderson.[79]

Front page headline from the Louisville *Courier-Journal*, October 13, 1941. Tom Penney (smoking a cigarette), and Robert Anderson (far right.)

Authorities were notified to be on the lookout for the car. There were no clear suspects, and it took a couple of weeks after the shooting for Skeeter Baxter, Tom Penney, and Bob Anderson to be arrested for the crime. Seven days after Hugh Cramer identified Anderson's car, Penney was pulled over in Fort Worth, Texas for running a red light. In the car were two guns, and several loose cartridges that matched those in the Miley's apartment. Penney was returned to Lexington, and after being interrogated nonstop for 24 hours, confessed to the murders. He named Anderson as his accomplice and Baxter as an accessory, who admitted being the "inside man."

Penney claimed Anderson had double-crossed him by reporting the car stolen. He also claimed it was Anderson's idea to commit the robbery, to which Anderson replied, "I can't understand Penney's putting me on the spot this way. I've never done anything to him." Anderson consistently denied having anything to do with the plot, saying he was with his wife and mother-in-law that night, and had five other witnesses who would testify that he was at the club until 2 a.m. In a dramatic face-to-face meeting with Penney and Baxter at the police station, he called them "rats" and "liars."[80]

Marion Miley was buried October 1st, with Patty Berg and Helen Dettweiler among the mourners. Bing Crosby contributed $5,000 toward a reward for the capture of the killers and other entertainers also contributed. Fred Miley left the funeral sobbing to go to the hospital to be with his wife, who had not awakened from her coma. She died in his arms two hours later, and her heartbroken husband, who had lost his wife and only child to this violent crime, was himself hospitalized a couple of weeks later. Elsie was 53-years-old and Marion 27, and their murders made headlines throughout the country.[81]

The bombing of Pearl Harbor and the United States' entry into World War II pushed the investigation off the front pages, but by the end of the year all three men would sentenced to death in the electric chair. Newspaper stories of the time tell a complicated story of the plot and the trials of the men. Tom Penney would say he was "too soft" in confessing to the crime. "They didn't have much case against me. If I had it to do over again I never would confess." Penney asserted he had been led into the part he played, that the case never would have been solved had he not been cooperative. Of Anderson's refusal to confess, he said, "He's got sense. He won't burn. They haven't got a good case against him, and I'm sure [he's] not saying anything else."

Penney later had a conversion experience on death row after being introduced to two Catholic nuns who were touring the prison. He wrote letters to Chief Price, as well as with the sisters and a priest. He told Price he "never knew an officer could be so human before now." He admitted his guilt, and wrote the priest, saying that although he could not erase his mistakes, there was not a "day or a night I do not ask for forgiveness from God."[82]

One man wrote to Penney, imploring him to repent and telling him Jesus died so "that we sinners might be saved. Mr. Penney, the only hope you have for your soul is God's mercy through His beloved Son

Jesus." He assured Penney that "God loves you, but hates your sin – Jesus loves you and wants to save you from your sin."

Penney told his wife and mother that the experience had changed him, that he had been baptized, and that he was going to a better world. He left two small children behind, a four-year-old son and a two-year-old daughter, and said, "I'd like to see them amount to something, but I guess I never did much about it." Attorneys for Baxter contended he was not mentally responsible due to his addiction to liquor and narcotics, but the wheels of justice rolled over him. After their appeals were exhausted, all three men were executed on February 26th, 1943.[83]

Bob Anderson maintained his innocence to the end, but was identified as the buyer of the flashlight used that night, and both of the guns used in the crime belonged to him. As Miley biographer Beverly Bell makes clear in an excellent 2016 documentary produced by Beth Kirchner, Anderson went to see his doctor the day after the crime with what the doctor determined to be a human bite on his left leg (a fact the doctor later testified to.) County Patrol Chief John W. McCord, who had spoken to Elsie Miley before she slipped into a coma, testified that when Anderson was changing into prison clothes after being taken into custody, he noticed "there was a large splotch, a red mark on the inner front side of his left leg." Marion had bit him hard during the struggle, and one might conclude that this, along with other frantic resistance, prompted him to shoot her. She showed great courage in the face of evil and lost her life, as did her mother, to career criminals for the contents of the bags they stole – all of $139.50.[84]

Helen Dettweiler called her good friend Marion "one of the bravest girls I ever knew. We used to travel together a lot, and I always had a gun in the car. She used to say, 'Gosh, you'll never get a chance to use that. It will get rusty. Don't you know nothing like that ever happens?" What an eerie statement that was, foreshadowing the horrible event that took her life just a few years later. Marion was denied a future and a family of her own. One newspaper reported she was in a serious relationship with a chemist from Charleston, West Virginia, "and probably would have married him, had she lived."

Today, Miley's name surfaces when the Lexington Country Club conducts the Marion Miley Invitational, established in 1942, and the

Women's Western Golf Association presents the Miley bracelet to the low qualifier in its women's amateur and junior championships, but few modern competitors know who Marion Miley was. "On the links, in the midst of a tight match," wrote Arthur Watson in 1941, "she was grimness personified. She never admitted defeat until she was licked, which wasn't very often."[85] This is a good way to remember Marion Miley, who went down fighting to the end.

Chapter 5: John M. Shippen, Jr. – "The Father of African American Golf"

"He walked with giants," wrote New Jersey sportswriter Arthur "Red" Hoffman in the mid-1960s, yet his ancestry relegated him "to the deep woods of anonymity."[1] Born a month after Thomas Edison invented the light bulb, and dying a month after the assassination of Dr. Martin Luther King, Jr., Shippen's life spanned a transformative period in the history of this nation, and his own life was representative of the struggles and change that surrounded him. He was a flawed man, but one who had a passion for golf and tried to make the best of what life gave him.

"Maybe I should have kept going," Shippen said wistfully towards the end of his long life, "and gone to Yale like my brother, who's a teacher. I wonder until I look out the window and see that golf course. Then I realize how much enjoyment I've gotten out of the game, and I don't wonder anymore."[2] His choice would bring him as much pain as satisfaction, but it was his destiny.

John Matthew Shippen, Jr. was born December 3, 1879, in the Hillsdale section of present day Anacostia, then a predominantly white neighborhood in the southeast section of Washington, DC.[3] One of the family's neighbors was Frederick Douglass, the former slave and famous abolitionist and civil rights crusader, who purchased a home in the same area in 1877.

Like Douglass, Shippen's father and grandfather had also been slaves, and moved from Virginia to Washington, DC in 1867, part of a large influx of refugees who were drawn to the city after the Civil War. In 1872, Shippen's father graduated from the Preparatory Department of Howard University, where he had taken a three-year program featuring a core curriculum of Latin, Greek, mathematics, geography, and history. By receiving a "certificate of satisfactory study" in this rigorous curriculum, he was able to teach elementary students in the District's school system.

Two years after starting his teaching career, Shippen married Eliza Frye Spottswood on September 30, 1874. They settled in Anacostia and would have nine children together, John Matthew, Jr. being the fourth. Shippen's father taught school for several years before returning to Howard University to get a diploma in theology in 1883. As his salary was meager and his family had grown, he accepted a new job in 1888. The destination was Southampton in Long Island, New York, at that time a village of around 6,500 people. There, on the Shinnecock Indian Reservation, Shippen was both preacher in the local Presbyterian Church and teacher of grades one through eight at a one-room country school.[4]

The religious training of Shippen's father would help instill in his congregation a faith that the wicked would be destroyed, and that God would sustain them and help them overcome. Kelly Miller, a professor of sociology at Howard University, wrote in 1908 that the black church has "been and is the greatest enlightening, uplifting, and inspiring influence which actuates the life of the benighted masses." John Shippen, Sr. wanted his own family to cloak themselves in the same faith, and embrace the Presbyterian Church's emphasis on education, but his son John would go another way, finding his calling on the golf course. The

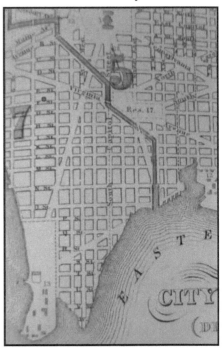

Map of Washington, DC, 1867. The dot above the "7" denotes where Shippen's father and grandfather lived on F Street, just south of the Capital Building.

family's move to the reservation was a fateful one, as three years after their arrival, golf was introduced to Shinnecock Hills, when Willie F. Davis arrived in July 1891 to build the first twelve holes.[5]

Among the 150 or so men hired to help build the golf course were, ironically, members of the Shinnecock tribe, as well as John Shippen, Jr. He became a caddie, and took to the game, which became so popular with the membership that the course was expanded to 18 holes in 1895. His younger sister Eliza Pearl Shippen wrote in 1973, "Shinnecock had a very good golf course and the boys served as caddies…It was here that John learned to play golf, became quite proficient, and later taught golf in other places."[6]

Organized sports in the late 1800s were, with few exceptions, limited to white men, most of them wealthy, in fields such as sailing, horse racing (as owners), tennis, and golf. Golf was just taking root in the United States when John Shippen was a boy, but was reserved for the wealthy. For those in the lower social classes, participation was limited to caddying for rich members of private clubs.

As for the hiring and training of black youngsters as caddies, Marvin Dawkins and Graham Kinloch, in *African America Golfers During the Jim Crow Era*, assert that the idea fit well "with Jim Crow America at the turn of the century. This image of blacks was consistent with the stereotypical white view of their subordinate role in society generally." Black caddies were thus "perceived in a similar light as the ubiquitous Pullman porters in passenger trains. Whites could think of blacks as…their personal golf course servant."[7]

Given these restrictive conditions, it is amazing that the man known as this country's first home-bred professional golfer even made it out of the caddie pen. John Shippen was a black man who played a white man's game. That was true when he began his professional career in 1895, and is still sadly true today.

Shippen would always be separated from the game's mainstream by race and class. He recalled, "I caddied two years and then I turned pro." Even though education was so important to his parents, Shippen dropped out of school and concentrated on golf to the exclusion of all else. Shippen, "a pleasant-faced boy, about 5'7", square-shouldered, and weighing between 140 and 150 pounds," saw his reputation spread.[8]

A newspaper article took note of his play, but suggested that Shippen's caddie background had been a hindrance. "If, when going around the links, he had had clubs carried for him instead of his carrying for someone else, there is no telling how good his play would be now." Shippen said in 1963, "As far as I know, I was the first American-born pro. When I first came around all the pros came from Scotland and England." He remembered he was able to "beat all of the members and anybody else who happened to come around the course," so the members entered him in the U.S. Open.[9]

The United States Golf Association (USGA), founded in December 1894, oversaw the championship. Its president, Theodore Havemeyer, represented the richest of the barons who ruled the Gilded Age. He was the "most conspicuous figure in that band of millionaires who compose the despotic Sugar Trust," reported one newspaper in 1889, and as one of the drivers of an elitist game, he and his upper-class friends wanted to keep golf booming in America.[10]

Two months ahead of the U.S. Open, a British publication suggested that since the introduction of the game here "the impatience to see the Great American golfer has become almost as strong as that awaiting the Great American novelist." It noted that there was a golfer, however, who was "either in the first class or certain to be in it before very long. He is a young negro boy named John Shippen." The article described his game as "good from first to last. It would not be at all surprising if before long [he] appeared in the open championship as one of the most threatening candidates for honors."[11]

The Fort Wayne News observed that the first "great American golfer" was expected to "come from the ranks of the upper classes, as the sport is most affected by them." Instead, it seemed that "one of the best, if not the best, of all the players" was Shippen, who had "developed such skill as astonishes everybody. Even with the small practice that he has had he can beat any amateur in the country, and very probably some of the professionals."[12]

John Shippen had an intimate knowledge of the course, which no doubt helped him in the championship. "Shinnecock might very easily be made the best course in the United States," noted *The New York Times*. "It has a splendid situation, and its grounds are admirably adapted for good lies." It was short, even for that era (only 4,423 yards, the longest hole being 356 yards), but was nevertheless lauded as having "taken a high position in the golfing world, largely on account of the singleness of purpose with which everything has been done for the best interests of the game."

The course, and the "popular and somewhat aristocratic village of Southampton" would become better known that summer, when visited "by several hundred golfers during the championship week [for both the Open and Amateur titles], and, judging from the increasing popularity of the game, the matches will be even more exciting and more hotly contested than was the case last year at Newport."[13]

JOHN SHIPPEN.

aver, that one of the best, if not the best, of all players of golf in this country is a little 16-year-old colored boy, named John Shippen, a caddy at the Shinnecock Hills Golf club, at Southampton. N. Y.

John Shippen, from the *Fort Wayne News*, May 28, 1896.

Saturday, July 18, 1896 was a beautiful day in Southampton, New York. Thirty-seven players entered the championship, including Shippen and Oscar Bunn, a Shinnecock Indian. Like Shippen, Bunn had been a caddie at the club, as had many other members of the reservation. However, the "professional golfers object to colored boys meeting them on equal terms," reported the New York *Sun*, "and they held a meeting on Thursday night to protest against it." As Shippen recalled over sixty-five years later, Theodore Havemeyer "told the other pros he was going to run the tournament as he saw fit, and he didn't care if they played in it or not, and furthermore, the tournament would be played if only Oscar and me were in it." In effect, "he told 'em to go to hell." Havemeyer's progressive stand won out, and Shippen and Bunn played. As Shippen's daughter Clara Shippen Johnson recalled, "It didn't bother my dad. Dad said he was used to it."[14]

There are alternative explanations for Havemeyer's decision. One asserts that he refused to ban Shippen and Bunn because both were 'native-born' Americans, their race notwithstanding. Another involves Havemeyer's personal financing of the U.S. Open, and desire to prevent the sport from being the target of social criticism. It became an issue of protecting his own class interests rather than upholding the civil rights of

Shippen and Bunn. During those early years, particularly, golf's "most wealthy participants were regarded as 'gentlemen-players' above the 'petty bickering' of the nation's masses."[15]

Oscar Bunn, 1899.

Shippen was thought to be of mixed African American and Shinnecock Indian descent until his daughter Clara Shippen Johnson corrected the record in 1986, just before the U.S. Open returned to Shinnecock that summer. One source of confusion might have involved a story in which Havemeyer placated the other players by telling them that Shippen was half-Indian, and therefore, acceptable. "And that isn't true, either," Johnson contended, "because those men also objected to Oscar Bunn, and Oscar Bunn was a Shinnecock Indian." It was Shippen's wife who was Native American, not his mother, and this led to years of confusion. He was called an "Indian" but never denied being African American. Clara Johnson was adamant: "My father was a Negro. Every time I meet somebody, I have to correct the story."

Following Havemeyer's decision, play began Saturday morning at ten o'clock in "splendid weather, excepting that a strong wind was blowing in the faces of the players as they drove off from the first tee." The U.S. Amateur, at that time the premier event in the land, had ended the day before over the same course. Players approved of what they saw of the course, according to *The Sun*, the only criticism being "the slippery putting surfaces. The ball on the slightest touch fairly shoots over the turf," and the greens "played many tricks with the contestants."[16]

The first to go off that Saturday were George Douglas and James Foulis, followed by John Shippen and Charles Blair Macdonald. Shippen played extremely well, and was tied for second place after the first round with four other players, two strokes behind Joe Lloyd's 76. Macdonald, the U.S. Amateur champion the year before, didn't fare as well, shooting a 90. Dissatisfied with his play, he withdrew, but surprisingly stayed and kept Shippen's score for the final round. "It probably did not improve his nerves," the *Chicago Tribune* said of Macdonald, "to see the smooth-faced colored lad going slowly but surely ahead of him."[17]

James Park played with Oscar Bunn, "the colored caddie, as an accommodation." Bunn didn't play his best, shooting a first-round 89 and ultimately finishing twenty-first, but merely taking part has kept his name alive down through the decades.[18] After a short break for lunch, the second and final round began at two p.m. Shippen played steady golf going into the final nine holes before stumbling, finishing with an 81 and a tie for sixth. For years, the long-held narrative has held that he took an eleven on the thirteenth hole. Newly discovered hole-scores from the New York *Sun*, however, contradict this. Nearly every account of Shippen's performance in 1896 makes mention of this disastrous hole, although at least two reference the 11th rather than the 13th hole.

Shippen recounted the story numerous times. In 1963, he claimed "I would have tied Foulis if I hadn't taken eleven on a par-four hole." Around the same time he told Red Hoffman about the thirteenth hole:

> It was just a little easy par-four with a little dogleg to
> the right. All I had to do was play it a little bit to the
> right. Well, I played it to the right, too far to the
> right and the ball ended up on a sandy, rutted road. I
> just kept hitting that darn ball along that road, and
> before I knew it, I had taken an eleven on the hole.

Shinnecock's thirteenth hole in 1896 was 200 yards long, in that era it could be deemed a par-four, but his description of a dogleg would suggest a longer hole. A contemporary map of the course indicates a road in front of the fifteenth green, running across the fairway in both directions, with the course description noting that a "road and artificial bunker are hazards."[19]

The July 19th edition of the New York *Sun* contains hole-by-hole scores for sixteen players, evidently hidden in plain sight at the

Library of Congress all these years. They show Shippen with a three on the thirteenth hole and a seven on the fifteenth, a 333-yard par-four. Is it possible he remembered it incorrectly?

False memories – in psychiatry referred to as confabulation – refer to the production of fabricated, distorted, or misinterpreted memories about oneself or the world. People who confabulate recount incorrect memories ranging from "subtle alterations to bizarre fabrications," and are generally very confident about their recollections, despite contradictory evidence. Yet there is no conscious intention to deceive. Our memories are "not based on exactly what happened," says cognitive neuroscientist Martin Chadwick of University College London. "There's something more approximate going on, often referred to as a gist memory. Rather than encoding every word, you're building up an overall concept that you store in memory."

On different occasions, our own memories of the same event, place, or person may vary in the specific details. Memory is a complicated thing, in the sense that it is the result of a combination of factors that we could never quite sort out, according to Edward S. Casey, author of *Remembering: A Phenomenological Study.* "Implicit in all remembering is a commitment to truth concerning the past, a truth that reflects the specificity of this past even if it need not offer an exact likeness of it."

Daniel L. Schacter, in *Searching for Memory: The Brain, the Mind, and the Past,* claims the "fragility of memory is partly attributable to the fact that the seemingly straightforward task of remembering the what, where, and when of our past depends on subtle interactions among different processes of which we are only dimly aware." Elizabeth J. Marsh has observed that the "simple act of retrieving a memory can change the memory…the perspective taken during retelling affects later ability to remember the original event in its entirety." She adds that "What people remember about events may be the story they last told about those events."[20]

There are other examples of golf stories becoming legend where the facts conflict with the tale. For example, Bobby Jones is famous for picking up his ball and quitting on the 11th hole during the third round of the 1921 British Open. Numerous accounts have him shooting a 46 on the front nine, although some newspapers and Jones himself said it was 43. Another legend has Tommy Armour making a 23 on a hole during a tournament in 1927, but numerous accounts have him with an 11 on the 486-yard 17th hole. So one can see how time can set fiction as fact.[21]

Round 1 hole scores from the New York *Sun* (39-39=78)

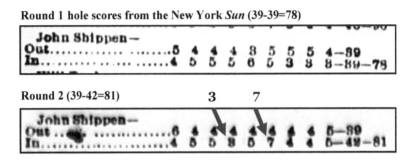

Round 2 (39-42=81)

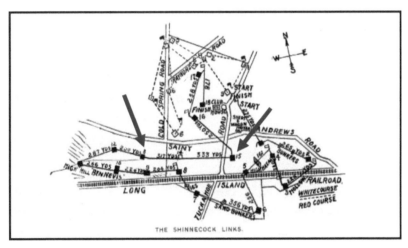

Layout of Shinnecock Hills, from *The Golfer*, April 1896. The arrows indicate holes #13 and #15 (note the road crossing the fairway.)

As historian Carl Becker said in 1931, what we call history is imperfect knowledge (or memory) of past events, "since we can never revive them, never observe or test them directly." We may accept as a fact that an event once occurred, but it has slipped away forever. All that is left to us is "some material trace" of that event, a written document, a photograph, a piece of film or video. We must therefore use what is left to us to "infer what the event was," and in doing so, we concede that history is relative, "always changing in response to the increase or refinement of knowledge."[22]

History is therefore "rather an imaginative creation," according to Becker, something each of us fashions out of personal experience. In constructing this far-flung pattern of remembered things, each individuals works "with something of the freedom of a creative artist," and the history he or she "imaginatively recreates as an artificial extension of his personal experience will inevitably be an engaging blend of fact and fancy, a mythical adaptation of that which actually happened."[23] This could aptly describe John Shippen's memory of that final round. With little other evidence available, it is difficult to ascertain exactly what happened, but when examining the twenty-nine rounds of hole-by-hole scores found in the New York *Sun*, they all add up to the correct round totals found in accepted USGA records, including Shippen's 78-81.

This suggests that the reporting at the time was accurate enough. It appears that Shippen, years later, somehow remembered the seven he shot as an eleven – and placed it on the wrong hole – and like an embellished fisherman's tale, his oral history has been adopted as the truth ever since. The *Sun*, in evaluating the way the championship was conducted, noted only one "blunder was made, the omission to arrange for the collection and prompt posting of the cards as each pair came in…There should have been an official to attend to this work alone."[24]

There was little press coverage, no radio or television or PGA Tour ShotLink to capture every stroke played. In those days scorecards weren't kept as a permanent record. After the fact, they were discarded, or given to the players or anyone else who wanted them as souvenirs. *The Golfer* magazine of August 1896 contains the hole scores of four players, which match those found in *The Sun*, and are as close to an accurate account of events as we can achieve.

Whether Shippen took an eleven or a seven in that final round, the fact is he failed to win. When his ball landed on that sandy road, his fate was sealed. It was "bad trouble in those days before sand wedges," he remembered. "I kept hitting the ball along the road, unable to lift it out of the sand…You know, I've wished a hundred times I could have played that little par four again." Shippen recovered to play the last three holes in four, four, five and finished tied for sixth with H.J. Whigham, who had won the U.S. Amateur the day before.[25]

The golfing world was impressed by Shippen's performance. *Outing* noted that "the caddies of our links have already produced…a competitor whose reputation and skill were sufficient to give the oldest hands a bad quarter of an hour [an old expression signifying an unnerving experience.]" The *Chicago Tribune* noted that a "group of Shinnecock caddies surrounded their youthful champion and showered congratulations upon him." It added that

> anyone who plays Shippen has got to forget his boyishness, and pay careful attention to his golf, for Shippen is, in view of the circumstance, the most remarkable player in the United States. His principle weakness was in putting, and this cost him fully five or six strokes in the first round.[26]

A New York paper noted he had been dubbed the "Little Wonder," and that it was "quite a sight to see this mere infant in golf go around with Macdonald, the former champion and an old St Andrews man in Scotland, and he beat him, too. In driving the boy distanced his older competitor four times out of five."[27] It was his youth, rather than race, that seemed to be emphasized in press reports.

Race, however, would always define John Shippen. "No sport worthy of the name ought to take note of creed, color, or rank," decreed Britain's *Golf* magazine, "and we should hope that American professionals will discard the sentimental prejudice, and be ruled by the generous instinct to allow all competitors…to freely compete for coveted honors in their midst." *Outing* noted that Shippen was "an example of what progress can be made in the game," while at the same time revealing the "cliquishness of some of our imported professionals, who tried to exclude him from their matches on account of his color."[28] Shippen would compete, but he would always be defined by his color.

Shippen's success in the U.S. Open galvanized his determination to pursue a career in golf. It had been a question, observed a newspaper article, whether he would follow in his older siblings' footsteps and continue his education "or to become a professional of the links, the inclination being strongly in the latter direction."[29] This decision must have been a great disappointment to his father.

For his son to play a game must have seemed to John, Sr. quite childish and irresponsible. Their old neighbor in Anacostia, Frederick Douglass, probably would not have approved of the younger Shippen playing a game. Douglass saw "sports and merriments" as an oppressive holdover from slavery times, when masters used them as an "effective means...of keeping down the spirit of insurrection." Douglass's reasoning, according to Dr. Jeffrey Sammons of New York University, "served to stigmatize play and sport as dangerous and wasteful, perhaps setting the tone for scholarly perception and representation of sport as trap or safety valve."[30]

African Americans tended to "depreciate and belittle and sneer at means of recreation," wrote historian and sociologist W.E.B. Du Bois, who gave considerable thought to the role of athletics in education. In his article "The Problem of Amusement," he called for an equal emphasis on work and play in education, contending they complimented one another. "Boys and girls should be encouraged if not compelled," he wrote, "to run, jump, walk, row, swim, throw and vault." Such a balance, he argued, is not only healthful but also cultural: "Where the balance between the two is best maintained, we have the best civilization, the best culture."

Sports provided more than simple exercise, they also channeled the need for amusement into productive activity. "We must rapidly come to the place where the man all brain and no muscle is looked upon as almost as big a fool as the man all muscle and no brain." Du Bois felt young people should be inspired to "unselfish work," but also realize that "amusement and recreation are the legitimate and necessary accompaniments of work, and that we get the maximum of enjoyment from them when they strengthen and inspire us for renewed effort in a great cause" – that of "the development of Negro character to its highest and holiest possibilities." However, as Du Bois became more militant, he saw little value in golf as a recreational or athletic endeavor; its association with middle-class, white elitism was simply too strong.[31]

As for Booker T. Washington, the only forms of physical recreation he valued were gardening and caring for animals. Beyond an occasional game of marbles with his children, all other games were useless. "I have never seen a game of football," he asserted.[32] As a minister, John Shippen's father recognized the importance of both religion and education in the lives of African Americans. Education, not athletics, was seen as a means through which African Americans could rise, and prove that they were the equals of whites, both socially and intellectually.

For Du Bois, education was also a political tool in the struggle against oppression. In 1930, at a Howard University commencement address, he said:

> Let there be no misunderstanding about this, no easy going optimism. We are not going to share modern civilization just by deserving recognition. We are going to force ourselves in by organized far-seeing effort by outthinking and outflanking the owners of the world today who are too drunk with their own arrogance and power successfully to oppose us, if we think and learn and do.[33]

Shippen's father and siblings were among those who, like Du Bois, understood that "outthinking and outflanking" the opposition required education. But John's life was tied to golf, and this created strains in familial relations for years to come.

When the 1897 U.S. Open was held in Chicago, Shippen did not participate, most likely because of the cost involved in travelling to the venue. *Outing* wrote that as one of the best professionals in the country, it was "hoped that Shippen will be enabled to play at Chicago, and his club ought to see to it that, despite his color, he is given every opportunity to show what he can do."

Opportunity for African Americans has always had a different meaning. Black men suffered the burden of being "inferior" in a culture which placed extreme importance on male superiority. If they excelled athletically, like Shippen, they were seen as a threat, and demeaned (as were most African Americans), with the epithets "nigger" or "coon." Moreover, their successes could be – and frequently were – diminished by attributing these to a "baser, less-evolved" nature.[34]

"Nigger is a very powerful, provocative word," argues Randall Kennedy, professor at Harvard Law School and author of a 2002 book on the subject. "It's first and foremost a slur that provides a window on some of the ugliest aspects of American history." As far back as 1837, Hosea Easton, an abolitionist minister of mixed race, wrote that the shameful word was "employed to impose contempt upon [blacks] as an inferior race...It flows from the fountain of purpose to injure."[35] John Shippen, his parents, and siblings would hear it often, as it was common not only in everyday conversation but in literature, including newspapers and magazines.

Abraham Lincoln, who freed slaves like Shippen's mother and father, shared the conviction of founding father Thomas Jefferson that whites were by nature superior to blacks. Jefferson, for example, in contemplating the ideal of physical beauty in *Notes on the State of Virginia*, placed whites at the top of the scale, apes at the bottom, and African Americans in the middle. The notion that black people were less than human was one engrained in the minds of people, especially Southerners. Slavery had been based on the theory of the racial inferiority and biological inequality of blacks.

In his seminal work on the history of African Americans, historian John Hope Franklin outlines the main postulates of the theory. A central tenet was that blacks were destined to occupy a subordinate position, unable to "throw off the chains of barbarism and brutality that have long bound down the nations of that race; or to rise above the common cloud of darkness that still brood over them." Through the ages the church had sanctioned slavery as a means of converting the heathen to Christian civilization, and as most believed, it was "the stepping ladder by which countries have passed from barbarism to civilization."[36]

Race has been a problem in the United States since John Rolfe recorded the first shipment of Africans to Virginia in 1619, and it still defines us. Racism was a de jure and de facto reality. John Shippen's father was a nine-year-old slave when Chief Justice Roger B. Taney, in the *Dred Scott* case of 1857, upheld the long-held belief that African Americans were "so far inferior that they had no rights which the white man was bound to respect." He ruled that no person of African ancestry could claim citizenship in the United States (which the Fourteenth Amendment settled in 1868.) As former Confederate President Jefferson Davis wrote in 1881, the Civil War "did not decide Negro equality."

In 1896, two months before John Shippen played in the U.S. Open, the Supreme Court handed down a decision in the case of *Plessy v. Ferguson* that upheld the constitutionality of state laws requiring racial segregation in public facilities. The Court maintained that social prejudices could not be overcome by legislation, and that "If one race be inferior to the other socially, the Constitution of the United States cannot put them upon the same plane."

Justice John Marshall Harlan offered the lone dissent in the *Plessy* case, arguing that in the eyes of the law, "Our Constitution is color-blind, and neither knows nor tolerates classes among citizens. In respect of civil rights, all citizens are equal before the law. The humblest is the peer of the most powerful." We are still aspiring to that end.[37]

Even through slavery had ended, attitudes hadn't changed. Text books taught millions of school children that blacks were "ignorant," "dishonest," and "extravagant." Most whites believed that "the Negro may be lazy," as John Clyde, a Columbia University sociologist, suggested in 1898. The relative autonomy of the city, he maintained, exacerbated negative traits, breeding "both sloth and inefficiency." Beliefs such as these, argues historian Marcy Sacks, "rationalized the implementation of housing restrictions, police harassment, and most importantly, occupational exclusion." These negative images of dangerous, slothful black men had profound consequences on their work experience. In 1896, Frederick Hoffman wrote in *Race Traits and Tendencies of the American Negro*, "the presence of the colored population is a serious hindrance to the economic progress of the white race."[38]

In 1901, President Theodore Roosevelt invited Booker T. Washington to dine with him at the White House. Being the first African American to do so, this unleashed the wrath of racist politicians. Future Governor of Mississippi James K. Vardaman described the White House as "so saturated with the odor of" Washington "that the rats have taken refuge in the stable." He added, "I am just as much opposed to Booker Washington as a voter as I am to the cocoanut, chocolate covered, typical little coon who black my shoes every morning." Senator Benjamin Tillman of South Carolina said that the President's entertaining

Washington would necessitate "killing a thousand niggers in the South before they will learn their place again."[39]

It was horrific, violent racist rhetoric such as this – by elected politicians, no less – that supported the lynching of blacks. The records of the Tuskegee Institute, the single most complete source of statistics and records on this crime, show that 4,743 persons (1,297 whites and 3,446 blacks) were lynched from 1882-1968. On June 13, 2005, the U.S. Senate formally apologized for its failure to act when it was most needed, admitting that it "considered but failed to enact anti-lynching legislation despite repeated requests by civil rights groups, Presidents, and the House of Representatives to do so."[40] This is the country John Shippen lived in, and the only thing that ameliorated his condition was that he lived in the North rather than the South.

Socially, African Americans were pariahs, and since their voting rights were systematically repressed, they were stripped of political power. Frederick Douglass once declared, "The feeling (or whatever it is) which we call prejudice, is no less than a *murderous, hell-born hatred* of every virtue which may adorn the character of a black man." The religious training of Shippen's father would help instill in his congregation a faith that the wicked would be destroyed, and that God would sustain them and help them overcome.

Religion provided succor, but in the racist nation no black person reflecting on his or her life had failed to ask the question, "what, after all, am I? Am I an American or am I a Negro?" So spoke W.E.B. Du Bois in a speech to the American Negro Academy in 1897. "Or is it my duty to cease to be a Negro as soon as possible and be an American? If I strive as a Negro, am I not perpetuating the very cleft that threatens and separates black and white America?"[41]

Later, in his 1903 book *The Souls of Black Folks*, he spoke of "two souls, two thoughts, two unreconciled strivings; two warring ideals in one dark body, whose dogged strength alone keeps it from being torn asunder."[42] Du Bois would argue that the "problem of the twentieth century is the problem of the color-line," one that still lingers. Recall the O.J. Simpson trial in 1995. Or consider the events in Ferguson, Missouri in 2014, and Charlottesville, Virginia in 2017, as well as daily headlines in newspapers in 2020 for evidence of serious societal racial strife that still produces shamefully violent consequences.

In 1944 Gunnar Myrdal wrote a book called *An American Dilemma: The Negro Problem and Modern Democracy*. Its main thesis was that the "Negro problem is a problem in the heart of the American,"

"A Typical Caddy," from *The Golfer*, September 1902.

Player at Pinehurst, NC – "Say boy, how many am I playing now?" "'Clare to goodness I don' know boss! What yo' want am a bookkeeper, not a caddie," from *The American Golfer*, April 1909.

a problem of "distinctly negative connotations" that suggests "something difficult to settle and equally difficult to leave alone." This racial problem, which Myrdal outlined exhaustively in his massive 1,500-page work, is in conflict with the "American Creed," as he calls it. People may think, talk, and act as if under the influence of high national and Christian precepts, but at the same time they are affected by personal and local interests, and long-held prejudices, which are "defended in terms of tradition, expediency and utility."[43]

In the era in which John Shippen lived, golf, in its typical country-club setting, was an elitist pursuit of white well-to-do patrons. What Shippen did went against the tide of what society expected of a black man, and also against what his own family wished for him, and caused a rift that would last most of his lifetime. At the end of 1898, when his father took the family back to Washington, DC, only John remained at Shinnecock.

Shippen was able to secure a job at Maidstone Golf Club after his performance in the Open, and although exact dates of service are difficult to ascertain, he remained there until 1899, when he took a job as the professional at Aronimink Golf Club, just outside of Philadelphia.[44] Upon his arrival at Aronimink, however, several female members objected to his hiring. One protested that the club "would be subject to a great deal of criticism, not to say ridicule, from the other Philadelphia clubs" for employing a black man in such a high-profile position.

Author Richard Wright, in recalling his own experiences as a black man in the South, remembered leaving a job where he felt harassed by his boss, and having his parents chastise him for it. "They told me that I must never again attempt to exceed my boundaries. When you are working for white folks, they said, you got to 'stay in your place' if you want to keep working." Whether or not the women members believed Shippen didn't know his proper "place," the male members defended the choice.

Almost unanimously, according to one commentator, they asserted that Shippen was "a good all-round player and an excellent teacher...[as well as] most gentlemanly, courteous, and deferential...without a trace of the brusqueness and almost intolerable overbearing ways of the average imported 'pro.'" The men saw his hire as being "of great benefit" to the club, and seemed unconcerned that a black man's presence might compromise the prestige of their organization. As a black man, life had taught Shippen to be "deferential" and not "brusque" in his interactions with white people. In the end, the men overruled the women's protest and Shippen got the job.[45]

Around that time he took the job at Maidstone, Shippen had married Effie Walker from the Shinnecock Reservation, but she passed away suddenly July 16, 1899 at the age of twenty-two. Shippen learned at a young age just how fragile life is. Two months later, with a heavy heart no doubt, he competed in his second U.S. Open, played at the Baltimore Country Club, where he finished in a tie for twenty-sixth.

Perhaps due to his rude reception when he arrived there, Shippen left Aronimink after a year to take a job in 1900 at the Marine and Field

Club in Brooklyn, the golf committee there noting that he was "well known as an excellent player and instructor." That year he tied for twenty-eighth place in the U.S. Open. Shippen was competing not only against local talent, but players with national reputations, an indication of the talent he possessed. Charles Thom, two years his junior, was the head professional at Shinnecock Hills for 55 years (1906-1961.) He competed in six U.S. Opens himself, finishing seventh in 1902. Of Shippen's style he said: "He had a vicious swing. I've never seen anything like it – yet he could control his club as if he had it on a string." Others described it as not a "picture book" golf swing. He had a short, "hoppy half-swing" or "three-quarter swing." Not aesthetic, but it got the job done.[46]

On May 27, 1901 Shippen married another Shinnecock woman, Maude Elliot Lee, with whom he had six children. After two years at the Marine and Field Club, he returned to Maidstone in 1902 or 1903, where he remained until 1913. Kenneth Davis, who may have the distinction of being the first white man to caddie for an African American, carried Shippen's bag in 1903 and 1904. He later went on to manage the Maidstone from 1931 to 1958. "He was an excellent driver. He could outdrive anyone playing at that time," Davis said of Shippen. "Many a player would bet him a dollar they could outdrive him. In all those years, until he left Maidstone…I never saw but one man who outdrove him." Shippen's grandson Hanno Shippen Smith recalled his grandfather's powerful forearms "were just huge…he was like Popeye."[47]

The same year he married Maude, another crisis arose. Shippen's father may have exhorted his parishioners to have faith in God and not lose hope in the face of unrelenting racism and economic oppression, but somewhere along the line he lost his own way. "Preacher Cuts His Throat," read the headline in *The Washington Post* December 27, 1901. The story reported that the "ex-Presbyterian minister" had committed suicide by cutting his throat with a razor. It was a shocking act that must have shaken the family greatly.

The report described how Shippen had asked one of his daughters to get his razor that morning, and when he didn't return to the house, his wife went to check on him short after nine o'clock. "She heard groans coming from the stable, and on entering was horrified to find her husband on the floor, the blood pouring from a gaping wound." A doctor was called, but Shippen, Sr. expired before he arrived. The article concluded by saying Shippen was well known in the community. "He left the ministry several years ago and engaged in the grocery business with his son," adding that he had been forced to leave his post at Shinnecock "on account of ill health."[48] His death made news in other parts of the country, including newspapers in New York, Ohio, Kansas, Mississippi, North Carolina, and South Carolina.

Not surprisingly, this event was not recorded in the Shippen family history written in 1994. Daughter Eliza would only say that after her father's death, their oldest sibling Clara provided for the five children who were still in school. Eliza would remember her father as "bright, scholarly, thrifty, ambitious, and hard-working. He often helped his children with Latin when they were in high school, and always encouraged them to study."

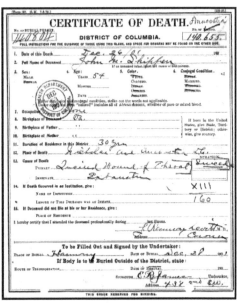

Death certificate of John M. Shippen, Sr., 1901. The cause of death is recorded as suicide.

We don't know how each member of the family reacted to John, Sr.'s suicide, but common reactions would most likely include anger, guilt, and feelings of shame. They may have thought "if only" when considering what they might have done to perhaps prevent the act, or blamed themselves for it in some way. Each of his brothers and sisters had to come to grips with what happened, and process it in their own way. Shame they felt could be linked to the stigma of suicide, especially since John, Sr. had been a minister, a religious and educated man.[49]

As Alison Wertheimer contends in her book on suicide, *A Special Scar*, survivors "may feel humiliated and believe that the suicide has brought dishonor and disgrace on the whole family." This can lead to feelings of not being normal or being an outsider, resulting in some cases to closed off communications, emotional estrangement, and isolation from others.[50]

His father's death must have had a unique impact on John, Jr., who had remained in Southampton to pursue his golf career. It could help explain his bouts with alcohol later in life and his strained relations with his siblings and children. It's possible it also pushed him away from a religious life, as he may have felt betrayed by his father and the faith he put in God. John had just turned twenty-two when he learned his father was dead, and he left behind no known diary or letters to offer insight into his and his family's reaction to what happened. He had a new wife and a new baby to take care of when 1902 arrived, and needed to find ways to support them, no matter how he may have felt inside.

Thus began a nomadic life for Shippen, looking for work in his lowly profession wherever he could find it to take care of his family. But he also loved playing golf for its own sake. In 1902, he tied for fifth in the U.S. Open, which would be his best finish in the event. He would miss the cut in 1908 and played his last in 1913, finishing tied for forty-first. While Francis Ouimet's victory that year spurred a great growth in the game in this country, Shippen's life was at a crossroad. His extended absences made for a troubled marriage, and there is some evidence that he drank. A 1941 club history of Maidstone noted that he was "a first-class player until the Indian's besetting weakness spoiled his game," referring to the belief that Native Americans – which he was not – were susceptible to alcoholism.[51]

Separated from their father in their formative years, an unquestionable estrangement from his children took place as the years passed. It seems that Shippen attempted to make amends by acquiescing to his wife's wishes and moving to Washington, DC in the early 1920s. There he worked as a laborer for various government departments, while moonlighting as a golf professional for several Washington area golf clubs.

William Carter met him as a teenager at the East Potomac Park Golf Course, site of the 1923 U.S. Amateur Public Links Championship. "He wore knickers and smoked a pipe and was a most pleasant man. He was very serious on the course but he was always patient and extremely helpful. He'd tell you right away how to straighten out what was wrong with your swing." His daughter Clara recalled that he tried other kinds of work "for four or five years, but he really disliked it. He had to be outdoors. He had to be near a golf course."

John Shippen was an outsider in his own family because he turned away from education in favor of golf, while many of his brothers and sisters – and his wife, children, and grandchildren – had college educations. Shippen's sister Eliza Pearl would earn a Ph.D. from the University of Pennsylvania, and her life was dedicated to education, as she began teaching in District of Columbia public schools in 1906 and retired in 1954 as a professor of English at D.C. Teacher's College (which became the University of the District of Columbia in 1977.) She

wrote in 1973 that her father "was very eager that all of his children go to college. He made sacrifices to accomplish his goal."[52]

Cyrus Shippen graduated from Yale University in 1899, where he was also a member of the football team. Shippen's sister Clara Russell Shippen graduated from Oberlin in 1897, and taught for several years in District of Columbia schools. Her alma mater was a popular choice for African Americans, since it resolved in 1835 that "the education of the

Cyrus Shippen, graduation photo from Yale University, 1899.

people of color is a matter of great interest and should be encouraged and sustained in this institution." Henry graduated from Oberlin Academy and later attended Howard's School of Pharmacy, but dropped out. Eliza Shippen observed that with Henry perhaps her father made a mistake, as she believed it would have been better to send him to the Hampton Institute (Booker T. Washington's alma mater) to learn a trade, since "he did things beautifully with his hands."[53]

After graduating from Yale, Cyrus returned to Washington and began teaching in the public school system. He moved to Paul Lawrence Dunbar High School in 1924, where he remained until his retirement in 1946. At Dunbar (the former M Street High School) he taught Civics, Economics, History, and Latin, and also coached the golf team. "He insisted on a high standard of scholarship and character at all times," wrote his niece Mabel Shippen Hatcher. "He loved to dance, play golf, and enjoyed card games of all sorts. He was especially fond of horse racing."

"C.S." as his nieces, nephews and special friends called him "was a kind and benevolent man. He was always willing to lend a helping hand to those in need. He helped his family, his friends, and many needy students." Dunbar was known for the excellent education it provided its students in a city that had segregated public schools. As all public school teachers in Washington were deemed federal civil servants in those years, its teachers received pay equal to that of white teachers in other schools in the district. Consequently, Dunbar attracted high-quality faculty, many with advanced degrees like Cyrus Shippen.[54]

Cyrus S. Shippen (middle row, third from left), with members of the Dunbar High School golf team, c.1935.

Cyrus Shippen influenced many lives, including Edward W. Brooke, III, Dunbar class of 1936. Brooke was the first black U.S. Senator elected by popular vote after Reconstruction (in 1966, from Massachusetts) and someone considered to have "moved the arc of history" in this country.

As Brooke recalled at the end of his life, "I think everything that happened to me after Dunbar – Dunbar had an impact upon it." In high school he had the idea of being a doctor, until he met Cyrus Shippen. He advised Brooke to turn away from the sciences and concentrate on civics.

> He said, "You know, you are a people person." And I said, "A people person?" He said, "Yes, I've noticed you with the kids around here. You're a people person. You get along; you know how to get along with people. And I think that'd be a better career goal for you." So that, in its way, had a great impression on me....

Even though Shippen wasn't "a counselor or anything like that," he cared, and was insistent. Brooke paused for a moment before telling the interviewer in a low, deep voice: "And he said, 'I believe in you,' and that was quite an inspiration to me."[55] Brooke followed Shippen's advice, and it changed his life.

As his niece Mabel said of Shippen, "We respect all of his efforts to make our lives better, to smooth our paths along the way, and to impart his love of knowledge to all he met." Cyrus's sisters Bessie, Eliza, and Carrie graduated from the M Street High School, and taught in the elementary schools of Washington, while Clara taught in Normal School No.2 from 1898 to 1918. His nieces Ruth and Mabel were also teachers.[56] All served education well during their lives, but Cyrus Shippen was the star of his family. Younger brother John, on the other hand, was a disappointment to many, including his own wife and children.

The family history points out that their mother Maude "was the second woman from the Shinnecock Reservation to graduate from a school of higher learning," doing so in 1899 from New Paltz Normal School (now the State University of New York at New Paltz, south of Albany, New York.) "Instead of teaching, she elected to get married." John Shippen's lack of education alienated him from his family. And because he wasn't a churchgoer, the black community didn't embrace him either.[57] Given the way his father died, it is not surprising Shippen may have turned his back on religion.

Maude Shippen taught for a number of years as her husband traveled. Daughter Mabel claimed her mother "couldn't stand it" on the reservation. Whatever the reasons behind the move to Washington a decade later, the daughters claimed their mother adjusted well to life there, making new friends and adopting "new ways of living under meager financial circumstances."[58]

As the Great Depression fell over the country, Shippen was fortunate to find work, moving to New Jersey in 1931 to take a job at Shady Rest Country Club in Scotch Plains, New Jersey. He found a permanent home there, remaining until his retirement in 1960. Founded in 1921, the club grew quickly and soon had 200 members, and was one of the first clubs formed by African Americans in the United States.[59]

Shippen became a fixture at the club and would have an impact on many lives. "In the beginning we called him Mr. Shippen," recalled former caddie Earl Nettingham, "but he made it a point to call him 'Ship.'" He took an interest in the boys who caddied there. He "never had any kids give him any problem, as far as fighting or anything like that or bad language. When they came over here and they started to caddie they looked up to Ship."[60]

Joe Delancey, who won National Amateur championships from 1953 to 1955 conducted by the United Golfers Association (to be discussed in the next chapter), grew up in Florida and as a teenager moved to New York. The first tournament he played outside of "the times set aside by whites for caddies," was at Shady Rest. He remembered Shippen as "a real nice guy who was always trying to be helpful. When he'd see a youngster, he would try to help him along."

Earl Nettingham remembered Shippen having his hand in everything: "He ran the golf shop, he cut the greens, he was the caddiemaster. Us caddies even paid him a fee. If we got $5 for twice around nine holes, we gave him 50 cents. Not for his own pocket, but for the clubs he made up for us kids to play with."[61]

The move to New Jersey, however, effectively ended his marriage. After her husband took the club professional job at Shady Rest, Maude Lee Shippen was listed as a "widow" for many years in Washington, DC city directories, as well as in the 1940 Census. When asked about the ill will many family members harbored against John

Shippen, his grandson Hanno Shippen Smith maintained that it was because of golf. "At the end of their relationship, she wanted a stable income and a stable home."

> My grandmother got tired of running around all of the different golf courses where he played, and where he worked...I don't think they ever divorced. I think he and my grandmother just separated. They cared about each other, and loved each other I'm sure, but golf just got in the way. He went back to the golf game and wound up at Shady Rest.

Dr. Calvin Sinnette, author of *Forbidden Fairways: African Americans and the Game of Golf*, spoke with Alberta Shippen, the widow of Shippen's son William Hugh, in 1995 for his book. In discussing the separation, she contended it was acrimonious and "her mother-in-law's family never forgave him for leaving."[62]

1940 U.S. Census rolls, with Maude Shippen listed as a widow ("Wd.") Daughter Clara and her son Hanno lived in the same residence, along with daughters Mabel, Beulah, and brother-in-law Cyrus.

On January 12, 1957, John Shippen's wife Maude passed away in Washington, DC at the age of 77, after being bedridden the last two years of her life due to a paralyzing stroke. Her husband did not attend the funeral. She had adjusted well to life in Washington, claimed her daughters Beulah and Mabel, who said her greatest concerns always focused on her children and their welfare.

Shippen's time at Shady Rest was also marked by a certain rehabilitation of familial relationships. "My father drifted apart from us as we grew older and there was a long stretch of years when we didn't even know where he was," said daughter Clara Shippen Johnson, who lived in Washington, DC. One day while she and her husband were playing at a course in New Jersey, a man asked her if she was John

Shippen's daughter. "He told me my father was at Shady Rest. We went up the next Sunday and had a wonderful reunion."

Clara's son Hanno Shippen Smith offered new insights into the family dynamics during a 2004 interview. "My mother was his youngest child, and they were very close. She would travel to see him. My two uncles Jack and Hugh would play with him quite a bit." His mother moved to Arizona after retiring from the Bureau of Engraving and Printing in Washington.

When Hanno came back to Washington to visit his aunts Beulah and Mabel, discussing his grandfather, he discovered they "were different from my mother. They took more toward the education side of the family, which was my grandfather's brother Cyrus. He was the education type...and he was their connection." This is a true assessment of the family dynamic, as the same sisters claimed that most of "the information regarding the roots of this clan was told to us by our uncle, Cyrus...when we were young girls."[63] He would be their role model, not their father.

By the time he retired in 1960, John Shippen had seen much remain the same in the struggle for blacks to play golf, but on November 9, 1961, a significant change for the better took place. That day the PGA of America removed Article III, section I from its constitution, which stated that only "Professional golfers of the Caucasian Race" were eligible for membership. In 1928 Dewey Brown, a light-skinned black man, had been granted membership in the PGA, but it was rescinded years later when his race was identified, and the constitution was amended to exclude blacks and other minorities. Years of pressure from California's attorney general Stanley Mosk led to the "Caucasian clause" being eliminated, and PGA president Lou Strong stated that its removal was "in keeping with the realization of changing world conditions and coinciding with principles of the United States government."[64]

When asked in the late 1950s about his experiences with racial discrimination in golf, Shippen gave a very diplomatic reply: "I didn't have any trouble," but admitted that African Americans didn't have an "equal chance," although restrictions were "breaking down." Shippen claimed, "I never could figure out how the PGA could do me any good, so I never saw any reason to join it."[65]

The year before he retired, Shippen saw William Wright win the 1959 U.S. Amateur Public Links, becoming the first African American to win a USGA event. He saw Pete Cooper win the Waco Turner Open in 1964, Charlie Sifford the Hartford Open in 1967, and many other black players compete on the PGA Tour by the late-1960s. John Shippen could take pride in leading the way, but he would leave others to sing his laurels.

When Red Hoffman interviewed him in the mid-1960s, he found a "small, soft-spoken man with genteel manners." Shippen, he said, had "an avowed reticence about discussing his exploits and not the semblance of a scrap book to refresh his memory." Perhaps a scrapbook would have helped recount what happened on those final holes at Shinnecock Hills. As Shippen's daughter-in-law Alberta said in 1995, he was "a gentleman from the old school. I never heard him talk about the 1896 Open."[66]

In earlier interviews, he recalled the old greats of the game. He counted as one of his finest moments playing in "a foursome with Harry Vardon at the Chicago Golf Club in 1900. He was the greatest golfer I ever saw." He claimed that his good friend Willie Anderson, Walter J. Travis, and Vardon, among others, would have held their own with Jack Nicklaus, Arnold Palmer and Gary Player. As is the case today, he spoke of a different game played in earlier times. "The condition of the courses, the few clubs of rather crude design and a ball that wasn't in the same class for length and accuracy with today's ball, penalized the first American golfers more strokes than I would try to estimate."[67]

A kidney ailment slowed him down in 1964, and he lived in a nursing home in Newark the last few years of his life. Shippen's daughter Clara would say her father's "memory was very hazy at the end and he couldn't remember things that had happened the day before, but he remembered every shot he made in that Open in 1896." John Shippen died May 20, 1968, and except for a few passing mentions of him by black sportswriter Sam Lacy and others in the years that followed, the memory of his groundbreaking achievements faded away. That is, until the U.S. Open returned to Shinnecock Hills in 1986. Shady Rest members were shocked to hear Jim McKay of ABC Sports introduce the telecast by saying, "James Foulis won the Open here ninety years ago, when John Shippen, the first black in the Open, took an 11 on the 13th hole." His legacy did live on, as did the myth of his score.[68]

In 2009, the same year Barack Obama became the first black President of the United States, the PGA of America bestowed posthumous membership to John Shippen, as well as Ted Rhodes and Bill Spiller, who were excluded from membership due to the "Caucasian only" clause in its by-laws from 1934 to 1961. Honorary membership was also given to legendary boxer Joe Louis, for his work in pushing for diversity in golf in the 1950s. PGA President Jim Remy said that the organization recognized "the importance of honoring these gentlemen with their rightful place in golf history."[69]

Hanno Shippen Smith was present to accept the award for the family. He regretted that "my grandfather's six children, who include my mom, Clara, could not have lived to see it. My grandfather taught my mother how to play golf and she transferred the love of the game to us." Clara Shippen Johnson, when recalling her father's near win in the 1896 U.S. Open just before her death in 1986, said "I'm sure my father's whole life would have been different if he hadn't got into that road."[70]

Ralph Wise, who caddied for Shippen and loved the man, remembered a sad vision of Shippen, often "sitting by himself, mumbling and almost crying, maybe because he never achieved his goals. He didn't talk much about the U.S. Open, probably because he didn't win it. He came close." Shippen told a reporter in 1963, "I came along fifty years too soon." Wise echoed this sentiment in 2004 when he claimed Shippen "came at the wrong time…We often wonder what history he could have made. This man could have turned history around. I think it bothered him terribly."[71]

John Shippen's show of emotion surely involved more than golf. A myriad of memories must have tumbled around inside his mind. Memories of a father he couldn't please and a suicide he couldn't prevent. Of a wife and children he left behind and the estrangements he couldn't repair. Of his first wife Effie, sister Susan, and son Jack, who all died much too young. Of not finding better jobs due to the color of his skin. Of growing old and not being able to play golf as well as he once did.

Shippen's shortcomings with his own family was something he couldn't deny, and it probably contributed to his drinking problem. He lived a rather lonely existence, according to many sources, and turned to liquor for comfort. He would sometimes be so impaired that he forgot matches he had scheduled. Ralph Wise remembered those days. "I knew where to find him. I'd bring him a pail of water and a clean shirt. All that he'd ask was could the caddie tee the ball up for him on the first hole. As he went out, he sobered up."

Shippen was an imperfect man, but he also had a positive influence on the lives of others. Ralph Wise grew up without a father, and found a surrogate in Shippen. "He taught me the game." His relationship with Shippen was special, and reveals a man behind the myth, a man who enjoyed eating hot dogs and Milky Way candy bars, who "spoke fondly of his daughter" Clara. He liked going to the movies and playing cards, but was not a "church-going person." Shippen also had an appreciation for sports figures such as boxers Jack Johnson, Jack Dempsey, baseball players Josh Gibson and Satchel Paige, and singers Marian Anderson and Lena Horne.[72]

Hanno Shippen Smith said his grandfather "forsook everything for the game of golf," and "pursued the game even in those times and faced a lot of adversity and continued to play." At the end of their lives, his aunts modified their opinion of their father. As Smith explained, they "were upset with their dad in terms of what happened in their life."

> I told them I did not like their approach toward their father. They took a very downside [dim] view of their father. I told my Aunt Mabel about some of my hopes relative to my grandfather and what I wanted to try to do about kids and the game of golf, [and] she perked up.

They visited the USGA headquarters and were shown the portrait of John Shippen done by artist Don Miller, donated in 1996 to commemorate the 100th anniversary of Shippen's near-miss at Shinnecock. It was then that "it hit her and hit her hard." Mabel ended up helping her nephew Hanno do a film about her father in 1999, called *America's First Golf Pro*.

Mabel's tone in the film was conciliatory, reminiscing about life on the reservation and the move to Washington when she was a child. She asserted that her father would "be remembered as a golfer...He's now acknowledged." Grandson Hanno Shippen Smith would maintain that for John Shippen to do the things he did in life, "he had to have a certain fiber, certain strength to contend in those times."[73]

Rising from his bed each morning in that tiny, spartan apartment in the Shady Rest clubhouse, John Shippen must have felt a sadness looking at his reflection in the mirror, lamenting the years he could never call back. His heart may have been heavy at times, yet his memories must surely have sought out happy times as well – his early success, the births of his children, the young men whose lives he impacted in positive ways.

Alone in the winter of his life, he may have wondered how life might have been different had he not found golf as a young boy at Shinnecock and instead continued his education. But then, as he told Red Hoffman, when he looked outside and saw the welcoming green grass of the golf course, he knew his choice had been the right one for him. Had he been a religious man, he might have been reminded that, as the Bible says, "To everything there is a season, and a time to every purpose under the heavens." He could find comfort in knowing that, as with everyone, "time and chance happeneth to them all."

When Tiger Woods won the Masters Tournament in 1997 to become the first African American to win a major golf championship, he said, "I wasn't the pioneer. Charlie Sifford, Lee Elder, Ted Rhodes, those are the guys who paved the way." Walking up the last hole, he "said a little prayer of thanks to those guys. Those guys are the ones who did it." While Woods's tribute to these men was certainly proper and respectful, there were many others – including many women – who opened the way for those who came later.

First among them was John Shippen, who lived the life that was given to him, and who may have found solace before he died in a passage from Dr. Martin Luther King, Jr.'s 1967 Christmas Eve sermon at the Ebenezer Baptist Church: "I am personally the victim of deferred dreams, of blasted hopes, but in spite of that I close today by saying I still have a dream, because...you can't give up in life."[74]

Chapter 6: The UGA, Pat Ball, Jimmie DeVoe, Lucious Bateman, and Maggie Hathaway – "Vanguards of Change for African American Golf"

John Shippen didn't play a U.S. Open after 1913, but his future work helped contribute to a new era for African American golfers, including his time in Washington, DC. The methods used by black Washingtonians became a template for African Americans in other cities seeking to dismantle Jim Crow golf. According to Marvin Dawkins and Jomills Henry Braddock, II, "the nation's capital deserves much more credit than sports historians have given for advancing the cause of black golf in the United States."[1]

Shippen moved with his wife to Washington in the early 1920s, and *Boyd's* city directories show John M. Shippen's name irregularly, beginning in 1922, as a laborer. In 1924 he appears again, working as a laborer for the State, War, and Navy Departments, and in 1927 as a laborer for Public Buildings and Parks. He also moonlighted as a golf professional, teaching and eventually organizing tournaments at the Lincoln Memorial Golf Course, the first black golf course in the city.

Completed in 1924, its founders were criticized by some for giving into Jim Crow constrictions. There were six courses in the city then, but this was the only one available to blacks. The *Baltimore Afro-American* wrote that men in business and professional circles had "adopted 'Jim Crow' golf as a sport and are submitting gleefully to segregation on account of race and are making ineffective the protests of others against other forms of segregation and discrimination."

Lieutenant Colonel Clarence O. Sherrill, Superintendent of Public Buildings and Parks (the agency Shippen would work for as a laborer a couple of years later) was responsible for the segregation. He decreed that black players were permitted to play on the East Potomac course only after 3:00 p.m. on Tuesdays, and the three-hole West Potomac Course after 12:00 noon on Wednesdays. The *Afro-American* article argued that by accepting these conditions, the golfers were putting Sherrill "in [a] position to say that he is giving the colored people what they want."[2]

John Shippen's services were also retained in 1924 by the newly formed Riverside Golf Club, "to render professional advice and help." The District's first African American golf club, it sponsored a tournament that fall at the nine-hole Lincoln Memorial course. Although the course featured sand greens, some of the top African American players on the East Coast participated. The event stirred "a great deal of interest both locally and nationally," reported the papers, as "upwards of 75 entrants are expected in the men's matches and about 30 entrants in the ladies' event."

Victor R. Daly, a real estate entrepreneur, established the club, and membership was $2. Although the club grew to around 100 members, many of them doctors, college professors and businessmen, it didn't last long. Members became dissatisfied with the way Daly ran things, especially when he couldn't account for the dues that were collected, and they left to form the Citizens' Golf Club in 1925, hiring Shippen as greenskeeper and instructor.[3]

East Potomac Park Golf Course, the city's first public golf course, had opened in 1921. Among the first to play there was President Warren Harding, who enjoyed his golf, but was an unrepentant racist. Speaking in Birmingham, Alabama that year he emphasized the "fundamental, eternal, and inescapable differences" dividing the races. He called upon blacks and whites to "stand uncompromisingly against every suggestion of social equality...Racial amalgamation there cannot be."[4]

The nation's capital was becoming more racially segregated as a whole, and by 1923 the only places in Washington where it wasn't apparent was on the trolleys and buses, at Griffith Stadium, and in the reading rooms of the public library and the Library of Congress. The city was so tolerant of racist sentiments that 40,000 members of the Ku Klux Klan marched down Pennsylvania Avenue on August 8, 1925 before large crowds and virtually no protest.

At the end of 1926, Washington's principal black paper, the *Tribune*, declared that segregation had "grown to the dimensions of a national policy." It was in full force in government departments, and "the Negroes themselves have about reached the stage of acquiescence in the practice." Fearful of losing their jobs, black civil servants didn't lodge complaints, leaving NAACP officials without provable grounds for protest.

It was in this setting that John Shippen and the Citizens' Golf Club tried to operate. The leadership of the club was representative of the city's black elite, claim Marvin P. Dawkins and Jomills Henry Braddock, II in their study of black golf in Washington. Due to their class status, they were "better able to emulate their white counterparts in promoting golf and showing off the social status that normally accompanied the game." Club president Dr. M. L. T. Grant, in his acceptance speech, spoke of great champions of the day Bobby Jones and Walter Hagen, and the lofty goal of becoming "the most wealthy Colored Golf Club in the world and produce champion players as well."[5]

Off the success of the Riverside Golf Club, a group of African American men met in early 1925 at the 12th Street YMCA in Washington to form a new organization of minority golf clubs and players. Its objective was to "gather all colored golfers and golf associations into one body," with leadership provided by Dr. George Adams and Dr. Albert Harris, both physicians in the city. Initially called the United States Colored Golf Association (the name would be changed to the United Golfers Association – or UGA – in 1929), it consisted of twenty-six clubs.[6]

Like black churches, businesses, and colleges, the UGA was created to mirror, at least to a certain extent, the same institutions of the dominant white society. It was also formed partially in response to the exclusionary practices of the Professional Golfers Association of America, founded in 1916. UGA tournaments helped the whole African American community when they came to town, as hotels, restaurants, barber shops, and other businesses benefited from the influx of revenue during a tournament.[7]

The inaugural National Colored Golf Championship was held at Shady Rest Country Club in Scotch Plains, New Jersey in July, 1925. Harry Jackson of Washington, DC led a field of 30 golfers, shooting a 299 for 72 holes. John Shippen was second, three shots back. Fox Movietone News had a representative at the tournament, "who took motion pictures of the clubhouse, golf links, gallery, players in action, and of the presentation of cups...." The black press helped promote golf among business and civic leaders by covering tournament play in major cities. Harry Jackson would repeat as champion in the first official UGA National Open in 1926 at Mapledale Country Club in Stow, Massachusetts, where Shippen finished fourth.[8]

In 1927 Shippen moved to another African American club, becoming the head professional at the National Capital Golf Club in Laurel, Maryland. The club's members were "drawn from the most prominent people in the city," and included Emmett J. Scott, who had been a chief aide to Booker T. Washington before joining the War Department in 1917, and James Cobb, who President Coolidge had appointed as the only African American judge to the District of Columbia Municipal Court. Shippen was still involved with organizing tournaments for men and women at the Lincoln Memorial course, as

In 1927, John Shippen lived here, at 2223 12th Street, NW, Washington, DC.

evidenced by a June 1927 article in *The Baltimore Afro-American* calling for entries to "be sent to John M. Shippen, 222[3] Twelfth street, northwest, Washington, DC."

In October of that year, the *Pittsburgh Courier* announced that all "colored golfers in Washington and Baltimore have been invited to compete" in an 18-hole medal play invitation handicap tournament at the National Capital Country Club. Some 40 or more teed off, including Harry Jackson, the former UGA National Open champion, and Shippen, the club pro "in charge of events." He and Jackson had played an exhibition match that July opening the nine-hole course, but when the Great Depression came two years later, the club wasn't able to survive.[9]

"The Negro was born in the depression," recalled one African American man. It didn't have much meaning to that section of the population and "only became official when it hit the white man." After the Wall Street crash in 1929 black workers lost their jobs rapidly, while in rural areas they were driven to starvation wages. By 1931 one-third of African Americans in Southern cities couldn't find employment, the next year the percentage rose to over one-half. By 1935 Atlanta saw 65 percent of its employable black population in need of public assistance.[10]

In urban areas blacks were pushed out of jobs by whites, desperate for any kind of job when only a year earlier they would never have taken them. Despite these horrible economic times, and constant battling against de facto and de jure discrimination, there was still a section of the black community with disposable income – professionals in the middle and upper classes – that found golf and a way to play it.

In 1927 Shippen finished second (by a whopping 20 shots) to Robert "Pat" Ball of Chicago in the UGA National Open at Mapledale. Ball, who grew up in Georgia, was described as having "had country charisma coated with big-city guile." As a young man, he caddied for Bob Jones at East Lake in Atlanta, and would have his own struggles with prejudice when trying to play in major championships conducted by the United States Golf Association.[11]

At the 1928 U.S. Public Links Championship in Philadelphia, he and fellow-competitor Elmer Stout were disqualified after the second round of qualifying. If not for this, Ball would have made it to the match play portion of the event, while Stout would have played-off for the final spot. (How Ball was even able to compete in an amateur event after earning money in professional ones is a whole other matter; he maintained that he was not a professional.)

Ball claimed that shortly after he arrived in Philadelphia he was "met with color discrimination," and warned that "because of the color of his race an attempt would be made to have him barred from the competition." He and Stout were accused of rules infractions, and sought the assistance of an attorney to get a hearing before a judge, asserting in court papers that they had been barred solely "on the grounds of color and race prejudice." Their attorney, Raymond Pace Alexander, a black graduate of Harvard Law School, in the mid-1920s began to identify with the black intellectual "New Negro" movement, which advocated self-help, racial pride, and protest against injustice.[12]

Alexander "made ridiculous specimens of each of the witnesses for the defendants," noted The *Pittsburgh Courier*, including the two men who brought forth the allegations, one of whom was supposedly asked by Ganson Depew, Chairman of the Public Links Committee, to "stay close from hole to hole, watching the strokes...." Judge Raymond C. MacNeille, who heard the case, ruled after four hours of testimony that on the "one hand there is no evidence that there was any intentional infraction of rules on the part of the complainants, and, on the other hand, there is no evidence of any intentional discourtesy or prejudice on the part of the committee against the complainants because of their color or otherwise."

MacNeille ordered the committee to remove the disqualifications and have the players reinstated, but that would have necessitated a replaying of earlier matches, an impractical solution. The judge addressed this by stating that after much discussion, the complainants, because of "their love of the game of golf" and "in the spirit of good fellowship and good sportsmanship," would "not interfere with the course of the game by participating in the contest at this stage." The *Philadelphia Record* editorialized that this was exceptional sportsmanship. "Better sportsmanship, indeed, than was displayed by the whites in charge of the tournament. It demonstrates that the Negroes were not demanding social equality, but social justice."[13]

Ball and Stout were cheered for exposing racism, the general feeling in the African American community being that the entire episode was "conceived in snobbery and cradled in the worst sort of racial prejudice." The *Philadelphia Tribune* chastised the "blue-blooded scions of golfdom" for being "hauled into a court of civil action to answer charges of discrimination...by shad-skinned sons of Africa." The USGA was definitely shaken by the episode. If either player had made it to the semi-finals of match play, they would have earned an automatic spot in the field of the U.S. Amateur, to be played a month later. There was a fear that this would have prompted the withdrawal of many Southern players, including perhaps even the great Bob Jones. "I feel we have successfully fought here a preliminary skirmish," wrote Ganson Depew to USGA Secretary Prescott Bush, "which might have had far-reaching results."[14]

Depew, the nephew of former U.S. Senator Chauncey Depew, believed the association could keep "the matter more or less under cover" by having all future entrants for the qualifying rounds of the U.S. Public Links answer certain questions on the application form, such as age, nationality, place of residence, how long they have played, etc., "in which one of the questions would be 'Are you white or colored.' If this were answered in the affirmative it would mean we would reject the entry under the Resolution of our Executive Committee of last November, but of course, without giving any reason...." The resolution was clearly meant to prevent black players from competing in USGA events, and consistent with the actions of many organizations at that time regarding access by minorities.

Ganson Depew, 1932.

At the time of the incident, Depew suggested reinstating the former practice of having a committee in each locality select the contestants, to ensure "only the right kind of subject."

> I assume the USGA wishes to be recognized as an organization which is thoroughly democratic in its fairness to all golfers in the playing of the game. It is an organization, however, to promote the development and best interests of golf and undoubtedly has the right to decide what will promote or retard it.[15]

The following year he wrote to the USGA's Chief Counsel John Jackson, saying he was "convinced on account of the attitude which the white players took almost without exception" to Ball and Stout's participation, "that if we accept entries of this kind it means the end of

143

our Public Links Championship, and in the development of golf among hundreds of thousands of public links players, I feel this would be a calamity."

Through all of this – even if the USGA's actions in disqualifying Ball and Stout were not proved overtly racist – Depew seemed totally oblivious to the injustice he was proposing in banning future African American entrants. When reflecting on the events in Philadelphia, he said what pleased him most "was Judge MacNeille exonerating our Association in his opinion from any discrimination or prejudice on the part of the Committee because of color or otherwise."[16] It wouldn't be the last time Ball and others encountered difficulties playing where they wanted to.

The actions of Ganson Depew were reflective of larger societal ills that shaped these attitudes. Racism was real, supported at times by scientists and historians who attempted to justify it as a natural state of relations between the races. Ulrich B. Phillips, for example, a born and bred Southerner, was the preeminent historian of his time on the subject of slavery. In *American Negro Slavery* (1918) and *Life and Labor in the Old South* (1929), he upheld the idea of African American inferiority. The slaves were, he wrote, innately "submissive," "light-hearted," "amiable," "ingratiating," and "imitative." As for slavery, "it is impossible to agree that its basis and its operation were wholly evil, the law and the problems to the contrary not withstanding." He described slavery as a necessary and successful mode of racial control.[17]

Other historians followed Phillips's lead. Just two years after Depew's actions, Samuel Eliot Morison and Henry Steele Commager wrote a best-selling textbook in 1930, *The Growth of the American Republic*. From it, students were taught that "Sambo" suffered "less than any other class in the South" from slavery.

> There was much to be said for slavery as a transitional status between barbarism and civilization. The negro learned his master's language, and accepted in some degree his moral and religious standards. In return he contributed much besides his labor – music and humor for instance – to American civilization.[18]

144

Although several white historians, including Carl Becker, William E. Dodd, and Frederic Bancroft were unwilling to accept Phillips's interpretations, one can see how these statements could inculcate people with prejudice and racism.

This is why men like W.E.B. Du Bios and Carter G. Woodson kept the emphasis on education. As Woodson wrote in *The Mis-Education of the Negro* (1933):

> When you control a man's thinking you do not have to worry about his actions. You do not have to tell him not to stand here or go yonder. He will find his "proper place" and will stay in it. You do not need to send him to the back of the back door. He will go without being told. In fact, if there is no back door, he will cut one for his special benefit. His education makes it necessary.

Even though he was the first black player to enter the Western Amateur in 1930, Pat Ball and all other black citizens were stuck in a corrupt system where they had to fight for their rights.[19]

When the UGA National Open was held at Shady Rest in 1929, with 80 to 100 golfers expected to compete, 50-year-old John Shippen, "the grand old man of golf and a match for any of the younger golfers," was singled out as one of the players to watch. Pat Ball won again, as Shippen's playing days were coming to an end, although his career was not yet finished. Fortunate to find work at the height of the Depression, he moved to New Jersey in 1931 to take a job at Shady Rest Country Club. He found a permanent home there, remaining until his retirement in 1960.

Founded in 1921, the club grew quickly and soon had 200 members. An article in the New York *Sun* the following year reported that from

> Harlem, Brooklyn, Newark [and] elsewhere in the metropolitan district prosperous negro merchants, lawyers, doctors, Pullman porters, waiters and janitors flock there by automobile and trolley car on Saturdays and Sundays to play tennis and golf and enjoy the luxurious ease of the country club life.

The nine-hole course began as the Westfield Country Club in 1897, but was sold to a group of black investors, led by Howard S. Block, when Westfield merged with the Cranford Golf Club to become Echo Lake Country Club. The new black-owned club was named Shady Rest Country Club, and was one of the first clubs formed by African Americans in the United States.[20]

One may note that the article quoted above used "negro" – with a small "n" – instead of Negro with a capital "N," in describing the members of Shady Rest. This regular occurrence since post-Civil War times was seen as a symbol of disrespect. In the mid-1920s, W. E. B. Du Bois began a campaign with book publishers, newspaper editors and magazines demanding that they capitalize the "N" in "Negro" when referring to African Americans.

In 1929, when the editor for the *Encyclopedia Britannica* informed Du Bois that Negro would be in lowercase in an article he had submitted for publication, Du Bois quickly wrote a heated response that called "the use of a small letter for the name of twelve million Americans and two hundred million human beings a personal insult." The editor changed his mind and conceded to the capital N, as did many other mainstream publications soon thereafter.

On March 7, 1930, *The New York Times* announced its new policy on the editorial page: "In our 'style book,' 'Negro' is now added to the list of words to be capitalized. It is not merely a typographical change, it is an act in recognition of racial respect for those who have been generations in the 'lower case.'" The U.S. Government Printing Office followed suit three years later and within a decade, capitalization would become the rule in the Supreme Court as well.[21]

Du Bois himself was the featured orator at a Decoration Day celebration (as Memorial Day was then known) at Shady Rest in 1923. As the *New York Age* described it, there "was a record crowd present and all enjoyed themselves" with open-air concerts, a matinee dance in the afternoon and a more formal dance in the evening.

Shady Rest was created, as were other black golf clubs in the 1920s (most near Boston, New York, Philadelphia, Baltimore, and Washington, DC) as an alternative to the elite white clubs they were prohibited from joining. There were "other black-owned or operated clubs," argues Lawrence Londino, who produced a 1994 documentary film on Shady Rest, "but none other combined golf with the clubhouse, restaurant, lockers, tennis courts, horseback riding, skeet shooting, croquet and social activities that were generally associated with country clubs of the era." Du Bois applauded Shady Rest's "tremendous energy and esprit de corps."[22]

When the club found itself in financial troubles in 1925, William Willis, Sr. assumed control. The owner of a taxicab business, Willis had the vision and financial skill that allowed Shady Rest to prosper. However, as the Depression descended upon the country, the club couldn't cope with mounting tax burdens, and after the situation was exacerbated by the conflicting interests of two groups of investors, the property was acquired by the township of Scotch Plains in 1938 through a tax lien foreclosure. His son William, Jr. recalled that people kept putting obstacles in his father's way, "saying that the place was closed, that they were going out of business." To counter that perception, "every week he would have a band come in out of New York." Duke Ellington, Count Basie, Ella Fitzgerald, Sarah Vaughan, and Cab Calloway were among those who appeared at Saturday night parties there.

"I guess we didn't at the time, but now we know how important it was," said Annie Westbrook in a 2009 interview. She grew up near Shady Rest and met her husband there in 1938, while Duke Ellington played "One O'Clock Jump." She remembered the "place would be packed. We would be dancing. It was a great time." The country club continued as a focal point of African American social life through the 1940s and 1950s. Sadly, Shady Rest came to an end in 1964, when the gentleman's handshake between Willis and the township was not renewed. It became the Scotch Hills Country Club, and was opened to the public.[23]

Horace Westbrook grew up near the course and caddied for Shippen in the mid-1930s. "Shady Rest was something unique. There was no other place open to us. The people could go there and feel like they owned it. They could do the same things the white people did at the white clubs. There was a sense of pride." In addition to golf, some of the best black tennis players in the country came to play tournaments there. Tennis great (and later LPGA professional golfer) Althea Gibson remembered it as "a regular stop on the American Tennis Association circuit in those years. It was a very pleasant atmosphere."

John Shippen was a mentor for many young men who served as caddies at Shady Rest during his tenure there. They were born in the 1920s, '30s, and '40s, and saw the world in a different way than previous generations. The Depression and World War II had a dramatic impact on daily life and culture and African Americans worked to transform the status quo. Charles Hamilton Houston, special counsel to the National Association for the Advancement of Colored People (NAACP), created litigation strategies to attack segregated schools and racial housing covenants, arguing several important civil rights cases before the U.S. Supreme Court. As he said in 1935: "The most hopeful sign about our legal defense is the ever increasing number of young Negro lawyers, competent, conscientious, and courageous, who are anxious to pit themselves against the forces of reaction and injustice."

Houston, known as "the man who killed Jim Crow," was motivated by his own experience as a soldier in World War I, when the "hate and scorn showered" upon black troops convinced him to "study law and use my time fighting for men who could not strike back." He would train and mentor a number of lawyers for this purpose, including Thurgood Marshall of *Brown vs. Board of Education* fame. The fight would be continuous.[24]

Racism on the golf course hadn't ended either. Pat Ball, UGA National Open champion in 1927 and 1929, continued to have issues with the USGA after his run-in with officials at the 1928 U.S. Public Links. After sending his $5 entry fee to play in the qualifying rounds for the 1933 U.S. Open, he received a letter from Prescott Bush, chairman of the Championship Committee. He informed Ball that his application was declined based on his conduct at the Public Links Championship in 1928. *The Baltimore Afro-American* claimed this was an excuse and "a screen behind which USGA officials can hide, thereby obscuring the reason that they are barring him because of color."

A couple of weeks later, John G. Jackson, chairman of the Rules Committee and future USGA President, wrote to USGA General Counsel Livingston Platt, stating it seems to me it helps our situation to emphasize the fact that it is the Open Golf Championship of the *United States Golf Association* – not of the United States. As you will see, the Association further reserves the right to reject any entry, and the only question in my mind would be whether you would think it necessary that the rejection of Ball's entry should be approved by the Executive Committee.[25]

In 1939, five black golfers, including Jimmie DeVoe of New York, were barred from entering qualifying rounds for the U.S. Open. Louis Rafael Corbin, a golf pro and trick shot artist, had mailed in the applications of James McCoy, James Bates and Clifford Taylor, while taking his in person to Joe Dey, executive director of the USGA. All of the applications were rejected, even though Dey maintained it wasn't on account of their race.

In the 1930s, DeVoe partnered with John Shippen to organize and sponsor numerous events while he was operating a golf school in Harlem. Later he moved to California, and among his students were Althea Gibson and Jackie Robinson. The *Baltimore Afro-American* reported that Jess W. Sweester, treasurer of the USGA "declined to give any reason for the non-acceptance of his entry, but it is obvious the ban was placed on DeVoe and his cohorts because of their color."[26]

Three months later Hitler invaded Poland to begin World War II, which took the lives of an estimated 50-80 million people, including six million European Jews in death camps. In the United States that year, Billie Holiday recorded a song about southern lynching. Titled "Strange Fruit," its lyrics hauntingly described the aftermath, and the shocking sight of "Black bodies swinging in the southern breeze."

A. Phillip Randolph, labor and civil rights leader, proposed a March on the Washington Monument in 1941 to protest racial discrimination in war industries, call for an anti-lynching law, and end the desegregation of the American Armed forces. His aggressive tactics became the standard by which the black press judged other civil rights groups. He empathically demanded the necessity for conflict. "We would rather die on our feet fighting for Negroes' rights than to live on our knees as half-men, as semi-citizens, begging for a pittance." President

Roosevelt moved to stop the march, and as a compromise signed an Executive Order that prohibited racial discrimination in the national defense industry.

When the United States entered the war six months later, the NAACP announced the following day that a "Jim Crow army cannot fight for a free world." The Association's Walter White would say, "Prove to us that you are not hypocrites when you say this is a war for freedom. Prove it to us."[27]

The year after the United States entered World War II, Pat Ball, former Northwestern University golfer Horace McDougal, Clyde Martin and his pupil, boxing legend Joe Louis, along with five other players, tried to qualify for the 1942 Hale America National Open at Chicago's Ridgemoor Country Club. This was an event created by the USGA as a substitute for the U.S. Open after cancelling its other three championships for the duration of the war, with gate proceeds going to the United Service Organizations (USO) and Navy Relief Society.[28]

The *Chicago Defender* claimed the USGA had "Hitlerized" the players. In a telegram sent to Martin, the USGA informed him, regrettably, that he could not compete in qualifying rounds, since the club announced "the privileges of that club and its courses are not available to you." The USGA attempted to shift the blame to the offending club, Olympia Fields, but lost the public relations battle. McDougal, a veteran of World War I, wrote a number of letters that appeared in black newspapers nationwide protesting the USGA.[29]

There were very few sponsors then who would welcome black golfers to their tournaments. George S. May, who ran the Tam O'Shanter tournament outside Chicago, was one. In response to the Olympia Fields controversy, and with prompting from Chicago Alderman Benjamin A. Grant, May opened play to "any American who is willing and able to qualify under the rules of competition which have been set up for all participants." Years later, in the face of continued discrimination against blacks, May claimed the PGA and certain white players didn't "want the fellow from the wrong side of the tracks to get into golf. They want to restrict the game and keep it for rich men…They fear a Negro will come along and win one of the tournaments." He wasn't alone in thinking so, even if he voiced a minority opinion.[30]

Over a million black Americans served in World War II, and after fighting for freedom from tyranny overseas, many returned home to suffer continued indignities under Jim Crow laws – sitting in the back of the bus, separate waiting rooms and water fountains, and not being allowed to eat in certain restaurants among them. But they would not suffer in meek silence.

What the Negro Wants, a book published in 1944, featured essays by the likes of Du Bois, Randolph, Langston Hughes, Mary McLeod Bethune, and other civil rights leaders, who were unanimous in demanding full equality. As a black Corporal in the Army said,

> I spent four years in the army to free a bunch of Dutchmen and Frenchmen, and I'm hanged if I'm going to let the Alabama version of the Germans kick me around when I get home...I went into the army a nigger; I'm comin' out a man.[31]

When the U.S. Open returned to Chicago in 1949 and the Medinah Country Club, its board of directors voted to "permit colored persons to participate in the National Open Tournament should they qualify." The year before, Ted Rhodes had been the first African American to play in the U.S. Open since John Shippen in 1913. He finished tied for 51st, and Richard S. Tufts of the USGA made mention of this in a letter to Medinah, saying "a Negro player did qualify in the sectional rounds last year and competed at Riviera. Everything went smoothly and it presented no problem at all." Rhodes did play in 1949, but missed the cut by a shot.

Negro Digest magazine ran an article in October 1948 prodding the world of golf to "turn an interracial front" to the world and open its tournaments and "tempting cash prizes" to all. "But at the moment big-time golf is a white man's game, and the clique who controls it is struggling grimly against the pressures of those who want to see the grand old sport Americanized once and for all."[32] John Shippen did all he could in his lifetime, and the baton would be carried by others to make it less of a "white man's game."

The USGA changed with the times under the leadership of Joe Dey, its executive director from 1934-1968. In 1956 Ann Gregory became the first African American to play in the U.S. Women's Amateur and in 1959 Bill Wright became the USGA's first African American champion when he won the U.S. Amateur Public Links Championship. Progress had been made since 1928 and Pat Ball and Elmer Stout's travails, but the struggle would continue.

****

James Ralph "Jimmie" DeVoe would have a longer career than Ted Rhodes or Pat Ball, spanning decades of change. He had amazing longevity and played high quality golf into his sixties. A contemporary of John Shippen's, DeVoe was born March 24, 1888, in Dowagiac, Michigan. He would not only be an excellent player, but an advocate for African American golfers; organizing tournaments and working as a dedicated teacher. He went on like Methuselah, yet few have heard of this man.

DeVoe told the *Los Angeles Times* in 1975 that his mother was a descendent of slaves and his father was an Iroquois Indian. "If you had any Negro blood in you, you were classed as a Negro. But Indians have had a lot worse treatment than Negroes all these years." The family moved to Long Island, New York, where he grew up caddying at Shinnecock Hills. "There were only the very rich or the very poor in Southampton," he recalled. "The rich lived on the ocean side; the rest of us, the poor, in shacks – oh, my, real shacks with no electricity or anything – on the other side, across the tracks down by the Sound."

He learned his golf in the early hours, when nobody was on the course. As he told an interviewer in 1972, black caddies weren't allowed to play the course, only the white ones. "Prejudice was strong then," he said. But there were six holes on the back nine that were obscured by trees where he and his mates would play long before sunrise, out of sight, and literally in the dark. They would basically run while playing those holes over and over again. "We'd play 36 holes before six, when the greens help came and we'd scatter."[33]

DeVoe would have many acts to a life which saw him travel across the country and do many things. The difficulty in recounting his

152

life is the paucity of evidence to verify his comings and goings. Dr. Jeffrey Sammons of New York University has done considerable research on DeVoe, and asserts that Devoe's own account of his life has many aspects that conflict with credible timelines and established facts.

This makes it difficult, according to Sammons, to discern between "fiction, distortion, simple lapses in memory, and faulty recall of details, bad reporting or a combination thereof." I would have to agree with this assessment, as we know from the previous chapter how capricious memory can be. DeVoe's life is one that should be remembered, as he was a supporter of junior and senior golf (his exploits are outlined briefly in Chapter 8), as well as being the first African American to gain membership in the PGA of America after it revoked its Caucasian clause in 1961.

Jimmie DeVoe's World War I draft registration card.

In his teens, DeVoe was supposedly part of a vaudeville group that travelled the country, and he claimed to have later spent time in Europe before World War I broke out in 1914. He returned to the United States and married Minnie Vasen in 1916. His draft registration card, dated June 5, 1917, shows he was living in Chicago at the time and was a self-employed window washer. It also indicated he had previously served three years in the Army infantry. DeVoe was drafted into the Army and sent to France, and came back a Sergeant from Bordeaux in 1919. DeVoe claimed these travels were a substitute for a formal education, but sorting fact from fiction is a difficult task.[34]

By 1920 DeVoe ended up in Cleveland, working in a hotel as a bell hop captain, and then found a job in golf working for Eddie Hass.

DeVoe said he met Walter Hagen in 1924 while working in a pro shop at a club in Coral Gables, Florida during the winter. Hagen walked into the shop that day and started a conversation with DeVoe as if he'd known him all his life, acting very jovial and friendly. "I was pretty dumbfounded at this golfing great being so down-to-earth. There was a man with class."[35]

The next spring, when DeVoe was back in Cleveland and working at Dover Bay Country Club, Hagen came in to the shop one day. "How the hell are you?" he asked, remembering Jimmie's name and asking what he had been up to since they last met. Hagen was to play an exhibition at Ridgewood Country Club the next day and DeVoe's boss gave him the day off to attend. He drove over the next morning at 8 a.m. and headed to the locker room, where he found Hagen sitting on a bench, changing into his knickers. He asked Jimmie if there was any place around there he could get a drink. DeVoe had a pint of liquor in his car, even though these were the days of Prohibition. In a hushed voice, he informed Hagen, who said, "I can't go out there like this," so Jimmie went and fetched the booze.[36]

Hagen had the locker room attendant fetch a couple of tumblers and the two sat there and shared a drink. Hagen liked the first one so much he poured himself another, but DeVoe contended Hagen never played drunk. Harry Cooper, a Hall of Fame player from the 1920s and '30s confirms this, saying in a 1990 interview, "Hagen drank but I never saw him under the influence," After finishing his libations Hagen asked DeVoe for a description of the course. Once given, he stood up and roared, "Aw hell, I feel like setting a record today," then went out and shot a 63.[37]

Perhaps he embellished this story, but in fact DeVoe was in Cleveland in the 1920s through to the first part of the 1930s, and the 1930 Census showed him still married to Minnie, although they parted ways sometime after this. *The Pittsburgh Courier* in 1930 reported that an Ohio Negro Golfer's Association amateur event was going to take place at Cleveland's Highland Park course on September 22nd and "Jimmy DeVoe, local pro in charge of this tourney, is being swamped with entries from all parts of the state...." By the early 1930s, he was back in the New York metropolitan area. A 1932 program of the Eastern

Golf Association showed him as the professional at the St. Nicholas Golf Club in New York, which was formed in 1926. DeVoe "carried a full stock of golf equipment" and was also a member of the Association's Greens Committee. There is also evidence that he also umpired Negro League baseball games in the 1930s.[38]

Jimmie DeVoe, 1932.

In 1936, DeVoe opened a golf school in Harlem's largest department store, L.M. Blumstein's, thought to be the first such operation owned by an African American. Two years earlier, the store had been the target of the Citizen's League for Fairplay, where "pickets started parading up and down the front" of the store until the owners saw the "justice of employing Negroes as clerks." It was reported that 75 percent of Blumstein's clientele was black, and the protests resulted in the hiring of African American clerical and sales help.

In addition to providing beginners a place to learn the game, DeVoe offered instruction to more advanced golfers. "An advocate of the Ernest Jones method of teaching golf," wrote *The Pittsburgh Courier*, "Jimmie puts great stress on swinging the club head."[39] That same year it was reported that DeVoe met with William J. Norman, who served on the USGA Public Links Committee. Norman told him that all eligible golfers were welcome to try to qualify for the event that year at Bethpage. This may have been an attempt to avoid the problems that occurred in 1928, as well as a reaction to the exclusion of entries in the 1933 U.S. Open. Whether this overture had any real effect is hard to determine.

In 1937 DeVoe is mentioned as being the professional and greenskeeper at the new Rising Sun Golf and Country Club in Ossining, New York. It hosted tournaments that drew outstanding black players, and that year teams of 36 golfers from New York and New Jersey competed there. The winning team was led by John Shippen, "the dean of our professional golfers," according to the *New York Amsterdam News*, whose "own game was an inspiration to his fellow players." Howard Wheeler, a powerhouse on the United Golfers Association circuit, who won the first of his six National Negro Opens in 1933, also won a tournament there that was conducted by DeVoe.[40]

Jimmie continued to operate his golf school, at times to the detriment to his own game. He and four other African Americans had their applications rejected for qualifying rounds for the U.S. Open in 1939, their race seemingly being the reason. Two months earlier, however, DeVoe questioned the notion that "color lines" kept them from getting into tournaments. He claimed the reason "we don't have Negroes playing in big tournaments today is that we don't have good enough players." Speaking specifically of the U.S. Open, "We haven't been able to find players who can play good enough golf to qualify. However, the fact remains that they don't bar aspirants because of color." I have found no comment from DeVoe regarding his application being rejected later that June.

DeVoe ended his relationship with Blumstein sometime before 1940, and began teaching at the Harlem branch of the YMCA. He began going to California in 1937, teaching for short periods and then returning to New York. DeVoe made the move to the West Coast permanently by 1942, perhaps drawn to the warmer climate and pushed by the considerable racial unrest in Harlem at the time. He began as the golf professional at the Baldwin Hills Driving Range in Los Angeles.[41]

In 1944, DeVoe became the first African American to play in the Los Angeles Open, held that year at the Wilshire Country Club. He recalled the moment he arrived at the course for a practice round the day before play began. A man approached him, saying they were only using white caddies. DeVoe said, "I don't give a damn what color he is, as long as he can caddie." The man was taken aback as DeVoe went to the pro shop and told Olin Dutra (the 1934 U.S. Open champion) what happened. Dutra set the man straight in no uncertain terms, and DeVoe played. "We got kicked around then," he remembered, "but since I got in the PGA I haven't had any trouble."

In 1946 DeVoe organized the Pacific Coast Open golf tournament for black golfers, sponsored by the Cosmopolitan Club of Los Angeles. Played in October, Ted Rhodes finished tied for 8th, Bill Spiller tied for 34th, and Jimmie DeVoe tied for 38th. Smiley Quick, a top amateur who won the 1946 U.S. Public Links and would latter hustle Joe Louis out of hundreds of thousands of dollars on the golf course, beat Stan Kertes in a playoff. (Kertes had once been Babe Didrikson Zaharias's teacher.) There was also a women's division, a first for the event.[42]

The Cosmopolitan Club, founded in 1944, had hired DeVoe as its professional and Tournament Director, who later became an important executive in the Western States Golf Association, an umbrella organization of black western clubs.

DeVoe continued to play in local events, as well as the United Golfers Association tour, finishing fifth behind Charles Sifford at Kansas City in 1953. Up-and-comer Lee Elder, the first black man to play in the Masters in 1975, finished eighth, 15 shots behind DeVoe. At the UGA National Open that year, DeVoe finished fifth with a four round total of 314, 12 strokes behind the champion Sifford, nearly half his age. At Houston in 1954, at the age of 66, Jimmie finished seventh behind winner Bill Spiller. Charles Sifford was second and Lee Elder fifth. Even though in his 60s, DeVoe could still hold his own in a competitive environment.[43]

In 1959 Jimmie went through local qualifying for the U.S. Open. Needing to shoot 148 to go to Southwest Sectional at Yorba Linda, he shot 161 (84-77). He was 71 years old, but would never retire. The same year he was hired by Harry Bassler as an assistant professional at the former Fox Hills Country Club in Los Angeles. DeVoe said Bassler was as good a businessman as he was a golfer, and "ran his shop like a department store." DeVoe worked for him for five years. "That qualified me for PGA membership, but in those days you had to have a class A Pro sign for you. Harry did." It was here that DeVoe frequently came into contact with the rich, famous, and powerful.[44]

Bassler had an interesting career himself. In 1931, at the age of 22, he became the professional at Lakeside in Los Angeles, where he taught people like Ty Cobb, Bing Crosby, W.C. Fields, Jean Harlow, and

Howard Hughes. When Bob Jones came to Lakeside to make his Warner Brothers movie "How to Break 90," he asked Bassler to work as a technical advisor. "When Bob asked me to play with him. I was trembling all over. I skulled about all afternoon and kicked it around in 82. Jones had 67 the first time he saw the course."

Bassler moved to Fox Hills Country Club in Culver City, California in 1942, where he oversaw its two 18-hole courses and 650 members. He served three years as president of the Southern California section of the PGA, and was respected by his members and peers; U.S. Open champion Lloyd Mangrum called Bassler "Teach." Bassler took a chance in hiring DeVoe, and deserves credit for being a friend to African American golf.[45]

William Wright, the first African American to win a USGA event (the 1959 U.S. Public Links), knew Jimmie DeVoe. According to Dr. Jeffrey Sammons, Wright believed DeVoe's knowledge of golf enabled him "to straddle the line between white and black golf like no one else had before." DeVoe had a quiet, unassuming, nature and could get along with anyone, proudly admitting that he was not a rabble rouser. In a 1975 interview, he referred to himself as a "Negro" – the old fashioned identifier – and not as black or Afro American, which were popular terms at the time.

DeVoe taught beginners, advanced players, and many celebrities. When Althea Gibson decided to give up tennis and take up golf in the early 1960s, with the goal of becoming the first African American to play on the LPGA Tour, she took lessons from DeVoe at Fox Hills. Among his other students were Bill Spiller, Jackie Robinson, Los Angeles mayor Tom Bradley, Mrs. Nat King Cole and the Mills Brothers. He also drew praise for instructing underprivileged youth, along with students of all races, ages, gender, and class.[46]

When the PGA of America repealed the clause limiting membership to "Caucasians only" in 1961 (it had been on the books since 1934), DeVoe became the first African American since a man named Dewey Brown in the 1920s to be a member. This was in 1962, when DeVoe was 74, and according to PGA membership records, it made him the oldest first-time member of the Association.

When he was in his late 80s – and looking like a man in his 60s – the cigar-smoking DeVoe could be found six days a week on the driving range at Westchester Golf Course in Los Angeles, where he had relocated to. He recalled the old days when it was difficult to play tournaments at white clubs. On those rare occasions black players were allowed, they got the worst starting times, either beginning or finishing in the dark. They had to change their shoes in the parking lot, not being allowed in the clubhouse. And if they scored well, they might be accused of cheating. "But you couldn't quit," he said. "That's what they wanted you to do, get mad and go home."[47]

Jimmie DeVoe was never hired at a private club, recognizing the cruel realities of those times. "There's always some club committee member around who will say, 'I don't want no nigger teaching my wife to play golf,' and that'll be that." Yet he claimed he was not bitter, saying the PGA had been "wonderful" to him. "The black people are getting their chance now. Sure it's been slow, but look how long it took before there were blacks in baseball and football."

Yet he had no illusions that the playing field was level. While playing in the Senior PGA in Florida in 1974, he told a reporter, "How often do blacks get to play a course like this one? That's another reason the blacks who are playing the Tour have had some troubles. We all started out playing on public courses that weren't kept up at all, so when we get out on a good course like this we're lost. But our day is coming."[48]

He was also very astute in his grasp of societal strictures that had to be changed in order for minorities of all kinds to find a better life. "You'll never get rid of ghettos without a good education, a chance to get a better job, and live in a better neighborhood." But he believed in the future, and enjoyed teaching juniors. "It's like taking a beautiful chunk of fresh clay and molding it to your liking, teaching him to play golf the way you think it should be played – with dignity and respect for the game."[49] What a beautifully succinct method.

Jimmie DeVoe passed away March 19, 1979 from complications due to a heart condition; five days shy of his 91st birthday. He was teaching six days a week at Westchester until his death, and had lessons on the books. From caddying at Shinnecock Hills to meeting Walter

Hagen, to working with John Shippen, and moving throughout his life to find work in the game he loved, DeVoe had a full life indeed. As he said about his longevity, "I don't have any recipe. I guess the Lord's on my side."[50]

****

Another man who enjoyed teaching young golfers, and who had a lasting effect on many lives was Lucious Bateman. (Numerous public documents indicate this first name, and he signed his World War II draft registration card as "Lucious," but all other sources I have seen use "Lucius." For the sake of clarity he will be referred to here as Lucius.) Born in Franklinton, Louisiana on January 1, 1906, his family moved to Biloxi, Mississippi shortly thereafter, and as a young boy he started caddying at the Edgewater Hotel and Golf Club. The professional there, Arthur T. Saunders was impressed with his attitude and when Bateman got a little older he helped Saunders give lessons.

He earned a little extra money doing this, recalled Bateman, "but more importantly I was able to listen to Mr. Saunders give lessons and I learned a lot about golf." Bateman became a good player. As he said of those years, he had "nothing to do but hit golf balls, so I started learning, right then." As the caddie master, Bateman passed on those playing tips to some of his friends among the 250 boys who carried clubs at the club. This would prove his first foray into teaching.[51]

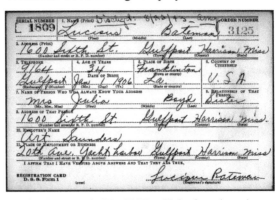

Lucius Bateman's World War II draft registration card. Note he spells his first name "Lucious."

Like Jimmie DeVoe, not much is known about Bateman's early life. He worked for a construction firm in Panama, and then served in the Army Air Corps during World War II, being discharged in 1943. He returned to Mississippi for awhile and then moved to California and got a job in San Francisco ship yards. After seeing "magazines with all those beautiful green courses in California," he decided to pick up and move, a decision made easier since he had a sister who lived in Oakland.[52]

Bateman had a lot of game. He set many records at local courses; a 63 at Alameda, 66s at Crystal Springs and San Mateo, 67s at Tilden and Hayward, and a 68 at Chabot. Earl Fry, the professional at Alameda (now Corica Park), liked Bateman and gave him an opportunity to teach by asking if he'd like to give lessons to the horde of eager and usually empty-handed juniors who hung around the course.

After four and a half years in the shipyards, Bateman returned to golf full-time, when he settled in 1947 at the Airways Fairways, a scruffy-turfed, fenced in driving range across from the Oakland airport, on the shore of San Francisco Bay. The owner, Rig Ballard, had seen Bateman's talents and gave him a job. He began as a handyman and later became a teaching professional. He would remain there until the place closed down, because he liked the work and was loyal to Ballard.[53]

Bateman dedicated himself to the young kids he taught, who called him "Loosh," and since he never married, they became his family. "He once told me girls take up too much of his time," said Don Baucom, who became a teaching pro in Sacramento. "He chased golf. He was totally addicted to the game." But Lucius was strict with his boys. Rig Ballard said Bateman wouldn't even talk to kids who lost their tempers over bad shots. "If they don't learn to be sportsmen as well as golfers, Lucius won't bother with them. He holds that in highest esteem. Being a gentleman is most important."

When future U.S. Open winner Ken Venturi was a junior player, Bateman was working with Don Whitt, who would also be a winner on the PGA Tour. Whitt was having trouble with club selection in tournaments, and the two worked out hand signals, somewhat akin to baseball. They used these while Whitt was playing, even though it was against the rules. In one tournament, Venturi was playing with Whitt and complained to officials about the signaling going on – rightly so,

Bateman admitted. Officials told him to cease and desist and stay away from Whitt. In addition to teaching, Bateman would continue to play against top-notch players, including Venturi a few years later.[54]

Of the countless youngsters Bateman coached, his most famous pupil was Tony Lema, winner of the 1964 British Open. The two met in 1947, when Loosh was playing in the Oakland City Championship, and where Tony was caddying. Bateman remembered Lema as a "bright looking kid and we just kind of liked each other from the start, so I started working with him...." At first he didn't think Lema would make a very good golfer. "He didn't seem to have much talent," Bateman said in 1966, "but he was – and is – a fighter."

Lema was so poor that Bateman had to buy him new golf shoes when his wore out. Bateman got him a job picking up balls at the driving range, and took Tony to the toughest East Bay courses where they would challenge anyone to best-ball matches. Lema held his own and then some in those money matches, Bateman recalled. He would "always come through in the clutch on key holes to help us win. Before every one of these matches, I'd tell Tony to 'know what you've got, play up to it and when the chips are down, don't choke.' He seldom failed." After winning the Oakland City championship at 18, Lema told Bateman his goal was to play on the PGA Tour.[55]

Lema did make the Tour, but in his early years had a reputation as a playboy and ladies man. "I told him he'd never make it on the Tour if he didn't settle down," said Bateman. Once married, Lema did settle down, and had a solid career before his tragic death in a plane crash in 1966. He never forgot his teacher, returning after winning a big tournament check to take Bateman out for dinner. "Tony didn't have a father, and that was a problem. But I became a sort of a father to him." Lema was a restless teen, skipping school often, and golf was the one thing that kept him balanced. Bateman knew Tony's mother well, and she said often that if not for him, she would have had "a boy in trouble."

"There's a kinship that goes beyond what color you are," said Bateman, who was pleased to see how Lema turned out given all he had going against him. Lema claimed that many kids might have been in jail if not for Bateman. "He knows kids – how they think, how to talk to them and what to do for them. As long as I've known him he's willing to help kids for nothing in return." Patrick Chapman recalled a kid by the name of Phil Torres, "who was really rough, the kind of guy you always wanted on your side. Bateman was the only one who could keep Phil in line." Golf, and Bateman's discipline, put some structure into his life and "saved him from a potential life of crime." Other young men realized the impact Bateman had on their lives, and were grateful.[56]

Dick Lotz, born in Oakland and a three-time winner on the PGA Tour, remembered a man who took kids on the borderline of "being good boys or bad boys," and helped them through adolescence. Bateman saved many a young man from juvenile hall, guiding them to be good citizens. "I think that is probably the more important thing about him than the golf aspect," said Lotz, who contends the nine core values the First Tee youth golf program follows were reflected in Bateman's teaching. "Man, Lucius invented 'em."[57]

Tony Lema with Lucius and his dog "Hacker."

Gary Plato, the retired PGA Head Professional at San Jose Country Club inducted into the Northern California PGA Hall of Fame in 2019, concurred, and spearheaded the efforts to recognize Bateman for his work. Plato says, "Lucius Bateman was a one-man First Tee Program back in the 50's and 60's," believing that had he been alive when the program came into being in 1997, "I am certain he would have been the National Chairman." Dick Lotz was impressed with Bateman's love for kids. He never charged him or the many others who he worked with, but he would adults. Bateman had the boys do a little work around the range in exchange for lessons. He molded nine PGA Tour players, including Lotz and his brother John, Don Whitt, and John McMullin, as well as several longtime teaching professionals.[58]

In 1962, about 100 of Bateman's present and former students held a banquet and tournament to honor him and his work. As he said simply at the time, "Golf is my life." Walt Roessing wrote in *Golf Digest* that it was fitting they gave Bateman a dinner, since over the years he had given a small fortune to his pupils. He paid green fees, provided equipment and contributed literally thousands of hours of free lessons. Over forty years later his students hadn't forgotten. Don Baucom recalled the group of kids who played golf with Lucius every Friday. Baucom didn't have money for green fees and spoke of Lucius paying for them, along with clubs and balls, and meals, never asking to be paid back.[59]

Gary Plato recalls an example of Bateman's generosity when he was a senior at San Jose State. Bateman asked if he was going to play in the Almaden Open, but Plato told him he didn't have the $50 entry fee (not a small amount in the early 1960s – more like about $400 today.) Lucius handed him $50 and said "'I want you to try to qualify and play.' I was lucky enough to be the medalist in the qualifying and played in the tournament. I didn't play well in the tournament, but I was in with Tony Lema, Billy Casper, Ken Venturi. A great experience. That was the kind of man Lucius was. He did this for many others over the years." Plato claims he would never have become a PGA professional if not for Lucius Bateman.[60]

Bateman said in 1965, "If kids who don't have any money ask for my help I give them all I can. I just ask them for one thing in return: to try. I do the rest. I get to know them and they get to know me." Whether it was a new shaft for Tony Lema's driver, or greens fees for Don Whitt, Lucius would pay. He also gave fatherly advice on all subjects: "school, money, girls, smoking, drinking and the future." Plato speaks of Bateman's incredible dedication to his boys. He worked "seven days a week doing what he loved most. It was not uncommon to see him give 25 lessons a day in the summer months. He still managed to squeeze in a round of golf on Friday afternoons after teaching all morning and returning to the range and teaching until nine in the evening."[61]

Bateman believed in a compact swing for control, with firm wrist action. "I do not care much for a really big swing," he said, advising a reasonably short backswing, depending on the student's physical capabilities. "I don't believe in remaking a golfer. I try to take what he has and make some good out of it." He also crossed paths with Johnny Revolta, winner of the 1935 PGA Championship and 17 other tournaments on the PGA Tour. Revolta was a master of the short game and Bateman often told stories of how much he learned about the game from him. Bateman's swing concepts, considered unorthodox at the time, are now the standard. Lotz and Baucom added that he was adept at course management, able to plot his way through a round effectively. Bateman was a "smart player," said Tal Smith, who was head professional at Claremont Country Club in Oakland. "Other guys might hit the ball better, but he out-thought them."[62]

"Bateman had a touch," said PGA Tour winner John McMullin. "He could see something when it broke down and he could fix it easily." Don Baucom agreed, saying Bateman had the best eye he'd ever seen for being able to diagnose a swing problem quickly and know how to solve it.

Art Spander wrote in 1972 that the temptation was to wonder what might have been had Lucius Bateman not been born a black man. Might he have made it on the PGA Tour, or been a club pro at a swanky club or a highly paid swing guru? Don Baucom played perhaps 300 rounds with Bateman, and contends that there is no doubt his mentor had the talent to play on the Tour. They would frequently play nine holes at Alameda and he saw Bateman "shoot 29 at least three times. He would shoot in the 60s every single day. He didn't play in a lot of tournaments, but he liked to play a lot of informal gambling matches."

Bateman was said to have beat Ted Rhodes and Charlie Sifford in matches. Gary Plato recalled Lucius often telling the story that of beating "Charlie out of $5, but Charlie never paid him." Plato believes if Bateman had been given the opportunity, "he definitely could have been one of the real good players on the Tour."[63]

"I could shoot in the 60s every day," Bateman maintained. "Some people said I could have made it as a pro. But heck, they didn't allow no colored players on the Tour then." The year before he died, he believed golf had "gotten rid of most of its hang-ups. The black golfer can go on Tour now and there's no fuss. But there's still not too many in the game...If Arnold Palmer was black, more kids would be playing golf." Twenty-five years later Tiger Woods would come on the scene, but today there are still only two African American players on the PGA Tour.

Bateman said, "I never tried to get much money out of golf. I wanted the poor kids to learn the game. I wanted them to love it the way I do." In November 1971 Governor Ronald Reagan congratulated Bateman on his long career. "Your efforts over the years have benefitted both the game of golf and the many young people who have had the opportunity to learn from you. The people of California and particularly the East Bay salute you."[64]

Even after suffering two strokes and a circulatory problem that prevented him from walking properly, Bateman didn't retire. He continued to work at Dougan's Sports Center in San Leandro after Airways Fairways closed. "I just can't quit," he told the *Oakland Tribune* in 1971. "A kid comes up to you, you've got to help him. Another one comes along, you've got to help him too." Bateman believed there was something "wonderful about spotting a kid with ability, then helping and encouraging him and seeing his progress. It's great to see one of them win a tournament, but it's even nicer to watch them turn into good citizens." Lucius Bateman passed away April 22, 1972 after suffering a heart attack and stroke. Both he and Tony Lema were elected to the Northern California PGA Hall of Fame in 2018.

Randy Herzberg, a teaching pro at Alameda's Corica Park, was one of Bateman's later students. He remembered the respect the young men had for Bateman, who knew if their behavior was just a little bit questionable, it would get back to him. John McMullin recalled getting upset once while playing and having Bateman respond by walking off the course. "He didn't tolerate a bad attitude. He did not have a good car and he lived in a shack, but me and a lot of the other kids never had to pay," he added. "He was one of a kind."[65]

John Lotz remembered picking balls on the range with his brother Dick after high school and then working on their games with Bateman. He would then drive them home. "We used to joke that like Sam Snead he had all kinds of money buried away in cans." The young men saw the decency in their teacher and friend, not his race. He said he never did want to get paid to teach golf, he just wanted to "help the kids." He seemed to understand the restrictions race had placed on him, but didn't show bitterness. "My mother taught me that everything happens for the best. What may seem like a tough break often works out the other way. I have no complaints."[66]

Gary Plato believes that Bateman transcended race. His students admired him as a man, and he "simply moved forward every day doing everything he could for as many people possible. He was truly a beloved figure." He wasn't confrontational, concludes Don Baucom. "Charlie Sifford and other talented black golfers were angry and fought the system. That was not Bateman's way." Plato added that Lucius "was extremely positive, I never saw him down or heard him say a bad word about anyone." Dave Harris had his own take on Bateman's response to prejudice. "He fought it by doing the right thing. For instance, he would give lessons to the son of the most prejudiced man in the world, but wouldn't hold his father's attitude against the boy. Lucius said he was just going to out-class them. That was his approach."[67]

Art Spander claimed Bateman was "a man from another era, a time when success was achieved by attaining an ideal, not an image." On those terms, he achieved resounding success. Jack Cummings didn't consider himself a "Bateman Boy" but knew Lucius well. "He was one of the finest men I've met in my life," and he felt fortunate to have known him. "I've always said since he passed away, if Lucius Bateman isn't in heaven, there is no heaven."[68]

****

Maggie Mae Hathaway played a little golf, but her lasting impact was off the course, not on it. Her activism began in Hollywood and spread to the world of golf, and she was a tireless crusader for real change. Born July 1, 1911 in the sawmill town of Campti, Louisiana, she was raised by a religious Methodist grandmother who was part Cherokee and Choctaw Indian. In 1939, Hathaway moved to Los Angeles with several of her cousins, where she hoped to find work as a piano player in a cabaret on Central Avenue, known then as Black Broadway. When that didn't pan out she became an extra in films, usually portraying sassy, witty ladies on screen.[69]

That year she played a maid and did a jitterbug dance in a Warner Brothers musical short, *Quiet, Please!* and was also a dancer in the Marx Brothers movie *At The Circus*. In 1943 she did a sexy dance with her partner in the cabaret scene in *Cabin In The Sky*, as they enter with other dancers and settle in around Duke Ellington as he plays the piano. That same year she appeared in *Stormy Weather* and was also a body-double for Lena Horne in that and other films. She was in the Ziegfield Follies of 1945 with Horne, Fred Astaire, and Judy Garland, among others. In most of her film appearances, whether she had a small or non-speaking part, her presence was always magnetic.[70]

Hathaway's activism began when she was cast in a 1944 film biography of Woodrow Wilson. Told she had to wear a bandana and sit in a field on a bale of cotton, Hathaway could hear the voice of her father, a Louisiana farmer, telling her "to get an education and never pick a piece of cotton." She returned the bandana to the director and left. In the spring of 1946, she led a picket of the dining room at the MGM studios, which didn't allow minority actors to eat there. The policy would be lifted, but she wasn't satisfied, targeting the Screen Actors Guild's discriminatory policies.[71]

Hathaway was also a singer who wrote and recorded blues and jazz records in the late 1940's and 1950s after leaving her movie career. Journalism was the focus of the last forty years of her life, beginning in 1962 with the *California Eagle*. When the paper was sold in 1963, she moved to the *Los Angeles Sentinel* and remained there for the rest of her career.[72]

Maggie began playing golf in the early 1950s, although the exact year is hard to determine. She said she took up the game after winning a bet with boxer Joe Louis. She went to Griffith Park to chastise him for playing in pro-ams with white players while deserving "black golfers like Bill Spiller weren't allowed to play," and found Louis on the eighth hole, a short par-3. After he hit his tee shot on the green she told him that wasn't so impressive. Annoyed, he told her if she could hit the green on her first attempt, he'd buy her a set of clubs. Maggie grabbed a club and swung away, all instinct and no technique. Somehow, she got the ball on the green and he was true to his word. She claimed that one swing changed her life, as she began taking lessons every week, and became good enough to win the women's division of the United Golfers Association's Houston Open in 1954.[73]

Hathaway soon discovered she couldn't play on many courses in Southern California and that most amateur and professional tournaments were exclusively for whites. She dedicated herself to changing that, and set up her first picket line at the Western Avenue Golf Course (now the Chester Washington Golf Course) in late 1958. "It was privately owned," Hathaway recalled, "and black golfers weren't accepted."

A decade later, when she asked to join the ladies' club, she was told she had to pass a playing ability test – if she could break 100 she'd gain membership. As she told it, "I went straight out and shot 88 to win the low honors and hurried back inside where the ladies were having cake and punch, only to be told that they hadn't voted me into the club after all."[74]

Maggie got so mad she picked up the cake and threw it through a window, followed by the punch bowl and a couple of chairs. "People ran every which way. I guess I just went a little berserk." The police were called to take her away. Undaunted, she applied again two years later, only to be told her trouble making ways were a problem. Returning to her car, she found that someone had slashed the tires. Furious, she took a pistol she kept in the car and ran back to the clubhouse, waving it around. "You've never seen a place clear out so fast." When she was finally admitted to the club after years of trying, she promptly resigned. "History had been made and I had other countries to conquer," she explained.[75]

In 1960 she organized the Minority Associated Golfers to secure meaningful golf related jobs and promote junior golf among minorities – even getting Jack Nicklaus to donate to her cause. She also sued the Women's Public Links Association, the all white union that established segregation in public courses. The cases took years to work themselves through the courts, but that didn't stop her from picketing. The group also targeted Los Angeles's Fox Hills Golf Course (where Jimmie DeVoe had taught) until it admitted black members in 1964. Hathaway called herself a militant, but said the only thing she regretted was picketing Bing Crosby's tournament. She later learned that he tried "to help blacks get into the tournament, but he couldn't do anything with the PGA."[76]

In 1963, Hathaway announced that six African American professionals were picketing the 39th annual Southern California PGA match play tournament. Speaking for the players, she said they would picket the tournament from 8 a.m. to noon on the first day. She charged the PGA with refusing membership to the six: Bill Spiller, Charles Sifford, Willie Jefferson, Rufus Jamerson, Roosevelt Nichols and Henry Barabin. Tournament chairman George Lake replied by saying the PGA removed its "Caucasian only" clause two years earlier and that membership was open to any professional meeting PGA requirements on length of service in club work or as a touring professional. He added that there was one black contestant, the seemingly ever-present Jimmie DeVoe.[77]

In 1962, with her friend Sammy Davis Jr., she co-founded the Beverly Hills/Hollywood branch of the NAACP to fight racism in Hollywood. As president of the new branch, her chief aim was to eliminate "racial discrimination in all departments of the motion picture, television, and recording industries," along with ending housing segregation. Her name made studio executives nervous, as they would often ask, "Is she picketing us?" Hathaway helped organize the NAACP Image Awards in 1967 as a way to honor the outstanding work of black actors who were shunned by the Oscars and other award shows. Late in life she appeared with comedian Arsenio Hall to promote them.

In the late 1960s she found an ally in football great and actor Jim Brown, who saw that she got press coverage for her protests. "Maggie's fearlessness was a wonderful, and scary, thing to behold. The core of her activism, like mine, was that we weren't asking for anything special." They just wanted to exercise their constitutionally guaranteed rights. Hathaway fought for the rights of everyone, and her efforts weren't exclusive to golf. For example, in 1962 there was a police shootout at the Nation of Islam headquarters in Los Angeles, in which seven unarmed Muslims were shot, and one, Ronald Stokes, was killed. During the trial of Nation of Islam members after the attack, several people carried anti-Muslim picket signs in front of the courthouse.[78]

Minister Abdul Allah Muhammad recalled in 2001 that Malcolm X was ready to confront the picketers, but Muhammad had a better idea. He made a phone call before they proceeded into the courtroom. After breaking for lunch they walked outside to find traffic snarled and the sidewalks crowded with people. In front of the courthouse, spreading over the entire block were picket signs in favor of the Muslims, recalled Muhammad. They were "carried by young Caucasian men and women who worked in the various downtown offices, and who had skipped eating lunch to be part of this demonstration. And there, standing on the courtroom steps, orchestrating the entire thing, was marvelous Maggie Hathaway!"

In 1971 she joined with Les Benson, a county recreation commissioner and chairman of a black coalition called the Park and Recreation Community Committee to complain to the city board that black employees were not in evidence at Rancho Park Golf Course (site of the Los Angeles Open then), especially as professionals. For example, one black employee there had come from Washington, DC three years earlier and was hired to pick up golf balls from the driving range, even though he had experience as a professional player. They urged the city to cancel the lease of Rancho's concessionaire. She would also be a Los Angeles County Commissioner, serving on the Alcoholism and Narcotics, Status of Women, Probations, and Martin Luther King Hospital commissions.[79]

Hathaway became a "personal hero" and a real friend to Jim Brown. He accompanied her to the 1975 Masters when Lee Elder made history as the first African American to play in the tournament. When her requests for credentials to cover the tournament for the *Los Angeles Sentinel* were turned down, she was able to obtain them through a Los Angeles radio station. She was the first black women to do so, but had to pay her own expenses. Brown stepped in and said he would pay her way there, and Maggie was able to get a pass from Augusta's caddie master (one of 15 Masters Chairman Clifford Roberts had provided) so that Brown could attend as her guest.[80]

Maggie recalled that many kitchen workers and grounds crew came out to watch Elder tee off. "I'll never forget a little boy who suddenly started saying the Lord's Prayer aloud, and Lee paused, walked

171

over, and thanked him." Then, after Elder hit his tee shot down the fairway, Maggie "fainted dead away." She was taken to the course infirmary, where she ran into Gary Player. "The Lord works in funny ways," she'd say. For years she had "been putting up pickets around that man" because he was South African, where apartheid was sanctioned by the government. But after a long conversation with him, she realized she had been wrong. "His heart wasn't that way at all." She said he'd done "a lot for young black golfers that people don't know about. He has to work harder than most to prove he's not a racist."

Hathaway covered her second Masters in 1997 and saw Tiger Woods win. A couple of months before, she wrote, "I just hope the press doesn't put too much pressure on him by constantly having a camera in his face or by asking too many personal questions." Woods would always have cameras and microphones in his face, and she didn't live to see the media circus that would surround him when scandal brought him down in 2009, nor the redemption he found in the years after, culminating in his triumph at the 2019 Masters.[81]

In 1998 the Jack Thompson course in South-Central Los Angeles was renamed the Maggie Hathaway Golf Course. Doris La Cour of the Western States Golf Association said at the dedication, "I am proud that she has been the pioneer who lighted the pathway that we all now seem to take for granted." Maggie said of that day, "You know, in all those years of protests I never cried until they named that golf course for me." The course has become a training center for many novice golfers, and its First Tee youth and women's programs have helped bring the game to many African Americans.[82]

Maggie Hathaway died September 24, 2001, at her home in the Baldwin Hills section of Los Angeles. James Dodson said of her in a *Golf Magazine* article months before her passing that she deserves to be called the Rosa Parks of golf in this county. When she was younger Maggie had a dream of getting good enough at it to be a professional. That didn't happen, but she said, "I get a beautiful feeling when I look out now and see black and white golfers playing together." She believed they would be better people because of the lessons the game taught them, and "every time one of those kids gives me a hug and says thank you, my old heart just gets young again."[83]

Chapter 7: Golfers with Challenged Bodies – "Adapt, Adjust, and Overcome"

Golf writer O.B. Keeler, who covered Bob Jones in his glory years, claimed "Golf is the closest game to the game we call life. You get bad breaks from good shots; you get good breaks from bad shots – but you have to play the game where it lies." Bill Campbell, one of golf's great amateurs and former USGA president, contended that "Golf is a game of misses and how you react to them. That applies also to life. We know that bad bounces and bad breaks occur. You don't always get what you deserve. But we always hold out the hope that from a bad place, we might make a great recovery."[1]

Dennis Walters had dreams of playing on the Professional Golfers Association Tour in 1974 when a horrific golf cart accident left him paralyzed from the waist down. Difficult, dark times followed, as he was forced to come to grips with what had happened to him, and ask himself "what now?"

He might have given up and given in to despair, and who would have blamed him? But he chose to fight on and created a new life for himself, doing so without abandoning his love for golf. When Walters was paralyzed in that tragic accident, he received a letter from Ben Hogan. In part it read: "We know the human body is a great machine and can absorb many shocks. Even though it may seem slow, recovery is possible provided one has faith, hope, will and determination."

Walters became a trick shot artist, working hard every day and travelling around the country entertaining audiences of all ages. In 2019, he was elected to the World Golf Hall of Fame. A hell of a comeback, I'd say. As he put it in 1977, "I still like to hit good shots, but I don't get mad at the bad ones anymore…Just being able to play is the big thing."[2]

The game has had countless people who have played the game in spite of physical limitations, many of them doing it much better than so called "able-bodied" people. Many people have heard of Dennis Walters, but we can see examples of others in the past century who persevered and demonstrated the durability of the human spirit. Poet Khalil Gibran once wrote, "Out of suffering have emerged the strongest souls; the most massive characters are seared with scars."

173

A strong soul was embodied in a man named Thomas McAuliffe. In spite of losing both arms in a horrible accident when he was nine-years old, he learned to play golf. The accident happened when he was hurrying home to get a baseball bat for a pickup game with friends. Taking a short cut home through a quarry, he saw the little gravity car loaded with stones coming down the slight incline on the narrow gauge tracks. He and his friends had jumped inside it a few times and ridden it down for fun.

Thomas McAuliffe performing a trick shot, 1930.

As his legs sped up to scurry across the tracks he suddenly tripped, falling on the rails. "In a flash he realized his danger and threw his arms out in front of him to push back his body. Instinctively he knew his head and shoulders were directly in the path of the heavy iron wheels. Frantically, he pushed back from the impending danger and then – everything was a blank." He had pushed his head away in time but his arms were severed by the wheels of the cart. After only two weeks in the hospital Tommy was back at school.[3]

In 1915, the then 22-year-old told his story to *The Golf Monthly*. He had special flat rubber grips on his clubs, with ribs running at 90 degrees from the shaft. His caddie would put the club under Tommy's chin and he would turn his head and shoulders to swing the club. He would make two or three movements back and forth – similar to a waggle – and with a "combined swing and jerk of the body and shoulder," he was able to hit the ball 120-150 yards with a driver. "I guess mine is a real case of necessity being the mother of invention." He once shot an 86 for 18 holes on a course in Buffalo, and played golf his whole life. He would go on to marry, and he and his wife had four children.[4]

174

McAuliffe was certainly a positive thinker. "I never permit the thought of my accident to take possession of my mind," he declared, "nor do I think of anything being impossible for me to overcome. When the time comes, I just go ahead as best I may, and somehow, someway, I generally get there without any great difficulties."[5]

****

Jimmy Nichols recalled the day of the "first big crash" of 1929, as he described it. It was March 24, 1929, when the car he was driving collided with a freight train outside of Fort Worth, Texas. Fortunate not to be killed, the crash cost the 23-year-old Nichols his right arm. He also suffered two broken legs and severe facial injuries, spending 129 days in the hospital before he could be released. A welterweight boxer with a promising future before him, he had just turned pro. After the accident, like Dennis Walters forty-five years later, he had to figure out what to do next.

Nichols had never played golf before, and one day, as he was sitting around with nothing to occupy himself, a couple of friends stopped by. "We're heading to the golf course Jimmy," said one. "You want to come along?" "What'll I do out there?" Jimmy asked. "You can follow us and maybe keep score," said the other. "Hell, I don't know. But it beats sitting around here. Come on, it's a nice day. Get out for some fresh air." Jimmy went, he watched, and it seemed like an enjoyable game to him.

Being a competitive sort, he wanted to give it a go, first trying to play with left-handed clubs, but he couldn't get any power on the ball. Then one day he grabbed a two-iron out of another player's bag, took a right-hander's stance and swung with his left arm. The shot flew 175 yards down the fairway. "I couldn't have hit that far left handed if the course was all downhill," he recalled in 1961. He kept practicing and playing. A year later he broke 80 at the old Oakhurst course in Fort Worth (where Ben Hogan had been the pro in the early 1930s.)[6]

Nichols remembered that he "practiced from daylight till dark. Anybody seein' me out there must have thought I was nuts and maybe I was." He turned professional before the 1930 Fort Worth City championship. Ben Hogan and Lee Ramsay reached the 36-hole final that year, and during a break for lunch between rounds, somebody suggested Nichols hit some shots to entertain the 300 or so restless fans, since he had earned something of a local reputation as a one-armed golfer. "So I hit some and they passed the hat and there was $156 in it. Without signing a card or anything, there I was, a pro."

He began playing exhibition matches, being a unique drawing card, to say the least. While playing an exhibition in Massachusetts, Milton B. Reach, an executive for the Spalding Sporting Goods Company, saw him and was so impressed that he signed him to a contract. Nichols told *Golf Magazine* in 1961 that he had played 250 exhibitions one year, perhaps 10,000 in all. At 5'10" and 200 pounds he had plenty of power, which he attributed "not to muscles but to clubhead speed and to meeting the ball solidly." He once made a hole-in-one on a 336-yard hole in Georgia, and played some of his best golf just after World War II.[7]

In 1946 he shot a three under 69 at the Springfield Country Club in Massachusetts at the annual Elks-Shriners tournament, to finish as low professional. In 1947 he tried to qualify for the match play portion of the PGA championship in St. Louis, but missed out, shooting 76-80.

Nichols kept playing and doing exhibitions. In 1971, he went on a three-week tour of Vietnam for the USO with two LPGA players, Renee Powell and Mary Lou Daniel. They did golf clinics in hopes of bringing "a little bit of home" to the troops.[8]

Jimmy was given the Ben Hogan Award in 1962, presented to an individual who overcomes serious injury or illness to actively be involved in golf. Nichols's motto had become, "In golf and life, it's not what's missing that counts, it's what you have left." He gave "courage and hope to fellow handicapped persons," wrote Ray Fitzgerald in *Golf Magazine*, "and made service amputees say to themselves, 'If this guy can do it, so can I.'"

Nichols may have offered inspiration to those returning from the war. Dale S. Bourisseau, who lost his leg in Anzio, teamed up with an organization of disabled people in Cleveland, Ohio in 1952 called Possibilities Unlimited, Incorporated. Bourisseau helped organize regional competitions of amputee golfers. By 1954, the group was incorporated as the National Amputee Golf Association (NAGA), supported by the PGA and the USGA. It helped veterans get back into their "normally lively mental and physical stride." Herb Graffis, noted editor and golf promoter, said it did a tremendous "job with golf as an emphasized element of physical and social therapy." The NAGA currently has over 2,000 members in the United States and some 200 players from 17 other countries.[9]

Dale Bourisseau said the "loss of a limb to many an amputee is much more than a physical thing; it can be a great mental shock, with the haunting fear that perhaps now he won't be accepted by society, that he won't be able to support himself and his family, and that he is now some sort of a 'freak.'" Today the disabled golfer is still reluctant to take up the game for fear of rejection. Marcia Bailey, an LPGA Master Professional, spent years teaching the physically challenged and said, "It's not easy for them to come out here...They have been told they can't do this and they can't do that. As a result, they confine themselves."[10]

I admire courage, and remember a young man I saw from time to time years ago when I lived in Washington, DC and used to go to the now defunct White Flint driving range. He was about 16 or 17 and had a growth or deformity enveloping his head. His jaw and face were very large, somewhat like the "Elephant Man." He drew stares from the people out there, but he just put his token in the ball machine and got his bucket and started swinging. And the kid could hit good shots. I never talked to him but thought it was great that he was out there just trying to hit a golf ball well, and like the rest of us, he could lose himself in the game. Watching him I was thankful that I was whole and healthy, and was inspired by the kid's spirit. The people introduced in this chapter have their own stories we can all appreciate and applaud.

Like Jimmy Nichols, Bob Morgan won the Ben Hogan Award, but he wasn't a professional golfer. An ex-Navy pilot and a stuntman in Hollywood, by 1962 he had been working 17 years doubling for the stars of that era – John Wayne, Humphrey Bogart, Charlton Heston, Burt Lancaster, Gary Cooper, Bill Holden, and James Arness. The 6'3" 200 pound Morgan was on location near that Spring in Globe, Arizona, where MGM was shooting *How the West Was Won*.[11]

On April 9th, 1962 he was standing in for George Peppard. The scene called for him to crouch behind a pile of 20 chained fiberglass logs – each weighing 300 pounds – on a moving freight train. He was preparing himself for the cameras to start to roll, the train bed vibrating below him. The cables holding the logs strained, and in an instant something snapped. Morgan, with no time to react, was pummeled as 6,000 pounds of logs crashed down on him, sending him under the train as two flat cars and the caboose ran over his left leg.

Chuck Hayward, his friend and fellow stuntman, saw the whole thing unfold, and frantically rushed to his aid, thinking he was dead. Morgan was unrecognizable, as his face had been ripped apart, and what was left of it was a black mass battered by dust and dirt. As an article in *Golfing* magazine described the scene: "His right eye hung loose from its socket. His left leg, brutally mangled, appeared torn from the hip. His right leg was broken in numerous places. Blood gushed from several severed arteries." Morgan regained consciousness shortly after the event and remembered, "Bones were sticking out everywhere. I looked like an ivory porcupine."[12]

Other crew members joined Hayward, pushing Morgan's eye back into its socket and bandaging him up as best they could before loading him into a car and rushing him to a small hospital nearby. The emergency room there wasn't equipped to handle such trauma, so he was given blood transfusions and taken by ambulance to Phoenix, 70 long miles away. That he even survived the ride was a miracle.

"The doctors just looked at me and shook their heads," Morgan recalled. He refused to have the left leg amputated. He had also suffered a compound fracture of the femur on his right leg, had broken his pelvis, and had crushed the lower vertebrae in his back. He died twice on the operating table and was brought back to life each time by a team of seven surgeons who worked feverishly to assess the extent of the damage and stabilize him.[13]

His left leg turned gangrenous and had to be amputated two inches above the knee. Doctors didn't tell Morgan they had to take his leg before doing so, and after the fact they had a psychiatrist break the news to him. "They knew the kind of guy I was, a physical guy who made his living physically." His wife at the time was Yvonne DeCarlo, who appeared in numerous movies, including *The Ten Commandments*, and is best remembered for her role as Lily Munster in *The Munsters*.

Yvonne had told the doctors how much Bob loved to play golf, and how much it meant to him. "They realized I was the kind of guy who says, 'I'd rather be dead than crippled.'" When the doctors talked with him after the amputation, he had one big question. "Can I play golf again?" When they said "yes," he felt a bit of hope emerge deep inside him. But he wasn't out of the woods yet. "When the doctors first looked at me," said Morgan later, "they figured I had two of three days at the most."[14]

De Carlo recalled that even after the operation, "Bob was completely toxic, and it looked as if we were going to lose him after all. But I prayed and prayed. And he held on...or God let him hold on." For two weeks his body fought the toxins in his system, and almost burned up, running temperatures of 105 and 106 degrees for awhile. Finally, the fever broke and he stabilized. He body had been assaulted and he lost a leg, but was going to live. "I don't think I could have made it without my wife," said Morgan. "I drew strength from her the whole way she held up under the whole terrible ordeal." He claimed it was the love of family and friends that saw him through it.

Morgan also said his doctors had "performed miracles." Now, as a survivor, he had to determine how to go forward. He resolved to accept his "new normal," because if he didn't, he feared he might either drink himself to death or let a dark depression swallow him up. As he said, "I wasn't going to follow either of those routes." When he had recovered sufficiently, he was transferred to the Los Angeles Orthopedic Hospital. During his ordeal he had three plastic surgeries on his face and lost half his body weight, dropping down to 105 pounds. It was to be a long, arduous recovery. A month before being released from the hospital he told reporters, "I don't consider myself handicapped. I'm going to be doing just about everything I did before. Golf is my goal. When I get back to playing golf again, I'll figure I've made it."[15]

Bob left the hospital on December 10, 1962, and two days later he was back on the golf course, hitting "little 8-iron shots." He had been a member of famous Riviera Country Club, site of Ben Hogan's 1948 U.S Open victory, and was a 2-handicap player before the accident. "Some doctors told me that without this goal, I might still be in a wheelchair."

He was given a lot of help, as many friends came to his aid. Ed Furgol, the 1954 U.S. Open winner, who himself had a physical handicap – he had a withered left arm as the result of a childhood playground accident that shattered his elbow – helped Morgan by suggesting he play and practice in street shoes instead of golf shoes. "Ed said with street shoes I wouldn't have a tendency to overswing and lose my balance. He was 100 percent right." Tommy Bolt, the 1958 U.S. Open champion, helped him with his swing and told him to open his stance so he could transfer his weight through the ball better. The advice helped and Morgan began to regain some of his form.[16]

Bob got back to a nine-handicap by 1964, when he won the Ben Hogan Award. "I got a tremendous lift when I received a wire from Charles Bartlett," informing him that he had been selected to receive it. Inspired, the following day Morgan went out and shot a 77 at Riviera. The day after that, the Willie Hunter Pro-Am took place at Riviera, where he was paired with Bobby Nichols, ironically the Hogan Award winner the year before. "That was the day I shot 73." Morgan had the opportunity to talk with Ben Hogan at the award dinner. "He listened and watched as I demonstrated my swing. Then he said, 'You've got it going on the right track, Bob. Just keep going at it.'"[17] Bob Morgan did keep at it. He continued to play golf, and even made it back to working in movies, not allowing his near death that horrible day in Arizona to keep him from doing what he wanted with the rest of his life.

Another person who kept at it was Patrice Cooper. When she won the club championship at Hazeltine Golf Club in Minneapolis in 1986, she had "about a seven handicap." Then a recurrence of cancer in her left arm the next year forced its amputation just below the elbow. That didn't mean the end of her golfing days, however. She was fitted with a prosthetic arm that had a locking clasp at the end, which accommodated the thick end of a golf grip. Before the amputation, her handicap had been lowered to a four, and with her artificial arm, it miraculously dropped to one. "When I play I see myself playing with two arms." One artificial and one real, it didn't matter to the scorecard.[18]

In 1996, she qualified for the U.S. Women's Mid-Amateur at the 6,129 yard Mission Hills Country Club in Palm Springs, California, shooting 82-78 to make the match play portion. "I thought she played great," said Gail Flanagan, who played in the same group as Cooper for the two days of stroke play. "She could handle any kind of shot, any kind of lie, and she's a smart player...I didn't expect her to hit the ball as far as she did, as well as she did, but she hit it out there as far as a lot of players." When she lost her arm she worked on improving her technique to compensate, and became more consistent, while still being able to drive the ball 200 yards. "The day after I lost my arm, I told my husband, 'This is not going to change a thing.' The body is amazing, what it can do. The body *and* the mind. I have always played golf in the mind." As Ben Hogan once said, "Don't believe the doctors. They told me I'd never walk again, but I knew they were wrong."[19] Although she lost her first round match 3 and 2 in that Women's Mid-Amateur, Cooper won numerous championships in the women's division of National Amputee Golf Association, and her spirit was shared by others, like Bob Wilson and Mike Reeder.

Bob Wilson was a lieutenant commander in the Navy, running routine takeoff and landing exercises on the USS Kitty Hawk, when his life changed one day in 1974. He was in charge of the busy deck, with F-4 jets coming in and out every two or three minutes. Inadvertently, he took three steps backward and stepped over the "foul deck line," the painted line that marks the area occupied by the large cables that grab the tailhooks on the aircraft and bring them to a stop. "When a jet hits the deck, it's travelling at 170 miles per hour," Wilson recalled, "and so is the cable when it catches the jet. Within two seconds of stepping over the foul deck line, in came a jet, and off went my legs. Clean, just below the knees."

Bob was a 4-handicap player and was afraid he'd never be able to play again. While recovering in the hospital, he picked up "a copy of *Golf World*, and on the cover was a photograph of Bic Long, who had just won the National Amputee Golf Association championship at Pinehurst. Man, did that give me a spark." Wilson came back to not only play, but would later become the Executive Director of the National Amputee Golf Association. While at that post in the mid-1980s, he received a letter from an amputee who was disqualified in a tournament for having an artificial hand.[20]

Wilson called P.J. Boatwright of USGA and asked why the rules then prevented "artificial devices." His letter prompted an extended back and forth between Boatwright, members of the USGA rules department, and Wilson. "P.J. really was guided by the spirit of the rules," remembered Wilson. Not long after, the rule was changed to permit use of an artificial limb that assists in gripping the club. Wilson told *Golf Digest* in 2005, "Never show pity for a disabled person. The determined person resents it, and the quitter embraces it. Either, way, everyone loses."[21]

A remarkable man named Mike Reeder lost both of his legs below the knee in 1970 when he stepped on a booby trap while serving in the Vietnam War. He was 21, and after receiving a Bronze Star and Purple Heart for his service, returned home to find a good job, get married and raise a family. "My philosophy is to adapt, adjust, and overcome," he said. "There's no obstacle that can't be overcome." He started playing golf almost by accident at age 40, when he went to a golf shop one day to buy a gift for a friend. The clerk asked him if he'd like to try a shot into the hitting net, and Mike figured, "why not." He took a 5-

wood and wheeled himself into position. A few practice swings allowed him to feel the weight of the club in his hands and measure the motion necessary to reach the ball.[22]

From his wheelchair he swung that 5-wood, and as it came into the ball it contacted the sweet spot of the club face, sending a feeling of satisfaction up his arms. Like Ben Hogan said, a well struck shot goes from your hands, up you arms, and right into your heart. After that first shot Reeder knew this was a game he had to try, and in less than four months, he broke 90.[23]

Reeder became a true golf nut and got his handicap down to eight at one time. His best round, an even-par 72, came in 2001 at the Forrest Crossing Golf Club (now Franklin Bridge Golf Club), in Franklin, Tennessee, where he also worked as a ranger. Reeder adapted his wheelchair especially for golf, with a rod he would push into the ground to steady it as he swung. When he got to the green, he would get out of the chair and walk on his stumps, putting with a 22-inch putter. The manager of his club said of him in 2008, "He always has a smile on his face. He's always upbeat. People are amazed." Reeder maintained that "Golf is the only game where everyone has a handicap. Mine is just a physical one."[24]

Bob Wilson of the National Amputee Golf Association said in 2008 that Mike was a "good ambassador for anyone who plays golf with a disability." Reeder made national news and was featured on ESPN in August 2010 when he became the first golfer to complete a round at the Old Course in St Andrews, Scotland using a wheelchair. He shot 89 at nearby Kingsbarns his first day, adjusting to the time change and acclimating himself to the ground and weather conditions. The second day, he improved with a 77 at St Andrews's Jubilee course, opened in 1897, which features huge hillocks on many holes, making it in many way more difficult than the Old Course.

Thus prepared, Reeder finally tackled the granddaddy of them all, the Old Course, where golf has been played on for over 500 years (Chapter 10 discusses this history.) On a blustery day he shot a 79 – missing a five-footer on the last hole for a 78 – but still fulfilling his goal of breaking 80. He impressed the curious onlookers who had gathered to watch him, as well as Jack Nicklaus. "To go to St Andrews," Nicklaus said, "prop yourself up and hold your wheelchair stable and hit it solid enough to get around the golf course – that's pretty astonishing."[25]

About nine months after his round, Reeder met Nicklaus in person, who noticed his left-handed clubs. "God didn't think I had enough handicaps," quipped Reeder. On shooting that 79, he said, "You can do anything you can set your mind to, and I think that is one example that I will claim." Nicklaus would say, "There are a lot of things that are very special that we have in this country, and a lot of people are very inspirational. I think you look back and say, 'Hey, that guy really wanted that.'"

Mike Reeder passed away on October 24, 2014, losing a battle with brain cancer. When speaking four years earlier about crossing the ancient Swilcan Bridge on the 18th hole at St Andrews, he said: "I am surrounded by the history, not only of the game but of the players that have all walked through this fairway and over the bridge, and the ghosts are close."[26] I'm sure a part of Mike's spirit resides there now as well.

****

Mike Reeder once said that one has to find it in themselves to "be self-confident. Perseverance is the key in everything you do." Charley Boswell would have certainly agreed with that ideal. He had been a three-letter athlete at the University of Alabama (football, baseball, and track), and had gone to the 1938 Rose Bowl. While there he and his team toured the movie studios and at the Warner Brothers commissary, and were interviewed about their experiences by a young radio reporter by the name of Ronald Reagan.[27]

Boswell was fortunate to even be there. Growing up in Birmingham, he broke his hip in the first game of the 1934 high school season. He recalled, "The doctors told my father that there was a strong possibility that I might be crippled for the rest of my life." He was in a cast for two months, but fortunately the break healed properly. This proves how capricious life can be. Had he not healed, and been hobbled so badly that he would have been rejected for service in World War II, he might have been better off in a way. But life doesn't work that way, and we are all products of its vicissitudes.

Boswell was drafted in May of 1941 and eventually sent to Europe, where he was the captain of a tank company. There, he was in the thick of the fierce fighting during the Battle of the Bulge. On November 30, 1944, while pulling one of his crew from a burning Sherman tank, Boswell's face was ripped with the hot shrapnel from an exploding shell. He was taken to a hospital in Heerlen, Germany, and described waking up there. "I could feel bandages covering the entire upper part of my body. But all I sensed was a pervading and painful numbness. *And I couldn't see.*"[28]

The doctors thought he might get partial sight back in at least one of his eyes. "After each operation on my eyes, the doctors told me that my chances of seeing again looked better," but he felt they were just trying to soften the blow. "One thing I always did was to beg each doctor not to kid me." Finally, they told him there was nothing more that could be done for him; his sight would not return. Charley was sent back to the States to recuperate and undergo therapy at Valley Forge hospital, near Philadelphia. It was there he met a man who would change his life, Corporal Kenny Gleason, his rehabilitation specialist. It was 1945, and Boswell was understandably despondent, struggling with his blindness.

Gleason began playing golf as a youngster in Charlottesville, Virginia and trying to get Boswell out of his funk, prodded him to go to the golf course with him. Smell the flowers, feel the sun on your face, swing a club. "You've made a bad mistake," Boswell told him. "I'm blind." "I know, Captain," Gleason said. "Come on, you'll enjoy it." Boswell offered a salty retort, telling Gleason he thought he was crazy, and had never played golf. Gleason kept persisting, and finally cracked Boswell.[29]

One day Gleason drove them to the course and took Charley to the practice tee, showing him how to hold the club and take his stance. Now swing the club, he said, back and forth, back and forth. Feel the weight of the club and just swing it back and through. Gleason teed up a 2-wood and told him to give it a go. "Here goes nothing, I thought as I started the swing," recalled Boswell in his autobiography. "An instant later, I heard a neat, solid click as the wood hit the ball. 'Where'd it go?'

I asked." The shot sailed 200 yards down the middle. When Gleason told him how it flew, Bowell thought he was joking, but Gleason assured him he was telling the truth.[30]

Boswell recalled that moment years later, when he received the Ben Hogan Award in 1959; "If I had whiffed, I think I would have dropped the club and walked away." He didn't, and it was a turning point for him. "Something new was brewing in me – confidence. The good Lord must have been out there with us on that golf course, for only He could have known how desperately I needed something – anything – to turn me around." He would say in 1976, "That shot, the insistence and patience of Kenny, and a big smile from the Man Upstairs, changed my life."

Gleason guided Charley around for a few holes that first time out, and he made a couple of 5s and 6s. Gleason's presence at Valley Forge, "was a large part of the miracle" that helped change Boswell's destiny. His wife Kitty, who he described as "properly soft and fluffy" but who also possessed a "steel in her being," sensed the improvement in his spirits as soon as she picked him up for the ride home that afternoon. He had to convince her, though, that he had really played golf.[31]

He and Gleason would play almost daily for the next few weeks, but after the euphoria wore off Boswell found the times off the course hard to deal with, as he had to learn Braille and accept his new life. A low point came that Christmas. While his wife and two-year-old daughter Kay were trimming the Christmas tree, he began to know what it really meant. He asked his daughter to tell him what the lights looked like. "But there they are Daddy. Look at them yourself." The remark, innocent as could be, was nonetheless a gut punch to Charley, who walked slowly to a room in back of the house and closed the door behind him. He stayed there a long time.[32]

"Beneath my smile," Boswell wrote in his autobiography, "there was more sorrow and bitterness than anyone has ever known until now." He was still struggling inside himself when he got a call in the spring of 1946 from an old friend, Grant Thomas, asking him to play golf with him. Thomas would end up being his coach for years, helping him negotiate the course. Boswell's enthusiasm for the game was reignited, and this time he didn't look back. At the end of 1946 he played in his first National Blind Golf Tournament, where he was beat by Clint Russell (a Ben Hogan Award winner in 1957.)

Russell was blinded in 1924 when a tire he was changing on his car exploded in his face. He continued playing golf and in 1931 appeared in a "Ripley's Believe it or Not" newspaper article after shooting an 84 at his club in Duluth, Minnesota. The day after the 1946 tournament, he and Boswell played an exhibition match with Bing Crosby and Bob Hope, in which Boswell teamed with Hope to win. Crosby predicted Charley was "going to do some great things for blind golf in the years to come. He's really a man to watch."

Hope and Boswell began a life-long friendship that led to millions of dollars being raised for eye related causes. Another friend was the legendary football coach at his alma mater, Paul "Bear" Bryant. "He's a winner, a real champion in every sense of the word," Bryant said of Boswell, "and it applies to everything he undertakes. If you know him, you have to love him."[33]

Charley Boswell ultimately won 17 U.S. and 11 International championships, and served as president of the U.S. Blind Golf Association (USBGA) from 1956 to 1976, an organization that had only 11 members when it was formed in 1948. His best score of 81 couldn't have been accomplished without his coaches. "I couldn't hit it a lick without a coach's help," he said, "and I'll never cease to be grateful for having had the support of the men who have made possible this tremendously important part of my life." Boswell founded an insurance company, raised a family and served as Alabama state revenue commissioner before passing away October 22, 1995, so he had a full, productive life outside of golf. The game, however, was a wonderful friend to him. President Eisenhower said that Charley winning the Ben Hogan Award was "a superb testimony to the unconquerable spirit of a brave man and a strong encouragement to everyone who has tried to become proficient in the game of golf."[34]

Pat Browne, Jr. followed Boswell as the best blind golfer in the world, with 70 golf victories worldwide, and 23 U.S. Blind Golf Association national championships (including 20 in a row from 1978 to 1997.) He also holds the USBGA tournament record with a score of 86-83-169, and won the Ben Hogan Award in 1988. Browne lost his sight at age 32 in 1966 when a speeding car jumped a median and crashed into the car in which he was a passenger. Among the injuries he suffered was a severed optic nerve, which left him blind. He was a scratch golfer prior to his accident and didn't want to give it up. "I loved the game and I thought it was worth taking a chance to see if I could hit it again. I wanted to know if I could do it again and we did it and once I hit it solid, I was hooked again." With his coach Gerry Barousse, Browne shot an 85 at the Old Course at St Andrews and an 80 at Pinehurst, two of the most famous courses in the world.[35]

Browne said he hoped blind golfers could help change the perceptions of the public, "to show that because you're lacking one of the senses doesn't mean you can't be a productive member of society." He also believed he was able to adjust to his blindness without being bitter, because "[I] had faith that God wouldn't give me more than I could handle."

When Browne passed away April 21, 2107, one of the stories told about him involved a nine-hole exhibition match with two-time U.S. Open champion Payne Stewart in 1990. Stewart was blindfolded the entire match and played with the aid of a coach. Stewart shot 62. Browne shot 42. Stewart later told a friend: "If I practiced every day I couldn't beat Pat Browne."[36]

Paul McCormack lost 80% of his vision as a result of asbestos and chemical gases that seeped into his eyes while working on the Ground Zero site after the 9/11 attacks in 2001. In 2016 and 2017 he won the USBGA championship, believing "You can sit at home and be depressed about it, or you can put your pants on like everybody else and live life."[37]

****

At the end of 1950, Skip Alexander was coming into his own on the PGA Tour. After returning from service in the South Pacific during the war, he had won three tournaments and played in the 1949 Ryder Cup. The 32-year-old had just finished sixth in the Kansas City Open on

September 24th and had signed to do an exhibition tour in Venezuela. He was to leave for the tour from New Orleans on September 27th, but wanted to see his wife and daughter before leaving. The Civil Air Patrol offered transportation to Louisville, where he would then catch a flight to his home in Lexington, North Carolina.

Over Evansville, Indiana, one of the fuel tanks was exhausted, and when the pilot reached to switch to the other tank, the selector valve sheared off. "We were out of gas," remembered Alexander. "I went back to my seat, moved a table so it wouldn't hit me, fastened my seatbelt and prepared for what I thought would be a bumpy landing, nothing more."[38] Instead, a few horrifying minutes later, the plane would crash, and Skip would be the only one on it to survive.

Stewart Murray "Skip" Alexander, Jr. was born in Philadelphia on August 6, 1918, while his father was serving as an infantry captain in France during World War I. After being badly gassed, Captain Alexander returned home when Skip was five months old. Four years later, the

family moved to Durham, North Carolina, moving into a house near the Hillandale Golf Club. "I was thrown out on the golf course and grew like a weed," Skip recalled. He was ambidextrous, and as a boy initially played golf as a left hander, but since it was hard to find decent clubs, became a right-handed player.[39]

Skip and his younger brother Chuck virtually lived on the course as kids, playing and caddying before and after school, and on weekends. Skip learned early on to control his temper. While playing with his father one day, in a fit of anger he threw his club after a bad shot. That was all the golf he played that day, as his father sent him home, and it was the last club Alexander threw. Skip was the Hillandale club champion before he went to Durham High School, and credited his

Skip Alexander's high school yearbook photo, 1936.

father, who had been an all-around athlete at Lafayette and Washington and Jefferson, with the success he enjoyed in golf.[40]

Skip's father hated being called "Stew," so he gave his son the nickname that would stick with him throughout his life. After high school, Alexander attended Duke University, where he was captain of the golf team for two years, winning the Southern Conference championship twice. In 1941 he won the prestigious North and South Amateur at Pinehurst and was the medalist in the U.S. Amateur, where he lost in the second round after beating former champion Johnny Fischer in his first match. He turned professional thereafter, saying, "That amateur stuff is for rich people."[41]

Alexander was driving to Miami for his pro debut when the Japanese bombed Pearl Harbor. The country's entry into World War II put his career on hold. In his 44 months as a lieutenant, he was busy with more important things than golf, but did win a Pacific area service tournament in Honolulu just before being discharged in early 1946. He played in the Greensboro Open that year and made his first money, and also appeared in his first U.S. Open, tying for 35th. Skip went to work as an assistant to Dugan Aycock in Lexington, North Carolina, and his game sharpened under Aycock's mentorship. "Dugan brought my game around," he said. "Man, I'd been hacking around and getting wilder and wilder off the tee," said Alexander in 1948, when Aycock told him he wasn't getting his hands high enough on his backswing. He worked on it and gained an extra 30 yards on his drives.[42]

Other people had told him the same, including Craig Wood in 1941, but Aycock "was the first one who had ever wanted to do anything about it. Bingo! He had me in Lexington. And bingo! He had me out on the course, boss-whipping me, I'm telling you, making me play till my tongue was hanging out." Skip won three small events in 1947, and teamed with Dick Metz to beat Lawson Little and Lew Worsham 2 and 1 in a scorching 13 under-par effort in the first round of the 1948 Miami Four-Ball matches. Little, winner of a U.S. Open and two U.S. Amateurs, told Skip after that he had played one of the greatest rounds he'd ever seen. "I can't call you a boy any longer."[43]

Alexander was one of the bigger men on Tour, 6'2" and 210 pounds, with a powerful swing. In February 1948 he won the Tucson

Open, closing with a final round 62, after shooting a 63 in round two. His score of 264 beat players like Ben Hogan, Sam Snead, Bobby Locke, Cary Middlecoff, Jimmy Demaret, and Lloyd Mangrum. At his first Masters that April – which was host Bobby Jones's last – he tied for 35th, but his power was on display when he sent his second shot with an 8-iron over the green on the par-5 15th. The next month he won the National Capital Open outside of Washington, DC, beating Bobby Locke by six shots He shot four rounds in the 60s, including a 68 in the final round, while Locke, Hogan, and Middlecoff faded, each shooting 74. In June Skip finished 11th in the U.S. Open, and only Ben Hogan, Lloyd Mangrum, Jimmy Demaret and Bobby Locke made more money than he did in 1948.[44]

These two victories secured him a place on the Ryder Cup team for 1949, where he lost his only match in foursomes play with partner Bob Hamilton. Although he failed to win on the Tour in 1949, he did finish third behind Sam Snead in defense of his National Capital Open, and tied for 6th in the Canadian Open, finishing among the top-20 on the money list. In 1950 he won the Empire State Open in Albany, New York, beating Ky Lafoon in a playoff, and finished 8th on the money list. Life was good. He married Kathleen "Kitty" Reade in 1948, and had a baby daughter, Carol, who they called "Bunkie." Son Buddy would come along in 1953.[45]

Alexander was trying to live up to the expectations of sportswriters and peers who two years earlier had predicted that he'd soon be "endorsing as many checks as Hogan or Mangrum or any of them." He had played well since then and most likely secured another spot on the Ryder Cup team in 1951. Then came September 24th. He was playing in the Kansas City Open, and had tried to arrange an earlier starting time on Sunday in order to catch a commercial flight for Louisville and then home to North Carolina.

He was going on an exhibition tour to Caracas, Venezuela and the West Indies that would pay him $2,000 (about $20,000 today.) Joining him would be Jimmy Demaret, Jackie Burke, Jr., Bob Toski and Chick Harbert. Burke said, "Skip was a wonderful, kind man," and part of a new breed, as he and Cary Middlecoff were two of the first college graduates to play on the Tour.[46]

Tournament officials couldn't change Stewart's tee time, but had arranged for him to catch a flight on a Civil Air Patrol (CAP) plane, an auxiliary of the Air Force. In exchange for playing some exhibitions for them, the CAP would ferry players from places where commercial flights weren't available to airports where they were. This was the maiden flight of the CAP-PGA arrangement, and sadly would be the last. Burke recalled that there was bad weather around Kansas City, but Alexander still got on the C-47 transport plane based out of Sioux Falls, South Dakota.

After taking off, it was a fairly routine flight until they got over Evansville, and the pilot couldn't get fuel to flow in the second wing tank. "We were at 6,000 feet, all runways cleared to land, a bright, moonlight night," Alexander recalled in 1997. He listened to it all on the radio and thought, "Well, we'll just pick a runway and do the best we can." The pilot tried a basic approach, but as Alexander explained, with no engine, the plane didn't glide very well. The plane came down hard and crashed only a quarter mile from the municipal airport, on the railroad tracks in front of the International Harvester Company plant beside U.S. Highway 41.[47]

The other three men aboard were killed in the crash, leaving only a terrified Alexander trying desperately to escape the fiery hull. He undid his seatbelt and got to the door somehow. Surrounded by flames and his left ankle shattered, he yanked at the white-hot door latch, searing his hands. Unable to open the door, he instinctively threw his body into it. It finally gave way and he jumped out into the fire. "I hit the railroad tracks about 50 feet away, and that was as far as I could go. I tried to beat out the flames and wipe them off my hands and face with my hands. Somebody kept beating me with a cap." The men who had rushed to the scene then left. "This fella can't live, let's go for somebody else," Skip remembered them saying. When they couldn't get to the others "they came back and found I was alive."[48]

Jackie Burke said his friend was a big, strong man, but when he "busted his way out of that airplane...he was just charred." Arriving at the Deaconess Hospital in Evansville, Indiana, he was still conscious, and was able to call his wife. He told her about the accident before passing out. "Looks like they'll keep me here a week or two."

Alexander was alive, but burned over 70 percent of his body. His nose was flattened on the side of his face, his face and ears burned badly. He remembered his hands, the most important part of a golfer, "looked like they'd been dipped in a bucket of molasses," all the skin gone. The plastic surgeon reattached the nose and his hands spent two months in saline-solution-filled bags. As he said, "I was helpless for a long time."[49]

Bob Hamilton, Skip's foursomes partner in the 1949 Ryder Cup, lived in Evansville, and so Kitty stayed with him and his wife. She said that nothing could have prepared her for how her husband looked. Skip was a big man, over 200 pounds, but now appeared twice that size, "totally bandaged like a big mummy on that little hospital bed." Her steadfast love and support throughout the ordeal played a key role in Skip's recovery. He was hospitalized in Evansville for three months, then spent five more months at the Duke University Hospital.

Just before Christmas, the Evansville *Courier* reported that Alexander had planned to fly home to Lexington, North Carolina, "but both little fingers still need surgery...The cast on his broken left ankle is due to be taken off soon to allow some movement of the leg." The ankle couldn't be set at the time of the crash "so it had to be rebroken and set properly about a month later. That's why it's taking so long."[50] His friends raised money to pay for his medical bills, and planned benefit matches early the next year.

Skip was back home in January 1951, and dropped in "on the boys at the Lexington Municipal Club," reported *Golf World*, before going to St. Petersburg, Florida. Even though on crutches, he had "been driving his car and his spirits have soared appreciably. Just getting back home has been a great tonic." Skip attributed his survival to "God and the skill of the physicians who worked on him." It was reported that he looked well for a man who has been through an ordeal. "His hands are giving him the most worry." He would need more skin grafts and would shuttle in and out of the Duke Hospital for these surgeries.[51]

Doctors wanted to amputate Alexander's little fingers, but he persuaded the orthopedic surgeon to instead freeze the last two knuckles of the fingers in a curled position, and do the same for the last knuckles of his ring fingers. Having the fingers permanently bent rather than straight would allow him to hold on to the club easier. Wilson Sporting

Goods even constructed a short golf club with a grip as a guide for the surgeons. Afterwards, Skip would flex them all day long to regain flexibility. He also strengthened them with a skill he learned from his nurses. "I must have knit a thousand potholders," he would say of that unusual therapy.[52]

In March of 1951 a match was played to raise money for Alexander, organized through the efforts of his friend Dugan Aycock. Players included Ben Hogan, Jimmy Demaret, Byron Nelson, Lloyd Mangrum, Jackie Burke, Jr., Sam Snead and Cary Middlecoff. The next month the Charlotte Country Club hosted "Skip Alexander Day," which took in about $8,000 (about $85,000 today) to help defray his medical bills.[53]

At the end of April, Skip was able to shoot a 72 playing with Dugan Aycock. The round pepped Alexander up, according to Aycock, who called it the greatest thing he'd ever seen in golf. To accommodate his injured hands, Alexander made the butt end of the grip smaller and used a combination overlapping and interlocking grip to hold on to the club. While recuperating at Duke, Alexander's cousin Dr. Clyde Anderson had helped get him the job at Lakewood (later St. Petersburg) Country Club in St. Petersburg, Florida, which he began later that year.

Skip came back to the Tour in the summer of 1951. He played in the Sioux City Open, shooting a 287, tiring in the final round with a 78 to tie for 27th. He decided to defend at the Empire State Open in September, and *Golf World* reported that "if everything goes well he will continue on the circuit with the hope of winning a spot on the 1951 Ryder Cup team." He was in 9th place in the points system that determined the team, with ten making it.[54]

Dugan Aycock had started a movement to have Alexander named as non-playing Captain of the team, as Ben Hogan had been in 1949 after the horrific car crash that almost took his life. Aycock thought it impossible for his friend to be able to play. While in the hospital, Alexander came to the stark realization that he wouldn't be able to perform on the Tour regularly anymore. But the Ryder Cup was still a goal, and kept him "hanging in there and trying to play." He was determined to grind it out, make the team, and play.

In the end, he edged out Marty Furgol to earn the last spot on the team, but didn't know if playing-Captain Sam Snead, who he was friendly with, would play him. When Dutch Harrison fell ill, Snead's selection of his lineup was made easier. Alexander joked years later that he didn't know if Snead was "sending the lambs to the slaughter or what," referring to facing John Panton, arguably the strongest player on the British side. For his part, Snead was adamant 46 years later, asserting that Skip was a man everyone on the team liked and wanted there. "And I wouldn't have put him in the Ryder Cup match if I didn't think he could do well."[55]

Skip never forgot that November 4, 1951, a cold and rainy day in North Carolina, as he prepared for his 36-hole match over the famous Pinehurst #2 course, playing at a then-demanding 7,007 yards. Only Ben Hogan and one other player had a better score than him in the morning rounds, as Skip shot a 74 with 22 putts. His opponent was John Panton. "I was all banged up. My hands were bleeding...every time I played a hole, I wondered if I could play the next, because I stiffened up a lot during the break." He began to tire on the final 18, the growing pain in his hands and ankle making it difficult to continue. He didn't know if he could make it, but he gutted it out. "I kept telling myself, 'Hurry up and win.'" He did hurry up, beating Panton 8 and 7, contributing to the most lopsided U.S. victory at that time, 9½ to 2½. Of his match, he said in 1960, "That was my most gratifying victory of all."[56]

Alexander would endure numerous plastic surgeries and skin grafts after the accident. "His hands looked like big scarred paws," says his son Buddy, the 1986 U.S. Amateur champion; very scarred, with no pores and no hair. Skip had no hair on his legs, and would walk with a limp, as his ankle bothered him the rest of his life.[57]

In 1952, Alexander filed a $279,000 lawsuit against the Federal government and the Civil Air Patrol for injuries suffered in the crash, and outlined his loss of earning power and medical expenses. In his complaint, Alexander charged the pilot, Lt. Colonel Oliver A. Singleton, with negligence, alleging that the plane had a faulty valve or fuel selector switch. Alexander testified "that he had 17 operations, both ears were nearly burned off, his face and eyes burned severely, hands burned and disfigured, legs burning from mid-thigh to ankle, back, shoulder and neck burned," Dr. Kenneth L Pickrell of Duke University Hospital testified in 1954 that he still needed perhaps 20 more plastic surgery operations. That year the case against the Civil Air Patrol was dismissed by a judge on the grounds that the plane and the pilot were under the control of the Air Force.[58]

It took four years to work through the courts. In 1956 Alexander lost his final appeal for compensation, and to add insult to injury, the United States Supreme Court declined to review a circuit court decision which overruled an award of $75,000 made earlier by a federal district court. As his son Buddy says, it's hard to imagine that kind of justice being meted out today, but things were different in those days. His father was part of that generation that just kept going when faced with tough times, and Skip didn't dwell on it. His attitude was to just "keep on keeping on" with his life, which is just what he did. Buddy says his father always said he was lucky to have survived the crash, and that's what was important and emphasized.[59]

Alexander played occasionally on the PGA Tour after his Ryder Cup triumph, coming back in March 1952 at the St. Petersburg Open, close to home, the start of a four tourney swing. He finished 27th at the Masters the next month, and missed the cut at the U.S. Open. In December he was co-champion with Jim Ferrier of the one-day International Four-Ball Tournament at Miami Beach. Both shot 65s, beating the likes of Claude Harmon, Julius Boros, Art Wall, Jim Turnesa, and Vic Ghezzi. In 1954 he finished 46th in the Masters, missed the cut in the U.S. Open, and won the West Coast Florida Open. He would qualify for the 1956 and 1957 PGA Championships, losing each year in the first round of match play.[60]

On February 20, 1959 he won the National PGA Club Professional Championship by two shots with a four under par 284. "I won it for Buddy," he said, dedicating the win to his son, "who had his sixth birthday today." He kept playing at a high level and competed in the PGA Tour's St. Petersburg Open and Florida Citrus Open (now the Arnold Palmer Invitational) into the late 1960s. This brief summary demonstrates that Skip didn't just ride off into the sunset after the 1951 Ryder Cup, but kept competing when he could, given that his bad ankle made it difficult to walk.[61]

In January 1960, Alexander won the Ben Hogan Award, and also played in the St. Petersburg Open that March, finishing tied for 50th. He downplayed the Hogan award, which sits proudly on his son Buddy's mantle, saying he didn't deserve to be in the company of the previous recipients. "They are the deserving ones."[62]

In 1964, Skip played an exhibition in Tampa with Jack Nicklaus, Arnold Palmer, and another club professional. He shot a 72, Nicklaus a 71, Palmer a 70 and the host pro a 74. *The Tampa Times* covered the event and wrote a sidebar about the first time Nicklaus met Skip. "I was ten and I was watching the PGA in Columbus," recalled Nicklaus, as it was played in 1950 at his home course, Scioto Country Club. "I was excited about golf then and wanted to get some of the players' autographs, but I was too little to get near them. Skip didn't even know me, except that I was a little kid, but he took me through the locker room and I got all of their autographs." Skip would be defeated in that PGA Championship by Lloyd Mangrum in a second round match that came down to the final hole. Three months later, he'd get on that plane in Kansas City.[63]

Skip didn't look back much, says Buddy, and "99 percent of the time he was fine. But once in a while, when the majors came around he'd say, 'Gosh damn, I'd like to be able to play.'" Skip once lamented the fact that four years of college and four and a half years in the service during the war detracted from the learning experience he could have had playing on the Tour. "In terms of experience, I was really a 23-year-old 32-year-old man learning to play golf," he said. "I think I could have done a lot better."[64]

He was bigger and stronger than Hogan and Snead and many thought he might have had the chance to be one of the best players on Tour when the accident happened. Cary Middlecoff, three-time major winner and Skip's best friend on Tour, was one of them, having witnessed Alexander's continued improvement. "But considering the two hands he was left with and how beat up he was, I think he did as well as it was possible to do."

The hands are vital to playing great golf, and as golf writer Jack Horner wrote in 1948, Skip had "tremendous hands." But the accident forever changed the way those vital tools performed. Middlecoff thought that "Hogan probably came closer to dying, but I think Skip was hurt worse." Given his hands and poor vision – he was color blind and had 20/600 vision without his glasses and said it cost him two to four shots a round – his accomplishments are not only admirable, but heroic.[65]

Skip's son Buddy (Stewart M. Alexander, III) did something his father never did, win the U.S. Amateur. He also coached the University of Florida Gators for 27 years, leading them to NCAA golf championships in 1993 and 2001. He claims his father was not a stage father. They would talk after most of his tournament rounds to discuss what he might do to improve, "but it wasn't one of those things where he lived his life through me." Skip was a "stern taskmaster who had his way of doing things and that was that," according to Buddy, who began helping him out on the range when he was around 11 years old. "He was a pretty tough father, but eventually I realized everything he had done. He became my best friend and my idol."[66]

His father ruled every room he ever walked into, according to Buddy. He was a big man with a big personality and possessed of a good sense of humor. The members at Lakewood loved him. Skip said when he won the Ben Hogan Award that "my problems are all small ones," and that the accident "only speeded up my becoming what I had hoped to be in the end anyway, a happy club pro." Buddy admired his father and the manner in which he lived his life, saying he inspired many people.[67] That he did.

Skip Alexander passed away October 24, 1997, and left behind quite a legacy. His son Buddy and grandson Tyson both played in the U.S. Open, making three successive generations of one family to do so. They were the second of only three families to achieve this honor – preceded by the Herrons (Carson, Carson, Jr., and Tim) and followed by the Loves (Davis, Davis, Jr., and Drue.) As Skip said once looking back on his life, "I'm the luckiest sumbitch alive. I couldn't ask for anything more than what's happened to me." Then, displaying the tongue-in-cheek sense of humor that served him well in life, added, "Well, I could do without that airplane wreck."[68]

The people featured in this chapter offer just a few examples of character and grit. "However mean your life is, meet it and live it."[69] These words of Henry David Thoreau could describe the lives of all these people, who faced tremendous physical and emotional trials in their lives, yet persevered and overcame. The strength and resilience of the human spirit – indeed, its stubborn persistence – was a common denominator in facing their struggles. They never gave up or gave in to the suffering that afflicted them, and all offer inspiration to anyone going through their own trials.

Chapter 8: Senior Golfers – "Aging is First and Foremost a State of Mind"

At the age of 59, golfing legend Tom Watson lost a playoff for the 2009 British Open, the oldest golf championship in the world. He was one missed putt away from becoming the oldest player to ever win a major championship (the oldest being Julius Boros, who won the 1968 PGA Championship at age 48.) At age 68, Watson won the Par-3 contest at the 2018 Masters Tournament, beating players in the prime of their careers. It goes to show that golf truly is a game for a lifetime.

Grantland Rice, the famed sportswriter, wrote in 1921:

> Golf, in the main is this – the only game in the world that can lead those beyond fifty or sixty back to a competitive sport that will return again all the thrills and throbs that once ended for most men at twenty-five. It is the only competitive sport in the world that can lead a veteran back to boyhood; the only sport that can give you a game to play until you are within mashie [5-iron] distance of the grave.[1]

In 2018, 24.2 million people played golf on a real course in the United States. Of those, about 8.5 million, or 35%, were age 50 and over (including about 1.7 million women). Some 4.2 million were age 65 years and up, including almost 2 million 70 and over (including some 350,000 women.) As Tom Watson has said, golf is like the opera, you might hate it at the beginning and may grow to like it over time, but if you don't love it from the beginning you never will. For those who do love it, it hooks them for life. David Forgan wrote a "Golfer's Creed" in the late 19th century. To him, golf "means going into God's out-of-doors, getting close to nature, fresh air, exercise, a sweeping away of mental cobwebs, genuine recreation of tired tissues.... It is a cure for care, an antidote to worry." Michael Murphy, in his classic book *Golf in the Kingdom*, spoke of golf in terms of "walkin' fast across the countryside and feelin' the wind and watchin' the sun go down and seein' yer friends hit good shots and hittin' some yourself. It's love and it's feelin' the splendor o' this good world." Even though the game can

201

drive one crazy, at the same time it's addictive, and can be therapeutic to many.[2]

For me, I find myself at peace on the golf course or driving range, trying to hit the ball where I want it to go. Even though back surgery a dozen years ago limits my being able to hit the ball as far as I used to, it's still fun. I see the ball fall 20 yards shorter than it did a few years ago and I get a little depressed, but it isn't the end of the world. I feel a connection to the earth out there, breathing the fresh air and feeling the breeze against my cheeks.

As Sherwin Nutland writes in *The Art of Aging*, "Whatever else aging may represent to us, it is first and foremost a state of mind." Victor Hugo spoke of the relativity of age when he wrote, "Forty is the old age of youth; fifty the youth of old age." The late President George H.W. Bush personified this ideal, skydiving to celebrate his 90th birthday. "Just 'cause you're an old guy," he used to say, "you don't have to sit around drooling in the corner. Get out and do something. Get out and enjoy life." Janet Travell was the personal physician to President John F. Kennedy, and lived into her 90s. She used to say that she would rather "wear out than rust out," and I agree wholeheartedly with that motto.[3]

There are plenty of older people continuing to play golf well into their later years. And since I am a golf historian who has studied the game for 45 years, I have found many examples of people who don't let age hold them back, and their stories give me hope. Attitude is all important in life, and we need to keep a sense of humor as we age. Charles Price wrote a very good piece for *Golf Magazine* in 1979, as he was reaching "senior" years. "At 50 there are a lot of things you can't do that you could do at 25, not all of which you care to do anyhow – such as climb the Washington Monument or play 54 holes in one day…At 25 I thought the bunker on the fifth fairway was unfair because I couldn't carry it. Today I think it is eminently fair, because I can't reach it."[4]

George Bush loved golf too as he got older, and he kept moving, kept doing, until ill health slowed him down. When my back acts up and I can't swing a club, two words comfort me – patience and perseverance. Then I think of what others have done. As baseball great Satchel Paige once said, "How old would you be, if you didn't know how old you were?"

Old Tom Morris, one of the game's icons, played in the British Open until he was 75. Sam Snead tied for third in the 1974 PGA Championship at age 62, and shot his age or better (67) in two consecutive rounds on the PGA Tour in 1979. He would also shoot an incredible 60 when he was 71 years old at the Homestead's Lower Cascades at Hot Springs, Virginia, tying the course record set by his nephew J.C. Sam shot 30 on each side, with 12 birdies. His approach to the final hole hit green but took a bad bounce, leaving him a long birdie putt. "The course must have been saying, 'Damn you, you've had enough,'" said Sam.[5]

Ben Hogan shot his age in 1977 with a 64 at Shady Oaks in Texas, on a 6,975-yard course. Joe Jimenez shot a 62 at the age of 69 on the Senior PGA Tour. Jerry Barber, who won the PGA Championship in 1961 at age 45, shot his age or better in each round of the 1992 U.S. Senior Open, when he was 76 years old, hitting his drives 210-225 yards and still wielding a deadly putter.[6]

Chuck Kocsis was a great amateur player who was one of the best senior players of all time that very few people have heard of, with an impressive career that spanned 60 years at the highest levels of the game. Byron Nelson called him one of the most remarkable golfers he'd ever known. Chuck started playing golf with his brothers when he was six or seven, and began caddying when he was 10 at the Redford Golf Club, designed by Donald Ross in 1921.[7]

In 1930, at the age of 17, Kocsis won the first of six Michigan Amateurs, and beat Francis Ouimet in the first round of the U.S. Amateur. The next year he won the 1931 Michigan Open, beating the immortal Tommy Armour, who was so miffed at losing to an amateur that he walked off without shaking Chuck's hand. "The rudest, unkindest guy I ever knew," said Chuck in 2000. Kocsis was the NCAA champion in 1936, runner-up in the 1956 U.S. Amateur, and a Walker Cup team member in 1938, 1949, and 1957. He also played in nine U.S. Opens. In 1988, at age 76 he captured the last of five International Seniors Championships in Scotland (he won the 1970 event by 21 shots over 72 holes.)[8]

Byron Nelson experienced Kocsis's talent firsthand in a July 1948 exhibition at Red Run Golf Club with Bobby Locke, and Bob

Gajda, who played in numerous U.S. Opens. Chuck went out in 32 and Nelson in 34. "Byron came up to me," Kocsis recalled, "and said, 'No amateur is going to beat me.' He said it in a very nice manner." Nelson was just very competitive, and as an elite professional, he didn't want to lose to anybody. He shot a 30 on the inward nine to Kocsis's 34, finishing with a 64 to Chuck's 66.

In November of that same year, Kocsis was on a hunting trip when the car in which he was a passenger ran off the road and rolled over near Great Falls, Montana. "I was caught halfway out the door and broke my back." He was hospitalized for two weeks, and his X-rays were sent to his doctor back home. He called in a specialist, Dr. Eugene Secord, who reviewed them and told Kocsis without an operation there was no way he could recover.[9]

The operation involved taking six inches of bone from Kocsis's right leg and grafting it to his back. "It turned out very well," Chuck remembered. He was on a Stryker frame bed for ten weeks, and then instructed to be careful with physical exertion, wearing a back brace. In April 1949, he "went to the club and hit a few shots with a real easy swing." His doctors played a round with him later and Chuck was happy with his performance, a 73. "After witnessing my round, Dr. Secord said I could play all the golf I wanted. That was good news."

Kocsis came back to play as well as he ever had. And he played with everyone: Presidents Eisenhower, Kennedy, and Ford, Gene Sarazen, Ben Hogan, Arnold Palmer, Cliff Roberts, Grantland Rice, Babe Ruth, Bob Hope, Bing Crosby, Joe Louis, and Tommy Armour, among others. One of his methods to keep him sharp was to take "five or six balls and play them all the way around. It was my best practice. That way, you're always hitting different shots…not standing there (on the range) and hitting the same shot every time."[10]

On August 26, 1972, at the Edgewood Country Club, 35 miles northwest of Detroit, he shot his age on the 6,435-yard par-71 course, going 30-29. Kocsis played in the 1973 U.S. Amateur, and at age 60, was the oldest player in the field. He won his first two matches by convincing margins before facing 20-year-old Buddy Alexander in round three. Alexander recalls he was hanging around the putting green with Bill Rogers (1981 British Open champion) when a "little old man" in shorts and white socks walked by. Rogers said to Buddy, "Look at this guy, somebody is going to get him and it will be like having a bye and you have to play Andy Bean [future 11-time winner on the PGA Tour]."[11]

Kocsis wasn't big, about 5"8" and didn't hit the ball a long way, but he was a great player. Buddy was 1 up going to 18th, a short par-4. He played a cautious second shot 25 feet past the hole while Chuck hit his to eight feet. Faced with a fast downhill putt – Buddy said the Inverness greens were some of the fastest he had seen – he just wanted to lag it close. He remembered the "ball was going so fast it might have rolled off the front of the green, but it hit the middle of the hole, jumped up, and fell in." Kocsis left his putt to force the match into extra holes on the lip of the cup. He shook Alexander's hand, and "was polite, but you could tell he wasn't pleased. He was a real competitor." Alexander believes Kocsis is one of the great underrated amateurs of all-time, which is true. In 15 U.S. Amateurs, he won 71 percent of his matches.[12]

In 2002, at age 89, Kocsis went out with a foursome at Pine Trace Golf Club, in Rochester Hills, Michigan. Playing from the middle tees (6,003 yards long), he made four birdies in his par round, with a 38-34=72. Amazing.

Vartan Kupelian, author of a wonderful little book called *Forever Scratch*, tells a story that sums up the greatness of Koscis. They were playing together in a charity scramble event in the late 1980s, when they arrived to the par-3 fifth hole, about 200 yards long. Kupelian hit a 5-wood to the middle of the green. "I can't carry the ball onto the green any more – too far for me," said Chuck as he considered his tee shot. "The only way I can get it close to that pin is to hit a 2-iron short of the bunker and have it hop over the sand, onto the green, and take the roll toward the pin." Kupelian remembered thinking, "Right. I'm sure this guy is going to pull off that miracle shot. Sure." Kocsis proceeded to hit a laser-like 2-iron that hit just short of the bunker, bouncing over it and rolling eight feet from the hole. "That's how good Chuck Kocsis was with a club in his hands," concluded Kupelian.[13]

Ed Ervasti, a native of London, Ontario, Canada, did not have the golfing resume Chuck Kocsis did, but he did play in two U.S. Opens in 1949 and 1956. Like Kocsis, he won a Michigan Amateur (in 1947), and played with the likes of Ben Hogan, Arnold Palmer, and Byron Nelson. He also played with ball-striker extraordinaire Moe Norman, who touted Ervasti's short game. "Oh my, what Ed can do around the greens and with the putter."[14]

At the age of 84 Ervasti still had a 6-handicap, playing 200 to 300 times a year. At 93, he shot a 72 on a 96-degree day. How's that for stamina? The 21 shots under his age is a record. By age 98 he had shot his age about 2,500 times, and was still playing about 100 times a year. He maintained the secret to his longevity was exercise. "I walk every morning for almost two to three miles. I have for 20 to 30 years." He also was a firm believer in proper technique in the golf swing, saying, "If you strive for form you can play forever."[15]

These were all great golfers, but the stories of average players over the years also give me inspiration. Henry DeVries of San Mateo, California, started playing golf at 60, and even after losing his left leg below the knee in a car accident, he wasn't deterred. "One beauty of golf is that you must concentrate and think of nothing else. That's why, on the course, I am never aware that I have lost a leg." At age 92, he was playing 18 holes five days a week, and his daughter believed, "Golf has really kept him going." He walked the course until he was 87, then bought a golf cart and kept going. DeVries believed golf was "the world's finest sport because it has no age limit," adding that it "provides just the right exercise, and you can have lots of fun to boot."[16]

George "Dad" Miller of Anaheim, California, shot three consecutive 79s on a regulation course when he was 92 years-old, and had three holes-in-one in his life, two coming after age 82. After three heart attacks, the last at age 92, he finally had to employ the use of a cart. "I hated to give up walking, but as long as I don't have to give up golf it was OK. I know I owe my good physical condition to golf." At age 97 he still played four times a week. Miller claimed, "You don't get old playing golf, you get old when you stop playing." The secret to his longevity? "To kiss all the women you can."[17]

For Louis Barch, 92, there was no questioning the role golf played in his life. "I think it's one of the reasons I lived so long," he said in 2000. The Rutland, Vermont native walked the course, never riding a cart, and praised the game's benefits. "It's been the camaraderie, a chance to get acquainted with the fellows. I like the exercise and the scenery, and the game is good for your health."

Jean McCabe, 79, of Staten Island, New York, suffered from chronic pulmonary disease, and when her doctor said it would get worse she asked if it would affect her ability to play. "I wasn't going to let anything keep me from playing golf." She continued to play two or three times a week, despite needing an oxygen tank. "I guess I've shown that you don't have to be considered an invalid. You can get out and do almost anything you want." Marge Ryan of California shot her age at 75 and said, "If you have the determination and the dedication, you can do it."[18]

Ann Lidle of Peoria, Illinois was shooting "49 or in the 50s for nine holes" at the age of 97. What's more, she walked the course. She would see her doctor each spring before starting golf. "He said if I feel like it to go out and play, but slow down a little. I'm trying to, but it's hard when you've jumped around all these years." She enjoyed her Monday morning sessions with other seniors. "It's a fun group…I don't care about prizes, I just love to play." Elsie McLean made a hole-in-one the age of 102, getting her a spot on the *Ellen DeGeneres* show. "If you want to keep playing golf," she said, "you've got to enjoy yourself, quit complaining about your aches and pains and stay away from doctors."[19]

Cy Perkins, 97 of Hood River, Oregon admonished people, "As you get older, you can't get discouraged about how far you hit the ball…Keep playing until you can't bend over and tee it up." He shot his age 473 times. George Selbach played nine holes three times a week at age 104, when *Golf Digest* named him the Oldest Avid Golfer in America. As a young man he played professional football from 1918 to 1921, including a game against the legendary Jim Thorpe. He shot a 77 at age 96, and made two holes-in-one when he was 97. "If I did everything the doctors wanted me to do, I'd be dead. I use common sense."[20]

Cy Breen, 95, of Cathedral City, California played 90 holes on his 90th birthday to raise money for cancer. "The most important thing about age is attitude," said the man who played once or twice a week, went to the range twice a week, and practiced putting every day. "If you're a complainer, if your attitude is terrible, that's when you're going to have problems." Bob Exter, 94, always tried to stay healthy. "I'm very careful about diet, and every morning I do my calisthenics, some sit-ups and some stretching."

Sid Beckwith, at 96, played golf in Clermont, Florida every day but Sundays, and shot an 86 on a 6,088-yard course. "I go out every day and try to get better. That's what makes the game fun." He also exercised after he played, getting on an elliptical machine for 20 minutes. He shot his age over 1,000 times, the first time at 72 (with a 71.)[21]

Walter Estby was 93 when he drove from his home in Burlington, Washington to Mesa, Arizona, to attend a five-day golf school, looking to improve his game. "I guess you're never too old to improve," he said. Five years later he was still at it, shooting in the low 90s while playing about twice a week, and able to drive the ball 200 yards on occasion. His secret? "I've never weighed much more than 160 pounds. I think eating kills more people than drinking." He lived to be 106. Duffy Martin of Guthrie, Oklahoma, could still shoot in the low 80s at age 90. "I tell people to stay away from the whiskey and cigarettes and play golf every chance they get. If people will play more golf and exercise, age is just so many numbers."[22]

As we learned in a previous chapter, Jimmie DeVoe taught and played golf into his 90s. He first played in the PGA Senior Championship in 1969, at age 81, and won his division with a 79. In 1972 he shot 79-89 to win again. At the tournament in 1974, he shot 45-42=87 for two separate nine-hole rounds, missing his age by two strokes. "This is the first time I've come out here that I haven't shot my age," he said, irritated at himself. "But I still won by 14 strokes, so that isn't bad." He didn't like the format, complaining, "Anyone who can't play 18 holes riding a cart doesn't belong on the course."[23]

Steve Melnikoff of Cockeyville, Maryland said in 2019 that his 32-handicap golf game followed a strict schedule: "I play Tuesdays, Thursdays, and Saturdays. Sometimes guys get upset with me because I won't play two days in a row. But it's just too hard on me. You see, I'm 99 years old." He was 24 years old when he landed on Omaha Beach during the D-Day invasion of Normandy. He was shot in the neck near St. Lo, where his best friend was killed. Melnikoff recovered and returned to the fighting, serving to the end of the war. He returned home, married, and worked for Bethlehem Steel. In his later years he was able to share his story with young people through the Greatest Generations Foundation. "People call us the greatest generation," he said. "Well, I think golf is the greatest game."[24]

Jimmie DeVoe gave credit to the Lord. At the age of 88, he claimed he hadn't been sick a day in his life, but admitted he was slowed down by arthritic knees. He still hit a large bucket of balls each day and walked 18 holes once a week, scoring between 83 and 88. "I feel like a young whippersnapper. I feel like I could go out and shoot 68 like I used to." But he knew his body couldn't do the things it used to. He spoke for all seniors when he pointed out one undeniable truth: "Your muscles won't respond to your will." But it didn't keep him from trying to be better. Sid Beckwith was 96 and still reading instructional articles trying to find an edge. "Sometimes I'll try a swing for two or three holes, give it up for another swing and then go to a third one, all in one round. One of these days, I'm sure I'll find the right one."[25]

That's the beauty of the game; we keep trying to get better until the end, and continue to enjoy the ride. Ninety-two-year-old Henry DeVries said, "It's the world's finest sport because it has no age limit...Golf provides just the right exercise, and you can have lots of fun to boot." And no matter how many holes he and his friends played, he claimed "I always feel just as fresh as when we started."

Jimmie DeVoe believed golf is a romantic game, because it's something you're truly in love with. "Golf is like a lover – you can't get it off your mind. I guess you could call it unrequited love, because you never possess it." He added that life is short, and "you'd better make something of it while you can."[26] Amen, brother, amen.

Chapter 9: Pebble Beach – "The Fifth Hole and the Women Connected to its History"

Pebble Beach. The name evokes indelible images of golf history played out over one of the most magnificent meetings of land and sea in the world. The iconic course where Bob Jones suffered a stunning first-round defeat at the hands of Johnny Goodman in the 1929 U.S. Amateur; where Jack Nicklaus struck a glorious 1-iron into a gale on the 17th hole to clinch the 1972 U.S. Open; and where ten years later he was denied a record fifth title when Tom Watson holed a magical pitch shot from the rough on the same hole.

Much has been written about these and other events that give Pebble Beach its heart and soul, but it's doubtful if anyone knows how Camilla Jenkins, the granddaughter of the first U.S. Women's Amateur champion, affected the evolution of its par-3 fifth hole. It's a tale as intriguing as anything Jones, Nicklaus, or Watson could conjure up, and one that deserves telling. First, we have to go back to where it all began.

Jack Neville, who designed the course with Douglas Grant in 1916, recalled years later that doing so "took a little imagination, but not too much. Years before it was built, I could see this place as a golf links. Nature had intended it to be nothing else. All we did was cut away a few trees, install a few sprinklers and sow a little seed." *The American Golfer* wrote in 1929 that the architects, by "enlisting Father Neptune and Old Mother Nature" created "the most devastating ocean hazards of any course in the world." If this wasn't enough of a challenge for players, they flung "at their frazzled nerves such natural beauty that no man with the whiff of anything but dollars in his soul will be able to hold his mind steadfast on his game." This speaks to the end result of Neville and Grant's work (and later H. Chandler Egan's), but belies a more complicated story. What is today Pebble Beach was largely developed by one company, and inspired by the vision of a single person: Samuel Finley Brown Morse.[1]

Between 1880 and 1919, the Pebble Beach area was owned by the Pacific Improvement Company (PIC), a consortium of four railroad barons which included Leland Stanford. The company also developed the famous 17-Mile Drive, much of which meanders along the spectacular

Pacific coastline. But it was Morse, hired in 1915 as the manager of the PIC, who championed the construction of the Pebble Beach Golf Links.

Morse was enamored with the natural beauty of the place, and found that "the effect of the Monterey Peninsula is to make one want to shout, to run rather than walk." He believed a golf course would help attract visitors and also raise property values. Former PIC manager A.D. Shepard's development plan, which would have crammed more than 400 lots of 80-feet each along the current course's 6th to 13th fairways, was scrapped. Morse convinced the PIC that the course should be laid out along the coastline, and set aside land in the hills for the sale of lots. Doing so preserved the scenic vistas that we now take for granted at Pebble Beach.

Bust of Samuel Morse at Pebble Beach's "Wall of Champions."

Morse went about buying back lots that had been sold but were not built on. One of the first lots he sold in 1915 was a 5½-acre parcel on a bluff overlooking Stillwater Cove. The buyer, William T. Beatty, an industrial magnate from Chicago, had paid a little more than $6,000 for it, and refused to sell it back to Morse. This infamous Lot 3, Block 137, would be a coveted piece of real estate for the next 80 years.[2]

"That was the first deed that I signed after becoming a member of the Pacific Improvement Company," Morse would later recall. "I remember saying at the time, 'I'll probably regret this.'" He offered Beatty "his choice of any property in the whole area in exchange for it, but he couldn't be tempted with anything else. The result was, we designed the course around the property." Beatty was so adamant that he placed a restriction on the property to prevent it from ever being sold.[3]

Nevertheless, Morse was confident that the area had great potential as a resort for the rich and their guests, who could enjoy a variety of recreational activities there. He put together a consortium that bought the property from the PIC in 1919 for $1.3 million, forming the Del Monte Properties Company. "Sam was passionate about the lands he acquired," wrote his grandson Charles Osborne, "and he let that passion rule his life." He ruled as an autocrat, and "personally approved the design of every house built in Pebble Beach and every tree cut down" from 1919 to his death in 1969.[4]

The 160-yard par-3 fifth hole built to skirt the Beatty's property went uphill, and required a tee shot threaded between trees and over a ravine, with out of bounds on either side. Some deridingly called it golf's only dogleg par-3. In 1951 it was described as a "tricky 3 to 6-iron shot and the mental hazard is terrific."

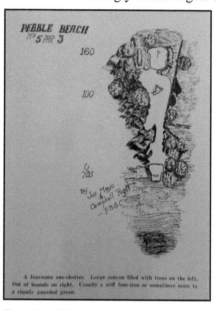

Golf writer Jim Moriarty noted that the "most charitable description of Pebble Beach's original fifth hole is that it was the shortest way for players to get from four to six. Uphill and blind, it was an anomaly. A plow horse among thoroughbreds." Arnold Palmer described it as "an awful, terrible hole." Robert Trent Jones wrote in 1982 that the hole "seems out of place when matched with the spacious holes preceding it and the majestic

Drawing of Pebble Beach's original 5th hole, 1929.

holes to follow. In fact, it is out of place." But Sam Morse was stuck with it.[5]

William Beatty had commissioned Julia Morgan to design and build a home on the site. The first woman to graduate from the University of California, Berkeley with a degree in civil engineering in 1894, and the first to attend L'Ecole des Beaux-Arts in Paris, Morgan designed nearly 800 buildings before her death in 1957. (She is best known for her work on the Hearst Castle in San Simeon, California.) After retiring from business, Beatty and his wife moved to Pebble Beach full-time in 1931. He enjoyed the property only two more years before dying in 1933, and his widow Valerie put the property up for sale in June 1940 for the sum of $95,000. Between financial difficulties brought on by the Great Depression and the coming of World War II, Sam Morse was unable to purchase the property.[6]

Pebble Beach's original 5th hole, up the hill to the right, 1920.

The Beatty estate, known as "Live Oak Meadow," was charming enough to be used in the 1939 movie, *Daughter's Courageous*, starring Claude Rains and John Garfield. "Twenty-three live oak trees with beards of Spanish moss, scores of cypresses twisted by the shifting ocean breezes, and graceful eucalyptuses line the grounds," a newspaper reported. "The Beatty home was singled out for the Warner picture of family life because it so closely represented the kind of attractive and comfortable abode which any American household would choose if 'its ship came in.'" After Mrs. Beatty died in 1941, the property was relisted in October 1943 for $40,000.[7]

It was bought in March 1944 by Matthew C. Jenkins. Raised on the East Coast, he spent one lackluster semester at Williams College in Massachusetts before heading west, coming to California in 1921. Over the next 30 years he would marry and divorce while working on ranches in the San Joaquin Valley, and owning a couple himself. In 1947 the property was used again by Hollywood, for the filming of *The Ghost and Mrs. Muir*. The swimming scene with Gene Tierney and Natalie Wood was done at Stillwater Cove, and when Tierney climbs a stairway to a coastal bluff where she finds George Sanders drawing her in her bathing suit, the stairs belonged to Jenkins and led to his property where the current fifth hole sits. In 1951 Matt Jenkins married Camilla "Mimi" Canfield at Saddle Rock Ranch, the Big Sur residence of Mimi's parents.

Mimi was born Camilla Hooper Brown on January 26, 1913, and received her nickname from her sister Halla. Having trouble as a toddler pronouncing her baby sister's name, Camilla became "Camimi," and then "Mimi." Her father was New York Congressman Lathrop Brown, who graduated from the famous prep school Groton in 1900 and from

Lathrop Brown, c.1915.

Harvard University in 1903. At Harvard he shared a room with a good friend from Groton, a young man destined to be a future president of the United States – Franklin Delano Roosevelt. Lapes, Lapie, or Jake, as his family and friends called him, Brown would act as best man at Roosevelt's wedding in 1905, with Roosevelt returning the favor at Lathrop's nuptials in 1911.[8]

After graduating from Harvard, Lathrop worked for his father's firm, Douglas Robinson, Charles S. Brown Company, as well as G. Schirmer Company, music publishers, and the Commonwealth Insurance Company. He served one term in Congress from 1913 to 1915; was a special assistant to the Secretary of the Interior Franklin K. Lane

215

from March 1917 to October 1918; and then a joint secretary to President Woodrow Wilson's Industrial Conference in 1919.

As a child, Mimi bounced on Wilson's knee, and grew up in an affluent and political household, with her father remaining active in Democratic party politics on a national level. Brown went with his close friend Franklin Roosevelt to the Democratic National Convention in 1920, which nominated Roosevelt for Vice-President. Filmmaker Pare Lorentz noted that the two "had traveled west together and had shared a hotel room in San Francisco. On the way east, FDR, as vice-presidential candidate, now rated the lower berth [in the Pullman sleeper.] The campaign tour developed FDR into a nation[al] figure." In 1933, Brown would attend Roosevelt's first inaugural, and later visited him in the White House.[9]

Lathrop and his wife Helen bought Saddle Rock Ranch in Big Sur, California, in 1924, and lived there part-time until 1946, when they moved from Boston and made it their permanent residence. In 1961, two years after the death of her husband, Helen Hooper Brown donated the entire 1,800-acre property to the state of California. She stipulated that it be used as a park and be named for Julia Pfeiffer Burns, the daughter of a pioneering homesteader, with whom she had a close friendship.

Governor Pat Brown praised Helen's generous gift, saying it "demonstrated her friendship for the people of the state in a manner that will never be forgotten."[10] The park's McWay Falls tumble down 80-feet over granite cliffs and freefalls into the sea – or the beach, depending on the tide, to provide the classic Big Sur postcard shot. The Browns had a home half way down the cliffs, opposite the falls. To get to the house, one had to take a tram from the highway down a long track that the family called "The Big Sur and Pacific Railroad."

Mimi Brown was twenty years old when she married Robert Warren Canfield in New York City on October 13, 1933, the same year William Beatty passed away. Robert, a Harvard graduate, was an expert with guns. A successful businessman, he was passionate about his shooting, which he had been doing since age seven. In fact, as *The Brooklyn Daily Eagle* reported in 1940, "he was so carried away by his hobby that he once presented his wife with a skeet gun for a wedding present. It made no difference to Bob that she had never shot a gun in her life." Under Robert's tutelage, Camilla won the New York Women's open shooting championship just 11 months later.[11]

Canfield was an All-American skeet champion in 1940 and held the world 20-gauge record of 319 straight targets at that time. His expertise would be utilized by the government when the U.S. entered World War II, as he became a gunnery specialist of the Air Forces Flying Training Command, stationed in Fort Worth, Texas. He entered the U.S. Army Air Corps in early 1942 as a captain and became an instructor, teaching the men how to shoot at moving targets.

Skeet shooters and hunters, "who shoot at rapidly moving targets, such as ducks, geese, rabbits, doves, and so forth, are our number one prospects," said Canfield in 1942. It was found that their training in leading a target helped them adapt "to aerial gunnery more readily." He added that the "skeet shooter has learned to lead his target instinctively, and if his plane ever is in a tight spot where there is little time for thinking, he'll do the right thing anyway."[12]

Bob Canfield Gave Impetus To Skeet Shooting in East

Few people are as enthusiastic over a sport as is Robert W. (Bob) Canfield, Locust Valley, L. I., shooting captain of the Hilltop Skeet Club, the leading unit of its kind in the East. In fact he was so carried away by his hobby that he once presented his wife with a skeet gun for a wedding present. It made no difference to Bob that she had never shot a gun in her life. She almost fainted when he trudged into the house with the gun slung over his shoulder. Under his tutelage she won the New York Women's open championship 11 months later.

Bob's encouragement of his mates has resulted in them nicknaming him "Pepper." Canfield is practically the daddy of active team skeet competition in the East. It was the success of the Hilltop Club which gave impetus for the mushrooming of skeet teams throughout the Atlantic seaboard.

Bob has been acquainted with shooting for 25 of his 32 years. When he was seven his father presented him with a rifle and told him to learn how to shoot. Two of his uncles, Albert W. Canfield and Robert B. Canfield, were characters of the flat lands of Montana during the riotous days from 1860 to 1870. Bob was educated at St. Paul's School. He later played football.

Bob Canfield

Robert Canfield, article in *The Brooklyn Daily Eagle*, March 24, 1940.

Mimi, herself a pilot, also served during the war. "She believed women could do anything," wrote *Golf Digest's* David Kindred in 1998. As a fifteen-year-old she pestered her parents about flying until they drew straws to, in her words, decide who would "take the brat up" in the air "so that she would stop talking. It didn't work at all." On her 80th birthday she took a flying lesson in a 747 simulator, telling the instructor, "Don't bother yourself, I know what I'm doing."[13]

Mimi ferried aircraft for the Civil Air Patrol, formed in 1941. Other women did the same, flying planes from factories to military bases in order to free male pilots for combat roles. They included Helen Dettweiler, a founding member of the Ladies Professional Golfers Association, who served her country as a WASP (Women Airforce Service Pilot) from 1943 to 1944. Despite such distinguished service, these women were considered civilians and would not be granted World War II veteran status until 1977. First Lady Eleanor Roosevelt claimed women were indispensable to the nation, but their roles and relative importance were still defined by their sex.[14]

As Mimi ferried aircraft, her husband Robert went to Buckingham Field in Fort Myers, Florida, where he was the assistant director of its Central Instructors School for aerial gunners. Having been promoted to Major in January 1943, he went overseas in July. "The fine recreational sport of skeet has added tremendously to the success of the war effort," wrote *The San Francisco Examiner*. "Dozens of its highest ranking exponents are in service in instructional capacities, but in the instance of Maj. Robert W. Canfield, one of the sport's outstanding aces, the supreme sacrifice has been made."[15]

While serving as a waist gunner on a B-17, the "Calamity Jane," testing a gun site he had developed, his plane was shot down over Germany on August 12, 1943. Some members of the crew were able to bail out, but he was among those killed in action. It was his only mission. Although widowed and pregnant with her third child, Mimi Jenkins continued to ferry planes until she grew so big she was ordered to stand down. Now without her husband, she went to California to be with her parents. It was there that Mimi would meet Matt Jenkins, beginning a new chapter in her life. Compared to what she had faced during the war, her later negotiations with the Pebble Beach Company, regarding the property she and Matt owned, were a trivial matter.[16]

As he had with William Beatty, Sam Morse tried to persuade Mimi and Matt to sell their property in the coming years. Morse was always pushing Jenkins to sell, said Mimi's daughter Pamela, but Matt argued that nobody "had enough money for him to give it up." The Julia

Morgan-designed home on the Beatty-Jenkins property was destroyed in a 1955 fire, an event which put Mimi's tenacity on display. Her daughter recalled, "As the fire roared, Mom threw on a brown skirt and yellow sweater. Then she carried out the family safe." The Jenkins's would rebuild on the same site and remained residents for the rest of their lives.[17]

Matt's passion for sailing lead to the creation of the Stillwater Yacht Club, and he and Mimi hosted numerous cocktail parties at their home in the 1950s and 1960s. They also had open houses every day at 5 p.m., informal affairs allowing friends to stop by and relax. Pebble Beach's own Sam Morse, as well as Ansel Adams, were among the guests. Mimi favored vodka and noted: "We do have parking, plumbing, and alcohol, so do stop by anytime."

When daughter Pam graduated from high school, Mimi and Matt chartered a bus to Pebble Beach for her and 40 Katharine Branson School classmates to attend a dinner dance at the Beach Club. The *San Francisco Examiner* reported, "The formal affair was followed by a party around huge bonfires on the beach after which the guests had breakfast at the Jenkins' Pebble Beach home before returning by bus to San Francisco." The article added, "It will be a long time before anyone duplicates the graduation party given for Pamela Canfield."[18]

Matt Jenkins had purchased the property in 1944, and although the golf course's fifth hole was on the other side of his backyard fence, he was never a golfer. Neither was Mimi, who married him seven years later. They became part of the background, as golfers blithely passed by their place daily. These included everyday amateurs who made pilgrimages to experience the famous course, as well as professionals who played in Bing Crosby's National Pro-Am tournament, which came to Pebble Beach in 1947. Most had no idea who the Jenkins's were. "Too busy chasing immortality to be curious," wrote David Kindred, "Jack Nicklaus passed the Jenkins place hundreds of times without knowing who lived there. 'Why would I?' he said."[19] Besides Nicklaus, the best players in the game all passed by their residence – Sam Snead, Ben Hogan, Byron Nelson, Billy Casper, and Tom Watson. And celebrities such as Sean Connery, Clint Eastwood, James Garner, Frank Sinatra, and Joe DiMaggio.

Mimi's daughter Pam recalls selling sandwiches during the Crosby to players and spectators alike, as there were no refreshment stands near the house in those days. Her autograph book contained the names of many who wandered by, including Jack Lemmon and Bob Hope (sadly, it was lost when the house burned down.) The U.S. Open came to Pebble Beach for the first time in 1972, and saw Jerry McGee and Bobby Mitchell both make holes-in-one on the fifth. For that event the tee had "been moved slightly right and the trees trimmed to nullify the long applied epithet of the 'world's only dogleg par-3.'"

It returned in 1982, and Bill Brodell, an unknown pro from Appleton, Wisconsin, added another ace. That same year Matt Jenkins passed away, leaving Mimi a widow for the second time. She was still not interested in selling. As she said, "Over my dead body will the Pebble Beach Company ever get this property."[20]

People might have known of Mimi Jenkins's resolute attitude in not giving up her home, but few, if any, knew of her family's social and political connections that impacted the history of this nation. Her grandfather was Charles Stelle Brown, born in New York City on March 19, 1851. At the age of 22, he opened his own real estate office in lower Manhattan. Among his firm's more notable transactions was selling the land on which the Brooklyn Bridge was built. In 1901 he formed a partnership with the brother-in-law of President Theodore Roosevelt, and the business is still active today as Brown Harris Stevens, LLC.

Perhaps Brown's "most notable contribution of a public nature to the well-being of the citizens of New York," claimed a 1937 biography, "was his service on the Tenement House Commission," which was appointed April 16, 1900, by Governor Theodore Roosevelt. At that time everything dangerous to public health was present in these fetid dwellings; "dark rooms and halls, closed skylights and air-shafts, defective and boxed-in plumbing, filth and disease, damp cellars, overcrowding...."

The conditions made infectious diseases such as tuberculosis commonplace. The odor, too, was also something one could not soon forget, as the "absence of any proper ventilation made the stench arising from the filthy halls and living rooms almost unendurable." More than two-thirds of New York's population lived in tenement houses, and there were more than eighty thousand of them in the city. In the late nineteenth century the Lower East Side and its tenements was one of the most densely populated places in the world.[21]

Governor Roosevelt believed that the movement to reform them was "vital to the well-being of our people," and urged action.

> Every wretched tenement that a city allows to exist revenges itself on the city by being a hotbed of disease and pauperism. It tends steadily to lower the tone of our city life and of our social life. The present movement for better tenement houses is an effort to cut at the roots of the diseases which eat at the body social and the body politic.[22]

The commission had 13 members, including Charles S. Brown, and consisted of builders, architects, lawyers, a former city health commissioner, and former chief of the New York Fire Department. Its goal was to ensure that future dwellings would have sufficient space, light, and fresh air in every room, proper sanitation, and fire protection, while making changes to the law requiring the alteration of old houses to make them fit for human habitation.

Lucy Nevins Barnes, about two years before her marriage to Charles S. Brown.

One tenement house inspector wrote that for the poor, the hungry, and the needy, the "teachings of Christ are forgotten. We do not know how our neighbors live, and we would rather not know. Not charity, but justice, is needed."[23]

The recommendations of Brown and the other commissioners were enacted into law by the

State Legislature, thus ameliorating the squalid conditions Jacob Riis – a friend of Roosevelt's – had outlined a decade earlier in his book, *How the Other Half Lives*. The Commission's work had a lasting positive effect.

Seven years after founding his real estate business, Charles Brown married Lucy Nevins Barnes. Born in Brooklyn, New York, March 15, 1859, she was the daughter of Henry Wheeler and Mary Caroline (Young) Barnes. An attractive woman who shared her husband's enthusiasm for sport, they were married in the New York's Fifth Avenue Presbyterian Church, June 3, 1880. When golf became popular in this country in the 1890s, Charles fully embraced the sport and became a member of one of the United States Golf Association's founding clubs, Shinnecock Hills. He would later hold memberships at Garden City Golf Club on Long Island, New York and the Jekyll Island Club in Georgia. "His favorite hobby was golf," noted his biography, "and even in recent years he played an extraordinarily good game for a man of his advanced age."[24]

Yet it was his wife who gained lasting fame as a golfer. Lucy Barnes Brown had four children from 1881 to 1889, the second being Lathrop Brown, Mimi Jenkins's father. Like her husband, Lucy enjoyed golf, playing frequently at Shinnecock Hills. The game offered women with one of the few acceptable expressions of their sporting interest given the social structures of the late 19th century, as they were believed to be physically fragile. The "woman on the pedestal," whose strengths were moral and emotional rather than physical, remained the ideal. Women were expected to be delicate and sensitive, cultivating compassion, gentleness, piety, and benevolence in their own special sphere – the home – where they were to raise children and be good mothers.[25]

Too much activity unnerved females, warned physicians, since it was believed the uterus was connected to the nervous system, and "overexertion threatened reproduction," with "weak and degenerate offspring" being the result. Since women were perceived to be physically weak, any recreation they partook in should be passive in nature. Accordingly, only select sports (such as golf, archery and croquet) were deemed suitable for not doing harm to their physical constitutions. "That the game is admirably adapted for a ladies' pastime there can be no doubt," wrote *Outing* magazine in 1890. "And it has the advantage of being an amusement in which the fair sex are not so heavily handicapped as in other games."[26]

As an upper-class woman, golf provided Lucy Barnes Brown with a way to express her athletic qualities in a socially acceptable way. Caroline Manice, a multiple champion of the Women's Metropolitan Golf Association (New York), had her own ideas on women playing sports. In 1904 she wrote that unlike men, who saw sport as "something to be enthralled in, to bet on and to fight over," women sought it for diversion, and they remained good friends no matter who won or lost.

Manice insisted that even in formal competitions, perhaps the central aim was "to renew old and make new friendships." It was suggested by most experts at that time that women who were too competitive displayed masculine characteristics. This hypothesis gave rise to a central and underlying tension in American women's sport that continues to this day – as Susan Cahn states, "the contradictory relationship between athleticism and womanhood."[27]

Lathrop Brown, Mimi Jenkins's father, was 12 when his 36-year-old mother competed in the inaugural U.S. Women's Amateur championship at Meadow Brook in Long Island, New York. Played

GOLF FOR HIGH HONORS.

MRS. CHARLES S. BROWN WINS THE FIRST WOMEN'S CHAMPIONSHIP.

Good Play on the Meadow Brook Links— Second and Third Prizes Won by Boston Golfers—Thirteen Players Start in the Competition in a Dense Mist and Fog.

New York claims the first amateur woman golfer of America, through the prowess on the Meadow Brook links yesterday of Mrs. Charles S. Brown, a resident of this city, who has learned the game to good advantage during her summer sojourns at Shinnecock Hills. Her victory was gained by the narrow margin of two strokes from Miss N. C. Sargent of the Essex Country Club, and the champion on the links near Boston, while third place in the competi-

Headline announcing Lucy Barnes Brown's victory, November 10, 1895.

November 9, 1895, a month after the inaugural U.S. Amateur, it was open to women belonging to member clubs of the less than year-old USGA (a condition which essentially excluded people of color and virtually all middle-class golfers, and would for decades to come.)[28] Democratization in the game would come later.

"The game was played under unfavorable conditions," reported *The New York Times*, "so far as both the weather and grounds were concerned." When play started shortly after 10 o'clock that morning, "a dull, heavy fog hung over the course, completely shutting off the sight of everything beyond the first bunker." Thirteen women entered that first event (by comparison, only 14 entered the inaugural U.S. Open that October.) A "large number of society people and enthusiastic golfers as well followed the contestants over the course of the match," reported the *Times*. "The contest for first prize was unusually close and exciting, and the many brilliant plays of Mrs. C.S. Brown of the Shinnecock Hills Golf Club and Miss N.C. Sargent of the Essex County Club were liberally applauded by the spectators. By steady play and excellent judgment in driving, Mrs. Brown succeeded in obtaining first prize."

On the final hole she made "good drives up the hill," and holed a putt of thirty feet for a six, "the best putt of the day." The New York *Sun* noted that Brown was "a graceful driver, but her great advantage was in finely directed approach strokes and putting." The event was described by the *Times* as "one of the gayest social events that have ever taken place at the Meadow Brook Hunt Club." Brown won "a beautiful cup offered by W.D. Winthrop and W.H. Sands," while a gold medal was given to the runner-up and a silver medal to the third-place finisher. "The title of champion lady golfer for the United States will be held until next year by Mrs. Brown. Then the $1,000 cup offered by Robert Cox, M.P., of Edinburgh, Scotland, will be played for on the Morris County (New Jersey) golf links."[29]

Many regarded Brown as "the strongest lady player in the United States, and her work yesterday was a beautiful exhibition of golfing." The *New York Herald* declared that it was "said at the club yesterday that the 132 strokes of Mrs. Brown was the best score for eighteen holes that any American woman has yet made. She was naturally very pleased with her victory, and was overheard to suggest that she thought she would mount in gold the ball which had won her the championship."[30]

This may have seemed an inauspicious beginning by today's standards, but scores are a very relative thing when observed through the prism of time. Equipment and course conditions were primitive. One must also consider what women had to wear while navigating the course.

This was at a time when the sight of a woman's ankle was almost scandalous, and when legs were still referred to as "limbs." Players were attired in long cloth or tweed skirts reaching from their waists to their ankles, with petticoats underneath that almost touched the shoe tops.

Jackets were worn by many, and blouses featured full-length sleeves and starched collars. Bulky, broad-brimmed hats adorned their heads, and heavy shoes or boots on their feet completed the restrictive wardrobe. Alexa Stirling, winner of three U.S. Women's Amateurs by 1920, played in high tight collars that nearly choked her. When looking at the ball as she swung, "my eyes must have appeared as though they would leave their sockets altogether," she would vividly remember.[31]

In the early years the attire was featured almost as much as the golf in many new reports. "The costumes of the ladies were very attractive and pretty. Gray skirts with brown leggings and white, blue, or red waists were the predominating features of the golf costumes." Lucy Brown wore a "gray dress, with scarlet blouse, black necktie and hat, and a cape of tartan plaid lining thrown over her shoulder." Sadly, decades would pass before personal appearance did not provide fodder for articles on women's golf.

The battle of the sexes would continue for generations. "When women in America first began to play golf," wrote two-time U.S. Women's Amateur champion Genevieve Hecker in 1902, "they were allowed at many of the big clubs to use the links only at certain hours on certain days when it was thought that their presence would not incommode the Lords of Creation...The women took their hardly won permission with joy, and proceeded to demonstrate that they could play good golf by taking on their detractors for a round and soundly beating them."[32]

Lucy Barnes Brown proved that she could play, and would continue to do so, although she never competed in another U.S. Women's Amateur. In 1899 *The New York Times* reported that since her big win in 1895, "Mrs. Brown has appeared but seldom in big events, although she keeps in constant practice every summer in Southampton. Her game yesterday showed that her hand has by no means lost its cunning, as she made the credible score of 111 strokes" to qualify for the match play portion of the Hudson Cup matches. Ruth Underhill, the 1899

U.S. Women's Amateur champion, also qualified with a 106. Although Brown was ultimately defeated in match play, it demonstrates that she maintained a high enough profile since 1895 to warrant attention from the *Times*.[33]

The early 1900's were filled with family events for Charles and Lucy Brown. Lathrop graduated from Harvard (1903), oldest son Archibald became a father (1904), Lathrop married (1911), and granddaughter Mimi's birth followed in 1913. On September 30, 1921, Lucy died at her summer home in Mount Kisco, New York. She was only 62 years old, and had been a member of the Colony Club and of the National Society of Colonial Dames in the state of New York. Lucy's husband Charles lived to see Mimi marry, but passed away a month before the birth of her first child, George, in 1935.[34]

Mimi Jenkins ended up living on the other side of the country, far removed from her native New York. She never became a golfer and never spoke of her grandmother's golf exploits. It is therefore somewhat ironic that her life took her to one of the most iconic golf courses in the world and impacted its evolution and destiny. After her husband Matt passed away in 1982, she continued to joust with Pebble Beach.

When the company wanted to build another course in the area in the mid-1980s, it went to the local government and the California Coastal Commission for the proper permits. They were to be granted on the condition that all the beaches have public access, including the one on Mimi's property. Realizing she had a bargaining chip, she next demonstrated a political savvy that would have made her ex-Congressman father proud. In exchange for access to the beach, Mimi asked that the company rebuild the pier below Stillwater Cove that had been washed away by a storm. The company agreed, and spent $850,000 on the new Matthew C. Jenkins Pier. In exchange, The Links at Spanish Bay, designed by Tom Watson and Sandy Tatum, came into being in 1987.

Mimi Jenkins passed away March 7, 1995 (a century after her grandmother's victory in the U.S. Women's Amateur), and soon after her children opted to put the property up for sale. For the first time, the Pebble Beach Company was in a position to purchase this missing link and fulfill the original vision of a hole along the coastline.[35]

The purchase price was $8.25 million, and the parcel was subdivided into three lots. The outer one, along the coast, was used for the new hole, while the two inner lots were sold as home sites. "Don Lucas, a prominent West Coast automobile dealer, purchased one," noted *The San Francisco Examiner*, "and the other went to Charles Schwab, the well-known investment broker," as both helped negotiate the deal. Magnificent homes now occupy each. "Even with this, the final cost of the hole, including land, design, construction, and permitting costs, came in right at $3 million – enough to build an entire golf course in most places."[36]

Jack Nicklaus was chosen to design the hole, and after numerous delays, including an extended battle over the removal of an ancient oak tree, it was completed in November 1998. When the company began moving dirt on the site before Nicklaus took over, it found abalone shell ornaments, mussel shell-carved fishhooks, and other antiquities left by the indigenous peoples who inhabited the area a thousand years ago. It also found a burial site.

The new fifth hole at Pebble Beach looking out onto Stillwater Cove. U.S. Open, 2019.

The late Dr. Gary Breschini, an anthropologist and expert on prehistoric Indian tribes of Monterey, along with his wife, Pebble Beach's archaeological consultant, assessed the findings. "Whenever you encounter human remains," explained Breschini, "you have to stop and inform the coroner." The coroner investigated, and after consultation with Native American representatives, the remains were "reburied in that

Homes to the left of the fifth hole at Pebble Beach looking in the direction of the old hole. U.S. Open, 2019.

area with as little disturbance as possible." Like Old Tom Morris finding human bones and skulls from an ancient burial ground when he built the new 18th green on the Old Course at St Andrews in 1866, and workers uncovering an Indian burial ground beneath the 12th green at Augusta National in 1932, the new fifth hole at Pebble Beach has its own connection with the spirits of the past.[37]

The new green is about the same size as the old one, although it slopes severely toward the ocean, and has a similar bunker set up, with two on the right and one on the left. "I think the hole looks like it's always been part of the golf course," said Nicklaus upon its completion. "It's nice to be part of the history of this course." On November 18, 1998, special guests, including the two surviving daughters of Samuel Morse, and Charlie Seaver, who played in the 1929 U.S. Amateur, attended a special luncheon to celebrate its opening. Missing were the children of Mimi Jenkins, who were never contacted.[38]

"The new fifth is probably a bit easier to play than the old fifth," reported a newspaper ahead of the 2000 U.S. Open, "unless the wind is howling." Thongchai Jaidee would make a hole-in-one there when the event returned in 2010. The new hole has been widely praised, but there are still those who think the old one wasn't all that bad, and lament its passing. It was an uphill tee shot that added a club or club and a half to the distance, with a large bunker looming on the right side.

"The right of the hole was bordered by the cart path," wrote a course superintendent who played it many times, "and immediately right of that, a stone wall running the length of the hole. The left side was hazard, a large eucalyptus grove, with branches almost hanging over the green. Precision was paramount. A miscue could be a card wrecker." Dan Forsman, a five-time winner on the PGA Tour, thought it was a great hole. "You get a little bit of wind blowing and you had to be precise."

Well-known golf course architect Tom Doak asserted in 2012: "It wasn't really a bad hole, just a disappointing hole, as you had to break away from the ocean to avoid someone's oceanfront house. It was a narrow tee shot through a little hourglass in the trees, playing a bit uphill to a very steep, terraced, back-to-front green. If you got over the back of the green, you were dead." It should be pointed out that the short seventh hole, one of the most photographed in the world, was thought to be a weak link in Pebble Beach's early years.[39]

"It seemed to be the consensus of opinion that Hole No. 7 must go," reported *The San Francisco Examiner* in 1920. "A putter is the only club in a regular bag that can make the grade, unless the shot be spared. But there is an excellent chance for a wonderful one-shot hole to be made out of the eighth...." The article proposed that a tee be placed before the chasm on the eighth fairway "with the ocean underneath." The hole would then create an "international reputation for itself as a ball loser and a nerve tester. The second rater could then choose to make the elbow route in two shots. And the fairway [thus] saved could be used to convert No. 7 into a real hole."[40]

A hundred years later the seventh remains, while the fifth hole is no longer the black sheep of the family. The players who competed in the 2019 U.S. Open, and the fans who watched them in person and on television and streaming video, will most likely never know who Sam Morse, Mimi Jenkins, or Lucy Barnes Brown were, but they should.

Sam Morse finally has the hole he wanted. As his grandson wrote in 2018, "His imagination never stopped sparking and he made things happen through force, charm, determination, teamwork, and grit."

Mimi Jenkins liked Sam Morse. He was a great friend, but his determination and charm could never move her to give up the home she loved while she was alive. Her grandmother Lucy Barnes Brown was a pioneer of women's golf by virtue of her victory in the 1895 U.S. Women's Amateur. One-hundred years later, her family was still making history.

To Mike Antoncich IV, his grandmother Mimi "was a lady of her class and time, humble and generous, not ostentatious in any way because she felt no need to impress anyone. And while she wanted to like everyone, she took no guff...Hey, to me, she was as big as Pebble Beach. It was cool."[41] The whole story of her family and life, and how she influenced the history of this iconic golf course is more than cool, it is truly remarkable.

The Brown family plot in the Green-Wood Cemetery, Brooklyn, New York. Lucy Brown's grave is on the first row, far right (small flat stone below ground) and husband Charles next to her (large flat stone.)

Chapter 10: The St Andrews "Rabbit Wars" of 1801-1821

Legendary golf writer Bernard Darwin devoted a small chapter of his 1932 book *Out of the Rough* to "The 'Ifs' of Golfing History." What if steel shafts hadn't been legalized and we still played with hickory? What if the gutta percha ball hadn't been replaced by the rubber-cored "Haskell" ball? What if the Old Course in St Andrews, Scotland had been rendered unplayable by rabbits and abandoned in the early 1800s? What? Actually, Darwin left the last one out of his book, but it's an interesting question to consider. People may know about hickory shafts and the Haskell ball, but have no idea what rascally rabbits had to do with the most famous golf course in the world.

Golf had been played for at least 250 years over the Pilmor Links of St Andrews when a brouhaha erupted between the gentleman golfers of the Royal and Ancient Golf Club (then known as the Society of St Andrews Golfers) and the family that leased the Links land, triggering the so called "Rabbit Wars" that almost brought things to a grinding halt. It sounds rather ominous, and conjures up images of a violent conflict, but it's a true story that happened on the most famous course in the world.

Archbishop John Hamilton was granted a license by the city of St Andrews, dated January 25th, 1552, to keep rabbits in the northern part of the links, reserving the common right of "playing at golf, football, schuting, at all gamis, with all uther manner of pastyme, as ever thai pleis" to the people. The "Rabbit Wars" began, as do many things, with politicians mucking things up.[1]

St Andrews was in decline by the end of the 18th century, as its population had declined nearly 30% from fifty years earlier. Samuel Johnson, on his tour of Scotland in 1771, referred to the "silence and solitude of inactive indigence and gloomy depopulation" of St Andrews. The Town Council was in need of cash to keep it afloat, and in February 1797 it persuaded two local merchants, John Gunn and Robert Gourlay to advance the town £2080 Sterling [about $340,000 today.] As security against the loan the two men acquired a bond over the links that gave them the right to sell "whole or part of the subjects" at public auction.

They did just that in November 1797, selling part of the land extending for some three miles along the coast, to Thomas Erskine (later the 9th Earl of Kellie) for £805.[2]

The area concerned in the sale was 280 acres bounded by the sea and the Swilcan Burn on the east, the Eden estuary on the north, and part of the lands of Strathtyrum on the west and south. The portion of the Old Course now forming the 1st and 18th fairways and lying east of the Burn was not included and has never been out of public ownership. In August 1799, Erskine sold the feu (right to the use of land for an annual payment) to Charles Dempster and his son Cathcart.[3] Trouble ensued soon thereafter.

The Dempsters rented the land for £130 a year (about $15,000 today) to one James Begbie, who bred rabbits on their behalf, selling the pelts and meat. For almost two years the rabbits did what they do best, until their numbers overwhelmed the Links, with the scrapes and holes they made in the ground becoming an increasing nuisance to the golfers.

The situation came to a head in October 1801, when George Cheape, Captain of the Society of Golfers, wrote a letter to the Town Council.

> The Golfing Society are extremely concerned to find the Golfing ground so much cut up and destroyed by the Rabbits in the Links, and which if not speedily presented must land in the total destruction of the golf ground. It is unnecessary for the Golfing Society to suggest to your Honors that the destruction of the Links will be a severe loss to the good city in point of emolument is it will have the tendency to put an end to the ancient society of golfers which has now subsisted here for time immemorial....[4]

Cheape hoped to persuade the Council to "see the necessity of doing something speedily," and members of the Society kept playing and complaining, but precious little changed.

When Hugh Cleghorn, owner of an 1,800-acre estate in Stravithie, became Captain in 1802, he upped the ante. Meeting minutes from January 15, 1803 show that the Society of Golfers believed the

Links had been "rendered almost entirely useless for golfing," by the Dempsters, "having converted them into a rabbit warren, by bringing new colonies of these animals from different places, by letting them to a tenant with a view to multiply the breed, and of profiting by the sale...." Cleghorn moved to have members of the Club contribute to a fund "sufficient for vindicating their right before the Court of Sessions...," and twelve members formed a committee "for the purpose of carrying on the prosecution against the Dempsters."[5]

Cathcart Dempster wrote to Cleghorn on January 25, 1803, offering to find a person to keep the Links in good order. He said he would pay the difference between this person's wages and the sum then expended by the Club for the repair

Rabbit near the 16th hole of the Old Course, during the 2015 Open Championship.

and upkeep of the course. This, however, did nothing to stop the move to prosecute Cathcart and his father. Contributions poured in – from as far away as India and the West Indies – as the fund reached almost £1,000.[6] For another two years a case was built against the Dempsters, and in February, 1805 the golfer's (plaintiffs) case, filling twenty-four pages, was ready. It was prepared by John Clerk, who had such a stellar reputation as a litigator it was once said that half the business before the courts went through his hands. The Dempsters, asserted Clerk, admitted in a newspaper article that they had brought in 200 rabbits, not content with the few found in the sandhills on the links. On May 17, 1805 the Court of Sessions ruled for the plaintiffs, and that December a "State of the Process" report was issued.[7]

The plaintiffs maintained that the inhabitants of the city, the gentlemen in the neighborhood, and "all others who chose to resort thither for the purpose of playing golf, have, for time immemorial, enjoyed the constant and uninterrupted privilege of playing golf" on the ground known as Pilmor Links or Links of St Andrews, and that privilege was being threatened. They pointed out that the magistrates and Town Council had historically restricted tenants' actions – they were not to plough up "any part of the said golfing course" or do anything that might injure the course.[8] In a time before lawn mowers and modern agronomy, the golfing ground was very rough to begin with, and the rabbits only made it worse.

At the time of purchase by the Dempsters, the tenant was James Ritchie, a butcher, who pastured only sheep on the Links. His lease did not expressly prohibit using the land as a warren, nor did it prohibit planting, enclosing, or other uses inconsistent with the privilege of golf. It was argued that the "tenant should not have it in his power to make use of the said links as a rabbit warren...."

If action was not taken, the links would "soon be rendered altogether unfit for the purpose of playing golf" and they moved that the Dempsters get rid of the rabbits and "keep and preserve the said Golf Links, or course of golfing, in the same state of good order, and entirely as they have been for ages in time past...." As Harry S.C. Everard wrote in *A History of the Royal & Ancient Golf Club St Andrews from 1754-1900*, the ground was to be preserved "for the comfort and amusement, etc. of the inhabitants and others."[9]

Witnesses testified to the condition of the course, with most agreeing that it had declined perceptibly. Charles Robertson, who for twenty-five years had served as the greenskeeper, had resigned from that position four years earlier because he could not keep up with the repair of the scrapes created by the rabbits. George Mitchell said

ADVERTISEMENT.

In an Advertisement, signed by Mr Cathcart Dempster, dated the 29th instant, he complains of an intention in the Magistrates of St Andrew's, and Society of Golfers, to destroy his, and his Father's Property.——For be it from them to infringe the legal property of any man, but this is a *Species of Property* without any right or title whatever, and assumed merely on their own authority.

An attempt to establish a Rabbit-Warren on the Links of St Andrew's, is most certainly unjustifiable in itself, because, at the time the feu of them was disposed of, the Magistrates never meant that this use should be made of them, and in which, by the issue of the Suit, lately determined, Mess. Dempsters have not been supported by that *Law* to which they say they have appealed. So very much the contrary, —on their protesting against Four of the Gentlemen of the Golfing Society, who went out in open day to assert their unquestionable right to destroy the Rabbits; and, on their applying to the Lord Ordinary for an interdict to prevent such conduct in future, the interdict was refused by his Lordship.

Part of an advertisement by the Town Magistrates protesting the Dempsters's rabbit warren, 1806.

that before the Dempsters and their tenant arrived, there were very few rabbit scrapes or occasions when his ball found one, but now he claimed on one occasion his ball found "a scrape three holes running."[10]

George Robertson, who had been a caddie for twenty-five years, claimed that before the Dempsters, rabbits were not numerous and people had the right to kill them. There had always been "small holes or scrapes likewise in the course, but there are fifty now for one there was formerly...." The total number of scrapes and holes was even entered into the record – 895, with the most being the 232 found between the 7th and 8th holes.

The Dempsters, for their part, denied that the links had been rendered unfit for playing golf, asserting they were "actually just now, and have been, since the commencement of the process, in the best possible order." The Dempsters admitted the golfers had a right to play (although this right was determined by custom and not law), but claimed nobody had the right to destroy the rabbits. On February 17, 1806 the St Andrews Town Council had joined the plaintiffs, claiming it never considered itself "at liberty to

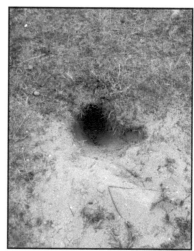

Hole dug by a rabbit on the 7th hole at the Old Course, 2016.

sell the lands for a rabbit warren on account of the long and uninterrupted servitude of golfing by the citizens, society of golfers, and others over their links."[11]

The plaintiffs' argument seemed to resonate with those whose opinion mattered. On May 18, 1806 court magistrates issued an interlocutor to the effect that the Society had the right to destroy the rabbits, and that it was the clear responsibility of the defendants to see that no damage be done to the golfing ground.[12]

Two months later a defiant Cathcart Dempster published a signed advertisement addressed to "the Inhabitants of St Andrews." "You have been stimulated by unsigned advertisements," he began, "in the name of the Magistrates and Golfers, to destroy the private property of my father and I on the Links of St Andrews, on the ground that you had an undoubted and legal right to do so – but I would advise you to pause, before you venture to act upon such vague authority." You can almost see the blood rushing to his face as he wrote down the words. "Far be it from me," he continued, "to encroach upon any of your *lawful* privileges, but...*killing of rabbits* on these Links is NOT one of them."

He next addressed the uproar "raised against the proprietors of the Links, for using them as a Rabbit-Warren, as if they had committed an unlawful deed. I must, however, inform those who make this noise, that they labour under a great mistake; for the doing so is *strictly lawful* being particularly recommended by ACT of PARLIAMENT."[13]

He had a point to make, and made it. As far back as 1726 the Town Council had allowed William Gib "to put and place his black and whyte rabbits or cunnings on the Links of this city and that during the Council's pleasure he shall have the sole and privilege and power" of disposing of them, provided that he should "not suffer the said Links when the golfing is used to be spoiled in any ways." The Council could recall the grant at a month's notice. The strongest point the Dempsters may have had to defend their position was a letter from Lord Kellie, captain of the Society of Golfers in 1798, to George Forgan in 1799, that authorized Forgan to "protect the rabbits or convert the ground into a rabbit warren." Lord Kellie promised him rabbits from Cambo, and in a deposition Forgan stated that he could have paid the rent in no other way but by using the Links as a warren. The precedent had been established. What was in question was whether the rabbits were spoiling the grounds.[14]

Dempster argued that at the time "the Town Council of St Andrews granted my father and I a Disposition to the Links, *they were actually under a tack* [lease] *for 19 years as a RABBIT WARREN*: and which tack we were taken bound to fulfil [sic]. But, you'll naturally ask, who granted this tack and who wrote it? Why, I'll tell you! The *then and present* CHIEF MAGISTRATE of St Andrews GRANTED IT, and the *then and present* TOWN-CLERK of St Andrews WROTE IT!!!"

Cathcart made a valid argument, and it gives one pause to consider the politics of the case. On the one hand there were the proper gentleman golfers, many of whom represented the inherited wealth of their forefathers, playing a rich man's game in their red jackets and resenting the pesky rabbits that were interfering with their leisure

236

pleasures. On the other hand were the Dempsters, successful merchants who were also members of the golfing society, but whose money perhaps was not "old" enough.

Charles Dempster set up the first bank in St Andrews. His son Cathcart began a canvas factory, introduced the selling of mussels as bait at the Eden Estuary, improved the harbor on several occasions, and proposed street lighting for the town. He also purchased property as a site for the new town hall, brought boats and crews to the town from Shetland to improve the fishing industry, and set up a subscription list by which the poor of St Andrews were supplied with meal at a discount. Even if they had the law on their side and had done good works, Charles and Cathcart were outnumbered. As Oliver Wendell Holmes supposedly said, "It's a court of law, not a court of justice."[15]

In a public reply a week later to Cathcart's testy defense, the magistrates of St Andrews and the Society of Golfers countered that a rabbit-warren on the links was "certainly unjustifiable in itself, because, at the time the feu of them was disposed of, the Magistrates never meant that this use should be made of them."

Referring to the suit that had been brought and the interlocutor issued two months earlier in favor of the plaintiffs, the Dempsters were not "supported by that *Law* to which they say they have appealed. So very much to the contrary – on their protesting against four of the GENTLEMAN of the GOLFING SOCIETY, who went out in open day to assert their unquestionable right to destroy the Rabbits, and on their applying to the Lord Ordinary for an interdict to prevent such conduct in future, the interdict was refused...." The killing of the rabbits had been upheld, but hostilities continued. New battle lines were drawn by the two sides, and détente would not be achieved for more than a decade.

"The irrepressible Mr. Dempster meantime continued his evil courses," wrote H.S.C. Everard; he "encroached, he ploughed up, he defaced." It was charged that Dempster had placed traps and "poison in the open grounds, in order to destroy the dogs who follow their masters to the Links, in which he has been but too successful." The minutes of the R&A from November 1806 indicate that a committee was formed "to guard against any encroachment made on the links, particularly a dyke [low wall] that Mr. Dempster is now making between the third and fourth holes."[16]

On December 29, 1806 an injunction was granted to keep outsiders from killing the Dempster's rabbits, but it didn't resolve tensions. In March 1807 a letter was presented to the Club by a member of the R&A, John Fraser, who complained of the "malevolent threatenings," indulged in by Mr. Dempster, whose tenant James Begbie "nearly murdered" Fraser two months earlier as a reprisal for events the previous June. What, if any, satisfaction the victim obtained is not known. One can only imagine how unsettling it was for the golfers who ventured out to play in such a hostile environment.[17]

The Dempsters did win an appeal to keep their rabbits from being destroyed by outsiders. The records are scant as to the specific behavior of the parties during those years, but more appeals and decrees followed until 1812, when the matter went to the House of Lords. After a four day hearing, Lord Eldon (the Lord Chancellor of England), found that there had been inconsistencies in the decisions of the lower court and referred it back to the Court of Session in Scotland.

On review, the court found as incompetent the finding that the plaintiffs had the right to destroy the rabbits, and recalled that part of the judgment. With regard to the golfing grounds, the Town Council had "no rights whatsoever in so far as respects it, so long as their feu duty continues to be regularly paid." In deciding the case, Lord Eldon noted that if it were possible to feed cattle on the land, golf balls might have found their way into what cattle occasionally leave behind them, and the golfers would have been "in a worse scrape than if he got into a rabbit scrape."[18]

> The Proprietor of these Links therefore has the highest legal authority in the Kingdom for the full enjoyment of his property. His conviction is that under the dicta of the Lord Chancellor he has the right of having a Rabbit-Warren there whenever he chooses…but on the contrary, wishing to evince his good will to the Honorable Company of Golfers, of which he is himself one of the oldest members, he has ordered his game keeper and has given

238

permission to his friends to destroy the Rabbits to
prevent the possibility of injuring the links – so that
at present few of those animals are to be seen.

There is no evidence of any further proceedings by the parties after this
point.[19]

Lasting peace finally came in 1821, when James Cheape
purchased the links. A wealthy landowner, he was a former Captain of
the Society of Golfers – in 1787, the year the United States Constitution
was written. As a young man, Cheape went to India and was employed in
the civil establishment by the East India Company, for many years at the
presidency in Bombay. He returned to Scotland and in 1782 acquired the
estate of Strathtyrum, which adjoins the southern boundary of the
Links.[20]

Cheape lived a quiet life on his estate, but was drawn into the
battle when crops on his Balgrove farm were destroyed by rabbits, which
consumed "the corn, turnip, and potatoe [sic] crops...." One of the
witnesses in the 1805 case, George Russel, who had owned a rabbit
warren of his own, estimated that there were 900 rabbits on the Links,
and testified that they could travel a mile to search for food, which they
found in abundance on Cheape's farm.[21]

It's hard to know why James Cheape bought the Links, but it
was fortuitous he became the owner when he did. Perhaps he wanted
more land; perhaps it was his love of golf. Whatever the reason, when he
became the owner in 1821, he changed the history of the course. His
agent John Govan notified him in a letter dated July 13th of that year:

I give you joy of becoming the purchaser of the
Pilmor Links, which I have this moment effected at
the upset price of £3150...I hope you continue to be
satisfied with your acquisition, which always
seemed to me to add very much indeed to the dignity
of Strathtyrum, whose eastern boundary will now be
washed twice a day, so long as the world remains, by
the German Ocean [North Sea].[22]

George Cheape, in a letter dated July 17, 1821, congratulated his
brother on becoming "the Laird of St Andrews Links, and I sincerely
hope you will enjoy them...I don't say they will ever be a profitable

concern...[but] I have no doubt but the people will be very happy they have at least come into your hands."[23] Little did George know that today St Andrews would have seven courses – with golfers coming from all over the world to play some 45,000 rounds a year on the Old Course alone. In 1979 the green fee was £5. Forty years later, in 2019, it was £190 during the high season (£90 in low season.) Certainly George, it has become a profitable concern.[24]

Cheape also took steps to define the boundaries of the course by having it surveyed and marked with "march stones" denoting the edges of the golfing grounds. On March 24, 1768 the Town Council had approved an agreement "relative to the settling the marches and placing march stones betwixt the lands of Strathtyram [sic], and the North Haugh and Pilmour Links belonging to the town," but nothing more was done. On March 18, 1777, a petition was submitted by the lease holder, Robert Nicol, asking that the "Golf Links should be marked out so that he might not encroach thereon by ploughing or otherwise."[25]

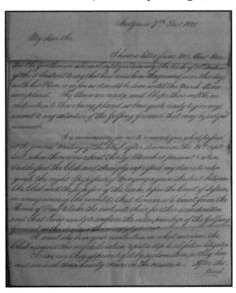

Letter from James Cheape discussing the placing of boundary stones, December 7, 1821.

The boundaries stones were finally set when Cheape purchased the Links. In a letter to Colonel Bethune of Blebo dated December 7, 1821 he explained: "I have a letter from Mr. Alex Martin, the Gentleman whom I employed to survey the links of St Andrews...to say that he would be on the ground as on this day, with his Plan, so as far as it could be done until the March Stones were placed. The stones are ready and I hope there will be no obstruction to their being placed, as I am ready to give my consent to any extention [sic] of the Golfing Ground that may be judged reasonable."[26]

In the same letter Cheape made note of a meeting he had on September 28th with thirty members of the Club, and his desire to relinquish the right to pursue any legal action with regard to his right to use the land for any means he wished. He "was ready to confirm the entire privilege of the Golfing Ground, as the Society at present proposed it." Cheape reminded Bethune how the members had received his "declaration to put a stop to all future litigation. I may say, they approved of it by acclamation as they honoured me with three hearty cheers on the occasion." James Cheape's magnanimity thus effectively ended the Rabbit Wars. The survey he commissioned is the oldest known plan of the Old Course and defined not only the boundaries of the course, but also outlined each hole and its yardage.

James Cheape died in 1824, leaving no children. He was succeeded by his brother George, twenty years his junior, who was Laird of Strathtyrum until his death in 1850. It was George who was the first to warn the Town Council in 1801 of the damage being done to the course by the rabbits. His grandson James, himself a member of the R&A, sold the Links to the Club in 1894 for £5000 (about $800,000 today), but the family remained in control of the estate.[27] In the family papers preserved at the University of St Andrews there are account books kept by this James Cheape. They indicate him selling, from 1904 to 1910 to Robert Pratt, butcher in St Andrews – what else – rabbits! Today you still see a hare or two while taking a stroll around the Old Course, but the war waged against them ended two hundred years ago, allowing the course to survive – and thrive – in peace.

The legacy of the Cheape family is still present on the Old Course today. The Cheape's Bunker, on the second hole and about 150 yards in front of the 17th tee remains, and the Strathtyrum course, built in 1993, is another reminder of his influence. The march stones are still there, and most evident on the fairway of the fifth hole, where one sees what looks like small green tombstones – they are covered by plywood and artificial turf to blend in with the grass. On one side they have a "G," denoting the golfing ground, and on the other a "C," indicating Cheape's land.

One can see how much wider the course is now. As the game became more popular and the course was getting more crowded in the late 1800s, more room was needed for the players. When Old Tom Morris came back to St Andrews from Prestwick in 1864 to be the keeper of the green, he almost singlehandedly cleared much of the gorse from the right side of the course, widening it substantially. What was once the edge of the course is now the middle of the fifth fairway, as evidenced by the march stones.

March stones, covered in the fairway on the 5th hole (left), and one uncovered by the author next to the 9th tee.

It's amazing to think that golfers from Allan Robertson, Old and Young Tom Morris, Harry Vardon, Bobby Jones, Sam Snead, Arnold Palmer, Jack Nicklaus, Tom Watson, and Tiger Woods have all walked by those stones put in the ground in 1821. It's a wonderful connection to the past, and golfers from all over the world who play the course each year pass by them without even knowing what they are. Neither do they know of the trouble rabbits caused over 200 years ago and how different things might have been had James Cheape not bought the Links. It's a story that for the most part remains hidden in the shadows, and one I wanted to share here. It's a fun story, no?

Chapter 11: Not Quite Good Enough – "Sexism, Class, and Racism in Women's Golf"

The late British golf writer Peter Dobereiner once wrote, "Golf has been soaking in the male chauvinist piggery for 500 years and so it cannot be eradicated overnight."[1] Sexism has been, and to a lesser extent still is, a fact of life for female golfers. Women have also been divided amongst each other along racial and class lines.

Mildred "Babe" Didrikson is the archetypical example of a pioneering female athlete whose femininity and sexuality were constantly questioned from the time she arrived on the national scene until she married in 1938. She took the 1932 Olympic Games by storm, winning two gold medals and one silver in track and field, impressing all with her overwhelming athleticism. A *Dallas Morning News* editorial argued that Didrikson was "too good for her own sex," adding that she was a living example of how rigorous athletic activity could create "a new super-physique in womanhood." This evolution, it was feared, could threaten male superiority in areas other than sports. Sportswriter Grantland Rice found Babe's talent overwhelming and her wit refreshing, and featured her in many articles, introducing her to the nation. He hailed her as "the athletic phenomenon of all time, man or woman."[2]

However, she was too masculine and not pretty enough to avoid future scrutiny. A 1933 *Redbook* article, for example, casually mentioned that she liked men just to "horse around" with and not "make love" to, adding that Babe's fondness for her best girlfriends far surpassed her affection for any man. In the early 1930s the press ridiculed her for her "hatchet face," "door-stop jaw," and "button breasted" chest. [3]

Sportswriter Paul Gallico, in an article for *Vanity Fair* in October 1932, described her as a "muscle moll" and "girl-boy" and more than a dozen times used word boy to describe her. Gallico claimed she was the vanguard of a breed of women "who made possible deliciously frank and biological discussions in the newspapers as to whether this or that woman athlete should be addressed as Miss, Mrs. Mr., or It."[4]

Nine years later, in his book *Farewell to Sport*, he remembered her at the Olympics as "a tomboy who never wore makeup, who shingled her hair until it was as short as a boy's and never bothered to comb it...She had a boy's body, slim, straight, curveless, and she looked her best in a track suit. She hated women and loved to beat them. She was not, at that time, pretty." He contended that she became a great athlete "simply because she would not or could not compete with women at their own and best game – man-snatching. It was an escape, a compensation."

Didrikson used her subsequent fame to tour with basketball and baseball teams across the country and was paid for her athletic endeavors – the American dream come true for the daughter of Norwegian immigrants. She was introduced to golf while in high school, and when she took it up again after the Olympics, was fully absorbed by it. As she told a reporter in 1933, "Most things come natural to me, and golf was the first that ever gave me much trouble."[5] She began to take lessons and practiced long hours while working a full-time job, making it her goal to win the U.S. Women's Amateur.

Peggy Kirk Bell, a good friend of Didrikson's, said that in those years girls in sports were "tomboys and a little weird they thought. Women were supposed to stay home and cook." Women were meant to be school teachers, nurses, secretaries, and housekeepers, or not work at all but raise children. Bell's father didn't allow her to work and financed her golf "because he thought it was respectable. I wanted to go play softball and he said girls don't do that." Anthropologist Margaret Mead contended in 1935 that women had two choices in life – she could proclaim herself "a woman and therefore less an achieving individual, or an achieving individual and therefore less a woman."[6]

From its beginnings in this country, as we learned with Lucy Barnes Brown, golf offered women an acceptable outlet for sporting activity given the restrictive social mores of the time. As late as 1936, just four years after Didrikson's Olympic triumphs, Professor Donald A. Laird argued in a magazine article titled "When Ladies Compete" that, as a general rule, it was a "good thing" if women weren't interested in athletics. It had been "noted by many scientific observers that feminine muscular development interferes with motherhood," and there were those who feared women becoming "a race of maternally functionless Amazons." The author of the article said women didn't "look pretty flexing their muscles and sweating like a bunch of truck horses, and they're certainly getting nowhere aping men athletes. More sane sports, more enjoyable sports; less accent on the Amazon, and a little more on the woman."[7]

Babe Didrikson's athleticism set her apart from other women, and because she wasn't pretty enough, Paul Gallico said she couldn't "compete with the other girls in the very ancient and honored sport of mantrapping." Westbrook Pegler, who played with Didrikson, Gallico, and Grantland Rice after the Olympics, said that "Babe probably did not know it but she was a beautiful woman – from the mouth down," saying she had a "shapely" body and beautiful legs. "I certainly do not mean to be unkind in saying this," he added, but he was.[8] Sentiments like these stung Babe, especially when writers said she didn't have much interest in men.

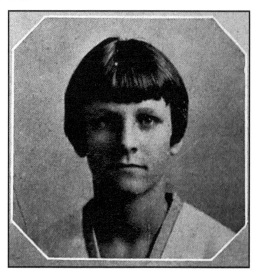

Yearbook photo of Babe Didrikson, Beaumont High School, 1928.

She created a marketable persona for public consumption and hustled for whatever she could get. She had been born poor and didn't want to remain that way. She also didn't live to please the press. Didrikson began to act more mannish, and seemed to glory in a coarse demeanor. "Her physique, her trousers and plain shirts, her short-cropped hair," wrote biographer Susan Cayleff, "and her sheer competence in the male realm of competitive sports presented an intimidating image" to a society that saw these traits as a threat to the ideal image of femininity, and put into question her sexual orientation.[9]

One article in a Dallas newspaper made note of her "almost wholly masculine" features and "husky voice." When the reporter tried to ask her if she wore brassieres and other feminine lingerie, she was indignant. "The answer is no. What do you think I am, a sissy?" To her, "sissy" was synonymous with a lady "loser."

Being thrust into the national spotlight was a heavy burden for an unsophisticated young woman to carry, and Babe had difficulty coping. Arthur Daley of *The New York Times*, after meeting Babe in 1933 and discussing her future plans, left the interview feeling sorry for her. Babe was an unsympathetic character, and almost overnight became a symbol of the negative effects competitive sport could have on women. In her home state of Texas signs were posted in women's gyms: "Don't be a muscle moll."[10]

Dr. Belle Mead Holm, a former dean of the Women's Physical Education Department at Lamar University, said Babe had to overcome the "viciousness" and "cannibalism" displayed by women who despised her. Paul Gallico suggested that "women golfers seem to be the worst sports and cattiest of all the strenuous sisters...." Edward T. Kennedy, swimming coach at Columbia and Olympics official believed that men were more frank when dealing with each other, and didn't repress themselves. "Men pop off where women may not speak up for themselves in case of poor treatment but nurse a grudge until it grows out of proportion to its importance." Dr. Holm contended Didrikson had to be fierce to survive. "Babe simply had to have a warlike spirit."[11]

Bertha Bowen, Babe's good friend and mentor, said that in those days it "wasn't ladylike to be muscular," and her physicality created tension on all sides, as both her gender and sexuality came into question. "Of course, that's where her courage came in. I never understood how she had the strength to overlook the snubs and slights and the downright venom of a lot of women."[12]

Having taken up golf in earnest after the Olympics, Didrikson played in the 1935 Texas Women's Amateur. By competing against top players, she felt this was a good way of testing the progress she had made. Few expected Didrikson to win her first major event, so it came as a shock to many when she beat Peggy Chandler 2 up in the final. Chandler, an accomplished player and fellow-Texan, who won the event in 1932, resented women like Babe. Before the competition began she said, "We really don't need any truck driver's daughters in this tournament," a clear swipe at Babe's working-class roots, and the powerful woman who outdrove her by 40 or 50 yards.[13]

Paul Gallico marveled at her win, but couldn't help taking a jab, hypothesizing that "maybe it was Mrs. Chandler's neat and feminine clothing that made Didrikson mad. The Texas Babe seems to be working out a lifelong vendetta on sissy girls." Babe said, "I always felt like I was going to win. It was just like events in the Olympics. Every time I took a step a little chill would jump up in my stomach and I knew I was OK." She added that her opponent "certainly is a marvelous player and it's difficult for me to realize I have defeated her."[14]

There were many who were less than thrilled with her victory, given her background and history of playing sports for pay. Chandler appealed to Joe Dey, the executive director of the USGA, asking that Babe not be allowed to "get away with this." As Paul Gallico claimed, women held grudges after losing; they have alibis, and make cutting remarks. "No man ever takes a game as seriously as a woman does. And a man views his opponent with complete personal detachment." He added that unattractive girls are "usually comparatively good sports. Pretty girls are not." Chandler would later describe Didrikson's victory as a "fiasco."[15]

Dey, who attended college before dropping out to begin a career as a sportswriter, and soon to marry into a wealthy family, may have shared the same class prejudices Chandler held. Golf was not as democratic then as it is now, and its history in this country has been "interwoven with money, privilege, exclusivity, and social class." Bertha Bowen said that Chandler was a "fine person and a fine golfer. But Babe just didn't fit; she just didn't."[16]

This was playing out at a time when most people in the country were suffering deeply from the Depression, with unemployment still at 20 percent. Hungry World War I veterans had marched to Washington, DC in 1932 demanding bonuses that had been promised them for their service, only to be removed by Federal troops. In Oklahoma and Kansas, families crammed into broken down vehicles and headed for California to escape the ferocious dust storms that destroyed their farms. John Stenbeck would portray them in *The Grapes of Wrath*, and their real lives were captured by James Agee and Walker Evans in *Let Us Now*

Praise Famous Men. They were outcasts, unwanted, the great unwashed. Poor whites have been characterized as "trash" for generations.

In 1938, sociologist Howard Odum sent a survey to academics across the country, asking what "poor white" meant to them. Among the replies were "shiftless," "lazy," "unambitious," and "no account." They were an ill-defined class somewhere between white and black. Like African Americans, they were blamed for their own failures, as if social forces had nothing to do with their station in life. One respondent to Odum's survey said of the poor white, "No one knows what to do with him."

Babe Didrikson came from nothing, and Bertha Bowen contended her life had been "really hard and rough...She faced not being welcome, not being wanted, and she was determined to break that barrier. She was fighting a system and she won." Childhood friend Raymond Alford said he and Babe came from poor families and neighborhoods. "Sports were a way of getting to be equal, and I think that's what carried Babe through and made her work so hard." Didrikson was from a different world and for the genteel ruling class of golf, the question was, what to do with her?[17]

Connie Sullivan of the Women's Southern Golf Association wrote to John Jackson of the USGA on April 24th, after Didrikson had qualified for the Texas Women's Amateur, asking for clarification on her amateur status. "We don't want her playing in a [Women's Southern Amateur] until she has been declared eligible by the USGA under whose rulings we run the Southern."[18]

The next day she wrote to Archie M. Reid, Chairman of the USGA's Amateur Status Committee in response to a letter he sent her. (This is the man who carried Eben Byers to the clubhouse after his 1906 U.S. Amateur triumph.) Sullivan said it had provided "a rather valuable piece of information regarding Ballyhoo Babe. I thought she was already an outlaw" but intimated that the situation as to her amateur status was not clear. "Now, I see how really difficult the situation's got us right out on the tip of a limb while she sits in the crotch with a saw in her hand. However, I'll see if I can get a little Hawkshawing [detective work] done down there under the Lone Star."[19]

Sullivan believed that since the Amateur Athletic Union pronounced Didrikson a professional athlete, "we should be able to use that to our advantage in some way." She wanted to "know in advance how to handle it should she enter the Southern this year. I'll let you know what I hear from Texas. In the meantime, here's hoping the limb holds!" Didrikson won the tournament on April 27th, and was looking forward to the U.S. Women's Amateur that August. She told reporters, "Sure, I plan to compete in the national, but don't say I am going to win it."[20] Immediately after the conclusion of the tournament, the USGA launched an investigation.

Peggy Chandler and her husband Dan had a friend from Dallas, Charlie Dexter, who was on the USGA Executive Committee. He and Joe Dey worked with Reid to look into the matter. On April 30th, Connie Sullivan wrote to a colleague, asking for more information on Didrikson. "The question of Babe Didrikson looms large, and I'm afraid to put it off any longer in case she should enter the Southern." Sullivan asked if anybody in the Texas State Golf Association did any investigating before accepting her entry, and if so, who? Sullivan ticked off a list of questions concerning Didrikson's actions; including whether she had ever had expenses paid to go to tournaments, or received any salary from any golf equipment company. Sullivan said she didn't know Didrikson personally, but "got the impression that no matter how much we say she is an amateur, that she will always be a professional at heart."[21]

That same day, A.M. Reid was quoted in newspapers asserting that although "Miss Didrikson is a professional in some sport other than golf is not necessarily a controlling factor. We know very well we will have to take up the question of her eligibility in a couple of months so we've decided to be prepared when the case comes up." On May 6th, Babe officially entered the Women's Southern Amateur. Two days later Connie Sullivan wrote to Reid, saying she was working to try to get Didrikson's entry withdrawn. If she succeeded, Sullivan felt confident that Didrikson would not "attempt to enter other competitions this year, which will relieve you of a definite decision, and by next year, she may have become a more desirable entry. If she does not withdraw, then we are still standin' in de need o' prayer and a decision."[22]

Six days later, on May 14th, Reid told Sullivan to reject Didrikson's entry and announced that the USGA would not allow her to enter the U.S. Women's Amateur. "After we considered all of the facts in the case, we agreed the decision made was for the best interests of the game." So much for a two month investigation. Didrikson biographer Don Van Natta, Jr. contends that banishing her was "intended to protect the game as the province of the wealthy and, at the same time, boost the chances of the high society golfers to win future tournaments."[23]

Bertha Bowen responded by hiring a lawyer for Babe, and sent a telegram to the USGA urging them to reconsider. Ben S. Woodhead, president of the Beaumont Country Club, which Babe represented, asked the USGA to grant a full and fair hearing. These appeals, however, fell on deaf ears. Bowen saw clear class conflicts at play. "I was just furious at those people who had been so cutting to her. The fact that she was poor and had no clothes did not mean she had to be ruled a professional." In fairness to the USGA, a precedent had been set years earlier, in 1927, when Mary K. Browne was suspended for playing tennis for money.[24] The odd thing about the Didrikson case, however, was the contradictory actions of the USGA before and after the suspension.

Archie Reid had approved Babe to play in the Texas championship. "The mere fact that Miss Didrikson is a professional in some other sport would not in itself bar her from amateur golf," he wrote in a letter to the Women's Texas Golf Association on February 18, 1935. The language matches what he said two months later. Didrikson told reporters after she qualified for the event on April 23th that there would be no more playing professional sports for her.

> When I firmly decided to become a golfer with the hope of someday winning the national championship, I wrote the United States Golf Association concerning my amateur status. They replied that I was an amateur. Just to be sure I sent them another letter. And guess what they wrote back? It was: "Why do you write again, we told you once you were an amateur."[25]

A.M. Reid said on April 30th that, "The question to be decided will be if her professional activities in other sports have been to the detriment of the game of golf. Another matter which will receive consideration is her endorsement of articles in public advertisements." The U.S. Women's Amateur was scheduled for August, but two weeks later the question was decided – Babe was out.

Another curious inconsistency involves the fact that Didrikson was not stripped of her Texas title. Paul Gallico wrote the day after the decision,

> Our amateur rules are cockeyed, but, such as they are, the amateur governing bodies have to stick to them. But certainly to be consistent I would imagine that the USGA would ask Mildred to hand over her Texas women's championship medal to Mrs. Chandler and strike her name from the records as a winner.[26]

He had a point, but it never happened.

Ralph Trost of *The Brooklyn Daily Eagle* contended that the matter of Didrikson's professional activities in other sports would not have been an issue had Connie Sullivan not inquired into Babe's activities in baseball, basketball, and billiards. "Until someone makes a polite inquiry of the United States Golf Association about a person's amateur status," Trost wrote, "the golf solons say nothing, do nothing. They are not trouble shooters." Paul Gallico agreed, claiming that if Sullivan had not queried the USGA, but accepted Didrikson's "entry the way the Texas tournament did, she would have been permitted to play."[27]

The USGA decision elicited much criticism in the press. Gallico wrote that Babe "would do amateur golf more good than harm and inject excitement in what is at best not a very dramatic affair." Helen Hicks, 1931 U.S. Women's Amateur champion, said "They're throwing away the greatest boost they've had in amateur golf in years, simply because she had to live, and found a livelihood in other athletic fields." Hicks said if Babe could attract 3,000 fans to the final of the Texas amateur, she might draw 10,000 at the Women's Amateur.[28]

Henry McClemore concluded, "The United States Golf Association is nuts...I can't recall a single instance where amateur officials ever did the nice, sensible thing. They follow their hard-bitten rules like a blind mule down a furrow." Jimmy Demaret said it was the "biggest joke of the year. It is so silly I even hate to think about it."[29]

Many, like Bertha Bowen, saw the ban also being motivated by class prejudices. "If the mighty Mildred were merely a shy girl who plays a fine game of golf and blushed when congratulated on winning," wrote Cy Peterman of the *Philadelphia Evening Bulletin*, her professional activities may have been overlooked. "As it was, the prospect of the swashbuckling Babe, with the national golf crown askew [on] hastily brushed tresses, gruffly dismissing her triumph as 'just part of the game' may have frightened the USGA ladies."

Homer Mitchell, president of the Employers Casualty Insurance Company, Didrikson's employer, said "Babe simply lives on the wrong side of the tracks. Golf is a snooty game. Babe's lack of social standing probably had something to do with the recent ruling of the USGA." He said she never received a penny for playing golf.[30]

Didrikson wrote to USGA President Prescott Bush after her suspension, asking what she had done that was detrimental to the best interests or spirit of the game. Was it her earlier professional career, some social impropriety, or "ghost written" articles for a news service? If not, she asked, what was it? "I feel sure you will agree that I am entitled to now for what I am being penalized." She also asked how she could be reinstated. In the end, she relented, saying "What the USGA says goes, and there's no use crying about it."[31]

Mary K. Browne Case Recalls Reasoning of U. S. Governing Body

By RALPH TROST

When a proposition like the Babe Didrikson case arises folk always pop up with the pertinent question, "Does a professional in one sport necessarily become a pro in all sports?"

Dealing with golf specifically, the answer is, "It does and it doesn't." Until some one makes a polite inquiry of the United States Golf Association about a person's amateur status, the golf solons say nothing, do nothing. They are not trouble shooters.

And when a question is presented to the committee it never brands a player "professional." It merely advises the

Headline from *The Brooklyn Daily Eagle* regarding Didrikson's suspension, May 15, 1935.

Didrikson would be reinstated three years later. In the meantime, she kept working, and with the help of Bertha Bowen, who became like a

252

second mother, went through a physical transformation. It was reported the Bowen took her to "Neiman-Marcus for seven hundred dollars' worth of new clothes, advised her on a more feminine hairdo, and applied subtle makeup...." Bowen maintained that "Babe was eager to be proper." The press took note. Henry McLemore wrote of Babe in 1937: "Her hair is worn in a soft brown, curly cluster about her face. Her figure is that of a Parisian model."[32]

Paul Gallico claimed that he hardly recognized her when he saw her in 1935. "The tomboy had vanished." He remembered looking at her, grinning, and she knew why. She told him, "Yeah, and Au got silk on underneath and Ah like it." Gallico claimed she "had come into her woman's birthright by a curiously devious route, but she had got there, which, I imagine, was more than she ever expected." The transformation made her less threatening, and with her marriage to George Zaharias in 1938, whispers regarding her sexuality stopped.

Years later, Babe would acknowledge the strain of being a trailblazer. "I feel as though I have been a prisoner in this thing," she told *Sport* magazine in 1948. "I've been like that gal who fought to get the women the vote, you know, the one who started the battle for women's suffrage." Women athletes had a long road ahead of them to gain respect, and as Paul Gallico claimed, "No matter how good they are, they can never be good enough, quite, to matter."[33]

Sexism was a constant obstacle for women golfers at all levels of the game. According to Marilynn Smith, who became a professional golfer in 1949, "career women were viewed suspiciously; professional female athletes led the list. It took us a long time to gain respect. Women were expected to get married and have children."

Women played the game because they enjoyed the competition, but even this was seen as unfeminine. Babe Zaharias would arrive in the locker room, and as Walter Hagen had done to the men twenty-five years earlier, ask her fellow-competitors, "Ya gonna stick around and see who'll finish second this week?" Betty Hicks summarized Babe's aggressive demeanor on the course as "openly, hostilely, aggressively, bitterly, laughingly, jokingly, viciously and even sometimes lovingly competitive."[34]

This competitive spirit was antithetical to what was expected from sportswomen. Women were supposed to play for the joy of the activity, not to win. A physical education professor said in 1936, "Sports are primarily for enjoyment, not for the purpose of unsuccessfully imitating men." Betty Hicks recalled that while she was attending college in California in the 1940s, students were not permitted to keep score in physical education classes. The "only 'nice' sports for girls and women," she said, "were croquet, swimming, tennis, and golf, as long as the competition did not reach any level of ferocity."[35]

This ethos continued into the 1960s, as Carol Mann, winner of the 1965 U.S. Women's Open, spoke of how competition and winning didn't fit the feminine ideal. Mann won the Western Women's Junior in 1958, but felt embarrassed to receive the trophy. Looking back on it in 1992, she concluded it was "a major gender issue. It's a female issue. We're not socialized for success, for being spot-lighted. We're socialized to kind of be in the background to support the males...Achievements aren't women things. That's what men do. Women don't win trophies."

Mary Mills, the 1963 U.S. Women's Open champion, born in Mississippi, claimed that Southern women were "supposed to support the male and be creative at home. Sports for women were not that acceptable." [36]

Kathy Whitworth won a record 88 tournaments on the LPGA Tour, and as a self-described tomboy, played many sports with boys when she was young. "I played baseball and basketball and all of them. And then of course, as I got older," she would recall, other sports had to be given up, as "it wasn't acceptable." She tried tennis before turning to golf at age 15. She fell in love with it, not only because it was challenging, but because as a young woman, it gave her "an outlet to play a game that was just dependent on me. And I was accepted."[37]

Golf was acceptable for women but they still suffered the critical comments of men regarding their physical appearance, which were more cutting than Peggy Chandler's "truck driver's daughters" comment directed at Babe Didrikson in 1935. *Life* magazine contended before World War II that most good woman golfers looked like fireplugs.

"They're squat and stolid with pudgy round faces and piano legs…they have almost no sex appeal."[38] This was an image they would struggle against for decades.

Look magazine ran a 1970 article in which the female writer asserted: "Women golfers know they are considered, as they delicately put it, 'unfeminine.'" As Ruth Jessen, winner of 11 LPGA events said in 1965, "People have the idea that a woman athlete is a big sloppy Amazon with whiskers." Players were painfully aware of the rumors surrounding them, but carried on.[39]

Independent women, especially in the sports realm, went against the grain of societal norms, and were an easy target for those who wanted to label them as less than normal. Hall of Fame member Marilynn Smith admitted that the golfers then "had an Amazon image, and I always tried to erase that stigma by wearing earrings and pearls, by being well groomed, and by behaving like a lady." Showing an aggressive attitude on the golf course was taken for masculinity, and she wanted to avoid that.[40]

In 1972, ahead of the U.S. Women's Open at Winged Foot in Mamaroneck, New York, a local sportswriter expressed thoughts that in today's culture would most likely get him fired. "I suppose what we male chauvinist pigs would really like to see Rachel Welch walking down the 18th fairway, wearing nothing but a three-iron," he began. "Really, that's not true. I'd settle for Gloria Steinem teeing off in hot pants." Women's golf lacked sex appeal, according to him.

What the LPGA needed to make it successful was "some sexy gal who hits it 240-yard drives and has the right kind of physical equipment on and off the course." He concluded by noting, "Tick off the five or six greatest names of women's golf. Babe Zaharias, Patty Berg, Louise Suggs, Betsy Rawls, Mickey Wright…none of them great lookers."[41]

At the conclusion of the championship, Frank Gifford of ABC Sports also alluded to the masculine image of women golfers in an interview with Susie Berning after her victory. Before a national television audience, he declared that she had helped dispel "the myth of the lady golfer. I mean, I've never seen so many charming and attractive ladies in all my life." He interjected this telling comment before congratulating Berning on her second Open title.[42]

The LPGA Tour actively crafted an image of its players that exuded femininity. Leonard Wirtz, its tournament director in the 1960s, told them "you're ladies first, golfers second," and he had the final vote on everything. He also used sex appeal to help draw spectators. Marlene Hagge would say in 1966: "He doesn't want any of us to get too heavy – we just wouldn't present a very good picture to the public if we were overweight." He made sure they presented themselves as feminine to the public and guidelines to players in the mid-1960s included the following: "Wear lipstick at all times," "Do not wear too short of shorts, nor too tight."[43]

These guidelines were reminiscent of the All-American Girls Professional Baseball League (featured in the movie *A League of Their Own*), which adamantly specified, "Always appear in feminine attire," as masculine hair styling, shoes, coats, and t-shirts were barred at all times. As Susan Brownmiller wrote in her book, *Femininity*, the fear of not being feminine enough, "in style or in spirit," has been used "as a sledgehammer against the collective and individual aspirations of women since failure in femininity carries the charge of mannish or neutered, making biological gender subject to ongoing proof."[44]

In the 1970s the LPGA found two players who were the antithesis of the Amazon image – Laura Baugh and Hall of Fame member Jan Stephenson. Baugh won the U.S. Women's Amateur in 1971 at the age of 16, turned professional in 1973. She appeared in a toothpaste commercial for Colgate, and made more money in endorsements than from playing golf.

Hughes Norton, a vice president of International Management Group (which managed Baugh, and at one time Arnold Palmer, Jack Nicklaus, and Gary Player as well) said that the LPGA then "had no one along the lines of appeal that Laura represented. You had some reasonably good-looking women who couldn't play very well and some great players who looked awful – typical women athlete types." He added that it didn't "hurt ticket sales to have a Jan Stephenson with good-looking legs. I don't think they should hide that image. It's part of women's golf."

Stephenson, an Australian who was Rookie of the Year in 1974, embraced the selling of sex appeal. She appeared as a model in many issues of *Fairway* magazine, which Volpe began in 1976 as an annual insert in *Golf Magazine* to promote the LPGA. It featured players in bathing suits and evening wear, and was created "to gain respect, recognition, and yes, even love for 300 women professional golfers." The LPGA cultivated "a snappy, fashionable image designed to prove that a girl doesn't have to look like an athlete to be one."[45]

Tony Andrea, an LPGA marketing consultant, claimed in 1981, "I think we can sell the Tour without sex, but the appeal of good-looking women should not be ignored. It's part of the overall marketing and selling of the sport." Some players resented this campaign, recalled Hall of Famer JoAnne Carner, "because they felt we should be judged by our golf ability, not by sex appeal. But I was sick of the old image of women athletes as lumberjacks. I think that effort helped turn things around." Jane Blalock, 27-time winner on the LPGA Tour, believed women's sports had been "stigmatized by a large, hefty, masculine image…the product of an antiquated thinking by a society that felt women should stay at home."[46]

As for Baugh, she struggled with the Barbie doll image. "You want to be out there because you are a good golfer, not because you are wearing something." Jan Stephenson, when asked what advice she would give to young women, said, "look like a woman, but play like a man." The media certainly objectified women. *Golf Digest* ran a close-up photo of Marlene Hagge's rear end in 1972, with the caption, "Are you a Ladies PGA Tour butt?" Hagge wrote an article five years later that pointed out "the LPGA encourages us to look as attractive and fashionable as we possibly can. We have a committee that advises young players on everything from shoes to hairdos."[47]

Televised women's golf, what little there was of it, had very few female commentators. ABC hired Renee Powell and Cathy Duggan to add their expertise to the 1974 U.S. Women's Open. When Duggan introduced the audience to JoAnne Carner, she was corrected by Chris Schenkel, working beside her; "*Mrs.* Don Carner, 133-pounds, and svelte." He then treated viewers to "another view of what we think is a lovely gal's swing." Frank Gifford described one player as "5'5", 122 pounds," adding that she was a "very attractive dresser."[48]

Gifford's and Schenkel's words, along with other broadcasters referring to the women as "girls" and "gals" reflected the underlying sexism of the times, as the USGA's own record books attached a "Miss" or "Mrs." prefix to female competitors' names until 1979. The LPGA still wants to promote its players, but stresses accessibility and showcasing their varied personalities. As LPGA Commissioner Mike Whan said in 2015, "We're not trying to just show you the shots. We're trying to tell the stories of these athletic, attractive, talented golfers." On special occasions the LPGA puts on fashion shows to highlight its best players in evening wear (akin to *Fairway* magazine years earlier); Michelle Wie, Paula Creamer, and Lydia Ko have all been models.[49]

Jan Stephenson, when asked in 2003 if she would like to undo her sex kitten image, replied, "Absolutely. I wish I hadn't done any of it. I wish I had done nothing but practice and work out." Nancy Lopez, who won the same number of major tournaments as Stephenson, labeled her as "the player who worked the hardest on her game." Yet the "whole sex-appeal thing," as Lopez called it, has stuck to Stephenson. Regrettably, she is perhaps remembered more for that than for her 16 tournament wins, including the 1983 U.S. Women's Open.[50]

The average woman player had her own troubles with male chauvinism. At the turn of the 20th century, many felt women had no business on the course. According to one writer, "They can neither stand still nor stop chattering," adding that golf "is too serious a thing to be interrupted by frivolity." Ten years later, in 1910, it was claimed that women were "barely tolerated. The average woman with a golf club is a source of terror and vexation to male players."[51]

They also had to struggle for a place to play. A *New York Times* survey in 1916 concluded that most clubs limited play to males on weekends and holidays, either all day or during certain prime times, which handicapped women's effort to grow the game for their sex. Women have continued to deal with prejudices directed at them. An article from 1936 quoted a club caddie as saying women golfers were "avoided on general principle."

Few can hit as hard as they can kick and when two play together, conversation lengthens the already tiresome round…The typical woman walks the few yards the ball has progressed since her last shot; then says, "Now, what shall I do?" The obvious answer is, "Give up," but professional etiquette interferes and one is tactful.[52]

Thirty years later a caddie in New York claimed half the caddies in the county "will be drunk tonight. Got to be. Only way we can keep our sanity." When I began playing golf in the 1970s, this feeling was still prevalent. My own prejudices were finally put to rest while in college, when I played with a young woman who was as good, if not better, than I was.

At the private club level, it was rare for a woman to be on the board of governors. If they did, reported *Golf Digest* in 1969, "there would be a general house cleaning of stale by-laws." Clubs still restricted women. The Blind Brook Club in New York, for example:

Women members or the families of members (wives and daughters residing with a member) may enjoy the privileges of the club on Tuesdays and Thursdays which are not holidays, during normal operating hours, and on Sundays, and Tuesdays and Thursdays which are holidays, after 12 noon in the case of the clubhouse, and 1:30 p.m. in the case of the course.

Most clubs had by-laws such that automatically suspending women's membership if she got divorced.[53]

Women continued having their access to courses restricted into the 1990s, highlighted in a Massachusetts legal case in 1995, when nine women sued Haverhill Golf and Country Club and won $1.9 million in damages five years later. Judge John C. Cratsley issued a permanent injunction barring the club from engaging in discriminating practices against women regarding membership, waiting lists and tee times. The women couldn't play from 11 a.m. to 2 p.m. on Wednesdays, nor on Sundays until after 11:30 a.m. They were also put on waiting lists, although men who applied after them were granted memberships before they were.

The club maintained that it did not discriminate and blamed the jury and the judge. But the attorney for the plaintiffs stated in an affidavit that they made more than 20 attempts to discuss and resolve the issues over the years. "All were either ignored or dismissed by the club." The women were not doing it for the money, and the settlement could have been reduced had the board negotiated. The Massachusetts Court of Appeals affirmed that the male officers of the Club had applied rules in a way that made women "second class members." This form of discrimination had economic side effects, the Court ruled.[54]

> Playing golf was not one of the unalienable rights of 1776, but it is naïve not to recognize the degree to which golf links and the country club are the locale for developing professional and business contracts. Golf and the country club lubricate the advance of careers. Deals are cut on the fairway and in the clubhouse.[55]

A 1995 review of Los Angeles and San Francisco metropolitan area golf courses found that 33 of 74 private clubs banned women during prime weekend hours. A pro at Green Hills Country Club, with 200 women golfers, said that many of the younger members "want to rebel against the rules. But most of our older ladies were brought up thinking it's just a privilege that they're let out on the golf course."[56] Quite a telling statement of old prejudices.

Sometimes women weren't even allowed in the clubhouse. In 1991, when the children of the great Glenna Collett Vare wanted to give one of her trophies to the Metacomet Country Club in Rhode Island (where she learned to play the game), her daughter Glenna had to wait outside. "It never occurred to me that I was a second-class citizen," said an outraged Glenna. "Our mother would never have stood for such treatment," added her brother Ned. When the club refused to put into writing that it did not discriminate against women, Glenna and Ned decided against donating the trophy.[57]

The game is hard enough to play without these obstacles. Cultural perceptions and prejudices are deterrents that are hard to change. I have heard from women who say they get funny looks on the driving range, as if men are waiting to see if they can hit the ball. I've seen men offer advice to women they don't know at the range, perhaps as a pick-up ploy, which is always amusing because invariably they can't hit the ball a lick themselves. And a woman just a little older than I am remembered not being allowed to play on a Saturday morning as a guest at a club, even though she was the member of another private club. Old prejudices die hard.

****

As Babe Didrikson discovered, class divided women among themselves. So did race, as there were no African American or other minorities playing the game at the highest levels when Babe got her start in the 1930s. Until the 1950s they were simply excluded by the white establishment.

Many good books have been written that explore the history of African American women in golf, including those by M. Mikell Johnson, Rhonda Glenn, Liz Kahn, Dr. Calvin Sinnette, and Pete McDaniel. I offer here just a brief look at a few women who had a lasting impact on the game.

Ann Gregory had an unusual childhood, being orphaned as a child and raised by a white Southern family. She was a good athlete, and took up golf in 1942 while in her mid-20s. Improving quickly, she began winning tournaments in her native Indiana and in United Golfers Association events, and soon distinguished herself.

In 1948, George S. May invited her to play in his World Championship of Golf at Tam O'Shanter in Illinois. She played with Babe Zaharias and got her attention by reaching the green in two on a long hole. "Ann, what did you hit on that green?" Zaharias asked her. When she responded it was a 2-iron, Babe said, "Hey, you cut that out. I'm the big cheese around here!"

May told Gregory if she encountered any trouble from anyone to let him know. "He was beautiful to me...The galleries were just beautiful. The people were beautiful. This was what really inspired me because it seemed like everybody was interested in my game."[58]

In 1956 she made history by becoming the first African American to play in the U.S. Women's Amateur. Her first round opponent, Carolyn Cudone, a Curtis Cup player who would win five consecutive U.S. Senior Women's Amateur championships, recalled a parking attendant telling her father, "Your daughter better win today, or you'd better not come back to this parking lot."[59] Gregory gave her a good match, but lost 2 and 1. "I'm happy to do as well as I did," she told reporters. "At least I did last longer than a snowball – and my husband told me I wouldn't."[60] In 1971 Gregory nearly won the U.S. Senior Women's Amateur, but lost by a single shot when her old friend and rival Cudone parred the final hole.

Gregory maintained that she rarely felt race prejudice. "The only time I felt it was at Congressional Country Club when they didn't allow me in for the dinner." That was at the 1959 U.S. Women's Amateur. Joe Dey, executive director of the USGA, told her the Club would not allow her to partake in the players' dinner. "I didn't feel bad," insisted Gregory. She didn't consider herself an activist. "I just wanted to play golf." The USGA had changed with the times since the 1920s, and Joe Dey was a religious man, carrying a copy of the Rules of Golf and the New Testament in his blue blazer. Frank Hannigan, who began working with Dey in 1961, maintained that his actions "all pivoted on his Christianity. He thought he was doing good deeds through golf." Jack Nicklaus said of Dey, "He just always wanted to do the right thing."[61]

Prejudice was rife in the U.S. at that time, as Martin Luther King, Jr. began the modern civil rights movement with the Birmingham bus boycott in 1955. During the 1940s and early 1950s, black golfers filed lawsuits in Atlanta, Baltimore, Miami, Houston, and Nashville seeking to desegregate municipal and public golf courses, but de jure segregation was still present in the South.

JoAnne Carner remembered competing in the 1955 U.S. Girls' Junior in Florence, South Carolina. She saw a sign that said, "Colored water" and wanted to try it. "So I went over and I stood in line, not noticing it was only the black caddies who were there." When she got to the drinking fountain and discovered it was just regular water, she couldn't understand it. "And then I stood back and looked again and saw that there were only blacks drinking the water. As I said, I'd never run into any prejudice like that before."[62]

Ann Gregory recalled when she played in the 1960 U.S. Women's Amateur in Tulsa, Oklahoma. The manager of a white hotel would not honor her reservation and sent her to a shabby black hotel with no air-conditioning. "Racism works best when you let it affect your mind," she contended. "It was better for me to remember that the flaw was in the racist, not in myself." Ann Gregory played in seven U.S. Women's Amateurs and six U.S. Women's Opens, never winning a USGA event. But, as her friend Jolyn Robichaux said, her success "dispelled many myths that black women couldn't play golf."[63]

Renee Powell, a very gracious woman who was kind enough to write a blurb for my first book, played on the LPGA Tour from 1967-1980. She remembered Ann Gregory as a determined and confident golfer, a warm-hearted, inspirational individual who set an example for others to follow. "She set the stage for every other black female golfer who came into golf after that." In the coming years Powell and Althea Gibson would dispel the same myth in the world of professional golf.

Althea Gibson gained fame as a tennis star, winning the U.S. Open and Wimbledon titles in 1957 and 1958. After giving up tennis, she turned to golf as a way of making a living, but it wasn't easy. "I know when I tried to have lessons with Betty Hicks in 1957 at Los Coyotes, California, I couldn't because the club wouldn't allow it."[64] Gibson would face similar challenges from racism as Ann Gregory had, but would not be deterred.

"I have a God-given talent for being able to do things with a ball," she told sportswriter Will Grimsley in 1962. "I have gone as far as I can in tennis. Now I intend to do the same thing in golf." Her athleticism allowed her to become a competent player – although slow and too mechanical – and she turned professional in 1963 at the advanced age of 36.

Marlene Hagge would describe trouble Gibson had in the 1960s, "especially in the South, and we said we wouldn't play unless Althea could be treated like everybody else. I'm proud of the LPGA and what we did." Hagge started rooming with Althea when a hotel said it "lost"

Gibson's reservation and she invited Althea to stay with her. Hagge said Gibson "had a tremendous amount of talent, but she came into golf too late," believing she would have been a star had she started earlier. "She achieved a lot just by being out there." Renee Powell would say "if Marlene liked you and she believed in something, she would fight your battle, and she wouldn't care what kind of cat was out there. She would fight."[65]

Gibson acknowledged that her game was not competitive, as the best finish she had in her career was a tie for second in 1970. "It was not only frustrating, it was embarrassing...I was often too upset, frustrated, and depressed to sort it all out." Her best year was 1967, when she finished 23rd on the money list. "I tried to set an example for future young Negro women," Gibson would say, which in itself was important.[66]

Renee Powell experienced her first run-in with racism at the age of eight when friends said their parents didn't want them playing with her because she was black. Golf became her escape and the course was where she "could go to and feel secure." Her father gave her lessons, and at 12 she played in her first United Golfers Association event in 1958. She was discriminated against as a woman and a person of color, but found acceptance from the USGA when she played in the U.S. Girl's Junior in 1962. "But I remember Mrs. Pennington, who was chairman of the of the Girls' Junior Committee at the time, telling my dad, 'The only thing the USGA requires is that you have a golf game.'"[67]

Her father William Powell built Clearview Golf Club in East Canton, Ohio in 1946, a response to the racism he experienced after returning from World War II. "My love affair with the game of golf started at the age of nine and never wavered," said Powell. He was denied playing the game he loved on nearby courses, so he built his own, which is on the National Register of Historic Places. "In life you have to believe in yourself even if no one else does," Powell maintained. "Stand tall, stand firm and never give up." Bill Powell was a trailblazer, and earned the PGA of America's Distinguished Service Award in 2009 before passing away later that year. His daughter Renee has also been a pioneer in her own right.

Problems would persist, however, even when she turned professional in 1967. In an interview with *Contemporary Black Biography*, Powell recalled relying upon her faith while traveling in the South. "I remember crossing the Vicksburg Bridge, traveling through Selma, Alabama. I was lucky to be alive. Thinking about those difficult times and the things that could have happened to me while I was traveling. It was the strength of God. I was doing what He wanted me to do. I was there for a reason."[68]

At one tournament in Florida her life was threatened by a man who wrote that if she wanted to live she better get out of the South. It was terrifying. "How would you feel," she would ask in a 2011 interview, "if somebody said they wanted to kill you because you played golf in your own country?" Powell called her parents, who tried to console her. She ended up playing, but feared for her life the whole time. She found strength in her faith, and remembered how she admired the courage of Harriet Tubman, the black abolitionist who before the Civil War guided slaves to freedom in the North via the Underground Railroad. "I thought, God put me here for a reason," Powell recalled. "He's going to protect me. Maybe He won't let anything happen to me...I've always been like this. You don't quit. You don't give up."[69]

Powell would play on the LPGA Tour until 1980. In 1971, joined by her friend Mary Lou Daniel and one-armed trick-shot artist Jimmy Nichols, she went on a three-week USO Tour to Vietnam. There, they hosted golf clinics in hopes of bringing "a little bit of home" to troops abroad.[70] Renee continues to work with women veterans by introducing them to the therapeutic value of golf, in a program called "Clearview Hope." In 2015 she and six others (including the late Louise Suggs) became the first female members of the Royal and Ancient Golf Club of St Andrews, which, along with the USGA, administer the game of golf throughout the world. Renee Powell has certainly left quite a distinguished mark on golf.

The history of women's golf has been replete with tales of their struggles to be taken seriously and secure equal access and opportunities.

This chapter has endeavored to share a few stories that shed light on areas many people may not have considered. As Hall of Famer Patty Sheehan says, "The majority of players have forgotten where we came from. I appreciate the history, the grand old women of golf who played their hearts out." Amateur or professional, they did so not for great monetary reward or lasting fame, but because they had a passion for the game. Their stories speak to the wonderful spirit and character of the game.

Chapter 12: The Rest of the Story – "Honorable and Dishonorable Mention"

There are a number of interesting stories in golf that most people have never heard about – at least I doubt they are common knowledge – and I thought it would be fun to end the book with a few I have gathered over the years. To paraphrase Paul Harvey, "Now for the rest of the story."

Interesting Names in the U.S. Open

I watched my first U.S. Open in 1974, and was pulling for Arnold Palmer. He finished tied for sixth with Tom Watson, who would supplant Arnie as my all-time favorite. Two great names in the world of golf which will be remembered as long as the game is played, while others will not.

"A good name is more desirable than great riches," the Bible tells us, "to be esteemed is better than silver or gold." The world of golf has been full of interesting and odd names since the game began, and many have been represented in the U.S. Open.

There are "fishy" names: Dan Herring and John Bass (both 1954), meet Chick Trout (1926.) And rhyming ones: Jim Pringle (1931) meet Ed Kringle (1962) – we don't know if he had a brother named Kris. Others are religious: George Christ and Ben Lord (both 1922), meet Neil Christian (1927) and Andy Pope (2015.)

Skee Reigel (1946), meet Skeeter Heath (1983), James West (1919) meet 1978 and '85 champion Andy North, Jack Hoerner (1941), don't sit in a corner, get out there and play. Jack Croke (1908) didn't after finishing 45th, but played eight more times.

Terry (1972) and Mike (1994) Small, meet Ted Huge (1953). Smiley Quick (1946), meet Smylie Kaufman (2014). Loddie Kempa (1954), meet Brooks Koepka (2017 and '18 champion). Rocky Rich (1929), meet Monte Money (1979.)

There have been more "skis" than you'll find at a Polish family reunion: Kasmir Zabrowski (1938), Walter Nagorski (1949), Richard Karbowski, John Zebroski and Gary Domagalski (all 1981), Walter Zembriski (1982) Bruce Zabriski (1986.) They sound like blue collar guys who might want to have a cold beverage after the round with Chet Beer (1929) and Sam Adams (1997.)

What would golf be without aristocratic sounding names? Austere Claeyssens (1925), Celestino Tugot (1955), Casmere Jawor (1966), Harcourt Kemp (1971), Pierre-Henri Soero (2005), and Estanislao Goya (2013.) Hard to imagine Mr. Tugot sharing a brew and pretzels with the likes of Mr. Nagorski.

As we come down the stretch, here are some names, a mixture of funny and odd, that just tickle me: Nemo Sherba (1938) – was he looking for Dory? Verl Stinchcomb (1938), Scudday Horner (1946), Guinea Kop (1948), Cleophas McVicker – wasn't he a Senator from South Carolina around 1873? (1948), Ockie Eliason – sounds like a farmer from North Dakota (1966), and David Smail (2003) – any relation to Judge Smails from *Caddyshack*? Too bad the Judge never played in a U.S. Open. I can see him now, putting his ball on a peg as an impatient Ben Hogan glares at him. Turning to Hogan, he growls, "Do you mind, sir! I'm trying to tee off."

The War of the Worlds

When I was a teenager I recall watching a TV-movie about Orson Welles's "The War of the Worlds" radio broadcast in 1938, and the panic it caused across the country. Recently I learned that Craig Wood, winner of the 1941 Masters and U.S. Open, and Vic Ghezzi, winner of the 1941 PGA Championship, heard the broadcast while driving from a tournament and believed it was real. Herb Graffis, golf writer and founder of the National Golf Foundation, wrote about it the following year:

> Frank Walsh tells this one on Craig Wood to illustrate how seriously the boys take their work. Craig had just won last autumn's Pine Valley invitation tournament by a margin that left the rest of the field far, far, behind. He and Vic Ghezzi were driving home from the tourney and listening to the radio in Wood's car. They tuned into the sensational "Men from Mars" broadcast.[1]

On Sunday, October 30, 1938, Orson Welles and the *Mercury Theatre on the Air* shocked the nation by using seemingly real news bulletins to describe a Martian invasion based on H.G. Wells's book *The War of the Worlds*. Listeners heard a reporter breathlessly describing the scene at a farm in Grovers Mills, New Jersey (a real place), where it was believed a meteor had landed. But upon closer examination, it's discovered to be an extraterrestrial craft, smooth and cylindrical.

Suddenly, a hatch screws open. "Good heavens," the terrified reporter told listeners, "something's wriggling out of the shadow like a gray snake. Now it's another one, and another. They look like tentacles to me." The aliens unleash a heat ray that kills the state police who arrived on the scene and they advance toward the gathered crowd. "Now the whole field's caught fire," as an explosion rumbled over the airwaves. "The woods...the barns...the gas tanks of automobiles...it's spreading everywhere. It's coming this way. About twenty yards to my right...." Silence then fell upon the audience. Reports continued to explain that a Martian army was marching across the earth.[2]

For those who tuned in late and didn't hear the introduction clearly informing listeners that it was all make believe, like Craig Wood and Vic Ghezzi, many didn't know what to make of it. Herb Graffis described their anxiety near the outskirts of Trenton:

> As they sped through the night, listening intently, they rather expected any moment to round a bend in the road and bump into invaders from another world. Eventually Craig found his voice. He sighed and said: "Just my luck! Here I play a tournament on the world's toughest golf course with the best players in the country and beat the best of them by two handsfull of strokes. What a lousy break! Tomorrow there won't be a soul alive to read about it."[3]

It was only toward the end of the broadcast that an announcement was made reiterating to the audience that they were listening to a play and not real events. When it concluded Orson Welles came on to explain that the performance was *The Mercury Theatre's* "own radio version of dressing up in a sheet and jumping out of a bush and saying Boo!"

The next day *The New York Times* reported that a "wave of mass hysteria seized thousands of radio listeners throughout the nation" as the dramatization led thousands to "believe that an interplanetary conflict had started with invading Martians spreading wide death and destruction in New Jersey and New York." Stories of people fleeing their homes or seeking sanctuary in churches thinking the end of the world had come were featured in cities such as San Francisco, Chicago, St. Louis, New Orleans, Minneapolis, Los Angeles, Atlanta, and Pittsburgh.[4]

Craig Wood's performance at the 72-hole invitational tournament at Pine Valley, New Jersey, one of the world's most difficult courses, has largely been forgotten. In shooting 71-69-71-75-286, Wood was the first to shoot a sub-par round shot there (in round two) and he beat Frank Walsh by 14 shots. The select field included Wood's car mate Vic Ghezzi and top players such as Gene Sarazen, Johnny Farrell, Ed Dudley (who would later be President Eisenhower's teacher), Wiffy Cox, and Willie Turnesa (that year's U.S. Amateur champion.) Wood's score was 16 shots better than the total Jimmy Thomson and Sam Snead had each shot the year before to tie for the title.[5]

As a letter to the editor in *The New York Times* stated, "The bad taste and lack of restraint in the Halloween 'joke' broadcast cannot be too harshly condemned…Make no mistake, it was not the ignorant, nor the believers in ghosts, who took this thing seriously." Poor Craig Wood and Vic Ghezzi were caught in the middle of the frenzy, and thus will have a connection to the lore of Orson Welles and "The War of the Worlds." I have found only two brief mentions of this incident, one in a 1954 article by Herbert Warren Wind and the other in a 2000 club history of Pine Valley. I've provided here more substance to this odd tale very few people know about.[6]

Bill Campbell and Ben Hogan

Bill Campbell was one of the great amateur golfers in the history of the game, and a natural, never taking a lesson. At 15 he played in his first U.S. Amateur, and would win it in 1964 at age 41. His life was devoted to golf, which included serving as the USGA president from 1982 to 1983 and as Captain of the Royal and Ancient Golf Club of St Andrews in 1987. He was also a recipient of the Bob Jones Award, given

270

in "recognition of distinguished sportsmanship in golf," and in 1990 was elected to the World Golf Hall of Fame. Campbell married Joan Dourif in 1954. A widow, she had four children, and they would have two more together. His stepson Bradford was an actor, and was nominated for an Academy Award in 1975 for his wonderful portrayal of the character Billy Bibbit in *One Flew Over the Cuckoo's Nest*.

An entire book can be written about Bill Campbell, but it was something he did while president of the USGA that is noted here. He described the USGA as a "many-splendored thing" that "means many things to many different people."[7] One thing it has done is offer special exemptions from qualifying to players it deems are worthy of competing in the U.S. Open. The first to receive one was Ben Hogan in 1966, who finished 12th at Olympic that year behind winner Billy Casper. In 1983 the U.S. Open returned to Oakmont for the 30th anniversary of Hogan's victory there in 1953.

Campbell invited Hogan and his wife Valerie to attend the event. In a letter to Hogan at the end of 1982, he wrote, "Simply put, the '83 U.S. Open cannot be complete without you." Then, on February 4, 1983 he sent another letter. "We have announced three special exemptions – Palmer, Player, and Trevino – but actually voted another one, involving you – a unanimous Executive Committee vote...We did not announce this special exemption for you until I could discuss it with you, lest we seem presumptuous. Please know that we do, very much, want you to play in the '83 Open."[8] The 70-year-old Hogan didn't mind Campbell announcing the exemption, but declined to play or attend. As it turned out, Arnold Palmer finished tied for 60th, Gary Player tied for 20th, and Lee Trevino ended up not playing. Mr. Hogan was content to have 1966 be his last hurrah.

One Club Experts

Chick Harbert, winner of the 1954 PGA Championship, made two interesting bets with members of the Battle Creek (Michigan) Country Club in October of 1942. The club professional there at the time, he wagered he could finish a round in less than two hours and break 75, using only a 4-iron for all the shots. He ended up collecting on both bets, taking 1 hour 58 minutes to shoot a 74 on the 6,732-yard course, twice nicely getting out of greenside bunkers in the process.[9]

At age 66, Chuck Kocsis played the Red Run Golf Club in Royal Oak, Michigan with a 3-iron and shot 34-34=68, 4 under par. "I did that a lot of times," he said. "I played a lot with one club."[10]

In a one-club tournament in 1983, professional Terry Beardsley shot a 76 using just a 4-iron at the 6,464-yard Olympia Resort course in Oconomowoc, Wisconsin.[11]

Scoring Records – Good and Bad

The 17th hole at the TPC Sawgrass is one of the most famous holes in the world, an island green surrounded by water. Only 132-yards long, this little par-3 can be a challenge for the best players in the world on their best day, and for the average player can be a torture chamber. *Golf Digest* told the story of Ray Walker of Lake City, Florida, who played it in the mid-1980s with three friends. They arrived on the tee loaded for bear, with a huge shag bag of balls. It wasn't enough.

When Ray splashed his first tee shot, there was no need for concern. Another followed, then 5, 10, 20 more, none finding land. Why he didn't pick up after a half dozen no one knows, but he kept firing, ball after ball, swatting, lunging, hitting at the ball like a Happy Gilmoresque driving range whack-a-ball-guy. We don't know how many groups played through, but he kept at it, draining the shag bag, his bag, his friend's bags and dozens more balls procured during the unfolding disaster. When he finally surrendered and put an X on his card, he was hitting 655 after putting 327 consecutive balls in the water. By way of comparison, Angelo Spagnolo shot an 18-hole score of 257 at TPC Sawgrass in 1985 to win *Golf Digest's* "America's Worst Avid Golfer" contest, and "only" took a 66 on #17.[12]

Sometimes you play a round of golf and have one good nine holes and one bad one. But how is this for a record comeback – Lawrence G. Knowles had an incredible 27 shot difference between nine hole scores in 1935 when he shot a 63-36 = 99 at the Agawam Hunt Country Club in East Providence, Rhode Island. The next greatest disparity I have found is 20 shots, by Jack Crowley at the Sebring Nassau in Mid-Pines, North Carolina in 1952. After making five birdies on the front nine, he was pressed on the back nine and fell apart. His scores: 626 344 425 – 36 946 485 677 – 56 = 92.[13]

Breaking 60 has become more common now on the PGA Tour with advances in clubs, balls, and agronomy. Jim Furyk shot a 58 in 2016 to set the record score up to now. Here are some other impressive scores:

- Considering the clubs and balls at the time, the most impressive score may have been the one shot in 1914 by John Black, a 31-27=58 at the 6,300-yard Claremont course in Oakland, California.
- On May 12, 2012, Rhein Gibson, a 26-year-old Australian professional shot a 55 on the 6,698-yard par-71 River Oaks Golf Club course in Edmond, Oklahoma. He had 12 birdies and two eagles.
- In 1994, Wayne Myers shot a 28-29=57 at the 6,449-yard par-72 Southern Oaks Golf Club in South Carolina
- On August 29, 1989, Willie Kane shot a 30-28=58 on the 6,229 yard par-70 South Course at Tucson's Randolph Park municipal golf course.
- On July 6, 1976, 13-year-old Douglas Beecher shot 33-25=58 on 6,000-yard par-71 Pitman Country Club course in Sewell, New Jersey.[14]

One of the most incredible stretches of nine holes in history was played on November 10, 1971 by Tom Doty, a 22 year-old assistant professional at the Brookwood Country Club in Wood Dale, Illinois. He already held the course record with a 64 when he went out in 26 on the 3,300-yard front nine. The scores: 354 211 244 = 26. He played with four members who attested the score. The head pro Emil Esposito admitted nobody believed it could be real, but concluded, "You have to go by the man's honesty and you have to go by the members. You got four guys who play golf [with] Tom, and you got to go by their honesty."[15] It was reported in *Sports Illustrated* and *Golf Digest*.

Doty had an eagle-3 on the short 465-yard first hole, then two bogies on the next two holes (a 380-yard par-4 and 230-yard par-3.) On the 500-yard fourth, after a solid drive he hit a towering 3-wood that hit in front of the green, took a couple of hops and rolled into the hole for a double eagle deuce. Wow. The fifth was a 360-yard par-4 dogleg left. Doty had been able to cut the corner and drive the green before, and with a strong wind behind him, hit a solid shot that drew around the corner. His playing partners said it was either on the green or just short. As the group neared the green, the ball wasn't in sight. "I got a hunch," said one of the men. "I wouldn't be a bit surprised if that ball went into the hole."[16] It did.

As they reached the 170-yard sixth tee, nobody said a word. The wind had shifted and was into them, with the hole located on the back of the green. Doty used a 4-wood, knocked the ball down in the wind, and it headed right at the hole. "You guys go up there," Doty said. "I'm not going because I think I hit it in the hole." They drove their golf carts to the green and yelled back that it was indeed another ace.

"My mind was just gone," Doty said, recalling hitting his tee shot on the 360-yard seventh. "I didn't know what I was doing. It was like having a putt for $50,000. I couldn't even get the club back. I had to walk away and set up to it again and just try to hit it on instinct." He almost smothered the shot, as the ball came out low and left, finishing in the rough. His 9-iron had to be hit over a tree. Having settled down a bit, he clipped it perfectly, the ball sailing high and dropping softly on the green, rolling as if drawn by a magnet once again into the hole.

This most unfathomable stretch of holes concluded, Doty said at that point he was "ready to put my clubs away or sell them and take up some other sport." He parred the last two holes (420 and 415-yards long) and took only five putts for the nine holes. A 33 on the back nine, including a missed one-foot putt on the last, gave him a 13-under par 59 with 16 putts on the 6,435-yard course.[17]

Then there was the case of Patrick Wills, a 59-year-old retired Marine, who shot a 57 during a 2015 tournament on the 6,021-yard Laurel Hill Golf Club in Lorton, Virginia. More miraculous than the score was the fact that it included three holes-in-one, two coming on par-4s. Three playing partners witnessed the feat, and the aces came on the

7th (278 yards), 10th (311 yards), and 14th (176 yards.) The director of golf at the club, Gene Orrico, verified the score.

Wills entered the day with 22 career aces, and like Tom Doty, realized there were people who wouldn't believe it. "But I know what I shot," he said, "my playing partners know what I shot and the people at the tournament do as well. I mean, I'm an accomplished amateur. I set my first course record when I was 16, shot a 65 or 66, and I've added a few since then. Anyone that has ever played a competitive round with me, they know what I'm capable of." But he added, "I had never imagined anything like this in my whole life. I was literally out of my mind."[18] As Ripley would say of Doty and Wills, "Believe it or not."

Bobby Jones's Caddies

Joe Horgan began caddying in 1893 for John Reid, who many regard as the "father of American golf" – he established the St. Andrews Golf Club in Yonkers, New York in 1888. Horgan began his big-time work at the inaugural U.S. Open in 1895, when he caddied for the winner Horace Rawlins, the start of a long career that had him carry the bag for the winners of six U.S. Opens, two U.S. Amateurs, four U.S. Women's Amateurs, plus numerous other titles. In those days the bags were small, but large enough to hold seven clubs. "When I won the championship with Rawlins that time in Newport, he counted me out 15 iron men [dollar coins] and added three of his clubs which I cashed in for two bucks a piece." Horgan was not particular about the rank and sex of those he worked for, but said he was "more at home with the pros and I leaned more to professional golf. Moreover it pays better."[19]

He carried the bag for Harry Vardon in the 1920 U.S. Open, which Vardon almost won at the age of 50 until running into bad weather derailed him on the back nine of the final round. Horgan also carried for Walter Hagen, Gene Sarazen, J.H. Taylor, Ted Ray, Beatrix Hoyt, Glenna Collett, and Bobby Jones. He recalled telling Jones, "'When you were a kid I used to think you were never going to be a champion because you lost your temper too much.' 'I guess there is something in that remark, Joe,' said Bobby. 'From all accounts I must have been a pretty fresh kid.'" One might recall his 1916 match with Eben Byers for evidence of that admission. At the 1950 U.S. Open, a 72-year-old Joe

275

Horgan told a sportswriter he was pulling for Ben Hogan. "After Ben's wonderful comeback from that accident, I gotta root for him." Horgan died in 1953, and with him an era ended.[20]

Horgan once told Bobby Jones he was a fresh kid. Luke Ross, who carried the bag for Jones in 12 major championships, knew the fresh kid who transformed himself into a champion. "It still seems strange to me," Ross recalled in 1969, "that a young Italian lad from Cleveland would become attached to the man who would carry the most hallowed name in golf." He began caddying as an 11-year-old at the Mayfield Country Club on Cleveland's East side.

In 1920 his life changed when his boss Bertie Way invited him to go to the U.S. Open at Inverness Golf Club in Ohio. He ran into Leo Diegel, who was playing and asked if he'd like to caddie. Ross said yes, but wanted to do so for Bobby Jones, who was playing his first Open. Ross was lucky enough to get Jones's bag and recalled the first time he saw him early the next morning, getting out of a car. "He wore a brown suit and a flat straw hat, tilted a bit to one side. His face was tanned and his big smile made me sure that here was a fellow I could root for to the finish, win or lose."[21]

After Diegel made the introductions, Jones asked Ross a few questions and then told him to grab his bag and meet him at the practice tee. He began shagging balls for Jones, which was easy duty. "All I had to do was watch where the first ball landed, take a couple of steps backward and catch the rest on the first bounce."

Jones was in contention to win, but a final round 77 put him in a tie for eighth, due in large part to poor putting, four shots back of winner Ted Ray. When the 1920 Open was over, Bobby said he'd see Luke at the U.S. Amateur in September, and that was the start. It was also the last of what Jones called his "kid" tournaments, as he began controlling his temper better, and quit throwing clubs as much. In their first few events together, Jones would throw a club and Ross would chase after it, and another poor shot would usually follow. Then Stewart Maiden, Jones's teacher, suggested that whenever he threw a club, Ross should walk slowly back to his player. This, Ross claimed, gave "him time to cool off. It seemed to work."[22]

When the USGA ended the use of private caddies at the U.S. Open and Amateur in 1926, the team of Jones and Ross was broken up. "My associations with Bobby also affected my life after I gave up caddieing [sic] to become a professional. A lot of people would take lessons from me thinking that I could teach them to swing the club like Bobby did. His name helped me a lot."

The USGA banned professional caddies "because their visits are considered to have had a demoralizing effect on local club carriers." It was called "an initial step to discourage a travelling corps of between 50 and 100 veteran campaigners – experienced carriers who follow their golf idols from tournament to tournament." It affected not only Luke Ross, but others such as Joe Horgan, considered the "dean of caddies."[23]

Jones's last win came at the 1930 U.S. Amateur at Merion, which completed his famous Grand Slam. On top of the golfing world, he announced his retirement soon after. Howard Rexford caddied for him that week, and recalled the experience in 1981 when he was 70 years old. Howard was supposed to caddie for Chick Evans, thanks to his brother Alfred's intercession, but then told Evans that the caddie master had arranged for him to caddie for Jones instead. "Mr. Evans told me, 'Son, if you've got Jones, you've got the best man, keep him.'"[24] After carrying Jones's clubs all week – Howard remembered there were 18 in his bag in the years before the 14-club limit – he waited outside the clubhouse, wondering how much he'd get paid.

Rexford didn't really care, he said, the experience had been enough. Jones came out to thank him and put some money in his hand. Howard pocketed it and waited until he was away from the clubhouse to count it. "I had $150 in $10 bills [about $2,300 today.]" Quite a payday considering the usual caddie fee at Merion then was a dollar a round. Five years later he sent Jones an invitation to his wedding. Jones couldn't attend, but sent a cut-glass fruit bowl that would be treasured by the couple. Rexford kept Jones's winning ball for a few years, but then lost track of it. It was a Spalding Dot, the ball Jones preferred. "I wish I had it now. It would be priceless."[25]

Other Caddies

Racism was deep inside of golf in the early 20th century, as we have seen in previous chapters. African Americans were prevalent among the caddie corps, and the year John Shippen moved to Shady Rest Country Club, an article appeared in *The American Golfer* in which the author noted a friend's love of Pinehurst caddies:

> He loves the old fashioned real black darkies of the South and initiated me into their rich sense of humor, their quaint stories and their superstitions about spooks, "hants" and luck. He makes them sing with their banjoes, guitars, washboards, and kazoos.

He went on to say his friend felt golf was no longer golf to him "without a black Southern caddie, afraid of everything and ready to laugh at anything."[26] This was the prevailing culture of the times and it's little wonder that when Bob Jones and his partner Clifford Robert opened Augusta National in 1932 that they staffed it with all black caddies. Or that the first clubhouse employee Roberts hired was Bowman Mulligan, "large and strong and a fine-looking black man...."[27]

On the professional level, caddies by the 1950s saw their roles shrinking. Duke Hancock, a friend of Cyril Walker's, contended that in "the old days the top players relied on me for the choice of club to use. But if I offered a recommendation to many of today's stars, they'd really chew me out." As Ben Hogan explained, "I've spent 30 years putting my game together. Do you think I'm going to let some stranger tell me what to do with it?" Hancock caddied for Gene Sarazen at the Bing Crosby tournament in 1958, saying Sarazen still asked him what club to use 75 percent of the time.[28]

Hancock also claimed that some of the best players of the late 1950s were "great alibiers. When they make a bum shot they'll blame it on the caddie...We probably had more truly volatile players back in the Twenties than today but they seldom blamed anyone but themselves." Before players had regular caddies, they relied on whatever was available each week. Sometimes funny things would happen. Lew Worsham was playing in Denver once when he was confronted with a downhill chip to a fast green. He chose a safe shot with the putter. His caddie was totally unimpressed and told him so. "Whoever told you you could play golf? That's a chip shot, not a putt. Man, take your wedge and cut it up there."[29] Could you imagine a caddie doing that today? I'd love to see it.

****

Fans

Golf had its own version of a "groupie" fan in the early 1980s, a guy who was seen on TV frequently. You couldn't miss him, with his rainbow afro-wig and shirt that had "John 3:16" emblazoned across the front of it. Rollen Frederick Stewart, or "Rockin' Rollen" as he came to be known, was just another actor trying to make a buck when he realized that "wearing the wig and acting crazy" could make him a living promoting various products. He had been living on a ranch in Cle Elum, Washington, with his life revolving around sex and drugs. "I wasn't happy, though, and one night I had a religious experience and was born again as a Christian." He sold his ranch and began traveling to spread the Word.[30]

He sold everything he owned except his car, which he slept in, but was not worried about the future. "Christ will come back before my money runs out," he said. Already having gained noticed at other events like the 1979 Super Bowl and 1980 Olympics, he began following the Tour in 1981, when he was 36, and in 1983 attended 28 tournaments. Stewart even attended the Royal Wedding in 1981, and was on television "just before Charles kissed Princess Di out on the balcony of Buckingham Palace. I couldn't have prayed for more." Stewart was befriended by Larry Nelson, the 1983 U.S. Open champion, who bankrolled him on a trip to that year's Masters and British Open. "I had to check my wig at the gate," said Stewart sheepishly.[31]

Frank Chirkinian, for over 35 years the director of golf telecasts for CBS Sports, remembered Stewart in a 2003 interview. As Stewart kept showing up at "virtually every telecast for a two-year period during the 80s," it began to irritate Chirkinian more and more, who was said to have once offered a $50 bounty for the infamous wig. He didn't like "having this man distracting viewers from the show we worked on so hard."

One day I'd had enough. I had Stewart brought into my office. "As a Christian, I'm embarrassed by you and what you're doing. If you continue, I'm going to have you arrested at every single tournament site. You're going to be spending most of your time with your funny wig behind bars." That was the end of Rollen Stewart, at least for us.

The story had a tragic ending, as Stewart later lost his senses and was sentenced to three life terms in prison for taking a hotel maid hostage in 1992.[32]

In 1926 Bob Jones won the U.S. Open at Scioto Country Club in Ohio, and was famous for penalizing himself a stroke when he caused his ball to move on a green (he also called a penalty on himself in the 1924 event.) Jones was the most popular player on the planet and a reporter for *The Brooklyn Daily Eagle* claimed that the gallery following him was the "worse mannered," most "inconsiderate rabble" he had seen in two decades of covering golf.

It violated every rule of etiquette and decency. Three or four times Bobby Jones had to check his swing as befuddled spectators ran directly into the line of his drive. If it hadn't been for its possible effect on the contender for the title, the gallery's unruly behavior would have been laughable. The crowd, made up of individuals who apparently had never seen a golf match, got completely beyond control of the marshals.[33]

The New York Times noted that about 2,000 fans surrounded the green on the final hole to see his birdie that clinched the title.

Two years later, the 1928 U.S. Open program cautioned fans, "Don't crowd too closely. In a large circle all can see without rushing. In a small circle only the best sprinters can see." Human nature being what it is, they didn't pay much attention and ran pell-mell around the golf course to see their hero Jones, and "let other players in the tournament fare as best they could."

Johnny Farrell was paired with Jones in the first two rounds and shot a 77 in round 1. William D. Richardson wrote in *The New York Times* that there was little doubt Farrell "would have played better golf than he did if he had not been jostled and jolted the way he was at the outset. It wasn't so bad for Jones. The crowd waited for him to play his shots."[34] They didn't extend Farrell the same courtesy, but despite these distractions, he beat Jones in a playoff by a single shot, due to better putting (he took 62 to Jones's 68 putts over the extra 36 holes.)

People remember the 1991 Ryder Cup as being the beginning of overly rowdy crowds in that event, but there were bad feelings in 1937 at Southport, England. "There were whoops of joy on the part of partisan spectators," noted Joe Williams in a newspaper article, when the U.S. side hit a poor shot or missed a short putt. Conversely, there was "nothing but a stiff silence when vital strokes happened to come off all right." Gene Sarazen was so offended he said he wouldn't play anymore in England after that year's British Open. He claimed that marshals had moved his opponent's ball when it appeared to be out of bounds. "It wasn't out of bounds after the gallery police got through with it. Or such was the charge of Mr. Sarazen."

Williams contended that the attitude of golf galleries was changing. "There was a time back in the Newport days when only the economic royalists played the sport when it was strictly a 'silence please' game." But in recent years spectators had become more animated and vocal, and felt they could "ignore the heavy restraints of tradition" and cheer openly for their favorites.[35]

At the British Open at Carnoustie the following week, Byron Nelson took a spill when he was accidentally tripped by a spectator. It led to a back problem that required a couple of trips to the chiropractor. Crowd control became more of an issue as increased numbers of people began attending golf tournaments. There was always a modicum of control, as in the early days marshals would follow groups that attracted the most spectators and hold a rope or a bamboo pole directly behind the players.

Byron Nelson was the victim of out of control spectators again in the 1946 U.S. Open. Marshals set up ropes almost on top of his ball on the 15th hole during the third round, and his caddie stepped on it as he ducked under the rope. Nelson was penalized a stroke, and said it "indirectly cost me the championship, but it wasn't the caddie's fault." He would go on to lose in a playoff to Lloyd Mangrum. *New York Times* columnist Arthur Daley described the gallery as a "mobile mob scene," and a "thundering herd [that] ravaged the countryside." He suggested that "the only way to hold spectator in check is to string the fairways with barbed wire."

At the 1947 PGA Championship at the Plum Hollow Country Club in Detroit, Australian Jim Ferrier had a unique solution to possible fan interference as he faced Michigan's Chick Harbert in the final match. Ferrier hired two policemen for $100 and stationed one on each side of the fairway to help maintain order. He beat Harbert 2 and 1 and said afterwards "that was the best $100 that I have ever spent."[36]

The problem of galleries getting out of hand took a huge leap forward when the USGA began roping fairways, green, and tees for the entire course at the 1954 U.S. Open. Golf course architect Robert Trent Jones suggested in 1952 that roping off target areas would give 15,000 spectators a chance to follow play and make it possible to protect the rough. "If the target area is roped off," he said, "then spectators would form a huge horseshoe and thousands could see the play." Jones noted that after the first round of the 1952 U.S. Open, the Bermuda rough had been effectively trampled down, thus neutralizing its value as a penalty. In some cases he said the rough was easier to play out of than the fairways.[37]

The USGA agreed with his idea "after heated discussion, and the idea caught on." The system was challenged immediately, as fans of Ben Hogan jumped the ropes. Joe Dey, executive director of the USGA, said years later that Jack Smaltz of Baltusrol had assured him that marshals could handle the situation, especially if they were allowed to halt play should the crowd disregard the ropes. Dey agreed, declaring at the time, "If they continue breaking these regulations, we will be forced to suspend play until order is restored."[38] The strategy worked, but fans were not satisfied.

The players appreciated not having spectators breathing down their necks as they tried to play a shot. Mike Souchak said, "There is no one around us at any time and we like that." He added that spectators still got closer to the players than they did at other sporting events. Claude Harmon, 1948 Masters champion, said at the time that the roping helped the players, keeping fans from frequently coming up "to chat and [recall] the time you played their course back in 1941."[39]

George S. May, famous golf promoter who was known for his innovations and also his acceptance of African Americans in his tournaments, interviewed 100 spectators in 1956, and only six thought roping courses was a good idea. "Mr. May's opinion," wrote *Golf World*, "is that if the PGA players insist on the tournaments being roped off, the attendance of all tournaments will go down rapidly because of the spectator's dissatisfaction." May said he would never rope his events from tee to green. The Masters and British Open had also been roping courses for crowd control, although fans could still be rude.

That same year it was reported that a spectator casually pulled clubs from Peter Thomson's bag while he was on the practice green and began inspecting them. Thomson was standing only eight feet away, and said nothing, but shot the intruder a harsh look. That couldn't happen today, as practice areas are cordoned off like a Presidential event. In golf, a ticket gives the fan "the feeling of belonging to the whole surrounding," although many lack manners, scurrying off to the next tee after their favorite player finishes putting, and talking loudly on cell phones.[40]

In 1977 Frank Beard, an 11-time winner on the PGA Tour, wrote in his column in *Golf Digest* that there are two basic types of spectators in the galleries. "Anywhere from 10 to 50 percent are true golf fans, and at most tournaments the figure is closer to 10 percent. The rest are 'entertainment people.' I define those as people who come to the golf course on a nice sunny day because it's the place to be." As proof of his hypothesis, he said "come out on a cold, rainy day sometime. The folks out there on those days are your true golf fans."

Beard observed a couple other things that are true today. One is that many of them don't even bother to watch the golf. "They just grab a hot dog and some beer and find a nice shady spot where they can watch the world go by – or pursue other pastimes." Now you see them in the merchandise tent or special pavilions, trying to win a new car in a drawing or checking the scores – or video – on their smart phones.[41]

Grantland Rice once wrote that "the golf spectator has to be a cross-country runner, high hurdler, high jumper and sprinter." Ben Hogan once said that the "golf fan certainly must be the strangest and the most faithful of all sports spectators." He fights traffic to get to the course, has to park far away, and when he finally gets inside – Hogan didn't foresee having to go through airport-like security – "he gets pushed around by [marshals] and queues up for a cold sandwich and a beer at double the price. Then he fights his way through a stampeding crowd to see perhaps a half dozen golf shots all day."[42] Not much has changed.

Golf is entertainment at the highest levels, and people enjoy seeing their favorites perform. We like to live vicariously through others and see how others do things we wish we could do. Spectators can support players but can also act like idiots. At the 2019 PGA at Bethpage, New York, I heard a drunkard say to one of the best players in the world, "Hey Rory [McIlroy], your driver makes my girlfriend horny." As one newspaper put it, "With the widening appeal of the game, spectators who have not an inborn appreciation of golf etiquette are becoming the rule rather than the exception at championships." That was written in 1926, proving the adage that the more things change, the more they stay the same.

Women

The late Barbara Romack, winner of the 1954 U.S. Women's Amateur and the first female golfer to grace the cover of *Sports Illustrated*, claimed in 1968 that a "lot of wild things happen to me, but this was the wildest." She was on Delta flight 843 going from Chicago to Palm Beach, Florida, with a stop in Tampa, when a man at the front of the plane wearing a cowboy hat and Levis stood up. "The stewardess was taking coffee into the cockpit," said Romack, "and he slipped in behind her," putting a gun to her neck. Soon after they entered the cockpit, "the pilot announced over the loudspeaker that we were going to Havana...No one got overly excited, I'll have to admit."[43]

When they arrived in Havana "some guy in an old shirt welcomed us. Then the military came on board and they took us all off. They served us coffee and lemonade, treated us very nicely and they even served us drinks." The 102 dazed passengers were also given cigarettes and pictures of the recently killed revolutionary Ernesto "Che" Guevara (quite a souvenir.) Even though she had to pay for the daiquiris at the airport, Romack said the crew "did a great job" during the ordeal and the Cuban authorities released the plane after three hours.

As for the hijacker in the white cowboy hat, she concluded that "all those guys in the white hats aren't good guys."[44]

Mary Elizabeth Anthony, better known as Bessie, was an excellent player at the Glen View Club in Golf, Illinois, and won the Women's Western Amateur in 1901, 1902, and 1903. She had as a regular caddie the great Chick Evans, later winner of the U.S. Amateur and U.S. Open, who she credited with teaching her many intricacies of the game. She was a determined player, and her goal was to win the U.S. Women's Amateur. When Bessie was introduced to Bernard Shea Horne at the Allegheny Country Club, a romance blossomed. "But, like the true golfer that she is," reported one newspaper, "Miss Anthony would not allow love to interfere with the game. With all a lover's impatience Mr. Horne urged an immediate marriage," but she "refused to distract her mind with the necessities of a trousseau until after the championship."[45]

In 1903, the U.S. Women's Amateur was played at the Chicago Golf Club, where Anthony beat J. Anna Carpenter in the final. The sweetest words Mr. Horne ever heard were "7 up and 6 to play," according to the Chicago *World*. "No soft whispers in the moonlight" the article went on, "no long kiss in some old-fashioned garden – just 7 up and 6 to play." After her victory, newspapers reported that Bessie had been engaged to be married, but no date had been set. "Why, no one knew, but now that she has become the national title-holder it is said that she was determined to win the championship before marrying," and a month later the couple tied the knot at the First Presbyterian church in Evanston, Illinois before 1,000 invited guests.[46]

Tragically, nine years later, the 32-year-old Anthony passed away after a sudden illness in her home in Keswick, Virginia, leaving her husband and three young sons behind. "She was called the daughter of the club," said Harry B. Clow of Glen View. Her fellow players all liked her for her good sportsmanship and companionship. "She was a wonderful player and a charming woman, and every member of the club took a warm interest in her prowess."[47]

A Few Final Things

William T. Linskill came to St Andrews, Scotland in the 1870s, becoming a town councilor in 1896 and later serving as Dean of Guild (head of the town's craftsmen.) He joined the Royal and Ancient Golf Club in 1875 at age 20, and enjoyed history, writing many articles for the *St Andrews Citizen* and other publications.

In a November 19, 1927 article, he described his experiences on the Links around 1873: "I can recall very vividly indeed those perfect early sunny spring mornings when Charlie Macdonald and I used to run down (one never walked then) to the Links, and get out our cherished pack of clubs from Tom Morris's shop." They would be greeted by "Old Tom and his pipe at the door to say a cheery word of encouragement to us wild boys."[48]

> There were no golfers about at that very early hour, but a few folk would be beating carpets on the grass to the north of Gibson Place (there was no road there then), and a few hefty women and 'sonsie lassies' would be washing clothes at the Swilcan Burn, and laying them out on the grass to bleach or spreading them over the luxuriant whins by the Ladies' Putting Green. Woe betide any luckless golfer who ventured to strike a ball on to those ladies' washings; their language was plain, loud and sultry.
>
> Not only was the actual playing space on the Old Course extremely narrow in those days, but the grass was awfully long, rank, and tangled (no lovely,

mown fairways) and buttercups and daisies abounded thicker than mushrooms. These prolific daisies were, were, in many places, so thick that they resembled snow, and a yellow or red ball was required...Young Tommy frequently met us on our return trip, and gave us a few tips on how to play the game.

I often wonder what the present day golfer would say to the Old Course as it then was, Black Forests of thick gigantic whins, deep natural bunkers, honey-combed with rabbit holes, a very rough fairway, and grassy putting greens, none too smooth.[49]

Linskill continued on December 3, 1927:

In the old days there was no trouble or bother whatever about getting off the first tee of the Old Golf Course – no worry and no waiting as there is now. One could practice driving, approaching, or putting when and where one liked quite unchecked. Ballots and crowds of players were undreamt of then, so were tee boxes.

As the sand required for teeing purposes was scraped up from the bottom of the hole, and as these holes were infrequently changed, their depth became great. After holing out one had often to reach down up to the shoulder to recover the ball from the bottom of the hole.[50]

What I wouldn't give to go back in a time machine and see with my own eyes the things Linskill described.

On April 14, 1912, the *Titanic* hit an iceberg on its maiden voyage and sank, with 1,500 souls perishing in one of the most famous disasters of all time. Harry Cooper, winner of 31 events on the PGA Tour and twice runner-up in the U.S. Open, was a seven-year-old boy coming to the United States with his family from England. "We left right after *Titanic*," he remembered, "and we came through the same ice flow, and we arrived in Halifax and we saw them bringing the bodies…in from the tugboat there."[51]

****

In 1948, a year after winning the British Ladies Amateur and two years after winning the U.S. Women's Amateur, Babe Zaharias announced to the press that she wanted to play in the U.S. Open that year in Los Angeles. In March, Joe Dey of the USGA acknowledged that she had sent a letter expressing this desire. He explained that official entry forms had not been printed and "it has been the practice in the past not to rule on an entry until it is received on the stipulated blank and is accompanied by the entry fee." Dey added that the rules under which the 1947 U.S. Open was played "would not have denied Mrs. Zaharias the right to play. But the rules are changed from time to time."[52]

On April 4th, it was reported that sportswriter Braven Dyer had taken an informal poll of members of the Southern California section of the PGA. "The group voted 45 to 19 to allow Mrs. Zaharias to play in the National. The inference was that the mighty Babe wouldn't cut the mustard anyhow, and no harm would come if a woman was permitted to enter." But three days later the USGA announced the rules had been changed:

> As the Championship has always been intended to be for men, the eligibility rules have been re-phrased to confirm that condition. Applicants must be men who are either professional golfers or amateurs with handicaps not exceeding three strokes. Thus, the

USGA has declined an informal entry submitted in behalf of Mrs. George Zaharias.[53]

It was reported that the "golfing fathers, taking alarm, have amended their rules to read 'for men only.'" Another sportswriter said that Babe should have been given a chance, as it would have added color to the championship. And if she didn't qualify, "the problem of women in National Open golf tournaments is settled once and for all. But no, the boys wouldn't take the chance."[54]

Zaharias should have waited until the entry forms had been printed and she might have been allowed to try to qualify. She had played in the Los Angeles Open years before, and it would have been something to see her try to make the field that year and compete against Ben Hogan and all the rest. Alas, it wasn't meant to be.

I could go on and on with other fun little stories from the long and varied history of golf, but the book would never end. In the words of one of my favorite comedians, Red Skelton, I'll just say, as he did at the end of his television show, "Good night, and may God bless."

Acknowledgements

This book could not have been written without the help of numerous people. Librarians and archivists lead the list. At the United States Golf Association, thanks to retired librarian Nancy Stulack – who was a superstar at what she did – and the Director of the Museum, Hilary Cronheim. The library's wonderful collections contributed heavily to the book, especially chapters featuring John Shippen, Pat Ball, and Babe Zaharias.

Also instrumental to the telling of John Shippen's story were collections at the Smithsonian's Anacostia Community Museum Archives; thanks to archivist Jennifer Morris and curator Alcione Amos. The staff at Howard University's Moorland-Spingarn Research Center helped me with items relating to John Shippen's family. At George Washington University and the Gelman Library's Special Collections Research Center, Jennifer King, an old friend, was as helpful and friendly as ever; at Yale University's Library Manuscripts and Archives division (which also helped with my chapter on Eben Byers), Genevieve Coyle went above and beyond. Thanks go to the Library of Congress for its newspapers collections and also the Washington DC Archives. At Georgetown University, Lynn Conway, University Archivist and Allan Hutchison-Maxwell, Office of Advancement, were gracious with their time.

The staff at the Kentucky Historical Society was very helpful in providing copies of parts of Marion Miley's diaries.

For the chapter on Pebble Beach, a very special thanks to Pam Grossman for talking with me about her family and great-grandmother, Lucy Barnes Brown, and for correcting a few errors in my research. Thanks to Michael Weishan, Executive Director of the Franklin Delano Roosevelt Foundation, Inc. at Harvard University for introducing me to Pam. Neal Hotelling, the historian at Pebble Beach, was also kind enough to provide new information. The final part of the story took me to the Green-Wood Cemetery, where Connie Thatcher and the genealogy team provided me with burial information on Lucy Barnes Brown.

The story of the St Andrews "Rabbit Wars" took me to Scotland. Thanks to Angela Howe, Director of the British Golf Museum, as well as

Hannah Fleming. At the University of St Andrews Richardson Research Library's Special Collections Division, retired director Norman Reid, Julie Greenhill, and Catriona Foote, especially, were extremely helpful and patient with my numerous and varied requests for documents. Julie's smiling face was always a welcome sight after a long day of trying to make out 200-year-old handwritten letters. At the St Andrews Preservation Trust Museum, thanks to curator Nicola Moss for allowing me access to its wonderful photographs. Thanks also to John Pearson and the British Golf Collectors Society for allowing me to use longer versions of articles I published earlier in its journal *Through the Green* (on Cyril Walker, John Shippen, and the St Andrews "Rabbit Wars.") I've been a proud member of the BGCS since 2012, which has a strong dedication to the history of the game.

Buddy Alexander took the time to answer my questions concerning his father Skip, and helped clarify and correct a few things in my research regarding him. Thank you Buddy very much for your help and humor. Thanks to Gary Plato for providing personal insights into Lucious Bateman that are a powerful testimonial to the man, and for allowing me to use a photograph he took of Bateman and Tony Lema (and Bateman's dog "Hacker.") Al Barkow, journalist and editor extraordinaire, also was kind enough to share some information on Mr. Bateman. My chapter on women in golf was informed by the wonderful work of the following: Rhonda Glenn, Pam Emory, Susan Cahn, Susan Cayleff, Liz Kahn, and M. Mikell Johnson, among others. Their contributions to the history of women's golf is impressive and far reaching.

Thanks also to the following: Timothy H. Horning, University Archives, University of Pennsylvania; Alison Stankrauff, University Archivist and Kelli Jurich, Office of Alumni Relations, Wayne State University; Kelly J. Helm, College Archivist, Washington & Jefferson College; Louisa Hoffman, Oberlin College Archives; and Don Holton, Historian, Exmoor Country Club.

And last, but certainly not least, thanks to Karen Greisman for proofreading the manuscript, as well as to my sister Lynda and brother-in-law Larry for reviewing the chapter on Pebble Beach and Lucy Barnes Brown. In writing this book I realize that life, as my late mother used to say, is for the living. We should all appreciate the pleasures of the day and keep working to contribute to this world with each day that is given to us. The people in this book inspire me to keep striving and not be derailed by thinking my best days are behind me, existing only in my memories. Where there is hope, there is indeed life.

Bibliography

Books

Abbott, Karen. *Sin in the Second City: Madams, Ministers, Playboys, and the Battle for America's Soul*. New York: Random House, 2007.

Adamson, Alistair Beaton. *Millions of Mischiefs: Rabbits, Golf & St Andrews*. Malvern: Peachfield Press, 1990.

Brownmiller, Susan. *Femininity*. New York: Simon & Schuster, 1984.

Cayleff, Susan E. *Babe: The Life and Legend of Babe Didrikson Zaharias*. Urbana, Illinois: University of Illinois Press, 1995.

Chafe, William H. *The American Woman: Her Changing Social, Economic, and Political Roles, 1920-1970*. New York: Oxford University Press, 1972.

Chambers, Marcia. *The Unplayable Lie: The Untold Story of Women and Discrimination in American Golf*. New York: Pocket Books, 1995.

Barkow, Al. *Getting' to the Dance Floor: An Oral History of American Golf*. New York: Atheneum, 1986.

Behrend, John and Peter N. Lewis. *Challenges and Champions: The Royal & Ancient Golf Club, 1754-1883*. St Andrews: The Royal & Ancient Golf Club, 1998.

Boswell, Charley with Curt Anders. *Now I See*. New York: Meredith Press, 1969.

Brown, Lathrop. *Charles Stelle Brown (1851-1935): A Biographical Memoir with Genealogical Notes*. New York: privately published, 1937.

Cahn, Susan K. *Coming on Strong: Gender and Sexuality in Twentieth-Century Women's Sport*. New York: The Free Press, 1994.

Canton, David A. *Raymond Pace Alexander: A New Negro Lawyer Fights for Civil Rights in Philadelphia*. Jackson, Mississippi: University Press of Mississippi, 2010.

Casey, Edward S. *Remembering: A Phenomenological Study*. Bloomington, Indiana: Indiana University Press, 1987.

Coleman, J. Winston, Jr. *Double Murder at the Lexington Country Club*. Lexington, Kentucky: The Winburn Press, 1981.

Collins, Gail. *America's Women: Four Hundred Years of Dolls, Drudges, Helpmates, and Heroines*. New York: Harper Collins, 2003.

Cose, Ellis. *Color-blind: Seeing Beyond Race in a Race-Obsessed World*. New York: Harper Collins, 1997.

Coventry, Kim. *Exmoor Country Club: The First Hundred Years*. East Greenwich, Rhode Island: Meridian Printing, 1996.

Crane, Malcolm. *The Story of Ladies' Golf*. London: Stanley Paul, 1991.

Dawkins, Marvin P. and Graham C. Kinloch. *African America Golfers During the Jim Crow Era*. Westport, Connecticut: Praeger, 2000.

Demas, Lane. *Game of Privilege: An African American History of Golf*. Chapel Hill: The University of North Carolina Press, 2017.

Dray, Philip. *At the Hands of Persons Unknown: The Lynching of Black America*. New York: Random House, 2002.

Du Bois, W.E.B. *Black Reconstruction in America, 1860-1880*. New York: World Publishing Company, 1967.

_____. *The Souls of Black Folks*. New York: Literary Classics of the United States, 1990.

Dunne, Edward J., John L. McIntosh, and Karen Dunne-Maxim. *Suicide and Its Aftermath: Understanding and Counseling the Survivors*. New York: W.W. Norton and Company, 1987.

Elzey, Chris and David K. Wiggins. eds. *DC Sports: The Nation's Capital at Play*. Fayetteville, Arkansas: University of Arkansas Press, 2015.

Everard, H.S.C. *A History of the Royal & Ancient Golf Club St Andrews from 1754-1900*. London: William Blackwood and Sons, 1907.

Fifty Years of the Maidstone Club, 1891-1941. New York, New York: Pace Press, Inc., 1941.

Fleming, David Hay. *Historical Notes & Extracts Concerning the Links of St. Andrews, 1552-1893*. St Andrews: Citizen Office, 1893.

Franklin, John Hope and Alfred A. Moss, Jr. 8th ed. *From Slavery to Freedom: A History of African Americans*. New York: McGraw Hill, 2000.

Gallico, Paul. *Farewell to Sport*. New York: Alfred A. Knopf, 1941.

Gates, Henry Louis, Jr. *Stony the Road: Reconstruction, White Supremacy, and the Rise of Jim Crow*. New York: Penguin Press, 2019.

Glenn, Rhonda. *The Illustrated History of Women's Golf*. Dallas, Texas: Taylor Trade Publishing, 1991.

Goodner, Ross. *Golf's Greatest: The Legendary World Golf Hall of Famers*. Norwalk, Connecticut: Golf Digest, 1978.

_____. *The 75 Year History of Shinnecock Hills Golf Club*. Southampton, New York: Shinnecock Hills Golf Club, 1966.

Graham, Julian P. *A Photographic Study of Pebble Beach Golf Links*. Carmel-by-the-Sea, California: Carmel Work Center, 1951.

Green, Constance McLaughlin. *The Secret City: A History of Race Relations in the Nation's Capital*. Princeton, New Jersey: Princeton University Press, 1967.

Grimsby, Will. *Golf: Its History, People, and Events*. New York: Prentice Hall, 1966.

Haultain, Theodore Arnold. *The Mystery of Golf*. 2nd ed. New York: Macmillan Company, 1910.

Hotelling, Neal. *Pebble Beach: The Official Golf History*. Chicago: Triumph Books, 2009.

Hudson, David L., Jr. *Women in Golf: The Players, the History, and the Future of the Sport*. Westport, Connecticut: Praeger, 2008.

Husband, Julie and Jim O'Loughlin. *Daily Life in the Industrial United States, 1870-1900*. Westport, Connecticut: Greenwood Press, 2004.

Isenberg, Nancy. *White Trash: The 400-Year Untold Story of Class in America*. New York: Viking, 2016.

Jack, Zachary Michael. *Let There be Pebble: A Middle-Handicapper's Year in America's Garden of Golf*. Lincoln, Nebraska: University of Nebraska Press, 2011.

Jarrett, Tom. *St Andrews Golf Links: The First 600 Years*. Edinburgh: Mainstream Publishing Company, 1995.

Johnson, M. Mikell. *The African American Woman Golfer: Her Legacy*. Westport, Connecticut: Praeger, 2008.

_____. *Heroines of African American Golf: The Past, The Present and The Future*. Bloomington, Indiana: Trafford Publishing, 2010.

Johnson, William Oscar and Nancy P. Williamson. *Whatta-Gal: The Babe Didrikson Story*. Boston: Little, Brown and Company, 1977.

Kahn, Liz. *The LPGA: The Unauthorized Version, The History of the Ladies Professional Golf Association*. Menlo Park, California: Group Fore Productions, Inc., 1996.

Kennedy, John H. *A Course of Their Own: A History of African American Golfers*. Lincoln, Nebraska: University of Nebraska Press, 2005.

Kennedy, Randall. *Nigger: The Strange Career of a Troublesome Word*. New York: Pantheon Books, 2002.

Kirkaldy, Andra. *Fifty Years of Golf: Memories*. London: T. Fisher Unwin, Ltd., 1921.

Kirsch, George B. *Golf in America*. Chicago: University of Illinois Press, 2009.

Kupelian, Vartan. *Forever Scratch: Chuck Kocsis – An Amateur for the Ages*. Ann Arbor, Michigan: Sports Media Group, 2007.

Labbance, Bob with Brian Sipio. *The Vardon Invasion: Harry's Triumphant 1900 American Tour*. Ann Arbor, Michigan: Sports Media Group, 2008.

Low, John L. *Concerning Golf*. London: Hodder and Stoughton, 1903.

McDaniel, Pete. *Uneven Lies: The Heroic Story of African Americans in Golf*. Greenwich, Connecticut: American Golfer, Inc., 2000.

Macy, Beth. *Dopesick: Dealers, Doctors, and the Drug Company That Addicted America*. New York: Little, Brown, and Company, 2018.

Martin, H.B. *Fifty Years of American Golf*. New York: Dodd, Mead & Company, 1936.

Matthew, Sidney. *Bobby: The Life and Times of Bobby Jones*. Ann Arbor, Michigan: Sports Media Group, 2005.

Miller, Kelly. *Race Adjustment*. 1908. Reprint, New York: Arno Press, 1968.

Moore, Kate. *The Radium Girls: The Dark Story of America's Shining Women*. Naperville, Illinois: Sourcebooks, 2017.

Moss, Richard J. *Golf and the American Country Club*. Urbana, Illinois: University of Chicago Press, 2001.

_____. *The Kingdom of Golf in America*. Lincoln, Nebraska: University of Nebraska Press, 2013.

Mrozek, Donald J. *Sport and American Mentality, 1880-1910*. Knoxville, Tennessee: The University of Tennessee Press, 1983.

Murphy, Michael. *Golf in the Kingdom*. New York: Viking Arkana, 1994.

Myrdal, Gunnar. *An American Dilemma: The Negro Problem and Modern Democracy*. New York: Harper Brothers, 1944.

Nickerson, Elinor. *Golf: A Women's History*. Jefferson, North Carolina: McFarland & Company, Inc., 1987.

Novick, Peter. *That Noble Dream: The "Objectivity Question" and the American Historical Profession*. Cambridge, England: Cambridge University Press, 1988.

Nuland, Sherwin B. *The Art of Aging*. New York: Random House, 2007.

Osborne, Charles. *Boss: The Story of S.F.B. Morse, the Founder of Pebble Beach*. Pebble Beach, California: Del Monte Publishing Co., 2018.

Outerbridge, David E. *Champion in a Man's World: The Biography of Marion Hollins*. Chelsea, Michigan: Sleeping Bear Press, 1998.

Quinones, Sam. *Dreamland: The True Tale of America's Opiate Epidemic*. New York: Bloomsbury Press, 2015.

Rader, Benjamin G. *American Sports: From the Age of Folk Games to the Age of Televised Sports*. Upper Saddle River, New Jersey: Prentice Hall, 1983.

Roberts, Clifford. *The Story of the Augusta National Golf Club*. New York: Doubleday and Company, 1976.

Rubio, Philip F. *A History of Affirmative Action, 1619-2000*. Jackson, Mississippi: University Press of Mississippi, 2001.

Schacter, Daniel L. *Searching for Memory: The Brain, the Mind, and the Past*. New York: Basic Books, 1996.

Sheff, David. *Clean: Overcoming Addiction and Ending America's Greatest Tragedy*. New York: Houghton Mifflin Harcourt, 2013.

Shipler, David K. *A Country of Strangers: Blacks and Whites in America*. New York: Alfred A. Knopf, 1997.

Shippen, Beulah A. and Mabel S. (Shippen) Hatcher. *The Family Recollections of Beulah A. Shippen and Mabel S. (Shippen) Hatcher* [Washington, DC?]: privately published, 1994.

Sinnette, Calvin H. *Forbidden Fairways: African Americans and the Game of Golf*. Chelsea, Michigan: Sleeping Bear Press, 1998.

Sitcoff, Harvard. *A New Deal for Blacks: The Emergence of Civil Rights as a National Issue, Volume 1: The Depression Decade*. New York: Oxford University Press, 1978.

Smith, Marilynn with Bob Cayne. *Have Clubs, Will Travel*. Goodyear, Arizona: Ambassador Publishing, 2012.

Spivey, Donald. ed. *Sport in America: New Historical Perspectives*. Westport, Connecticut: Greenwood Press, 1985.

Starck, Brent and John Cashman. *Lake Geneva Country Club Centennial: A Tradition of Lake and Country Elegance 1895-1995*. Lake Geneva, Wisconsin: Lake Geneva Country Club, 1996.

Stewart, Alison. *First Class: The Legacy of Dunbar, America's First Black Public High School*. Chicago: Lawrence Hill Books, 2013.

Tschetter, Kris with Steve Eubanks. *Mr. Hogan, The Man I Knew*. New York: Gotham Books, 2010.

Van Natta, Don, Jr. *Wonder Girl: The Magnificent Sporting Life of Babe Didrikson Zaharias*. New York: Little, Brown and Company, 2011.

Vaughan, Roger. *Golf: The Woman's Game*. New York: Stewart, Tabori & Chang, 2000.

Walters, Dennis with James Achenbach. *In My Dreams I Walk With You*. Chelsea, Michigan: Sleeping Bear Press, 2002.

Ward-Thomas, Pat. *The Royal and Ancient*. Edinburgh: Scottish Academic Press, 1980.

Ware, Susan. *Holding Their Own: American Women in the 1930s*. Boston: Twayne Publishers, 1982.

Wertheimer, Alison. *A Special Scar: The Experiences of People Bereaved by Suicide*. 2nd ed. Philadelphia: Taylor and Francis, Inc., 2001.

Wiggins, David K. and Ryan A. Swanson. eds. *Separate Games: African American Sport behind the Walls of Segregation*. Fayetteville, Arkansas: University of Arkansas Press, 2016.

Wolloch, Nancy. *Women and the American Experience*. New York: Alfred A. Knopf, 1984.

Wright, Richard. *Early Works*. New York: Literary Classics of the United States, 1991.

Theses and Dissertations

Bialowas, Anne Marie. "Swinging From the Ladies' Tee: Gendered Discourses of Golf." PhD diss. The University of Utah, 2009.

Bond, Gregory. "Jim Crow at Play: Race, Manliness, and the Color Line in American Sports, 1876-1916." PhD diss., University of Wisconsin-Madison, 2008.

Manuscript Collections

United States Golf Association Arnold Palmer Center for Golf History, Far Hills, New Jersey

African American Golf History Archive
Biographical and Subject Files
Rhonda Glenn Collection
Red Hoffman Collection
Scrapbook of Early Golf in America
Connie Sullivan Papers
Leonard Wirtz Collection

Anacostia Community Museum Archives, Smithsonian Institution, Washington, DC

Anacostia Story: 1608-1930, Exhibition Records
Mabel Shippen Hatcher collection on Cyrus S. Shippen

Kentucky Historical Society, Martin F. Schmidt Research Library, Frankfort, Kentucky

Tara Hopkins West collection on Marion Miley, 1930s-1941

University of St Andrews, Richardson Research Library, Special Collections Division, St Andrews, Scotland

Burgh of St Andrews Records
Cheape Family of Strathtyrum and Lathockar papers
Scrapbook of W.T. Linskill

Oral Histories

USGA Oral History Collection

JoAnne Carner, interview by Alice Kendrick, February 10, 1992
Harry Cooper interview by J. Robert Windsor, September 10 and 17, 1990
Carol Mann, interview by Alice Kendrick, July 8, 1992
Maureen Orcutt, interview by Joe Doyle, June 16, 1991
Kathy Whitworth, interview by Alice Kendrick, January 23, 1993

Interviews

Buddy Alexander
Pam Grossman

Internet Sources

Peter Aviles, "A Talk with Hanno Shippen Smith, Grandson of John Shippen, Jr.," Black Athletes Sports Network.net, November 27, 2004, http://blackathlete.net/2004/11/a-talk-with-hanno-shippen-smith-grandson-of-john-shippen-jr., accessed October 14, 2019

"Forgotten Fame: Marion Miley," a film by Beth Kirchner, KET Documentaries, https://www.pbs.org/video/ket-presents-forgotten-fame-marion-miley/, accessed August 10, 2019

"The Franklin Delano Roosevelt Foundation," https://fdrfoundation.org, November 1, 2019

"Lucius Bateman Tribute," Northern California PGA, https://www.facebook.com/NorCalPGA/videos/1076893448953/, accessed August 8, 2019.

Magazines

The American Golfer
Golf (U.S.)
Golf (U.K.)
Golf Digest
Golf Illustrated (U.S.)
Golf Illustrated (U.K.)
Golf Journal
Golf Magazine
The Golf Monthly (U.K.)
Golf World
Golfing
Golfweek
Holiday
Life
Look
The Metropolitan Golfer
The National Golf Review
Negro Digest
The New Yorker
Outing
PGA Tour Partners Magazine
The Saturday Evening Post
Senior Golfer
The Southern Golfer
Sport
Sports Illustrated
Sports Illustrated and The American Golfer
Through the Green
Tuesday Magazine
Women Sports

Journals

American Historical Review
American Journal of Sociology
American Studies
The Annals of the American Academy of Political and Social Science
Current Directions in Psychological Science
Feminist Studies
Financial History
The Georgia Historical Quarterly
Health Physics
History of Education Quarterly
Huntington Quarterly
Journal of African American Men
The Journal of American History
The Journal of Negro Education
Journal of Social History
Journal of the History of Medicine and Allied Sciences
Medical Anthropology Quarterly
Monthly Labor Review
New York Archives
Pharmacy in History
Scientific American
Studies in Popular Culture

Newspapers

Abilene Morning Reporter-News (TX)
The Advocate-Messenger (Danville, KY)
The Akron Beacon Journal
Alabama Tribune (Montgomery, AL)
Ames Daily Tribune (IA)
Arizona Daily Star (Tucson, AZ)
The Atlanta Constitution
Austin American-Statesman (TX)
The Baltimore Afro-American
The Baltimore Evening Sun
The Baltimore Sun
The Birmingham News (AL)
Bluefield Daily Telegraph (WV)
The Boston Globe
The Brooklyn Citizen
The Brooklyn Daily Eagle
Brooklyn Times Union
The Buffalo Sunday Morning News
Chicago Defender
Chicago Tribune
The Cincinnati Enquirer
Clarion-Ledger (Jackson, MS)
The Columbus Telegram (NE)
The Courier (Waterloo, IA)
The Courier Journal (Louisville, KY)
The Courier-News (Bridgewater, NJ)
The Daily Capital News (Jefferson City, MO)
The Daily Journal (Franklin, IN)
Daily News (New York, NY)
The Daily Oklahoman (Oklahoma City, OK)
The Daily Record (Long Branch, NJ)
The Daily Times (Mamaroneck, NY)
Dayton Daily News
The Decatur Herald (IL)
The Des Moines Register
East Bay Times (Walnut Creek, CA)
El Paso Herald-Post
Elmira Star Gazette (NY)
The Evening News (Harrisburg, PA)

The Evening World (New York, NY)
The Fort Wayne News
The Gazette (Montreal, Canada)
Harrisburg Telegraph (PA)
Hartford Courant
The Herald (Jasper, IN)
The High Point Enterprise (NC)
The Index-Journal (Greenwood, SC)
The Indianapolis Journal
The Inter Ocean (Chicago, IL)
Iowa City Press Citizen
Kingsport Times (TN)
The La Crosse Tribune (WI)
Longview News-Journal (TX)
Los Angeles Sentinel
Los Angeles Times
Marion Star (OH)
Messenger-Inquirer (Owensboro, KY)
The Miami News
The Minneapolis Star
The Monroe News Star (Monroe, LA)
The Morning Call (Allentown, PA)
The Morning News (Wilmington, DE)
The New York Age
The New York Amsterdam News
New York Daily News
New York Herald
The New York Times
The News-Herald (Franklin, PA)
News-Press (Fort Myers, FL)
Oakland Tribune
The Ottawa Journal (Ottawa, Canada)
The Paducah Sun-Democrat (KY)
The Palm Beach Post (West Palm Beach, FL)
Pensacola News Journal
The Philadelphia Inquirer
The Pittsburgh Courier
Pittsburgh Daily Post
Pittsburgh Post-Gazette
The Pittsburgh Press
The Post Crescent (Appleton, WI)

Reading Times (Reading, PA)
The Record (Hackensack, NJ)
The St. Joseph Herald (MO)
St. Louis Globe-Democrat
St. Louis Post-Dispatch
The St. Louis Republic
The St. Louis Star and Times
Salt Lake Telegram
The San Francisco Examiner
The Santa Fe New Mexican
The Semi-Weekly Spokesman-Review (Spokane, WA)
Shamokin News-Dispatch (PA)
Star-Phoenix (Saskatoon, Canada)
Star Tribune (Minneapolis, MN)
Sun (New York, NY)
The Tampa Times
The Tampa Tribune
The Tennessean (Nashville, TN)
The Times (Shreveport, LA)
The Tribune (Coshocton, OH)
USA Today
The Wall Street Journal
Warren Times Mirror (PA)
Washington Afro-American
The Washington Post
Wilkes-Barre Times Leader (PA)
The Windsor Review (Windsor, MO)

Photo Credits

p.30 *The Book of Sport*. New York: J.F. Taylor & Company, 1904

p.34 Newspapers.com

p.39 Newspapers.com

p.51 *American Golfer*, January 1929

p.52 *Golf* (USGA Bulletin), August 1906

p.54 *Yale Banner*, 1899 (Courtesy of Yale University Library
    Manuscripts and Archives)

p.55 *Golf*, October 1903

p.63 Newspapers.com

p.73 *American Golfer*, June 1924

p.75 *Golfer's Magazine,* April 1930

p.79 *American Golfer*, July 12, 1924

p.84 *American Golfer*, May 30, 1925

p.90 Newspapers.com

p.99 Ancestry.com

p.100 Newspapers.com

p.106 *Boyd's Directory of Washington & Georgetown*. 1867

p.109 Newspapers.com

p.110 *Golf Illustrated* (U.K.), October 6, 1899

p.113 New York *Sun* hole scores from the Library of Congress; layout of
    Shinnecock Hills from *The Golfer*, April 1896

p.121 "A Typical Caddy," from *The Golfer*, September 1902; Pinehurst,
    from *American Golfer*, April 1909

p.124 Washington DC Archives

p.126 *Yale Banner*, 1899 (Courtesy of Yale University)

p.127 Anacostia Community Museum, Smithsonian Institution

p.130 Ancestry.com

p.140 Photo by the author

p.143 *Golf Illustrated* (U.S.), May 1932

p.153 Ancestry.com

p.155 Eastern Golf Association Program, 1932 (Courtesy USGA
    Library)

p.160 Ancestry.com

p.163 Courtesy of Gary Plato

p.174 *American Golfer*, February 1930

p.189 Ancestry.com

p.212 Photo by the author

p.213 *National Greenkeeper*, October 1929

p.214 *Golf Illustrated* (U.S.), April 1920

p.215 Library of Congress, Prints & Photographs Division,
    LC-B2-1369-4

p.217 Newspapers.com

p.221 Courtesy of Pamela Grossman

p.223 Newpapers.com

p.227 Photo by the author

p.228 Photo by the author

p.230 Photo by the author

p.233 Photo by the author

p.234 Demptser advertisement, July 19, 1806 from Cheape Family of
    Strathtyrum and Lathockar papers (Courtesy of University of St
    Andrews, Special Collections Division)

p.235 Photo by the author

p.240 James Cheape letter to Colonel Bethune of Blebo, December 7,
    1821, from Cheape Family papers (Courtesy of University of St
    Andrews, Special Collections Division and Henry Cheape)

p.242 Photos by the author

p.245 *Pine Burr*, yearbook of Beaumont High School,
    Beaumont, Texas, 1928

p.252 Newspapers.com

Notes

Preface

[1] Charles B. Macdonald, "Golf: Ethical and Physical Aspects of the Game," *Golf*, January 1898, 20.

[2] Jolee Edmondson, "The Remarkable Jimmy DeVoe," *Golf Magazine*, August 1976, 65-66.

[3] Carl Becker, "Everyman His Own Historian," his speech before the American Historical Association in *The American Historical Review* 37 (January 1932): 222.

[4] Burleigh Taylor Wilkins, *Carl Becker: A Biographical Study in American Intellectual History* (Cambridge, MA: MIT Press, 1961), 54.

Introduction: "History is Ever Allusive and Likes to Stay Hidden"

[1] Frederick Jackson Turner, quoted from Patricia Nelson Limerick, "Turnerians All: The Dream of a Helpful History in an Intelligible World," *The American Historical Review* 100 (June 1995): 704.

[2] Carl L. Becker, "What are Historical Facts?" *The Western Political Quarterly* 8 (September 1955): 338.

[3] Carl Becker, "Some Aspects of the Influence of Social Problems and Ideas Upon the Study and Writing of History," *American Journal of Sociology* 18 (March 1913): 641; Becker, "What are Historical Facts?" 335.

[4] Becker, "What are Historical Facts?" 335.

[5] Sherwin B. Nuland, *The Art of Aging* (New York: Random House, 2007), 15.

[6] Brian Dimenna and Jeff Patterson, "Young at Heart," *Golf Digest*, November 2007, 136; Henry Hoople, "Dad Miller Still Breaks His Age…97," *Golf Journal*, April 1975, 42.

[7] "The Colonel" [pseudonym] "Obiter Dicta" *Golf*, December 1900, 401; "Mr. Webster's, 'Etc.,'" *Golfing*, May 1936, 21.

Chapter 1: Nathaniel Ford Moore – "From Gold Medal to Golden Syringe"

[1] Karen Abbott, *Sin in the Second City: Madams, Ministers, Playboys, and the Battle for America's Soul* (New York: Random House, 2007), 211.

[2] "Match Company Magnate Leaves Ten Million Will," *Wilkes-Barre Times Leader, The Evening News* (PA), November 10, 1916, 11; Abbott, *Sin in the Second City*, 211.

[3] Yohanna Von Wagner, "Tenement-House Inspection," *The American Journal of Nursing* 2, no. 7 (April 1902): 510; George Rosen, "Urbanization, Occupation and Disease in the United States, 1870–1920: The Case of New York City," *Journal of the History of Medicine and Allied Sciences* 43, no. 4 (October 1988): 393.

[4] Rosen, "Urbanization, Occupation and Disease in the United States," 422; Upton Sinclair, *The Jungle* (New York: Doubleday, 1906), The Project Gutenberg, https://www.gutenberg.org/files/140/140-h/140-h.htm, accessed October 1, 2019.

[5] Richard J. Moss, *Golf and the American Country Club* (Urbana, Illinois: University of Chicago Press, 2001), 2; James M. Mayo, "The American Country Club: An Evolving Elite Landscape," *Journal of Architectural and Planning Research* 15, no. 1 (Spring 1998): 29.

[6] George B. Kirsch, *Golf in America* (Chicago: University of Illinois Press, 2009), 11; Anne Marie Bialowas, "Swinging From the Ladies' Tee: Gendered Discourses of Golf" (PhD diss., The University of Utah, 2009), 84.

[7] H.L. Fitzpatrick, "Golf and the American Girl," *Outing*, December 1898, 294-295.

[8] Donald J. Mrozek, *Sport and American Mentality, 1880-1910* (Knoxville, TN: The University of Tennessee Press, 1983), 103-104.

[9] Kirsch, *Golf in America*, 11; George B. Kirsch, "Municipal Golf Courses in the United States: 1895 to 1930," *Journal of Sport History* 32, no. 1 (Spring 2005): 25.

[10] Kirsch, *Golf in America*, 9, 6.

[11] Bialowas, "Swinging From the Ladies' Tee," 89; Kirsch, *Golf in America*, 6.

[12] Lady Greville, ed., *The Gentlewoman's Book of Sports* (London: Henry and Co., 1892), 197.

[13] Theodore Arnold Haultain, *The Mystery of Golf*, 2nd ed. (New York: Macmillan Company, 1910), 244.

[14] John L. Low, *Concerning Golf* (London: Hodder and Stoughton, 1903), 6-7; David L. Hudson, Jr., *Women in Golf: The Players, the History, and the Future of the Sport* (Westport, CT: Praeger, 2008), 7.

[15] Kirsch, *Golf in America*, 12.

[16] H.B. Martin, *Fifty Years of American Golf* (New York: Dodd, Mead & Company, 1936), 137-138. Connecticut and Illinois had 57 courses; New Hampshire, 44; California, 43; Ohio, 36; Maine, 33; Michigan, 29; Wisconsin, 28; Rhode Island, 26; Vermont and Iowa, 20 each; Florida 17; Minnesota and Indiana, 16 each; Missouri, 14; Maryland 13; Virginia 11; Colorado and North Carolina 9; Georgia 8; Kentucky 7; Texas and South Carolina 5; Kansas 4; Alabama and North Dakota, 3 each; Arkansas, Mississippi, Delaware, South Dakota and the District of Columbia, 2 each; Louisiana, Arizona, New Mexico, Wyoming, Oregon, Nevada, Utah, and Oklahoma, 1 each. In 1905 *The Boston Globe* estimated that one million people played golf in the United States. See Kirsch, *Golf in America*, 6.

[17] "Golf Matches at Williams Bay," *Chicago Tribune*, July 29, 1900, 19; Brent Starck and John Cashman, *Lake Geneva Country Club Centennial: A Tradition of Lake and Country Elegance 1895-1995* (Lake Geneva, Wisconsin: Lake Geneva Country Club, 1996), 11.

[18] "Mr. Walter E. Egan," *Golf*, April 1902, 256; Essay by Walter Egan, "The Royal and Ancient Game of Golf at the Turn of the Century" (1967), 3, in Walter Egan biographical file, United States Golf Association Arnold Palmer Center for Golf History, Far Hills, New Jersey (hereafter cited as USGA.)

[19] H. Chandler Egan, "The Beginnings of My Golf," *Golf Illustrated* (U.K.), April 13, 1906, 49; "'Nat' Moore Dead at Levee Resort," *Chicago Tribune*, January 10, 1910, 2; Bob Labbance with Brian Sipio, *The Vardon Invasion: Harry's Triumphant 1900 American Tour* (Ann Arbor, MI: Sports Media Group, 2008), 98, 100.

[20] "Vardon Beaten at Lake Geneva," *Chicago Tribune*, July 15, 1900, 18; "Vardon Breaks Another Record," *Chicago Tribune*, July 14, 1900, 6; Labbance with Sipio, *The Vardon Invasion*, 98; Starck and Cashman, *Lake Geneva Country Club Centennial*, 20.

[21] Mark Frost, *The Greatest Game Ever Played: Harry Vardon, Francis Ouimet, and the Birth of Modern Golf* (New York: Hyperion Books, 2002), 14-15.

[22] "Golf in a Gale," *The Baltimore Sun*, July 17, 1902, 6; "'Nat' Moore Dead at Levee Resort," 2. In match play, the player with the lowest score on a hole wins the hole, and the match ends when one player has won more holes than there are left to play in the match.

[23] "'Aleck' Smith is First Golfer," *Chicago Tribune*, July 18, 1903, 8; Starck and Cashman, *Lake Geneva Country Club Centennial*, 15-16. It noted Moore shot a 76-77 at the end of June on the 5,542-yard course, "an excellent score for an amateur player."

[24] Ron Coleman, "Golf's Olympic Round," *Golf Journal*, July 1976, 29.

[25] Coleman, "Golf's Olympic Round," 30; *The Baltimore Sun*, September 25, 1904, 10; *The St. Louis Republic*, September 25, 1904, 28.

[26] Alexis J. Colman, "The Olympic Championship," *Golf*, November 1904, 283.

[27] *Golf Illustrated* (U.K.), September 2, 1904, 183.

[28] Minutes of the Royal and Ancient Golf Club of St Andrews, September 23, 1913, GM 010/RNA 70023, Business Meetings, 1903-25, Special Collections Division, University of St Andrews, St Andrews, Scotland; George S. Lyon, "The Beginnings of My Golf," *Golf Illustrated* (U.K.), February 23, 1906, 166.

[29] "Golf in the Olympic Games," *Through the Green*, September 2000, 14.

[30] Colman, "The Olympic Championship," 287-288; Kim Coventry, *Exmoor Country Club: The First Hundred Years* (East Greenwich, RI: Meridian Printing, 1996), 16; *Golf Illustrated* (U.K.), September 2, 1904, 183.

[31] "Will Start at Foot of Ladder," *Arkansas Democrat* (Little Rock, AR), November 11, 1904, 8; "Romance of an Auto Built for Two," *The San Francisco Examiner*, November 5, 1905, 49. Another account had them meeting in Palm Beach, Florida. See "Summer Girl Flirtations Which Turned Into Very Odd Romances," *San Francisco Examiner*, October 14, 1906, 34.

[32] "Won Society Girl on an Auto Tour," *The Philadelphia Inquirer*, October 19, 1905, 7; "Romance of an Auto Built for Two," 49.

[33] "Romance of an Auto Built for Two," 49.

[34] "Automobile Tour," *The Times Dispatch* (Richmond, VA), August 6, 1905, 1; "Romance of an Auto Built for Two," 49; *The New York Times*, February 10, 1907, 39.

[35] "Rich Wedding Gift Made by a Father," *The Indianapolis News*, December 5, 1905, 5.

[36] "'Nat' Moore Dead at Levee Resort," 2.

[37] *The Inter Ocean* (Chicago, IL), July 10, 1906, 6; "Nat Moore is Put in a Cell," *Chicago Tribune*, March 20, 1906, 7; "Nat Moore Wins at Santa Barbara," *Los Angeles Times*, March 25, 1906, 35.

[38] "'Nat' Moore Gives $20,000 Gotham 'Skidoo' Supper," *The Inter Ocean* (Chicago, IL), February 3, 1907, 3; "Investigate Death of Nathaniel Moore," *The Republic* (Columbus, IN), January 12, 1910, 2; "'Nat' Moore Dead at Levee Resort," 2.

[39] Abbott, *Sin in the Second City*, 212.

[40] Abbott, *Sin in the Second City*, 19; "Moore Victim of Drug Habits," *Chicago Tribune*, January 11, 1910, 1.

[41] "Nathaniel Moore is Being Rushed to Wisconsin Home," *The Inter Ocean* (Chicago, IL), August 20, 1909, 2; "Moore Victim of Drug Habits," 1.

[42] "'Nat' Moore Dead at Levee Resort," 2; "Investigate Death of Nathaniel Moore," 2; "Scion of Good Family Found Dead in Resort," *Pittsburgh Daily Post*, January 11, 1910, 3; "Judge Moore's Nephew Meets Mysterious Death, "*The Brooklyn Daily Eagle*, January 10, 1910, 3.

[43] David Sheff, *Clean: Overcoming Addiction and Ending America's Greatest Tragedy* (New York: Houghton Mifflin Harcourt, 2013), 95, 9.

[44] Sam Quinones, *Dreamland: The True Tale of America's Opiate Epidemic* (New York: Bloomsbury Press, 2015), 36; Sheff, *Clean*, 91-92.

[45] Quinones, *Dreamland*, 38; Susanne George Bloomfield, "'The Boy's Mother': Nineteenth-Century Drug Dependence in the Life of Kate M. Cleary," *Great Plains Quarterly* 20, no. 1 (Winter 2000): 7-8; "How Addictive is Morphine?" American Addiction Centers.org, June 10, 2019, https://americanaddictioncenters.org/morphine-treatment/how-addictive, accessed August 2, 2019. Eugene O'Neill's mother became a morphine addict in 1888 after the birth of her third child. Doctors had prescribed it for postpartum depression, a circumstance O'Neill portrayed in his autobiographical play, *Long Day's Journey into Night*. See Julie Husband and Jim O'Loughlin, *Daily Life in the Industrial United States, 1870-1900* (Westport, CT: Greenwood Press, 2004), 164.

[46] Beth Macy, *Dopesick: Dealers, Doctors, and the Drug Company That Addicted America* (New York: Little, Brown, and Company, 2018), 22.

[47] "Heroin, Morphine, and Opiates," History.com, https://www.history.com/topics/crime/history-of-heroin-morphine-and-opiates, accessed October 3, 2019; Audrey Redford and Benjamin Powell, "Dynamics of Intervention in the War on Drugs: The Buildup to the Harrison Act of 1914," *The Independent Review* 20, no. 4 (Spring 2016): 519.

[48] Husband and O'Loughlin, *Daily Life in the Industrial United States,* 166-167; Quinones, *Dreamland*, 53.

[49] F. G. Gosling and Joyce M. Ray, "The Right to Be Sick: American Physicians and Nervous Patients, 1885-1910," *Journal of Social History* 20, no. 2 (Winter 1986): 252.

[50] Gosling and Ray, "The Right to Be Sick," 252; Timothy A. Hickman, "'Mania Americana': Narcotic Addiction and Modernity in the United States, 1870-1920," *The Journal of American History* 90, no. 4 (March 2004): 1281; Marcus Aurin, "Chasing the Dragon: The Cultural Metamorphosis of Opium in the United States, 1825-1935," *Medical Anthropology Quarterly* 14, no. 3 (September 2000): 420.

[51] Abbott, *Sin in the Second City*, 211; Encyclopedia of Chicago: "Prostitution," http://www.encyclopedia.chicagohistory.org/pages/1015.html, accessed October 3, 2019. Alexander Wood of Edinburgh, Scotland invented the hypodermic syringe in 1853. See Quinones, *Dreamland*, 53.

[52] Abbott, *Sin in the Second City*, 89, 24; Melissa Lafsky, "The Golden Age of Chicago Prostitution: A Q&A with Karen Abbott," Freakonomics.com, August 1, 2007, http://freakonomics.com/2007/08/01/the-golden-age-of-chicago-prostitution-a-qa-with-karen-abbott/, accessed October 3, 2019.

[53] Norma Lee Browning, "Oldest Vice Queen Finds Reform at 70," *Chicago Tribune*, March 14, 1949, 1; "Scion of Good Family Found Dead in Resort," 3; "Moore Victim of Drug Habits," 1.

[54] "Moore Victim of Drug Habits," 1, 7.

[55] Abbott, *Sin in the Second City*, 213; "Moore Victim of Drug Habits," 1; Browning, "Dope and Death Doomed Levee, 'Queen' Recalls," 12; "Death of Nathaniel Ford Moore in Ill-Famed House Stirs up Chicago," *The La Crosse Tribune* (La Crosse, WI), January 10, 1910, 1.

[56] Moore Victim of Drug Habits," 1; "Death of Nathaniel Ford Moore in Ill-Famed House Stirs up Chicago," 1; "'Nat' Moore Dead at Levee Resort," 1.

[57] "Investigate Death of Nathaniel Moore," 2.

[58] "'Nat' Moore Dead at Levee Resort," 1; "Scion of Good Family Found Dead in Resort," 3; "Moore Victim of Drug Habits," 7.

[59] "Moore Victim of Drug Habits," 1; Encyclopedia of Chicago: "Prostitution."

[60] Edward Marshall, "Uncle Sam is the Worst Drug Fiend in the World," *The New York Times*, March 12, 1911, 64; Edward Marshall, "'We Are a Nation of Suicides,' Says Dr. H.W. Wiley," *The New York Times*, March 19, 1911, 57, 53.

[61] James Harvey Young, "Federal Drug and Narcotic Legislation," *Pharmacy in History* 37, no. 2 (1995): 61.

[62] Martin I. Wilbert, "The Number and Kind of Drug Addicts," *Public Health Reports (1896-1970)* 30, no. 32 (August 6, 1915): 2290, 2293; "Women Victims of Morphine," *The New York Times*, October 25, 1895, 6.

[63] "The Opiod Epidemic," Addiction Center.com, https://www.addictioncenter.com/opiates/opioid-epidemic/, accessed September 27, 2019; Quinones, *Dreamland*, 108, 126, 99; Macy, *Dopesick*, 20-21, 27. OxyContin gained FDA approval in 1995 and became widely prescribed by the early 2000s. Its manufacturer, Purdue Pharma was *the* company for pain management.

[64] "The Opiod Epidemic."

[65] "Death of Nathaniel Ford Moore in Ill-Famed House Stirs up Chicago," 6; "'Nat' Moore Dead at Levee Resort," 2; "Moore Victim of Drug Habits," 1, 7.

[66] "Moore's Widow Engaged," *The San Francisco Examiner*, May 24, 1911, 1. Arnold's great-great grandfather was a signer of the Declaration of Independence. See Elton Parks, ed., *Vicennial Record of the Class of Nineteen Hundred and Four Yale College* (New Haven, CT: Yale University, 1924), 404; "Match Company Magnate Leaves Ten Million Will," *Wilkes-Barre Times Leader, The Evening News* (PA), November 10, 1916, 11.

[67]Walter Egan and H. Chandler Egan biographical files, USGA; Coventry, *Exmoor Country Club,* 16.

Chapter 2: Eben Byers – "He Was Doing Alright Until his Jaw Fell Off"

[1] Dan Cooper and Brian Grinder, "The Playboy and the Radium Girls (Part 1)," *Financial History*, Spring 2008, 12.

[2] Byers's baptismal register shows him being baptized December 13, 1879, Presbyterian Historical Society (Philadelphia, PA), U.S., Presbyterian Church Records, 1701-1907, accession number: vault BX 9211 .P45232 T42 v.1, *Ancestry.com*, accessed November 28, 2019; Historic Pittsburgh.org, "Guide to the A.M. Byers Company Ledger Book 1864-1869," Senator John Heinz History Center, https://historicpittsburgh.org/islandora/object/pitt:US-QQS-mss639/from_search/0001488594c1e88f3ef3b3972eceacd4-2, accessed August 20, 2019; John G. Anderson, ed., *American Annual Golf Guide* (New York: Golf Guide Publishing Company, 1922), 1.

[3] "Mrs. Byers' Side," *St. Louis Post Dispatch*, August 19, 1894, 10.

[4] Ibid.

[5] Ibid.

[6] "Byers is Here in an Asylum," *The Times* (Philadelphia, PA), September 4, 1894, 1; "A Guardian for the Iron Master Byers," *The St. Joseph Herald* (St. Joseph, MO), October 16, 1894, 1.

[7] "Died at Kirkbride," *Pittsburgh Daily Post*, July 2, 1895, 1; Wikipedia.com, "St. Paul's School," https://en.wikipedia.org/wiki/St._Paul%27s_School_(Concord,_New_Hampshire), accessed July 24, 2019.

[8] William T. Moye, "The End of the 12-Hour Day in the Steel Industry," *Monthly Labor Review* 100 (September 1977): 21; Julie Husband and Jim O'Loughlin, *Daily Life in the Industrial United States, 1870-1900* (Westport, CT: Greenwood Press, 2004), 88.

[9] Husband and O'Loughlin, *Daily Life in the Industrial United States, 1870-1900*, 88.

[10] "Death of A.M. Byers," *Pittsburgh Post-Gazette*, September 20, 1900, 3; "Millions of A.M. Byers' Estate Go To Relatives," *Pittsburgh Daily Post*, October 6, 1900, 7. The will provided: "As the sons become of age he directs that such of them as desire may be employed in some suitable capacity in the business of A.M. Byers & Co., or the Girard Iron Company, their salaries to be fixed at $5,000 yearly [about $150,000 today]. From the time that the sons receive this salary they are not to depend upon their mother for support…Those sons who may not desire to enter the employment of one of these two concerns, when they reach legal age, are to receive the sum of $2,000 yearly [about $60,000 today.]"

[11] "Eben M. Byers Dies of Radium Poisoning," *The New York Times*, April 1, 1932, 11.

[12] Moye, "The End of the 12-Hour Day in the Steel Industry," 22-23, 25.

[13] Bob Labbance with Brian Sipio, *The Vardon Invasion: Harry's Triumphant 1900 American Tour* (Ann Arbor, MI: Sports Media Group, 2008), 184.

[14] "Oldcastle" [pseudonym] "The Amateur Championship," *Golf*, August 1902, 91.

[15] Recorder Weir, "Golfers in Action," *Golf*, October 1903, 236; "James Champion Golfer," *The New York Times*, July 20, 1902, 2; "James is Golf Champion," *The Brooklyn Citizen*, July 20, 1902, 5; "Louis N. James Takes National Golf Championship at Glen View," *The Inter Ocean* (Chicago, IL), July 20, 1902, 1.

[16] *Golf*, October 1903, 282.

[17] "Oldcastle," "The Amateur Championship," 79.

[18] "Pittsburgher Won the Title," *The Pittsburgh Press*, July 15, 1906, 18; "Eben M. Byers Won Amateur Championship," *The Brooklyn Daily Eagle*, July 15, 1906, 27.

[19] "Byers is Winner of Championship," *The Inter Ocean* (Chicago, IL), July 15, 1906, 29; "Eben M. Byers Won Amateur Championship," 27.

[20] Claire Burcky, "How Golf Came to Western Pennsylvania," *The Pittsburgh Press*, February 13, 1934, 24; Labbance with Sipio, *The Vardon Invasion*, 141.

[21] "Eben M. Byers Won Amateur Championship," 27.

[22] "Vardon and Ray Break Records," *The Times-Democrat* (New Orleans, LA), August 27,

1913, 10; "Vardon and Ray Defeat Local Golfers," *Pittsburgh Daily Post*, September 26, 1913, 14.

[23] Joseph Mark Passov, "A Man and His Game," *Golf Illustrated* (U.S.), September 1992, 33; Herbert Warren Wind, "The Sporting Scene – Mainly About Jones," *The New Yorker*, April 29, 1972, 118.

[24] Fred Brand, Jr. "A Byers Connection," *Golf Journal*, January/February 1993, 3.

[25] Michael W. Santos, "Laboring on the Periphery: Managers and Workers at the A. M. Byers Company, 1900-1956," *The Business History Review* 61, no. 1 (Spring 1987), 118; Roger M. Macklis, "The Great Radium Scandal," *Scientific American* 269, no. 2 (August 1993): 94; "Eben M. Byers Dies of Radium Poisoning," 11.

[26] Macklis, "The Great Radium Scandal," 95.

[27] Kate Moore, *The Radium Girls: The Dark Story of America's Shining Women* (Naperville, Illinois: Sourcebooks, 2017), xvi; Rick Lipsey, "A Great Amateur: Eben Byers," *Golf Journal*, October 1992, 45.

[28] Robley D. Evans, Ph.D, "Radium Poisoning A Review of Present Knowledge," *American Journal of Public Health and The Nation's Health* 23, no. 10 (October 1933): 1019.

[29] Cooper and Grinder, "The Playboy and the Radium Girls (Part 1)," 12; C. Prentiss Orr, "Eben M. Byers: The Effect of Gamma Rays on Amateur Golf, Modern Medicine and the FDA," *Allegheny Cemetery Heritage* 13, no. 1 (Fall 2004): 7.

[30] Roger M. Macklis, "Radiomedical Fraud and Popular Perceptions of Radiation," 292, at American Roentgen Ray Society.com, https://www.arrs.org/publications/HRS/oncology/RCI_O_c11.pdf, accessed July 12, 2019.

[31] Macklis, "The Great Radium Scandal," 95. It was estimated that the original bottle must have contained approximately one microcurie each of radium 226 and radium 228.

[32] Ron Winslow, "The Radium Water Worked Fine Until his Jaw Came Off," *The Wall Street Journal*, August 1, 1990, A1.

[33] Macklis, "The Great Radium Scandal," 96-97.

[34] Moore, *The Radium Girls*, 5-6.

[35] Winslow, "The Radium Water Worked Fine Until his Jaw Came Off," A1; Cooper and Grinder, "The Playboy and the Radium Girls (Part 1)," 12.

[36] Lipsey, "A Great Amateur: Eben Byers," 45; Macklis, "The Great Radium Scandal," 95; Winslow, "The Radium Water Worked Fine Until his Jaw Came Off," A1, A6.

[37] Winslow, "The Radium Water Worked Fine Until his Jaw Came Off," A6.

[38] Moore, *The Radium Girls*, 4-5, 20.

[39] Ibid., 35-36, 38-39.

[40] Ibid., 109, 172, 122.

[41] Ibid., 92.

[42] Ibid., 314, 329, 354, 370.

[43] "Radium Poisoning Kills Yale Man," *New Hampshire Register*, April 1, 1932; Macklis, "Radiomedical Fraud and Popular Perceptions of Radiation," 289; Macklis, "The Great Radium Scandal," 98.

[44] Macklis, "The Great Radium Scandal," 98.

[45] Macklis, "Radiomedical Fraud and Popular Perceptions of Radiation," 286; "'Radium Water' Held Cause of Golf Star's Poisoning," *The Pittsburgh Press*, April 1, 1932, 1, 4.

[46] "'Radium Water' Held Cause of Golf Star's Poisoning," 4.

[47] Moore, *The Radium Girls*, 272, 157.

[48] "Eben M. Byers Dies of Radium Poisoning," 1; "Many in Danger of Death from Radium Poison," *The Columbus Telegram* (Columbus, NE), April 1, 1932, 1.

[49] Macklis, *The Great Radium Scandal*, 94; "Death Stirs Action on Radium 'Cures,'" *The New York Times*, April 2, 1932, 12.

[50] Cooper and Grinder, "The Playboy and the Radium Girls (Part 1)," 13; Macklis, "The Great Radium Scandal," 94.

[51] "Death Stirs Action on Radium 'Cures,'" 12.

[52] Cooper and Grinder, "The Playboy and the Radium Girls (Part 1)," 13; Lipsey, "A Great Amateur: Eben Byers," 45; Winslow, "The Radium Water Worked Fine Until his Jaw Came Off," A6.

[53] Cooper and Grinder, "The Playboy and the Radium Girls (Part 1)," 13; "'Radium Water' Held Cause of Golf Star's Poisoning," *The Pittsburgh Press*, April 1, 1932, 1; "Death of Byers Spurs Drive on Panacea Quacks," *Daily News* (New York, NY), April 2, 1932, 246.

[54] "Death of Byers Spurs Drive on Panacea Quacks," 249; Martha Martin, "Radium 'Cures' Menace Many Wealthy Victims," *Daily News* (New York, NY), April 10, 1932, 3; Winslow, "The Radium Water Worked Fine Until his Jaw Came Off," A6.

[55] Macklis, "The Great Radium Scandal," 98; "Seaweed Tablets No Good in 30 Different Ways," *The Southern Democrat* (Oneonta, AL), January 21, 1937, 6.

[56] Macklis, "The Great Radium Scandal," 99; Winslow, "The Radium Water Worked Fine Until his Jaw Came Off," A6.

[57] Orr, "Eben M. Byers," 7; Robley D. Evans, "Inception of Standards for Internal Emitters, Radon and Radium," *Health Physics* 41, no. 3 (September) 1981: 437.

[58] James Harvey Young, "Federal Drug and Narcotic Legislation," *Pharmacy in History* 37, no. 2 (1995): 62; Moore, *The Radium Girls*, 378.

Chapter 3: Cyril Walker – "The Sad Tale of a Self-Destructive Man"

[1] George Bernard Shaw from BrainyQuote.com, https://www.brainyquote.com/quotes/george_bernard_shaw_109533?src=t_alcohol, accessed November 1, 2019; Ben Hogan, "Victory in 1924 U.S. Open Brought Trouble to Walker," *The Pittsburgh Press*, September 2, 1948, 33. Members of Fred Herd's club actually put up the bond to secure the trophy, not Herd himself.

[2] Cyril Walker, "Open Champion, Ridiculed at 18 by Superior, Winner Over Terrible Handicaps," *The Atlanta Constitution*, January 4, 1925, 24; Cyril Walker, "Scalding in Childhood, Small Size, Nervousness, Handicaps Champ Overcame," *The Atlanta Constitution*, January 5, 1925, 7.

[3] Cyril Walker, "Champion Began Real Climb at Hoylake after Leaving Office for Golf Course," *The Atlanta Constitution*, January 6, 1925, 9; Walker, "Open Champion, Ridiculed at 18 by Superior, Winner Over Terrible Handicaps," 24.

[4] Walker, "Champion Began Real Climb at Hoylake after Leaving Office for Golf Course," 9.

[5] Walker, "Champion Began Real Climb at Hoylake after Leaving Office for Golf Course," 9; "Record Broken at Pinehurst," *The Baltimore Sun*, January 16, 1922, 10; Grantland Rice, "Lighter, Larger Ball Will not Favor Stars," *Dayton Daily News*, May 4, 1924, 57; George Trevor, "Did He Win the Open?" *Sports Illustrated and The American Golfer*, May 1937, 40.

[6] Duke Hancock, "The Open Champion who Became a Caddie," *Golf Magazine*, November 1965, 77; Al Del Greco, "At Random in Sportdom" *The Record* (Hackensack, NJ), August 27, 1931, 16; O.B. Keeler, "Cyril Walker is Slow Golfer but Has His Reasons," *The Courier* (Waterloo, IA), October 11, 1927, 13.

[7] Keeler, "Cyril Walker is Slow Golfer but Has His Reasons," 13.

[8] "Loud Sweater is Too Much for Cyril Walker," *The Tampa Times*, March 17, 1923, 12.

[9] *Harrisburg Telegraph* (PA), April 13, 1923, 21; Walker, "Scalding in Childhood, Small Size, Nervousness, Handicaps Champ Overcame," 7.

[10] Keeler, "Cyril Walker is Slow Golfer but Has His Reasons," 13; Walker, "Scalding in Childhood, Small Size, Nervousness, Handicaps Champ Overcame," 7.

[11] Cyril Walker, "Walker Describes Methods of Training for Tourney," *The Atlanta Constitution*, January 7, 1925, 8; Cyril Walker, "How I Won the Open Championship," *The American Golfer*, June 28, 1924, 8; Cyril Walker, "Walker Calm and Confident Throughout National Open Championship Tourney," *The Baltimore Evening Sun*, January 3, 1925, 9. Until

1925, the U.S. Open was played over two days, at 36-holes a day.

[12] Walker, "Walker Calm and Confident Throughout National Open Championship Tourney," 9; Trevor, "Did He Win the Open?" 41.

[13] Trevor, "Did He Win the Open?" 41; Grantland Rice, "Not Always to the Strong," *The American Golfer*, June 28, 1924, 10; Walker, "Walker Calm and Confident Throughout National Open Championship Tourney," 9; O.B. Keeler, "One Hole at a Time," *The American Golfer*, July 12, 1924, 17.

[14] "Walter Hagen Beats Walker in Title Play," *Pensacola News Journal*, February 5, 1925, 5; "Walker Wins Golf Crown, Beating Sarazen One Stroke," *The New York Times*, November 15, 1925, S7; Hal Sharkey, "Team Play With the Pros," *The American Golfer*, May 1930, 45.

[15] "American Routed by British 'Pros' in Golf Cup Play," *Pittsburgh Daily Post*, June 6, 1926, 26. Foursomes is a form of play where two players as a team play one ball, alternating shots from tee to green.

[16] Oscar Fraley, "Some See Shadows Amid Sunny Oakland Hills Area," *The Monroe News Star* (Monroe, LA), June 15, 1961, 14; David Sheff, *Clean: Overcoming Addiction and Ending America's Greatest Tragedy* (New York: Houghton Mifflin Harcourt, 2013), 316; Hancock, "The Open Champion who Became a Caddie," 77.

[17] *The Baltimore Sun*, July 4, 1924, 15; Cyril Walker, "The Wrists When Putting," *The Salt Lake Tribune*, August 10, 1925, 9; "Cyril Walker Quits Post at Englewood," *Hartford Courant*, October 25, 1925, 4; "Cyril Walker is Given Job as Pro," *Warren Times Mirror* (Warren, PA), April 18, 1940, 10; "Coin Gone, So Champion Caddies," *The Cincinnati Enquirer*, April 11, 1940, 16; "Former National Open Golf Champ Joins Blue Ridge," *The Evening News* (Harrisburg, PA), April 18, 1940, 25; Don Donaghey, "That Little Old Caddy There is Cyril Walker," *The Daily Oklahoman* (Oklahoma City), March 31, 1940, 40.

[18] Donaghey, "That Little Old Caddy There is Cyril Walker," 40; "May Speed Up," *Iowa City Press Citizen*, February 1, 1929, 14; Al Barkow, *Getting' to the Dance Floor: An Oral History of American Golf* (New York: Atheneum, 1986), 51; Everett Clay, "He's Cyril Walker," *The Akron Beacon Journal*, April 11, 1940, 28.

[19] "Walker Cleared," *The Courier-News* (Bridgewater, NJ), August 26, 1931, 1; "Warrant Issued for Cyril Walker," *The Daily Record* (Long Branch, NJ), August 12, 1931, 12; "Boy Denies Cyril Walker Beat Him," *The New York Times*, August 14, 1931, 8; "Cyril Walker Case Continued a Week," *The Courier-News* (Bridgewater, NJ), August 19, 1931, 28; "Walker Out at Saddle River," *The Record* (Hackensack, NJ), January 3, 1933, 19; "Cyril's In Again – For 3 Months," *The Record* (Hackensack, NJ), November 7, 1942, 3.

[20] "Cyril Walker Arrested," *The New York Times*, May 28, 1933, 16; "Walker, Golf Pro, Cleared," *The Record* (Hackensack, NJ), September 27, 1933, 3.

[21] "Cyril Walker Back at Saddle River," *The Record* (Hackensack, NJ), April 13, 1934, 25; "Cyril Walker is Drunken Driver," *The Record* (Hackensack, NJ), June 14, 1934, 1; "Golf Star Fined $262," *The New York Times*, June 15, 1934, 18.

[22] "Cyril Walker," *The Record* (Hackensack, NJ), August 7, 1934, 17; "Accuses Cyril Walker," *The New York Times*, September 7, 1934, 24; "Girl Asks $100,000 in Suit Against Cyril Walker," *Chicago Tribune*, September 7, 1934, 23; "Cyril Walker Posts Bond in $100,000 Breach of Promise Suit," *The Minneapolis Star*, September 7, 1934, 24.

[23] Eddie Brietz, "Sports Round-Up," *Muncie Evening News*, February 19, 1937, 17; Gene F. Hampson, "Thru Sportsland," *The Courier-News* (Bridgewater, NJ), April 27, 1937, 17; "Walker Begins New Golf Job," *The Record* (Hackensack, NJ), June 28, 1937, 19.

[24] Sheff, *Clean*, 317-318; National Institute on Alcohol Abuse and Alcoholism.com, "Alcohol Facts and Statistics," https://www.niaaa.nih.gov/alcohol-facts-and-statistics, accessed October 2, 2019.

[25] "Cyril Walker Found Guilty," *The Record* (Hackensack, NJ), June 14, 1938, 4.

[26] Bob Considine, "Shed No Tear for Cyril Walker – Opportunities Were His," *The Des Moines Register*, April 24, 1940, 10.

[27] "Nelson-Picard Win in Crestmont Match," *The Courier-News* (Bridgewater, NJ), October 16, 1939, 20; Considine, "Shed No Tear for Cyril Walker," 10; "Parting Shots," *Wilkes-Barre Times Leader* (PA), July 2, 1930, 28. The *Courier-News* said almost $300 was raised (approximately $5,000 today.)

[28] Considine, "Shed No Tear for Cyril Walker," 10.

[29] Clay, "He's Cyril Walker," 28; "Coin Gone, So Champion Caddies," 16.

[30] Donaghey, "That Little Old Caddy There is Cyril Walker," 40; William James from BrainyQuote.com, https://www.brainyquote.com/quotes/william_james_132180?src=t_alcohol, accessed November 2, 2019.

[31] "Former National Open Golf Champ Joins Blue Ridge," *The Evening News* (Harrisburg, PA), April 18, 1940, 25; "Quits Post as Pro," *The Evening News* (Harrisburg, PA), May 14, 1940, 9.

[32] Lawrence Perry, "Cyril Walker Failed to Turn Fame Into Cash," *The Boston Globe*, June 12, 1940, 19; "Cyril Walker Gets New Job," *The Record* (Hackensack, NJ), June 18, 1940, 9.

[33] "Coin Gone, So Champion Caddies," 16; "Golf Champ Gets 60 Days as Drunk," *The Record* (Hackensack, NJ), April 15, 1942, 18; "Cyril's In Again – For 3 Months," 3.

[34] "Golf Champ Hits Matrimony Skid," *The Record* (Hackensack, NJ), July 8, 1944, 13.

[35] "From $150,000 Golf Champion to Caddie in 20 Years," *Detroit Free Press*, June 25, 1944, 14; Hancock, "The Open Champion who Became a Caddie," 77.

[36] "Ex-Golf Champ Jailed for Sleeping in Park," *The Miami News*, July 12, 1945, 11.

[37] "Cyril Walker, Golf Star in '20s, Dies," *The News-Herald* (Franklin, PA), August 7, 1948, 7; "Ace Golfer Cyril Walker Dies Broke, a Jail Lodger," *Daily News* (New York, NY), August 7, 1948, 129; "Cyril Walker, Ex-Golf Champ, Found Dead in Police Cell," *The Boston Globe*, August 6, 1948, 4.

[38] Pete Norton, "The Morning After," *The Tampa Tribune*, August 13, 1948, 17.

[39] Hogan, "Victory in 1924 U.S. Open Brought Trouble to Walker," 33; H.B. Martin, "Small Golfers with Big Records," *Golfing*, March 1950, 21.

Chapter 4: Marion Miley – "She Was Killed for $140"

[40] Rhonda Glenn, "The Tragic Death Of Marion Miley," April 30, 2010, https://www.usga.org/articles/2010/05/the-tragic-death-of-marion-miley-17179869434.html, accessed August 3, 2019; Liz Kahn, *The LPGA: The Unauthorized Version, The History of the Ladies Professional Golf Association* (Menlo Park, CA: Group Fore Productions, Inc., 1996), ii.

[41] 1920 Census, Danvers, Essex County, Massachusetts, T625, roll 689, page 13A, Enumeration District 29, *Ancestry.com,* accessed November 28, 2019; Gail Collins, America's Women: Four Hundred Years of Dolls, Drudges, Helpmates, and Heroines (New York: Harper Collins, 2003), 353; Hal Sharkey, "Team Play With the Pros," The American Golfer, May 1930, 78. Miley's mother is called Elsa in some accounts, and her baptismal record shows her name as Maria Elsa Ego, and her birth date as December 25, 1887. See Germany, Select Births and Baptisms, 1558-1898, *Ancestry.com*, accessed November 28, 2019.

[42] Arthur Watson, "Friends Praise Slain Golfer," *Daily News* (New York, NY), October 5, 1941, 136; Glenn, "The Tragic Death Of Marion Miley."

[43] "Forgotten Fame: Marion Miley," a film by Beth Kirchner, KET Documentaries, https://www.pbs.org/video/ket-presents-forgotten-fame-marion-miley/, accessed August 10, 2019; Watson, "Friends Praise Slain Golfer," 136; Charles Price, "Golf's Confounding Murder Mystery," *Golf Digest*, November 1989, 28.

[44] "Father Credited for Golf Ability," *Kingsport Times* (Kingsport, TN), February 18, 1937, 8; Watson, "Friends Praise Slain Golfer," 136; Marion Miley Wins Kentucky Title," *Star Tribune* (Minneapolis, MN), June 16, 1935, 21; Glenn, "The Tragic Death Of Marion Miley."

[45] Watson, "Friends Praise Slain Golfer," 136; Price, "Golf's Confounding Murder Mystery," 28.

[46] Glenn, "The Tragic Death Of Marion Miley"; "Victor Rallies on Final Round to Clinch Title." *The Miami News*, January 28, 1934, 34; "Jean Bauer Wins Augusta Tourney," *The Morning News* (Wilmington, DE), April 2, 1934, 9.

[47] "Miss Orcutt Wins Palm Beach Title," *The Boston Globe*, Feb 17, 1934, 7; "Helen Hicks Beaten, 1 up, in Florida Meet," *Chicago Tribune*, February 16, 1934, 30.

[48] Glenn, "The Tragic Death Of Marion Miley."; H.B. Martin, *Fifty Years of American Golf* (New York: Dodd, Mead & Company, 1936), 208; Ross Goodner, *Golf's Greatest: The Legendary World Golf Hall of Famers* (Norwalk, CT: Golf Digest, 1978), 35.

[49] Ned Vare, "Glenna: She Was, Simply, *The Queen,*" 1988 U.S. Women's Open program, 126; Bill Fields, "A Place in Time," *Golf World*, November 28, 1997, 18.

[50] "Marion Miley Named on U.S. Golf Team," *Reading Times* (Reading, PA), July 12, 1934, 13; Maureen Orcutt, interview by Joe Doyle, June 16, 1991, USGA Oral History Collection, 68; Glenn, "The Tragic Death Of Marion Miley." Dettweiler served her country as a WASP from 1943 to 1944, logging 750 hours ferrying B-17s from factories to military bases to free male pilots for combat roles. See Kahn, *The LPGA*, 19.

[51] "Marion Miley Captures Augusta Golf Tourney," *Bluefield Daily Telegraph* (Bluefield, WV), March 30, 1935, 10; "Marion Miley Wins in South Atlantic," *The Birmingham News* (Birmingham, AL), March 3, 1935, 19; Glenn, "The Tragic Death Of Marion Miley."; "Marion Miley Takes Trans-Mississippi Title," *The Morning Call* (Allentown, PA), June 23, 1935, 11.

[52] "White, Marion Miley Win Mexican Titles," *The Boston Globe*, November 4, 1935, 8; "Forgotten Fame: Marion Miley."; Arthur Watson, "Friends Praise Slain Golfer," *Daily News* (New York, NY), October 5, 1941, 136.

[53] "U.S. Women Golfers Not a Very Happy Group," *The Boston Globe*, May 21, 1936, 24.

[54] For a good article on Barton, see Bobby Burt, "Pam Barton, 1917-1943," *Through the Green*, March 2010, 24; "Miley Routs Didrikson 6 and 4 for Augusta Golf Championship," *The Courier-Journal* (Louisville, KY), March 28, 1937, 48.

[55] "Kentucky Girl Wins the Derby," *The National Golf Review*, December 1937, 55, 22.

[56] Roy White, "Miley Defeats Page for Title," *The Atlanta Constitution*, May 15, 1938, 15, 19; "Marion Miley Wins Southern Women's Golf Championship," *The Tampa Tribune*, May 15, 1938, 18.

[57] *The Cincinnati Enquirer*, June 19, 1938, 30; Kenneth Gregory, "Southern Crown Again Captured by Marion Miley," *The Paducah Sun-Democrat* (Paducah, KY), May 14, 1939, 15.

[58] Sam Livingston, "Down Sports Avenue," *The Paducah Sun-Democrat* (Paducah, KY), June 6, 1939, 6; Watson, "Friends Praise Slain Golfer," 136.

[59] "Forgotten Fame: Marion Miley."

[60] Watson, "Friends Praise Slain Golfer," 136; Marjorie Hoagland, "Champion Golf Now a Business Woman, Too," *The Courier-Journal* (Louisville, KY), October 1, 1939, 21.

[61] Miley diary, January-April, 1940-1941, Folder 4, Tara Hopkins West collection on Marion Miley, 1930s-1941 (MSS 249), Kentucky Historical Society, Martin F. Schmidt Research Library, Frankfort, Kentucky (hereafter THW Collection); "Forgotten Fame: Marion Miley."

[62] Miley diary, January-April, 1940-1941, THW Collection; Watson, "Friends Praise Slain Golfer," 136; Price, "Golf's Confounding Murder Mystery," 28.

[63] Miley diary, January-April, 1940-1941, THW Collection; Glenn, "The Tragic Death Of Marion Miley."

[64] Harry O'Donnell, "Dettweiler Sees Larger Field for Lady Pros," *Elmira Star Gazette* (Elmira, NY), August 16, 1940, 16; Richard J. Moss, *The Kingdom of Golf in America* (Lincoln, Nebraska: University of Nebraska Press, 2013), 222.

[65] "Marion Miley Striken by Appendicitis Attack," *The Miami News*, October 18, 1937, 11; Miley diary, January-April, 1940-1941, THW Collection; Watson, "Friends Praise Slain Golfer," 136.

[66] Miley diary, January-April, 1940-1941, March 31, 1940, THW Collection; Hoagland, "Champion Golf Now a Business Woman, Too," 21; Rhonda Glenn, "The Tragic Death Of Marion Miley."

[67] "Forgotten Fame: Marion Miley."; Kahn, *The LPGA*, 26. Hicks was named the Associated Press Woman Athlete of the Year in 1941. The trophy was donated in 1896 by Robert Cox of Edinburgh, Scotland, a businessman and member of the Royal and Ancient Golf Club of St Andrews. It was his way of encouraging women's golf in the United States.

[68] Elinor Nickerson, *Golf: A Women's History* (Jefferson, NC: McFarland &Company, Inc., 1987), 2; "Jack Bell's Sports Desk," *The Miami News*, February 2, 1941, 27.

[69] Watson, "Friends Praise Slain Golfer," 136; "Forgotten Fame: Marion Miley."

[70] Price, "Golf's Confounding Murder Mystery," 29; "Forgotten Fame: Marion Miley."

[71] "'Inside Man' Tells of Miley Holdup Slaying," *Daily News* (New York, NY), October 19, 1941, 20 ; "Slayer Says Miley Fought Bravely," *The St. Louis Star and Times*, October 13, 1941, 9; "Ex-Convict 'Breaks Down' at Fort Worth," *The Courier-Journal* (Louisville, KY), October 13, 1941, 3; "Third Suspect Tells of Robbery," *The Cincinnati Enquirer*, October 19, 1941, 21; "Penney's Confession Tells Details of Club Robbery," *The Courier-Journal* (Louisville, KY), October 13, 1941, 3.

[72] J. Winston Coleman, Jr., *Double Murder at the Lexington Country Club* (Lexington, KY: The Winburn Press, 1981), 11; "Penney's Confession Tells Details of Club Robbery," 3; "Third Suspect Tells of Robbery," 21.

[73] "Third Suspect Tells of Robbery," 21; Jack Turcott, "Hunt for Miley Slayer(s) Goes to FBI Microscopes," *Daily News* (New York, NY), October 5, 1941, 136; "Slayer Says Miley Fought Bravely," 9; "Ex-Convict 'Breaks Down' at Fort Worth," 1.

[74] Price, "Golf's Confounding Murder Mystery," 113; "Marion Miley, Golf Star, Killed, Mother Shot by Robbers," *The Tennessean* (Nashville, TN), September 29, 1941, 1; "Penney's Confession Tells Details of Club Robbery," 3.

[75] "Marion Miley, Golf Star, Killed, Mother Shot by Robbers," 1; "Ex-Convict 'Breaks Down' at Fort Worth," 3; Price, "Golf's Confounding Murder Mystery," 113; Death certificate of Marion Miley, Vital Statistics, Original Death Certificates, Microfilm rolls #7016130-7041803 (1911-1964), Kentucky Department for Libraries and Archives, Frankfort, Kentucky, *Ancestry.com*, accessed November 28, 2019. An examination of Marion Miley's body revealed that "one bullet had entered the top of her head on the right, passing out the left cheek below the ear; another entered her back near the spine, coming out over the left breast." See Court of Appeals of Kentucky, *Penney v. Commonwealth*, 292 Ky. 192 (Ky. Ct. App. 1942) • 166 S.W.2d 18, Decided Oct 23, 1942 (PDF of decision from Casetext.com.)

[76] Jack Turcott, "Police Admit they Have no Clues," *Daily News* (New York, NY), October 4, 1941, 47.

[77] Coleman, Jr., *Double Murder at the Lexington Country Club*, 9-10; "Marion Miley, Golf Star, Killed, Mother Shot by Robbers," 1.

[78] Coleman, Jr., *Double Murder at the Lexington Country Club*, 9, 11; "Forgotten Fame: Marion Miley."

[79] Turcott, "Hunt for Miley Slayer(s) Goes to FBI Microscopes," 136; "Ex-Convict 'Breaks Down' at Fort Worth," 3; "Third Suspect Tells of Robbery," 21; Price, "Golf's Confounding Murder Mystery," 113.

[80] Price, "Golf's Confounding Murder Mystery," 113-114; "Third Suspect Tells of Robbery," 21; Coleman, Jr., *Double Murder at the Lexington Country Club*, 15.

[81] Glenn, "The Tragic Death Of Marion Miley."; Price, "Golf's Confounding Murder Mystery," 113; "Fred Miley in Hospital," *Messenger-Inquirer* (Owensboro, KY), October 14, 1941, 9.

[82] "Too Soft," *The Cincinnati Enquirer*, October 14, 1941, 17; "Anderson's Attorney Hints New Evidence," *The Courier-Journal* (Louisville, KY), November 28, 1942, 9; "Forgotten Fame: Marion Miley."

[83] "A Young Man" to Tom Penney, October 13, 1941, Folder 15, THW Collection; Coleman, Jr., *Double Murder at the Lexington Country Club*, 16; "Too Soft," 17; "Raymond Baxter Placed on Trial," *The Owensboro Messenger* (Owensboro, KY), December 16, 1941, 5.

[84] "Forgotten Fame: Marion Miley."; Coleman, Jr., *Double Murder at the Lexington Country Club*, 15.

[85] Watson, "Friends Praise Slain Golfer," 136; Haskell Short, "Marion Miley Memorial Tournament to Draw Many Danville Golfers," *The Advocate-Messenger* (Danville, KY), June 10, 1942, 2; Glenn, "The Tragic Death Of Marion Miley."

Chapter 5: John M. Shippen, Jr. – "The Father of African American Golf"

[1] Red Hoffman, "John M. Shippen," feature for *Golf Digest* not published, c.1965, 1, Box 7, Folder 4, Red Hoffman Collection, USGA Arnold Palmer Center for Golf History, Far Hills, New Jersey (hereafter cited as USGA.)

[2] Philip St. Laurent, "The Negro in World History: John Shippen," *Tuesday Magazine*, April 1969, 30.

[3] John Shippen's birth certificate shows December 3, 1879 as his date of birth. Most biographical sketches list his birthday as December 5, and he wrote December 2, 1879 on his WWII draft registration card, https://en.wikipedia.org/wiki/File:John_Matthew_Shippen_WWII_Draft_Registration_card.pd f, accessed October 31, 2019; by an 1886 Act of Congress, Uniontown was officially named Anacostia. Nothing is known of John Shippen, Jr.'s grandmother. His father, John Matthew Shippen, Sr. (sometimes known as "Jr.," as his father was also called "Sr."), had two brothers, Phillip and Theodore, and a sister, Fannie.

[4] *Catalog of the Officers and Students of Howard University, District of Columbia, 1871-1872* (Washington, DC: Reed and Woodward, Printers, 1872), 28-30; Dr. Eliza P. Shippen, "The Rev. John M. Shippen, Jr.," 1973 essay, 1-2, Box 7, Folder 2, Anacostia Story: 1608-1930, Exhibition Records, Series I: Administrative and Research Files, Anacostia Community Museum Archives, Smithsonian Institution, Washington, DC (hereafter Anacostia Story Exhibition Records); *Bi-Centennial History of Suffolk County: Comprising the Addresses Delivered at the Celebration of the Bi-Centennial of Suffolk County, N.Y., in Riverhead, November 15, 1883*" (Babylon, NY: Budget Steam Print, 1885), 16.

[5] Kelly Miller, *Race Adjustment* (1908; repr., New York: Arno Press, 1968), 139. Princeton University, for example, was founded as a Presbyterian school; Faren R. Siminoff, "Shippen's Hole," *New York Archives* 7, no. 4 (Spring 2008): 13; "Shinnecock Hills Links," *The New York Times*, March 8, 1896, 25; Samuel Parrish, *Some Facts, Reflections, and Personal Reminiscences Connected with the Introduction of the Game of Golf Into the United States, More Especially as Associated With the Formation of the Shinnecock Hills Golf Club*, Shinnecock Hills Golf Club, 1923, 5.

[6] Dave Anderson, "The Tradition of the Tribe," *Golf Digest*, June 1995, 100; Dr. Eliza P. Shippen, "The Rev. John M. Shippen, Jr.," 2, Anacostia Story Exhibition Records.

[7] Marvin P. Dawkins and Graham C. Kinloch, *African America Golfers During the Jim Crow Era* (Westport, CT: Praeger, 2000), 18.

[8] R.H. Smith, Jr., "The Oldest Homebred Pro in America," *United Golfer and Other Sports* 3 (1938): 3; "A Negro Boy Golfer," *The Golfer* (U.K), May 20, 1896, 377.

[9] "General Sporting," *The Windsor Review* (Windsor, MO), June 11, 1896, 2; Harry Grayson, "Man who Integrated Golf: Shippen, First Negro Pro," *Ames Daily Tribune* (IA), June 18, 1963, 6; Hoffman, "John M. Shippen," 3, Red Hoffman Collection, USGA.

[10] "The Two Sides of the Sugar Trust," *The Evening World* (New York, NY), July 25, 1889, 1.

[11] "A Negro Boy Golfer," 377.

[12] "The Great American Golfer," *The Fort Wayne News* (IN), May 28, 1896, 2.

[13] "Shinnecock Hills Links," 25.

[14] "Great Golf by Foulis," *Sun* (New York, NY), July 19, 1896, 4; Grayson, "Man who Integrated Golf," 6; Hoffman, "John M. Shippen, 2 and "Slug: Box insert for Shinnecock Hills," c.1977, box 23, envelope labeled "Shippen material," Red Hoffman Collection, USGA; Marino Parascenzo, "Daughter Tells Tale of First Black Golfer to Lead the U.S. Open," *Pittsburgh Post-Gazette*, June 9, 1986, 13.

[15] Peter F. Stevens, "In the Eye of the Storm," *Golf Journal*, June 1996, 14-15; Dawkins and Kinloch, *African America Golfers During the Jim Crow Era*, 15.

[16] Parascenzo, "Daughter Tells Tale of First Black Golfer to Lead the U.S. Open," 13; Dan Burley, "Talkin' Out Loud," *New York Amsterdam News*, April 29, 1939, 18; "Foulis Was Best Golfer," *The New York Times*, July 19, 1896, 3; "Golf Players Ready," *Sun* (New York, NY), July 14, 1896, 5; "Is a Double Victory," *The Chicago Tribune*, July 19, 1896, 9.

[17] "Great Golf by Foulis," 4; Foulis Was Best Golfer," 3; "Is a Double Victory," 9. The first three U.S. Opens were played over 36 holes (1895-1897.)

[18] "Great Golf by Foulis," 4.

[19] Grayson, "Man who Integrated Golf," 6; Hoffman, "John M. Shippen," 4, Red Hoffman Collection, USGA; *The Golfer*, April 1896, 165. Ross Goodner, in *The 75 Year History of Shinnecock Hills Golf Club* (Southampton, New York: Shinnecock Hills Golf Club, 1966), page 21, wrote of Shippen on "the 11th hole, where he is reputed to have taken 11 strokes."

[20] "Confabulation," Wikipedia, https://en.wikipedia.org/wiki/Confabulation, accessed August 23, 2019; Simon Makin, "What Happens in the Brain When We Misremember," *Scientific American*, September 9, 2016, https://www.scientificamerican.com/article/what-happens-in-the-brain-when-we-misremember/, accessed August 3, 2019; Edward S. Casey, *Remembering: A Phenomenological Study* (Bloomington, IN: Indiana University Press, 1987), 283; Daniel L. Schacter, *Searching for Memory: The Brain, the Mind, and the Past* (New York: Basic Books, 1996), 132; Elizabeth J. Marsh, "Retelling Is Not the Same as Recalling: Implications for Memory," *Current Directions in Psychological Science* 16, no. 1 (February 2007): 17, 19.

[21] For accounts of Bobby Jones's 43 see: Howard Rabinowitz, "Bob Jones' First Retirement," *Golf Journal*, May 1993, 32; "Barnes Tied for Lead in Golf Tourney," *Brooklyn Times Union*, June 24, 1921, 1; "American Amaze Critics," *The Barre Daily Times* (Barre, VT), June 24, 1921, 2. For accounts of Tommy Armour's 11 see: "Tom Armour Shows 'Em How, and How!" *Daily News* (New York, NY), June 22, 1927, 216; "Tommy Armour Does One Hole in Eleven," *Brooklyn Times Union*, June 21, 1927, 61; "11 at Hole 17 Bans Champion," *The Evening News* (Harrisburg, PA), June 21, 1927, 1.

[22] Carl Becker, "Everyman His Own Historian," his speech before the American Historical Association in *The American Historical Review* 37, no. 2 (January 1932): 222.

[23] Becker, "Everyman His Own Historian," 228-229.

[24] "Golf Old Ocean's Rival," *Sun* (New York, NY), July 26, 1896, 6.

[25] St. Laurent, "The Negro in World History," 17.

[26] C. Turner, "Golf," *Outing*, September 1896, 141; "Is a Double Victory," 9.

[27] "Clever Golf by Professionals," *The New York Herald* [?], July 18, 1896, from "Scrapbook of Early Golf in America" (12F.MIS10), USGA.

[28] *Golf* (U.K.), September 25, 1896, 39; Price Collier, "Golf," *Outing*, April 1897, 98.

[29] "General Sporting," 2.

[30] Donald Spivey, ed., *Sport in America: New Historical Perspectives* (Westport, CT: Greenwood Press, 1985), 40; Jeffrey T. Sammons, "'Race' and Sport: A Critical, Historical Examination," *Journal of Sport History* 21, no. 3 (Fall 1994): 216.

[31] Daniel Anderson, "The 'Discipline of Work and Play': W. E. B. Du Bois, the New Negro Intelligentsia, and the Culture of Sports," *Studies in Popular Culture* 29, no. 2 (October 2006): 30; Lane Demas, *Game of Privilege: An African American History of Golf* (Chapel Hill: The

University of North Carolina Press, 2017), 51.

[32] Anderson, "The 'Discipline of Work and Play,'" 33.

[33] Ronald E. Butchart, "'Outthinking and Outflanking the Owners of the World': A Historiography of the African American Struggle for Education," *History of Education Quarterly* 28, no. 3 (Autumn 1988): 333.

[34] Price Collier, "Golf," *Outing*, October 1897, 88; Sammons, "'Race' and Sport," 267.

[35] "Booknotes," C-SPAN, March 3, 2002, https://www.c-span.org/video/?168015-1/randall-kennedy-nigger-strange-career-troublesome-word, accessed September 1, 2019; Randall Kennedy, *Nigger: The Strange Career of a Troublesome Word* (New York: Pantheon Books, 2002), 5.

[36] David K. Shipler, *A Country of Strangers: Blacks and Whites in America* (New York: Alfred A. Knopf, 1997), 177; John Hope Franklin and Alfred A. Moss, Jr., 8th ed., *From Slavery to Freedom: A History of African Americans* (New York: McGraw Hill, 2000), 211.

[37] Scott v. Sandford, 60 U.S. 393 (1856), Justica.com, https://supreme.justia.com/cases/federal/us/60/393/case.html, accessed September 3, 2019; Henry Louis Gates, Jr., *Stony the Road: Reconstruction, White Supremacy, and the Rise of Jim Crow* (New York: Penguin Press, 2019), 18. In 1892, after Homer Plessy had taken a seat in the whites-only railway car, he was asked to vacate it and sit instead in the blacks-only car. Plessy refused and was immediately arrested. "Plessy v. Ferguson, 163 U.S. 537 (1896)," Justica.com, https://supreme.justia.com/cases/federal/us/163/537/, September 3, 2019.

[38] W.E.B. Du Bois, *Black Reconstruction in America, 1860-1880* (New York: World Publishing Company, 1967), 711-712; Marcy Sacks, "'To Be a Man and Not a Lackey': Black Men, Work, and the Construction of Manhood in Gilded Age New York City," *American Studies* 45, no. 1 (Spring 2004): 42; Gates, Jr. *Stony the Road*, 70.

[39] Philip F. Rubio, *A History of Affirmative Action, 1619-2000* (Jackson, Mississippi: University Press of Mississippi, 2001), 71; Randall Kennedy. "Nigger: The Strange Career of a Troublesome Word, Chapter One - The Protean N-Word," *The Washington Post*, January 11, 2001, https://www.washingtonpost.com/wp-srv/style/longterm/books/chap1/nigger.htm, accessed September 12, 2019.

[40] NAACP.org, "History of Lynchings," https://www.naacp.org/history-of-lynchings/, accessed October 5, 2019; S.Res. 39 (109th): "Lynching Victims Senate Apology Resolution," https://www.govtrack.us/congress/bills/109/sres39/text, accessed October 23, 2019; Avis Thomas-Lester, "A Senate Apology for History on Lynching," *The Washington Post*, June 14, 2005, http://www.washingtonpost.com/wp-dyn/content/article/2005/06/13/AR2005061301720.html, accessed October 23, 2019.

[41] Gates, Jr., *Stony the Road*, 14; Ellis Cose, *Color-blind: Seeing Beyond Race in a Race-Obsessed World* (New York: Harper Collins, 1997), xxv-xxvi.

[42] W.E.B. Du Bois, *The Souls of Black Folks* (New York: Literary Classics of the United States, 1990), 8-9.

[43] Gunnar Myrdal, *An American Dilemma: The Negro Problem and Modern Democracy* (New York: Harper Brothers, 1944), xlvii, xlv, xlix.

[44] Calvin H. Sinnette, *Forbidden Fairways: African Americans and the Game of Golf* (Chelsea, MI: Sleeping Bear Press, 1998), 23. The Shippen family retained ties to the Shinnecock Reservation, and grandson Hanno Shippen Smith kept a home there. See *America's First Golf Pro: A Chip-in for Shippen*, VHS video. Produced by G. Theodore Catherine, IOKTS Productions, Takoma Park, Maryland, 1999; Smith, Jr., "The Oldest Homebred Pro in America," 3.

[45] Richard Wright, *Early Works* (New York: Literary Classics of the United States, 1991), 230; Gregory Bond, "Jim Crow at Play: Race, Manliness, and the Color Line in American Sports, 1876-1916" (PhD diss., University Of Wisconsin-Madison, 2008), 195.

[46] "Obituary – Long Island, Mrs. John Shippen," *The Brooklyn Daily Eagle*, July 21, 1899, 3; *The Brooklyn Daily Eagle*, April 9, 1900, 16; Ray Batt, "Shinnecock Indian was First Golf

Pro," unattributed magazine article, c.1958, and Ralph Wise, answers to a questionnaire in John Shippen files, Box 3, Folders 1-2, African American Golf History Archive, USGA.

[47] Beulah A. Shippen and Mabel S. (Shippen) Hatcher, *The Family Recollections of Beulah A. Shippen and Mabel S. (Shippen) Hatcher* [Washington, DC?]: privately published, 1994, 37-38; St. Laurent, "The Negro in World History" 30; *America's First Golf Pro: A Chip-in for Shippen*, VHS video.

[48] "Preacher Cuts His Throat, John M. Shippen, Former Presbyterian Minister, a Suicide" *The Washington Post*, December 27, 1901, 10; *Baltimore Sun*, December 27, 1901, 2. Although at least one newspaper report claimed he may have been murdered, Shippen's death certificate indicates suicide as the cause of death.

[49] Dr. Eliza P. Shippen, "The Rev. John M. Shippen, Jr.," 2-3, Anacostia Story Exhibition Records; Alison Wertheimer, *A Special Scar: The Experiences of People Bereaved by Suicide*, 2nd ed. (Philadelphia: Taylor and Francis, Inc., 2001), 152-153.

[50] Wertheimer, *A Special Scar*, 159; Edward J. Dunne, John L. McIntosh, and Karen Dunne-Maxim, *Suicide and Its Aftermath: Understanding and Counseling the Survivors* (New York: W.W. Norton and Company, 1987), 68.

[51] Sinnette, *Forbidden Fairways*, 24; *Fifty Years of the Maidstone Club, 1891-1941* (New York, New York: Pace Press, Inc., 1941), 108.

[52] St. Laurent, "The Negro in World History," 30; Dr. Eliza P. Shippen, "The Rev. John M. Shippen, Jr.," 2, Anacostia Story Exhibition Records.

[53] James Oliver Horton, "Black Education at Oberlin College: A Controversial Commitment," *The Journal of Negro Education* 54, no. 4 (Autumn 1985): 477; Shippen, "The Rev. John M. Shippen, Jr.," 2, Anacostia Story Exhibition Records.

[54] Shippen and Hatcher, *The Family Recollections of Beulah A. Shippen and Mabel S. (Shippen) Hatcher,* 36; Essay by Mabel Shippen Hatcher, "Cyrus S. Shippen, a Great Teacher and a Good Man," 1-2, Folder 1991.0013.3, Mabel Shippen Hatcher collection on Cyrus S. Shippen, Anacostia Community Museum Archives, Smithsonian Institution, Washington, DC (hereafter Mabel Shippen Hatcher Collection.) Cyrus Shippen contributed to Edwin Bancroft Henderson's revised edition of *The Negro in Sports*, published in 1949.

[55] Alison Stewart, *First Class: The Legacy of Dunbar, America's First Black Public High School* (Chicago: Lawrence Hill Books, 2013), 185, 187. Robert Weaver (Dunbar class of 1925) became the first black Cabinet member when President Lyndon Johnson selected him as the head of Housing and Urban Development in 1966.

[56] Mabel Shippen Hatcher essay, "Cyrus S. Shippen, a Great Teacher and a Good Man" 2, Mabel Shippen Hatcher Collection; Dr. Eliza P. Shippen, "The Rev. John M. Shippen, Jr.,"2, Anacostia Story Exhibition Records.

[57] Shippen and Hatcher, *The Family Recollections of Beulah A. Shippen and Mabel S. (Shippen) Hatcher,* 17; Sinnette, *Forbidden Fairways*, 24.

[58] *A Chip-in for Shippen*, VHS video; Shippen and Hatcher, *The Family Recollections of Beulah A. Shippen and Mabel S. (Shippen) Hatcher,* 33.

[59] St. Laurent, "The Negro in World History," 30; "Only Negro Golf Course in U.S. is Thriving in Suburban New Jersey," *Sun* (New York, NY), July 11, 1922.

[60] Larry Londino, "Shady Rest: Itself a Strong Ship," *Golf Journal*, June 1996. 17.

[61] Dawkins and Kinloch, *African America Golfer During the Jim Crow Era*, 102-103; Dave Anderson, "Remembering America's First Pro," *Golf Digest*, June 1995, 106.

[62] *Boyd's* city directories list her as a widow in 1934-35, 1937-39, as does the 1940 Census, District of Columbia, Roll M-T0627-00571, page 11B, Enumeration District: 1-526, *Ancestry.com,* accessed November 28, 2019; Shaun Powell, "Golf Pioneer Whited Out," *Newsday* (Nassau and Suffolk, NY edition), June 14, 2004: A57; Peter Aviles, "A Talk with Hanno Shippen Smith, Grandson of John Shippen, Jr.," Black Athletes Sports Network.net, November 27, 2004, http://blackathlete.net/2004/11/a-talk-with-hanno-shippen-smith-grandson-of-john-shippen-jr., accessed October 14, 2019; Dr. Calvin Sinnette, telephone

interview with Alberta Shippen, August 15, 1995, John Shippen files, Box 3, Folder 1, African American Golf History Archive, USGA.

[63] Shippen and Hatcher, *The Family Recollections of Beulah A. Shippen and Mabel S. (Shippen) Hatcher,* 31; Laurent, "The Negro in World History," 30; Aviles, "A Talk with Hanno Shippen Smith. Shippen's son, William Hugh Shippen, was a good amateur golfer, and tried numerous times to qualify for the U.S. Open. See Dan Burley, "Talkin' Out Loud," *New York Amsterdam News*, April 29, 1939, 18.

[64] Pete McDaniel, *Uneven Lies: The Heroic Story of African Americans in Golf* (Greenwich, Connecticut: American Golfer, Inc., 2000, 48; John H. Kennedy, *A Course of Their Own: A History of African American Golfers* (Lincoln, Nebraska: University of Nebraska Press, 2005, 138.

[65] Batt, "Shinnecock Indian was First Golf Pro," n.p.; Hoffman, "John M. Shippen," 2, Red Hoffman Collection, USGA.

[66] For a list of African Americans who played on the PGA Tour through 2000, see McDaniel, *Uneven Lies,* 165-167; Hoffman, "John M. Shippen," 1, Red Hoffman Collection, USGA; Anderson, "Remembering America's First Pro," 106.

[67] Grayson, "Man who Integrated Golf: Shippen, First Negro Pro," 6; Frank Strafaci, "Forgotten Golf Pioneer," *Golfing*, March 1957, 30.

[68] St. Laurent, "The Negro in World History," 30; "1986 U.S. Open (1/15)," You Tube.com, https://www.youtube.com/watch?v=KsR0cupsv6I, accessed August 3, 2019.

[69] Dave Anderson, "A PGA Member At Last," *Golf Digest*, November 2, 2009, https://www.golfdigest.com/story/golf_anderson_shippen_1109, accessed August 3, 2019; "PGA Bestows Membership on African American Pioneers," PGA of America.com, *November 14, 2009,* http://www.pga.com/pga-america-bestows-membership-african-american-pioneers, accessed August 3, 2019.

[70] "PGA Bestows Membership on African American Pioneers."; Parascenzo, "Daughter Tells Tale of 1st Black Golfer to Lead the U.S. Open,"13. Hanno Shippen Smith passed away September 26, 2010.

[71] Hank Gola, "Ahead of His Time: Little-known Linkster was First to Break Color Barrier," *New York Daily News*, June 17, 2004, http://www.nydailynews.com/archives/nydn-features/time-little-known-linkster-break-color-barrier-article-1.638760, accessed October 4, 2019; Grayson, "Man who Integrated Golf," 6; Bob Considine, "Plainfield Resident says John Shippen held back by Racism," *Courier News* (Bridgewater, NJ), June 17, 2004, A1, A12.

[72] Hank Gola, "Ahead of His Time."; Bob Considine, "Plainfield Resident says John Shippen held back by Racism," A12; Ralph Wise, answers to a questionnaire in John Shippen files, Box 3, Folder 1, African American Golf History Archive, USGA.

[73] Aviles, "A Talk with Hanno Shippen Smith, Grandson of John Shippen, Jr."; *America's First Golf Pro: A Chip-in for Shippen*, VHS video. Don Miller also painted the mural of Dr. Martin Luther King, Jr. that hangs in the Martin Luther King, Jr. Memorial Library in Washington, DC.

[74] Sinnette, *Forbidden Fairways*, 23; Ecclesiastes 3:1 and 9:11 (KJV); Marvin P. Dawkins and Jomills Henry Braddock, II, "Teeing off Against Jim Crow: Black Golf and Its Early Development in Washington, DC," in *DC Sports: The Nation's Capital at Play*, ed. Chris Elzey and David K. Wiggins (Fayetteville, AR: University of Arkansas Press, 2015), 71-72; Cose, *Color-blind*, 243. The John Shippen Memorial Golf Foundation was incorporated as a 501c non-profit in 1996 to help minority youth in golf. It has awarded scholarships to area high school graduates who demonstrate academic proficiency and have an interest and skill in golf. For more information, contact Thurman P. Simmons, Jr. at 1597 St. Ann Street, Scotch Plains, NJ 07076; email ShippenFoundation2@yahoo.com.

Chapter 6: The UGA, Pat Ball, Jimmie DeVoe, Lucius Bateman, and Maggie Hathaway – "Vanguards of Change for African American Golf"

[1] Marvin P. Dawkins and Jomills Henry Braddock, II, "Teeing off Against Jim Crow: Black Golf and Its Early Development in Washington, DC," in *DC Sports: The Nation's Capital at Play*, ed. Chris Elzey and David K. Wiggins (Fayetteville, AR: University of Arkansas Press, 2015), 58.

[2] "Two Golf Clubs in Washington," *The Baltimore Afro-American*, June 6, 1925, 8.

[3] Dawkins and Braddock, II, "Teeing off Against Jim Crow," 60; "Washington, DC Club to Hold First Colored Tourney in U.S.," *The Baltimore Afro-American*, October 17, 1924, 14; "Two Golf Clubs in Washington," *The Baltimore Afro-American*, June 6, 1925, 8; Calvin H. Sinnette, *Forbidden Fairways: African Americans and the Game of Golf* (Chelsea, MI: Sleeping Bear Press, 1998), 22; Marvin P. Dawkins and Graham C. Kinloch, *African America Golfers During the Jim Crow Era* (Westport, CT: Praeger, 2000), 25. Victor Daly was an author, graduating from Cornell University in 1919. By 1924 he had moved to Washington, DC and was at work on *Not Only War*, which would become the only World War I novel written by a black veteran. See Lane Demas, *Game of Privilege: An African American History of Golf* (Chapel Hill: The University of North Carolina Press, 2017), 62, 64.

[4] Constance McLaughlin Green, *The Secret City: A History of Race Relations in the Nation's Capital* (Princeton, NJ: Princeton University Press, 1967), 198; Dawkins and Braddock, II, "Teeing off Against Jim Crow," 57; Harvard Sitcoff, *A New Deal for Blacks: The Emergence of Civil Rights as a National Issue, Volume 1: The Depression Decade* (New York: Oxford University Press, 1978), 27.

[5] Green, *The Secret City*, 201-203; Terence McArdle, "The Day 30,000 White Supremacists in KKK robes Marched in the Nation's Capital," *The Washington Post*, August 17, 2017, https://www.washingtonpost.com/news/retropolis/wp/2017/08/17/the-day-30000-white-supremacists-in-kkk-robes-marched-in-the-nations-capital/?noredirect=on&utm_term=.f852e8d89b13, accessed October 30, 2019. A Pathe newsreel noted 40,000 marchers; Dawkins and Jomills Henry Braddock, II, "Teeing off Against Jim Crow," 61. In 1927, the Citizens' Golf Club changed its name to the Capital City Golf Club; in 1933 the club was renamed the Royal Golf Club.

[6] Raymond Schmidt, "Pars and Birdies in a Hidden World: African Americans and the United Golfers Association," in *Separate Games: African American Sport behind the Walls of Segregation*, ed. David K. Wiggins and Ryan A. Swanson (Fayetteville, AR: University of Arkansas Press, 2016), 182. By the close of 1929, the organization had been renamed the United Golfers Association (UGA.)

[7] Jeffrey T. Sammons, "'Race' and Sport: A Critical, Historical Examination," *Journal of Sport History* 21, no. 3 (Fall 1994): 267; Dawkins and Kinloch, *African America Golfer During the Jim Crow Era*, 21; Pete McDaniel, *Uneven Lies: The Heroic Story of African Americans in Golf* (Greenwich, CT: American Golfer, Inc., 2000), 54. The UGA's first president, B.C. Gordon, was also the president of Shady Rest Country Club, where John Shippen finished his career.

[8] "H. Jackson Wins First Golf Title," *The Pittsburgh Courier*, July 18, 1925, 12.

[9] Demas, *Game of Privilege*, 64; Green, *The Secret City*, 185; "DC Golf Tourneys July and August," *The Baltimore Afro-American*, June 18, 1927, 3; "Golfers Tourney Started," *The Pittsburgh Courier*, October 15, 1927, 16; "Eastern Golf Course Opens," *The Pittsburgh Courier*, July 30, 1927, 16.

[10] Susan Ware, *Holding Their Own: American Women in the 1930s* (Boston: Twayne Publishers, 1982), 8; Sitcoff, *A New Deal for Blacks*, 36; John Hope Franklin and Alfred A. Moss, Jr., 8th ed., *From Slavery to Freedom: A History of African Americans* (New York: McGraw Hill, 2000), 421.

[11] "Ball Wins Golf Title," *The Pittsburgh Courier*, September 27, 1927, 16. The paper reported

Ball won custody "of the championship cup for one year and $100 in money." Shippen won $75 McDaniel, *Uneven Lies*, 51; "Patrick Ball Wins National Championship," *Chicago Defender*, September 10, 1927, part 1, page 9. Ball shot 293, Shippen 313. Shippen's son John, Jr. ("Jack") also played, shooting 340. Five days later Ball won an invitational tournament at Shady Rest, with Shippen finishing 8th; "Ball Beats Shady Rest Golf Kings," *Chicago Defender*, September 17, 1927, part 1, page 9.

[12] Associated Press, "Ousted Negroes Seek Injunction to Halt Public Links Tournament," *The Washington Post*, August 3, 1928, 17; McDaniel, *Uneven Lies*, 51; "Golf Muddle Stirs Philly," *The Baltimore Afro-American*, August 11, 1928, 13; *David A. Canton, Raymond Pace Alexander: A New Negro Lawyer Fights for Civil Rights in Philadelphia (Jackson, Mississippi: University Press of Mississippi, 2010)*, 26.

[13] Bernice Dutrieuille, "Race Golfers Show Up Whites in Law Suit," *The Pittsburgh Courier*, August 11, 1928, 5; "Sport Editorial," *The Baltimore Afro-American*, August 11, 1928, 13; Kerr Petrie, "Kauffmann and Ogden Public Links Finalists," unidentified newspaper clipping, August [4?], 1928, 12, in subject files, "Minorities," USGA.

[14] Gordon Mackay, "Writer Raps Golf Officials but Praises Ball and Stout," *The Baltimore Afro-American*, August 11, 1928, 13; Demas, *Game of Privilege*, 103; Ganson Depew (Chairman of Public Links Committee) to Prescott S. Bush, August 4, 1928, subject files, "Minorities," USGA.

[15] Ganson Depew to John G. Jackson, February 19, 1929 and Ganson Depew to Prescott S. Bush, August 4, 1928, subject files, "Minorities," USGA.

[16] Ganson Depew to John G. Jackson (USGA General Counsel), April 16, 1929 and Ganson Depew to John G. Jackson, February 19, 1929, subject files, "Minorities," USGA.

[17] Sam E. Salem, "U. B. Phillips and the Scientific Tradition," *The Georgia Historical Quarterly* 44, no. 2 (June 1960): 182; John David Smith, "The Historiographic Rise, Fall, and Resurrection of Ulrich Bonnell Phillips," *The Georgia Historical Quarterly* 65, no. 2 (Summer 1981), 139.

[18] Peter Novick, *That Noble Dream: The "Objectivity Question" and the American Historical Profession* (Cambridge, England: Cambridge University Press, 1988), 229.

[19] Renford Reese, "The Socio-Political Context of the Integration of Sport in America," *Journal of African American Men* 3, no. 4 (Spring 1998), 22; McDaniel, *Uneven Lies*, 51.

[20] Elmer E. Brent, "Fourth Annual Championship at Shady Rest Country Club Aug. 31," *The New York Age*, August 24, 1929, 6; Sinnette, *Forbidden Fairways*, 22; "Only Negro Golf Course in U.S. is Thriving in Suburban New Jersey," *Sun* (New York, NY), July 11, 1922.

[21] Lori L. Tharps, "The Case for Black With a Capital B," *The New York Times*, November 18, 2014, https://www.nytimes.com/2014/11/19/opinion/the-case-for-black-with-a-capital-b.html, accessed October 28, 2019;
Sitcoff, *A New Deal for Blacks*, 333; Randall Kennedy, *Nigger: The Strange Career of a Troublesome Word* (New York: Pantheon Books, 2002), 114; Alison Stewart, *First Class: The Legacy of Dunbar, America's First Black Public High School* (Chicago: Lawrence Hill Books, 2013), xii; H. L. Mencken, "Designations for Colored Folk," *American Speech* 19, no. 3 (October 1944), 162. From 1850 to 1920, the United States Census Bureau classified people of African descent under these categories: black, negro, mulatto, quadroon or octoroon (depending on the visual assessment of the census taker, which could vary from census to census.) By 1930, only one of these categories was used: negro. Following the black power movement of the 1960s, *The New York Times* began using "black," as did the Associated Press, and by the late 1980s, "African American" became more prevalent.

[22] *The New York Age*, June 9, 1923, 3; "Decoration Day Observed at Shady Rest Golf Club," *The New York Age*, June 2, 1923, 6; Dawkins and Kinloch, *African America Golfer During the Jim Crow Era*, 25; Larry Londino, "Shady Rest: Itself a Strong Ship," *Golf Journal*, June 1996, 17; Demas, *Game of Privilege*, 50-51. Over time Du Bois grew increasingly pessimistic

about golf, although he signed up for membership at Atlanta's New Lincoln Country Club soon after he returned to the South in 1933 (he did not play the game.)

[23] Anthony Venutolo, "Shady Rest in Scotch Plains was First African American Club of its Kind," NJ.com, May 28, 2009, http://blog.nj.com/ledgerarchives/2009/02/country_club_life.html, accessed February 24, 2018; Londino, "Shady Rest: Itself a Strong Ship," 17; Anderson, "Remembering America's First Pro," 106.

[24] Nicholas Veronis, "A Black on the Greens," *The Sunday Star-Ledger* (NJ), June 16, 1991, 3; Sitcoff, *A New Deal for Blacks,* 218; NAACP.org, "NAACP History: Charles Hamilton Houston," https://www.naacp.org/naacp-history-charles-hamilton-houston/, accessed November 1, 2019.

[25] Pat Ball to USGA, April 29, 1933; Prescott Bush to Robert P. Ball, May 5, 1933; "U.S. Golf Body Won't Let Ball Enter Tourney," *The Baltimore Afro-American*, May 20, 1933, 16; John G. Jackson to Livingston Platt (USGA General Counsel), May 21, 1933, letters from subject files, "Minorities," USGA. Prescott Bush was the father of President George H. W. Bush and the grandfather of President George W. Bush. Ball would win two more UGA National Open championships in 1934 and 1941.

[26] "USGA Turns Down Golf Aces," *The New York Amsterdam News*, June 17, 1939, 15; "U.S. Golf Body Bars Players from Open," *Baltimore Afro-American*, June 3, 1939, 22.

[27] Sitcoff, *A New Deal for Blacks,* 316, 321, 324.

[28] Nat Rayburg, a sportswriter for the *Washington Afro-American*, observed In 1941 that Clyde Martin had "worked as clubmaker, golf instructor, and caddy for such stars as Walter Hagen, Tommy Armour and Ton[ey] Penna over 18 years...In many quarters, Martin is rated as the country's most outstanding [black] golfer." See Dawkins and Braddock, II, "Teeing Off Against Jim Crow," 64.

[29] Demas, *Game of Privilege,* 142-143; Telegram from the USGA to Clyde Martin, May 22, 1942, Box 2, Folder 6, African American Golf History Archive, USGA. Martin paid $5 for entry to qualify for Hale America National Open Golf Tournament, which was acknowledged May 8th by the USGA.

[30] "Tam O'Shanter Invites Negro Golf Entries," unattributed newspaper clipping, *Chicago Defender* [?], May 29, 1942, 12, Box 6, Folder 10, African American Golf History Archive, USGA; Sinnette, *Forbidden Fairways,* 164; John H. Kennedy, *A Course of Their Own: A History of African American Golfers* (Lincoln, Nebraska: University of Nebraska Press, 2005, 57.

[31] Philip Dray, *At the Hands of Persons Unknown: The Lynching of Black America* (New York: Random House, 2002), 368; The History Learning Site.co.uk, https://www.historylearningsite.co.uk/the-civil-rights-movement-in-america-1945-to-1968/education-and-civil-rights/, accessed November 5, 2019.

[32] E. Jack Barns (Chairman, Medinah Golf Committee) to Richard S. Tufts, February 28, 1949 and Richard S. Tufts to E. Jack Barns, January 21, 1949, subject files, "Minorities," USGA; Mark Harris, "Foul Play on the Fairway," *Negro Digest*, October 1948, 36.

[33] Lynn Simross, "Pro Wins Through the Rough," *Los Angeles Times*, August 17, 1975, 63; Margaret Roberts, "DeVoe Just Keeps Climbing the Heights," *Golf Digest*, May 1972, 80.

[34] Dr. Jeffrey Sammons, "Jimmie DeVoe," paper presented at 2010 USGA Golf History Symposium, November 7, 2010, 36, 39-40; DeVoe marriage certificate, Cook County, Illinois, Marriages Index, 1871-1920 and DeVoe World War I draft registration card, Cook County, Illinois, Roll 1439759, Draft Board, 14 and Lists of Incoming Passengers, 1917-1938, Records of the Office of the Quartermaster General, 1774-1985, Record Group Number 92, roll 235, all on *Ancestry.com,* accessed November 28, 2019.

[35] 1920 Census, Cleveland Ward 11, Cuyahoga County, Ohio, T625, roll 1365, page 9B, Enumeration District 216, *Ancestry.com,* accessed November 28, 2019; Fred C. Williams, "Jimmie DeVoe Responsible for New Interest in Golf," The Pittsburgh Courier, July 10, 1943. 19; Jolee Edmondson, "The Remarkable Jimmy DeVoe," Golf Magazine, August 1976, 66.

[36] Edmondson, "The Remarkable Jimmy DeVoe," 66.

[37] Harry Cooper interview with J. Robert Windsor, USGA Oral History Collection, September 10 and 17, 1990, 78; Edmondson, "The Remarkable Jimmy DeVoe," 66.

[38] 1930 Census, Cleveland, Cuyahoga County, Ohio, page 15B, Enumeration District 0356, FHL microfilm 2341506, *Ancestry.com*, accessed November 28, 2019; "Buckeye Golf Tourney Soon," *The Pittsburgh Courier*, August 30, 1930, 14; "Souvenir Programme of the Eastern Golf Association," 1932, Box 23, Folder 11, African American Golf History Archive, USGA; "Dial," *The New York Age* , July 25, 1936, 9.

[39] "Pickets to Continue Activity in Front of L.M. Blumstein Company's Store," *The New York Age*, June 16, 1934, 1; "Statement of Wm. Blumstein," *The New York Age*, August 4, 1934, 1; Sammons, "Jimmie DeVoe," 48; Williams, "Jimmie DeVoe Responsible for New Interest in Golf," 19.

[40] Jimmy Smith, "Negro Golfers Eligible to Enter Amateur Public Links Tourney," *The New York Age*, June 13, 1936, 9; "Swanky Country Club Elects Officers and Board of Directors," *The New York Age*, May 1, 1937, 4; "Jerseyites Win Rising Sun Meet," *The New York Amsterdam News*, August 21, 1937, 15; "Links Tourney at Rising Sun," *The New York Amsterdam News*, June 12, 1937, 16.

[41] Dan Burley, "Talkin' Out Loud," New York Amsterdam News, April 29, 1939, 18; Sammons, "Jimmie DeVoe," 52-53; "Entries Pour in for Coast Golf Tourney," The Pittsburgh Courier, September 21, 1946, 15; World War II Draft Cards (4th Registration) for the State of California, The National Archives at St. Louis, Records of the Selective Service System, Record Group Number 147, *Ancestry.com*, accessed November 28, 2019.

[42] Roberts, "DeVoe Just Keeps Climbing the Heights," 80; "Kertes, Quick Tie in Open," *Los Angeles Times*, December 5, 1946, 11.

[43] Sammons, "Jimmie DeVoe," 61, 64; "Entries Pour in for Coast Golf Tourney," 15; "Women Golfers in Coast Open Oct. 4," *The Pittsburgh Courier*, September 28, 1946, 16; "Charlie Sifford Wins Pro Honors in UGA Tournament," *Alabama Tribune* (Montgomery, AL), September 4, 1953, 7; PGA of America.com, "Jimmie DeVoe, Class of 2013," March 8, 2013, https://www.pga.com/pga-america/pga-feature/jimmie-devoe-class-2013, accessed August 2, 2019.

[44] Golfers Led in Qualifying by Andrews," *Los Angeles Times*, May 19, 1959, 79; Jimmy DeVoe file, Box 1, Folder 11, African American Golf History Archive, USGA; Roberts, "DeVoe Just Keeps Climbing the Heights," 81.

[45] Stan Wood, "Ex-caddie Becomes PGA Section Leader," *Golf Digest*, October 1957, 28-29.

[46] Sammons, "Jimmie DeVoe," 58-59; Simross, "Pro Wins Through the Rough," 63; "PGA of America.com, "Jimmie DeVoe, Class of 2013."

[47] "PGA of America.com, "Jimmie DeVoe, Class of 2013."; Edmondson, "The Remarkable Jimmy DeVoe," 64; Simross, "Pro Wins Through the Rough," 63-64.

[48] Simross, "Pro Wins Through the Rough," 63; Tom Sears, "DeVoe Disappointed Despite Win," *The Palm Beach Post* (West Palm Beach, FL), February 3, 1974, E2.

[49] Simross, "Pro Wins Through the Rough," 63; Edmondson, "The Remarkable Jimmy DeVoe," 65.

[50] PGA of America, "Jimmie DeVoe, Class of 2013,"; "One Putts," *Los Angeles Times*, March 25, 1979, 58; Sears, "DeVoe Disappointed Despite Win," E2.

[51] Walt Roessing, "California Builder of Champions," *Golf Digest*, January 1965, 42; Art Spander, "Quiet Glory of a Driving Range Pro," *Golf Magazine*, March 1972, 39.

[52] Roessing, "California Builder of Champions," 42; BIRLS Death File, 1850-2010, U.S. Department of Veterans Affairs, *Ancestry.com*, accessed November 28, 2019; Spander, "Quiet

Glory of a Driving Range Pro," 39.

[53] Roessing, "California Builder of Champions," 41-42.

[54] Al Barkow, "There Are Gurus...and There Are Gurus," a typed tribute to Lucious Bateman written for the Northern California Golf Association, Spring 2019, 4; "Golf Coach Insists on Sportsmanship," *The Semi-Weekly Spokesman-Review* (Spokane, WA), January 17, 1959, 11; Roessing, "California Builder of Champions," 42.

[55] George Ross, "Contemplate the Mirror," *Oakland Tribune*, July 27, 1966, 42; Spander, "Quiet Glory of a Driving Range Pro," 41; Roessing, "California Builder of Champions," 41.

[56] Spander, "Quiet Glory of a Driving Range Pro," 41; Ross, "Contemplate the Mirror," 42; Roessing, "California Builder of Champions," 41; Barkow, "There Are Gurus...and There Are Gurus," 3.

[57] Steward, "'Bateman Boys' Film a Tribute to East Bay Golf Mentor," July 11, 2009, updated August 15, 2016, https://www.eastbaytimes.com/2009/07/11/bateman-boys-film-a-tribute-to-east-bay-golf-mentor/, accessed August 5, 2019. The nine core values of the First Tee program are: honesty, integrity, sportsmanship, respect, confidence, responsibility, perseverance, courtesy, judgment.

[58] Gary Plato, email message to the author, December 16, 2019; Art Spander, "Quiet Glory of a Driving Range Pro," *Golf Magazine*, March 1972, 41; Steward, "'Bateman Boys' Film a Tribute to East Bay Golf Mentor."

[59] Norm Hannon, "Tourney, Banquet Slated for 'Loosh,'" *Oakland Tribune*, July 29, 1962, 42; Roessing, "California Builder of Champions," 41; Steward, "'Bateman Boys' Film a Tribute to East Bay Golf Mentor."

[60] Plato, email message, December 16, 2019; Barkow, "There Are Gurus...and There Are Gurus," 4.

[61] Roessing, "California Builder of Champions," 41; Plato, email message, December 16, 2019.

[62] Art Spander, "Quiet Glory of a Driving Range Pro," 79; Letter from Gary Plato to Len Dumas, Secretary of the Northern California PGA regarding honorary membership nomination on behalf of Lucius Bateman, 2008, 1; Roessing, "California Builder of Champions," 40-41.

[63] Steward, "'Bateman Boys' Film a Tribute to East Bay Golf Mentor."; Spander, "Quiet Glory of a Driving Range Pro," 39; Hannon, "Tourney, Banquet Slated for 'Loosh,'" 42.

[64] Spander, "Quiet Glory of a Driving Range Pro," 41; Ed Levitt, "Lucius, Thanks," *Oakland Tribune*, November 4, 1971, 39; Lucius Bateman Tribute, Northern California PGA, https://www.facebook.com/NorCalPGA/videos/1076893448953/, accessed August 8, 2019.

[65] Spander, "Quiet Glory of a Driving Range Pro," 41; Levitt, "Lucius, Thanks," 39; Roessing, "California Builder of Champions," 41; Steward, "'Bateman Boys' Film a Tribute to East Bay Golf Mentor."

[66] Spander, "Quiet Glory of a Driving Range Pro," 41; Roessing, "California Builder of Champions," 42.

[67] Plato, email message, December 16, 2019; Barkow, "There Are Gurus...and There Are Gurus," 5.

[68] Spander, "Quiet Glory of a Driving Range Pro," 41, 39; Roessing, "California Builder of Champions," 42; Steward, "'Bateman Boys' Film a Tribute to East Bay Golf Mentor."

[69] J. Andree Penix Smith, "Maggie Hathaway: Fighting for Freedom on the Front Lines," *Amsterdam News* (New York), March 30, 2017, http://amsterdamnews.com/news/2017/mar/30/maggie-hathaway-fighting-freedom-front-lines, accessed August 3, 2019; James Dodson, "A Lifelong Crusade," *Golf Magazine*, June 2001, 50.

[70] Maggie Hathaway biography, IMDb.com, https://www.imdb.com/name/nm0368889/bio?ref_=nm_ov_bio_sm, accessed September 22,

2019; Jason Lewis, "Maggie Hathaway Opened Doors for Blacks in Golf and Entertainment," *Los Angeles Sentinel*, March 22, 2012, B3.

[71] Smith, "Maggie Hathaway: Fighting for Freedom on the Front Lines."; Dodson, "A Lifelong Crusade," 50; McDaniel, *Uneven Lies*, 78.

[72] Sinnette, *Forbidden Fairways*, 145.

[73] Smith, "Maggie Hathaway: Fighting for Freedom on the Front Lines."; Randy Harvey, "Militant Maggie Hathaway Never Quits Fighting for Her Cause," *Los Angeles Times*, February 27, 1997, S8; Dodson, "A Lifelong Crusade," 52 ; "Down the Fairway," *The New York Age*, September 25, 1954, 20.

[74] Harvey, "Militant Maggie Hathaway Never Quits Fighting for Her Cause," S8; Sinnette, *Forbidden Fairways*, 145; Dodson, "A Lifelong Crusade," 48. Chester Washington began working at the *Los Angeles Sentinel*, the city's largest black-owned weekly, in 1962, where he became the editor. Los Angeles County Supervisor Kenneth Hahn dedicated the former Western Avenue Golf Course in Washington's name on March 18, 1982.

[75] Dodson, "A Lifelong Crusade," 48, 50.

[76] M. Mikell Johnson, *Heroines of African American Golf: The Past, The Present and The Future* (Bloomington, IN: Trafford Publishing, 2010), 214; Shav Glick, "Southland Golf," *The Los Angeles Times*, April 23, 1972, 57; Dodson, "A Lifelong Crusade," 52; McDaniel, *Uneven Lies*, 78; Harvey, "Militant Maggie Hathaway Never Quits Fighting for Her Cause" S8. In 1994 Hathaway became the first woman elected to National Black Golf Hall of Fame.

[77] "Golfers Tee Off Today in Match Play Tourney," *Los Angeles Times*, July 11, 1963, 42.

[78] "New Branch of NAACP is Formed," *Valley Times Today* (Hollywood, CA), August 13, 1962, 8; Smith, "Maggie Hathaway: Fighting for Freedom on the Front Lines."; Dodson, "A Lifelong Crusade," 53.

[79] Smith, "Maggie Hathaway: Fighting for Freedom on the Front Lines."; "Blacks Charge Bias in Hiring at Golf Courses," *The Los Angeles Times*, January 22, 1971, 30.

[80] McDaniel, *Uneven Lies*, 78; Harvey, "Militant Maggie Hathaway Never Quits Fighting for Her Cause" S8; Bill Christine, "Masters Tableau: Only Littler was White," *Pittsburgh Post-Gazette*, April 11, 1975, 11.

[81] Dodson, "A Lifelong Crusade," 54; Harvey, "Militant Maggie Hathaway Never Quits Fighting for Her Cause" S8.

[82] "Well Deserved," *The Los Angeles Times*, June 14, 1998, 52; Dodson, "A Lifelong Crusade," 194; Lewis, "Maggie Hathaway Opened Doors for Blacks in Golf and Entertainment," B3.

[83] Dodson, "A Lifelong Crusade," 50, 194.

Chapter 7: Golfers with Challenged Bodies – "Adapt, Adjust, and Overcome"

[1] Sidney Matthew, *Bobby: The Life and Times of Bobby Jones* (Ann Arbor, Michigan: Sports Media Group, 2005), 48; Jack Houvouras, "Bill Campbell: A Life in Balance," *Huntington Quarterly*, Issue 70 (Summer 2010), https://huntingtonquarterly.com/2018/09/26/issue-70-bill-campbell-a-life-in-balance/, accessed September 1, 2019.

[2] Dennis Walters with James Achenbach, *In My Dreams I Walk With You* (Chelsea, Michigan: Sleeping Bear Press, 2002), 137; Marven Moss, "People in Golf," *Golf Digest*, April 1977, 86.

[3] Khalil Gibran from Brainy Quote.com, https://www.brainyquote.com/quotes/khalil_gibran_386848, accessed September 5, 2019; "Bravest Boy in Buffalo Wins Unequal Battle," *The Buffalo Sunday Morning News*, November 23, 1913, 10.

[4] Vartan Kupelian, *Forever Scratch: Chuck Kocsis – An Amateur for the Ages* (Ann Arbor, MI: Sports Media Group, 2007), 27; "Bravest Boy in Buffalo Wins Unequal Battle," 10; "Still Plays Golf Without his Arms," *The Ottawa Journal* (Ottawa, Canada), June 15, 1936, 17.

[5] "The Armless Golfer and How He Plays," *The Golf Monthly*, January 1915, 772-774. The

article noted that he had shot 108 at the Buffalo Country Club. Twenty years later, he had improved greatly. See "Gossiping About Golf," *The American Golfer*, January 1934, 20.

[6] Ray Fitzgerald, "Righthanded Lefty," *Golf Magazine*, September 1961, 45-46.

[7] Ibid., 46-48.

[8] "Famous One-Armed Golfer Shoots a 69," *PGA Magazine*, September 1946, 29; Fitzgerald, "Righthanded Lefty," 48 ; "IMG Speakers - Renee Powell Golf Champion," and Bob Denney, "40 Years after Firebase Sherman - Vietnam Veterans Reach Out to Thank PGA/LPGA Professional Renee Powell for Her Work to Deliver Memories of Home," articles in Renee Powell biographical file, USGA.

[9] Fitzgerald, "Righthanded Lefty," 45; Herb Graffis, "Comeback in Sunshine," *Golfing*, March 1954, 3; "About," National Amputee Golf Association.com, http://nagagolf.org/about/, accessed September 6, 2019.

[10] Chuck Albury, "The Winner – By a Leg," *Golf Digest*, August 1964, 72; Jack O'Leary, "Ready, Willing, and Disabled: They're Golfers Too, and Just Like Us, They Want a Fair Shot," *Senior Golfer*, September/October 1996, 116.

[11] Lloyd Shearer, "Another Chance at Life," *Parade*, June 12, 1966, 6; Stan Wood, "Bob Morgan – He's Playing Borrowed Golf," *Golfing*, April 1964, 11.

[12] Wood, "Bob Morgan – He's Playing Borrowed Golf," 11.

[13] Bob Thomas, "A Return from Death," *St. Louis Post-Dispatch*, November 6, 1962, 34.

[14] Wood, "Bob Morgan – He's Playing Borrowed Golf," 10; Shearer, "Another Chance at Life," 6; Thomas, "A Return from Death," 34.

[15] Wood, "Bob Morgan – He's Playing Borrowed Golf," 11; Thomas, "A Return from Death," 34; Shearer, "Another Chance at Life," 6. Wood and DeCarlo were married from 1955 to 1973.

[16] Wood, "Bob Morgan – He's Playing Borrowed Golf," 40, 11, 42; Ed Furgol, "Winning the Open Changed my Life," *The Saturday Evening Post*, September 4, 1954, 72.

[17] Wood, "Bob Morgan – He's Playing Borrowed Golf," 42.

[18] "Real Success," *Golf Digest*, November 1997, 17; Rich Skyzinski, "A Strong Grasp of What's Needed," *Golf Journal*, November/December 1996, 21.

[19] Skyzinski, "A Strong Grasp of What's Needed," 21; "Real Success," 17; Kris Tschetter with Steve Eubanks, *Mr. Hogan, The Man I Knew* (New York: Gotham Books, 2010), 74.

[20] Guy Yocum, "My Shot – Bob Wilson," *Golf Digest*, September 2005, 137.

[21] Ibid., 138.

[22] Jeff Skirvin, "Adapt, Adjust, Overcome," *The Daily Journal*, (Franklin, IN), June 9, 2008, B1.

[23] Joe Biddle, "Double Amputee Will Feel Magic at St Andrews," *The Tennessean* (Nashville, TN), July 29, 2010, C1.

[24] Skirvin, "Adapt, Adjust, Overcome," B1; Biddle, "Double Amputee Will Feel Magic at St Andrews," C1.

[25] Skirvin, "Adapt, Adjust, Overcome," B1; Biddle, "Double Amputee Will Feel Magic at St Andrews," C1; "A 79 in the Old Course from a Wheelchair," *Golf Digest*, October 2011, 114.

[26] Ben Houser, "Making History in An Inspirational Way, ESPN.com, July 20, 2011, https://www.espn.com/espn/e60/story/_/id/6781849/tennessee-golfer-becomes-first-play-old-course-st-andrews-wheelchair, accessed August 4, 2019; "A 79 in the Old Course from a Wheelchair," 114.

[27] Skirvin, "Adapt, Adjust, Overcome," B4; Tom Siler, "The Champ Who's Never Seen the Ball," *Golf Magazine*, July 1959, 25; Charley Boswell with Curt Anders, *Now I See* (New York: Meredith Press, 1969), 28.

[28] Boswell with Anders, *Now I See*, 17, 11.

[29] Ibid., 69, 111.

[30] Ibid., 112.

[31] Siler, "The Champ Who's Never Seen the Ball," 60; Boswell with Anders, *Now I See*, 113,

68, 114; John Bibb, "Boswell's Big Shot," *The Tennessean* (Nashville, TN), June 25, 1976, 25.
[32] "Blind Champion," *Golf World*, April 21, 1948, 3.
[33] Boswell with Anders, *Now I See*, 150, 156; Steve Killick, "Blind Golfers," *Kingdom*, Winter 2019, 65; Bibb, "Boswell's Big Shot," 25.
[34] Boswell with Anders, *Now I See*, 157, 197; Siler, "The Champ Who's Never Seen the Ball," 58.
[35] Dominic Massa, "Champion Blind Golfer Pat Browne Jr. Dies at 84," April 21, 2017, WWL Tv.com, https://www.wwltv.com/article/life/announcements/obits/champion-blind-golfer-pat-browne-jr-dies-at-84/433212802, accessed September 5, 2019; Dodson, "18 Holes with Pat Browne," *Golf Magazine*, October 1992, 70.
[36] Paul Jaynes, "He Never Lost Sight of the Joys of Golf," *Pittsburgh Post-Gazette*, May 12, 1984, 36; Ray Kienzl, "For the Blind, Golf is Team Game," *The Pittsburgh Press*, February 4, 1979, 73; Massa, "Champion Blind Golfer Pat Browne Jr. Dies at 84."
[37] Killick, "Blind Golfers," 66.
[38] Tom McEwen, "Skip Alexander's Road Back," *Golf Digest*, April 1960, 70.
[39] James Achenbach, "Inspiration, Revisited," *Golfweek*, October 28, 2011, 50; Jack Horner, "One Skip and a Hop from Fame," *Sport*, August 1948, 88; Buddy Alexander, telephone interview with the author, August 29, 2019.
[40] Horner, "One Skip and a Hop from Fame," 88. Stewart Murray Alexander graduated from Washington and Jefferson College in 1915. See *General Alumni Catalogue of Washington and Jefferson College, 1802-1945*, University Archives, Clark Family Library, Washington and Jefferson College, Washington, Pennsylvania.
[41] Alexander, telephone interview, August 29, 2019; Furman Bisher, "Skip Alexander Thanks a Pal," *Sports Illustrated*, n.d., 63, in Skip Alexander biographical file, USGA.
[42] McEwen, "Skip Alexander's Road Back," 69; Bisher, "Skip Alexander Thanks a Pal," 63, 31.
[43] Horner, "One Skip and a Hop from Fame," 89, 56; Bisher, "Skip Alexander Thanks a Pal," 32.
[44] Abe Chanin, "Skip Alexander Captures Tucson Open Golf Crown," *Arizona Daily Star* (Tucson, AZ), February 2, 1948, 1; Bisher, "Skip Alexander Thanks a Pal," 63; Horner, "One Skip and a Hop from Fame," 56; Dillon Graham, "Alexander's 271 Wins Capital Golf; Locke Second," *The Philadelphia Inquirer*, May 3, 1948, 24.
[45] Mark Stewart, "The Incredible Comeback of 'Skip' Alexander," *PGA Tour Partners Magazine*, September/October 2001, 53. Foursomes is a form of play where two players as a team play one ball, alternating shots from tee to green. Buddy Alexander said that his sister Carol was born while Skip was away playing in the 1949 Ryder Cup in Ganton, England. The course had some dangerous, penal bunkers, so Skip nicknamed his daughter "Bunkie" because she was his own little hazard, a reflection of his rich sense of humor.
[46] Bisher, "Skip Alexander Thanks a Pal," 63; "Report on Alexander," *Golf World*, September 27, 1950, 5; "Unscheduled Flight," *Golf World*, October 4, 1950, 9; Achenbach, "Inspiration, Revisited," 50; Stewart, "The Incredible Comeback of 'Skip' Alexander," 53.
[47] "Unscheduled Flight," *Golf World*, October 4, 1950, 9; Stewart, "The Incredible Comeback of 'Skip' Alexander," 53; "Skip Alexander Injured as Plane Crashes; Three Die," *Arizona Daily Star* (Tucson, AZ), September 25, 1950, 6.
[48] Stewart, "The Incredible Comeback of 'Skip' Alexander," 53; McEwen, "Skip Alexander's Road Back," 70.
[49] Achenbach, "Inspiration, Revisited," 52; Stewart, "The Incredible Comeback of 'Skip' Alexander," 53.
[50] Stewart, "The Incredible Comeback of 'Skip' Alexander," 55, 54; "A White Christmas," *Golf World*, December 20, 1950, 6.
[51] "Skip Out of Hospital," *Golf World*, January 17, 1951, 3; "Follow the Sun," *Golf World*, January 24, 1951, 4.

[52] Alexander, telephone interview, October 7, 2019; Achenbach, "Inspiration, Revisited," 52; Stewart, "The Incredible Comeback of 'Skip' Alexander," 54.

[53] "Skip Alexander Match in Charlotte Today," *The High Point Enterprise* (High Point, NC), March 27, 1951, 4; "Winner Take All," *Golf World*, April 27, 1951, 13.

[54] "Winner Take All," 13; Alexander, telephone interview, August 29, 2019; Stewart, "The Incredible Comeback of 'Skip' Alexander," 54; "Skip Gives it a Whirl," *Golf World*, August 24, 1951, 16.

[55] "Skip Gives it a Whirl," 16; Stewart, "The Incredible Comeback of 'Skip' Alexander," 54-55; "Snead Heads Team," *The Courier-Journal* (Louisville, KY), October 10, 1951, 21; Alexander, telephone interview, October 7, 2019.

[56] Achenbach, "Inspiration, Revisited," 52; Stewart, "The Incredible Comeback of 'Skip' Alexander," 55; McEwen, "Skip Alexander's Road Back," 71.

[57] Alexander, telephone interview, October 7, 2019.

[58] "Skip Alexander Files $279,000 Injury Suit Against Government," *The Index-Journal* (Greenwood, SC), September 25, 1952, 9; "Skip's Suit Heard," *Golf World*, April 16, 1954, 6.

[59] "Skip Alexander Loses," November 16, 1956, 13; Alexander, telephone interview, August 29, 2019.

[60] Alexander, telephone interview, October 7, 2019; Oscar Fraley, "Skip Alexander Returns to Golf for Second Try Since Crash Landing," *Austin American-Statesman* (Austin, TX), March 3, 1952, 14; "Skip Alexander Ties Ferrier in 4-Ball Pro-Am," *Tampa Bay Times*, December 18, 1952, 21; Bill Beck, "Alexander Cops Skyway Open (205); Bolesta 2nd," *Tampa Bay Times*, September 7, 1954, 17.

[61] "Skip Captures Club Pro Title (284) at Dunedin," *Tampa Bay Times*, February 21, 1959, 9; Alexander, telephone interview, August 29, 2019.

[62] McEwen, "Skip Alexander's Road Back," 69.

[63] Paul Hemphill, "Good Show," *The Tampa Times*, February 22, 1964, 8. According to Buddy Alexander, after Nicklaus won the 1962 U.S. Open he played in the St. Petersburg Open as a silent thank you to Skip for the kindness he had shown him as a kid at Scioto (Alexander, telephone interview, October 7, 2019.)

[64] Alexander, telephone interview, August 29, 2019; Stewart, "The Incredible Comeback of 'Skip' Alexander," 55.

[65] Alexander, telephone interview, October 7, 2019; Stewart, "The Incredible Comeback of 'Skip' Alexander," 55, 54; Horner, "One Skip and a Hop from Fame," 57; McEwen, "Skip Alexander's Road Back," 69. Alexander was rejected when he tried to volunteer for the service after Pearl Harbor, but was drafted a few months later.

[66] Mark Stewart, "The Incredible Comeback of 'Skip' Alexander," 55; Alexander, telephone interviews, August 29 and October 7, 2019; Achenbach, "Inspiration, Revisited," 50.

[67] Alexander, telephone interview, August 29, 2019; McEwen, "Skip Alexander's Road Back," 71; Achenbach, "Inspiration, Revisited," 52.

[68] Alexander, telephone interview, October 7, 2019; Stewart, "The Incredible Comeback of 'Skip' Alexander," 55.

[69] Henry David Thoreau from Goodreads.com, https://www.goodreads.com/quotes/search?commit=Search&page=2&q=Thoreau&utf8=%E2%9C%93, accessed October 5, 2019.

Chapter 8: Senior Golfers – "Aging is First and Foremost a State of Mind"

[1] Grantland Rice, "The Youngsters," *The American Golfer*, March 12, 1921, 19.

[2] National Golf Foundation.org, https://www.ngf.org/golf-industry-research/, accessed October 7, 2019; Ryan Herrington, "National Golf Foundation sees Signs of Encouragement in Latest Annual Participation Report," Golf Digest.com, May 17, 2018, https://www.golfdigest.com/story/national-golf-foundation-sees-modest-signs-of-

encouragement-in-latest-annual-participation-report, accessed October 26, 2019; "Golfer's Creed" by Forgan, in *Golf*, September 1914, 174; Michael Murphy, *Golf in the Kingdom* (New York: Viking Arkana, 1994), 65.

[3] Sherwin B. Nuland, *The Art of Aging* (New York: Random House, 2007), 15; Victor Hugo from Brainy Quotes.com, https://www.brainyquote.com/quotes/victor_hugo_103906?src=t_age, accessed August 10, 2019.

[4] Charles Price, "Becoming a Senior," *Golf Magazine*, May 1979, 52.

[5] Satchel Page from Brainy Quote.com, https://www.brainyquote.com/quotes/satchel_paige_103901, accessed October 21, 2019; "A Phenomenal 60 at 71," *Golf Digest*, October 1983, 44.

[6] Kevin Robbins, "One for the Aged," *Golf Journal*, January/February 2000, 25; Brian Hewitt, "Jumpin' Jimenez," *Golfweek*, August 5, 1995, 1, 22. Jimenez shot 31-31=62, hit 16 greens, had 24 putts had a 295-yard drive on a 6,840-yard par 72 course.

[7] Vartan Kupelian, *Forever Scratch: Chuck Kocsis – An Amateur for the Ages* (Ann Arbor, MI: Sports Media Group, 2007), 8.

[8] Lynn Henning, "It Just Worked out This Way," *Golfweek*, May 15, 2000, 10; Kupelian, *Forever Scratch*, 2.

[9] Kupelian, *Forever Scratch*, 18-19, 98; John Gleason, "A Great Amateur – Chuck Kocsis." *Golf Journal*, September 1997, 52.

[10] Kupelian, *Forever Scratch*, 98, 7.

[11] Kupelian, *Forever Scratch*, 24; Buddy Alexander, telephone interview with the author, August 29, 2019.

[12] Alexander, telephone interview, August 29, 2019.

[13] Kupelian, *Forever Scratch*, 6, vi.

[14] "Super Senior," *Golf Magazine*, December 1998, 89.

[15] "Super Senior," 88-89; Brian Dimenna and Jeff Patterson, "Young at Heart," *Golf Digest*, November 2007, 136.

[16] Walt Roessing, "Still Swinging at 92," *Golf Digest*, October 1968, 34-36.

[17] Henry Hoople, "Dad Miller Still Breaks His Age...97," *Golf Journal*, April 1975, 20, 42; Lyla Dusing, "California's Dad Miller Going Strong at 101," *Golf Digest*, April 1979, 100, 99.

[18] Rich Skyzinski, "Breaking Eighty," *Golf Journal*, May 2002, 17-19; Robbins, "One for the Aged," 29. Margaret Dewberry shot her age, a 90 in 2000. Rose Montgomery shot 92 when she was 96 in 1992. See "She Can Almost Play Doug Ford Straight Up," *Golf World*, June 16, 2000, 8.

[19] "Senior Division," *Golf Digest*, November 1991, 16; Robbins, "One for the Aged," 25; Dimenna and Patterson, "Young at Heart," 136.

[20] Dimenna and Patterson, "Young at Heart," 134; "At 104, He's One for the Ages," *Golf Digest*, March 1991, 13; "Ageless," *Golf Digest*, October 1987, 14.

[21] Dimenna and Patterson, "Young at Heart," 134, 136; John Feinstein, "No Days off from Exercise," *Golf Digest*, May 2015, 124.

[22] Shelby Futch, "Still Great at 98," *Golf Digest*, December 2003, 116-117; Bill Fields, "'Breaking 90' With Ease," *Golf World*, February 2, 2007, 40.

[23] Margaret Roberts, "DeVoe Just Keeps Climbing the Heights," *Golf Digest*, May 1972, 80; Tom Sears, "DeVoe Disappointed Despite Win," *The Palm Beach Post* (West Palm Beach, FL), February 3, 1974, E1-2.

[24] Steve Melnikoff, "I Finally Started Talking About my War Experiences – Golf Helped With That," *Golf Magazine*, February 2019, 35-36.

[25] Jolee Edmondson, "The Remarkable Jimmy DeVoe," *Golf Magazine*, August 1976, 64-65; Feinstein, "No Days off from Exercise," 124.

[26] Roessing, "Still Swinging at 92," *Golf Digest*, October 1968, 36; Edmondson, "The Remarkable Jimmy DeVoe," 65-66.

Chapter 9: Pebble Beach – "The Fifth Hole and the Women Connected to its History"

[1] Neal Hotelling, *Pebble Beach: The Official Golf History* (Chicago: Triumph Books, 2009), 58; Prescott Sullivan, "The Low Down," *The San Francisco Examiner*, January 12, 1953, 32; Kenneth MacGowan, "Beautiful – But Tough," *The American Golfer*, September 1929, 17.
[2] Cameron Smith, "Follow the Money," *Golf Digest*, June 1992, 200; "Pebble Beach Historic Context Statement," Final Report, August 29, 2013, Prepared for Monterey County Parks Department by Page & Turnbull, Inc., San Francisco, California, 1, 60, https://www.co.monterey.ca.us/home/showdocument?id=37983, accessed October 4, 2019; Zachary Michael Jack, *Let There be Pebble: A Middle-Handicapper's Year in America's Garden of Golf* (Lincoln, NE: University of Nebraska Press, 2011), 132.
[3] Jack, *Let There be Pebble*, 134, 132; Charles Osborne, *Boss: The Story of S.F.B. Morse, the Founder of Pebble Beach* (Pebble Beach, California: Del Monte Publishing Co., 2018), 44.
[4] "Pebble Beach Historic Context Statement," 1; Smith, "Follow the Money," 200; Osborne, *Boss*, xvi.
[5] Julian P. Graham, *A Photographic Study of Pebble Beach Golf Links* (Carmel-by-the-Sea, California: Carmel Work Center, 1951), 20; Jack, *Let There be Pebble*, 132; Ron Whitten, "What You Might Not Know About Pebble Beach," Golf Digest.com, May 25, 2010, https://www.golfdigest.com/story/pebble-beach-not-know, accessed November 5, 2019; Robert Trent Jones, Jr., "Pebble Beach: Forbidding and Beautiful," *Golf Journal*, May/June 1982, 7.
[6] Susan Spano, "The Women Who Left Their Marks on California Parks," *The Santa Fe New Mexican*, July 30, 2000, 50; Hotelling, *Pebble Beach*, 65; "The New Fifth Hole," *The San Francisco Examiner*, June 4, 2000, 58.
[7] "Capitol," *Shamokin News-Dispatch* (Shamokin, PA), July 25, 1939, 9; "The New Fifth Hole," 58.
[8] "Ranch Scene of Nuptials," *The San Francisco Examiner*, August 2, 1951, 12; Neal Hotelling, email message to the author, July 29, 2019; David Kindred, "The Saga of Pebble's Fifth," *Golf Digest*, June 1998, 78; "Lathrop Brown and FDR: The Groton Years," The Franklin Delano Roosevelt Foundation, https://fdrfoundation.org/lathrop-brown-and-fdr-the-groton-years/, accessed November 1, 2019; Pam Grossman, telephone interview with the author, February 7, 2019.
[9] "Lathrop Brown, Ex-Bostonian, Congressman," *The Boston Globe*, November 29, 1959, 24. The company adopted the name Brown, Harris, and Stevens name in 1948. "Lathrop Brown," Biographical Directory of the United States Congress, 1774-Present," http://bioguide.congress.gov/scripts/biodisplay.pl?index=B000937, accessed November 4, 2019; Kindred, "The Saga of Pebble's Fifth," 78; "Lathrop Brown and FDR: 1905-1920," The Franklin Delano Roosevelt Foundation, https://fdrfoundation.org/lathrop-brown-and-fdr-1905-1920/, accessed November 3, 2019; "Lathrop Brown and FDR: Endgame," The Franklin Delano Roosevelt Foundation, http://fdrfoundation.org/lathrop-brown-and-fdr-endgame/, accessed November 3, 2019.
[10] "Lathrop Brown, Long After Harvard," The Franklin Delano Roosevelt Foundation, https://fdrfoundation.org/lathrop-brown-long-after-harvard/, November 3, 2019; "Julia Pfeiffer Burns State Park," Wikipedia.org, https://en.wikipedia.org/wiki/Julia_Pfeiffer_Burns_State_Park, accessed November 3, 2019; "Monterey Land Given to State," *Oakland Tribune*, September 15, 1961, 11. Helen had attended French boarding schools as a young woman and preferred the spelling Hélène.
[11] "Bob Canfield Gave Impetus to Skeet Shooting in East," *The Brooklyn Daily Eagle*, March 24, 1940, 36. Canfield was said to be a descendent of William Brewster, Mayflower passenger and religious leader of the Plymouth Colony, and theologian Jonathan Edwards; Pamela

Grossman, email message to the author, February 19, 2019.

[12] Whitney Martin, "Sports Trail," *The Daily Capital News* (Jefferson City, MO), August 5, 1942, 2; Oscar Fraley, "Skeeters Best Air Gunners," *Pittsburgh Press*, August 4, 1942, 21; Grossman, email message, February 19, 2019.

[13] Kindred, "The Saga of Pebble's Fifth," 78; Grossman, email message, February 19, 2019.

[14] Grossman, telephone interview, February 7, 2019; Liz Kahn, *The LPGA: The Unauthorized Version, The History of the Ladies Professional Golf Association* (Menlo Park, CA: Group Fore Productions, Inc., 1996), 19; Nancy Wolloch, *Women and the American Experience* (New York: Alfred A. Knopf, 1984), 461.

[15] "Major Canfield, Formerly at Gunnery, Dies in Action," *News-Press* (Fort Myers, FL), January 30, 1944, 1; H.L. Betten, "Rod and Gun," *The San Francisco Examiner*, November 28, 1943, 40.

[16] "Ranch Scene of Nuptials," 12; Grossman, telephone interview, February 7, 2019 and email message February 19, 2019.

[17] Kindred, "The Saga of Pebble's Fifth," 78; Hotelling, *Pebble Beach*, 65.

[18] Kindred, "The Saga of Pebble's Fifth," 78; Grossman, telephone interview, February 7, 2019; "Pamela's Party – A Hard One to Top," *The San Francisco Examiner*, June 12, 1962, 22.

[19] Kindred, "The Saga of Pebble's Fifth," 77.

[20] Grossman, telephone interview, February 7, 2019. The fire department was in Carmel and since the house had no address, they had trouble finding it in time to save it from destruction; "The Second Hurdle to Golf's Grail," *Golf World*, June 13, 1972, 22; Kindred, "The Saga of Pebble's Fifth," 77.

[21] Lathrop Brown, *Charles Stelle Brown (1851-1935): A Biographical Memoir with Genealogical Notes* (New York: privately published, 1937), 9-11, https://ia902807.us.archive.org/30/items/charlesstellebro00brow/charlesstellebro00brow.pdf, accessed November 5, 2019; Yohanna Von Wagner, "Tenement-House Inspection," *The American Journal of Nursing* 2, no. 7 (April 1902): 510; Francis R. Cope, Jr., "Tenement House Reform: Its Practical Results in the 'Battle Row' District, New York," *American Journal of Sociology* 7, no. 3 (November 1901): 334; Robert W. de Forest, "Tenement House Regulation-The Reasons for It-Its Proper Limitations," *The Annals of the American Academy of Political and Social Science* 20 (July 1902), 83.

[22] Cope, Jr., "Tenement House Reform: Its Practical Results in the 'Battle Row' District, New York," 335-336.

[23] Von Wagner, "Tenement-House Inspection," 510.

[24] Brown, *Charles Stelle Brown (1851-1935)*, 33, 11.

[25] Benjamin G. Rader, *American Sports: From the Age of Folk Games to the Age of Televised Sports* (Upper Saddle River, NJ: Prentice Hall, 1983), 23.

[26] Donald Spivey, ed., *Sport in America: New Historical Perspectives* (Westport, CT: Greenwood Press, 1985), 196; "Albion" [pseudonym] "Golf for Women" *Outing*, December 1890, 231.

[27] Donald J. Mrozek, *Sport and American Mentality, 1880-1910* (Knoxville, TN: The University of Tennessee Press, 1983), 138; Spivey, *Sport in America*, 194, 202; Susan K. Cahn, *Coming on Strong: Gender and Sexuality in Twentieth-Century Women's Sport* (New York: The Free Press, 1994), 3-4.

[28] This condition of requiring players to be members of "USGA Regular Clubs" was not changed until 1978 (taking effect in the 1979 for the U.S. Amateur, Women's Amateur, Senior Amateur, and Senior Women's Amateur championships.)

[29] "Champion Lady Golfer," *The New York Times*, November 10, 1895, 6; "Golf for High Honors," *The Sun* (New York), November 10, 1895, 9.

[30] "Champion Lady Golfer," 6; *New York Herald*, November 10, 1895, page 3 of typed transcript of an article in the 1895 U.S. Women's Amateur file, USGA.

[31] Malcolm Crane, *The Story of Ladies' Golf* (London: Stanley Paul, 1991), 145; Will Grimsby, *Golf: Its History, People, and Events* (New York: Prentice Hall, 1966), 204; Alexa Stirling, "Alexa Williamson Stirling: An Autobiography," *Golf Illustrated*, March 1917, 18.

[32] "Champion Lady Golfer," 6; *New York Herald*, typed transcript page 1-2; Genevieve Hecker, "Golf for Women," *Golf*, January 1902, 8.

[33] "Women Golfer's at Ardsley," *The New York Times*, November 15, 1899, 9.

[34] Archibald Brown became a prominent New York City architect and married the daughter of Shinnecock Hills founder and ex-USGA Executive Committee member Samuel Parrish. Archibald would also serve as president at Shinnecock Hills. He also donated his mother's trophy to the USGA in 1952 after finding it, forgotten, in a trunk. See "Through the Green," *Golf Journal*, July 2000, 5 and "How Times Have Changed," *Golf World*, August 22, 1952, 14; Brown, *Charles Stelle Brown (1851-1935)*, 12, 33.

[35] Kindred, "The Saga of Pebble's Fifth," 78; "Pebble Beach Held Hostage?" *Golf Digest*, December 1983, 35; Hotelling, *Pebble Beach*, 65.

[36] "The New Fifth Hole," 58.

[37] Whitten, "What You Might Not Know About Pebble Beach"; Jack, *Let There be Pebble*, 134-135; Andra Kirkaldy, *Fifty Years of Golf: Memories* (London: T. Fisher Unwin, Ltd., 1921), 166-167; Clifford Roberts, *The Story of the Augusta National Golf Club* (New York: Doubleday and Company, 1976), 32-33. When discussing the treacherous, swirling winds that tormented players over the years, Roberts claimed "some of the players are wondering if the spiritual displeasures of an Indian chieftain are causing the trouble."

[38] "The Missing Link," *The Palm Beach Post* (West Palm Beach, FL), June 15, 2000, 55; "The New Fifth Hole," 58; Grossman, telephone interview, February 7, 2019.

[39] "Fifth Hole Fits Golfers to a Tee," *Honolulu Star-Bulletin*, June 14, 2000, 37; "The Old 5th at Pebble Beach," Golf Course Architecture, GolfClubAtlas.com, http://www.golfclubatlas.com/forum/index.php?topic=51085.0;wap2, accessed November 5, 2019; "The Opening of a New Fifth," *Golf Journal*, January/February 1999, 5.

[40] Henry Roberts, "New Links Easier to Medal at Del Monte," *The San Francisco Examiner*, September 16, 1920, 10.

[41] Osborne, *Boss*, xv; Kindred, "The Saga of Pebble's Fifth," 78.

Chapter 10: The St Andrews "Rabbit Wars" of 1801-1821

[1] David Hay Fleming, *Historical Notes & Extracts Concerning the Links of St. Andrews, 1552-1893* (St. Andrews: Citizen Office, 1893), 1-2. There a many spelling variations of Pilmor in various sources: Pilmure, Pilmour, Pilmore, Pilmuir.

[2] John Behrend and Peter N. Lewis, *Challenges and Champions: The Royal & Ancient Golf Club, 1754-1883* (St Andrews: The Royal & Ancient Golf Club, 1998), 48; Alistair Beaton Adamson, *Millions of Mischiefs: Rabbits, Golf & St Andrews* (Malvern: Peachfield Press, 1990), 3, 2; Tom Jarrett, *St Andrews Golf Links: The First 600 Years* (Edinburgh: Mainstream Publishing Company, 1995), 25; Fleming, *Historical Notes & Extracts*, 16.

[3] Jarrett, *St Andrews Golf Links*, 27; Adamson, *Millions of Mischiefs*, 2; Fleming, *Historical Notes & Extracts*, 17. The disposition date in favor of the Dempsters was December 4, 1799.

[4] Behrend and Lewis, *Challenges and Champions*, 51; George Cheape to Lord Provost, Magistrates & Town Council, October 8, 1801, Box 70 (B65/22/70), Burgh of St Andrews Records, University of St Andrews, Richardson Research Library, Special Collections Division, St Andrews, Scotland (hereafter Burgh of St Andrews Records.)

[5] H.S.C. Everard, *A History of the Royal & Ancient Golf Club St Andrews from 1754-1900* (London: William Blackwood and Sons, 1907), 101-102; Behrend and Lewis, *Challenges and Champions*, 52.

[6] Everard, *A History of the Royal & Ancient Golf Club*; Jarrett, *St Andrews Golf Links*, 27.

[7] Adamson, *Millions of Mischiefs*, 6, 18; Behrend and Lewis, *Challenges and Champions*, 52.

[8] "State of the Process" report, December 17, 1805, 1-2, Box 11, Legal Papers, Cheape Family of Strathtyrum and Lathockar papers (MsDep 76), University of St Andrews, Special Collections Division (hereafter Cheape Papers.) Page 6 states that "The part over which golf is played, will measure from ten to twelve acres." In a meeting of town magistrates with James Lumsdaine, Esquire of Strathtyrum on October 26, 1769 it was agreed "that the part of the Links as presently golfed upon shall be kept entire, and not ploughed up nor enclosed by the Town of St Andrews or their tenants." See Fleming, *Historical Notes & Extracts*, 12.

[9] "State of the Process" report, 1-2, 5, Cheape Papers; Everard, *A History of the Royal & Ancient Golf Club*, 283, 290-291. The plaintiffs wanted the Dempsters to pay James Cheape and John Hood (his tenant at Balgrove farm) £50 for damage done to the property, and £100 to "said pursuers."

[10] Fleming, *Historical Notes & Extracts*, 35-36; "State of the Process" report, 19, Cheape Papers.

[11] "State of the Process" report, 23-24, 10, Cheape Papers; Everard, *A History of the Royal & Ancient Golf Club*, 285; Minutes of Town Council, February 17, 1806, Burgh of St Andrews Records.

[12] On February 17, 1806 the Town Council ruled that residents could destroy the rabbits. Twenty-six council members attended the meeting and only Charles Dempster and Robert Richard did not vote. See Fleming, *Historical Notes & Extracts*, 26, 42.

[13] Demptser advertisement, July 19, 1806, Box 12, Miscellaneous Correspondence, Cheape Papers.

[14] Minutes of the Town Council, September 24, 1726, Volume 3 – February 17, 1708-January 6, 1729, (B65/11/3), Burgh of St Andrews Records; Fleming, *Historical Notes & Extracts*, 8; Everard, *A History of the Royal & Ancient Golf Club*, 294.

[15] Cathcart Demptser advertisement, July 19, 1806, Cheape Papers. Information on the Dempsters provided to the author by the great-great-great granddaughter of Cathcart Dempster, Brenda Barnett, July 6, 2012.

[16] "Reply by Magistrates of St Andrews and Society of Golfers to the Dempsters," July 26, 1806, Miscellaneous Correspondence, Cheape Papers; Everard, *A History of the Royal & Ancient Golf Club*, 284, 102-103; Behrend and Lewis, *Challenges and Champions*, 54.

[17] Adamson, *Millions of Mischiefs*, 34; Everard, *A History of the Royal & Ancient Golf Club*, 103.

[18] Everhard, *A History of the Royal & Ancient Golf Club*, 300-301; Behrend and Lewis, *Challenges and Champions*, 55; Miscellaneous Correspondence, (undated "Notes"), Cheape Papers.

[19] Miscellaneous Correspondence, (undated "Notes"), Cheape Papers. This case was upon appeal remitted to the Court of Session for further consideration on December 3, 1813, but after that no further proceedings took place in the case.

[20] Miscellaneous Correspondence (genealogies), Cheape Papers; Jarrett, *St Andrews Golf Links*, 146.

[21] "State of the Process" report, 12, 64-65, Cheape Papers.

[22] Letters, 1819-1821, Box 7, Cheape Papers.

[23] Ibid.

[24] Pat Ward-Thomas, *The Royal and Ancient* (Edinburgh: Scottish Academic Press, 1980), 10; St Andrews Links Trust.com, "Green Fees," https://www.standrews.com/play/green-fees, accessed November 2, 2019.

[25] Everhard, *A History of the Royal & Ancient Golf Club*, 39-40.

[26] Letters, 1819-1821, Cheape Papers.

[27] Cheape died October 25, 1824. See Andrew Campbell, *Fife Deaths 1822-1854*, University of St Andrews, Special Collections Division; Jarrett, *St Andrews Golf Links*, 147-149.

Chapter 11: Not Quite Good Enough – "Sexism, Class, and Racism in Women's Golf"

[1] David E. Outerbridge, *Champion in a Man's World: The Biography of Marion Hollins* (Chelsea, MI: Sleeping Bear Press, 1998), 148.
[2] David B. Welky, "Viking Girls, Mermaids, and Little Brown Men: U.S. Journalism and the 1932 Olympics," *Journal of Sport History* 24, no. 1 (Spring 1997): 32-33. At the Olympics, Babe won the gold medal in the javelin and 80-meter hurdles, and the silver in the high jump.
[3] Susan K. Cahn, "From the 'Muscle Moll' to the 'Butch' Ballplayer: Mannishness, Lesbianism, and Homophobia in U.S. Women's Sport Author," *Feminist Studies* 19, no. 2 (Summer 1993): 349, 351.
[4] Don Van Natta, Jr., *Wonder Girl: The Magnificent Sporting Life of Babe Didrikson Zaharias* (New York: Little, Brown and Company, 2011), 140, 144.
[5] Paul Gallico, *Farewell to Sport* (New York: Alfred A. Knopf, 1941), 239; Susan E. Cayleff, *Babe: The Life and Legend of Babe Didrikson Zaharias* (Urbana, Illinois: University of Illinois Press, 1995), 118.
[6] Cayleff, *Babe*, 20; William H. Chafe, *The American Woman: Her Changing Social, Economic, and Political Roles, 1920-1970* (New York: Oxford University Press, 1972), 100.
[7] "When Ladies Compete," *Sports Illustrated and The American Golfer*, August 1936, 9, 8, 44.
[8] Cayleff, *Babe*, 92; Jack Newcombe, "The Incomparable Babe Didrikson," *Sport*, December 1959, 73.
[9] Cayleff, *Babe*, 2, 88.
[10] William Oscar Johnson and Nancy P. Williamson, *Whatta-Gal: The Babe Didrikson Story* (Boston: Little, Brown and Company, 1977), 74, 132; Van Natta, *Wonder Girl*, 141, 147.
[11] Gallico, *Farewell to Sport*, 242; "When Ladies Compete,"44; Johnson and Williamson, *Whatta-Gal*, 133.
[12] Rhonda Glenn, *The Illustrated History of Women's Golf* (Dallas, Texas: Taylor Trade Publishing, 1991), 136.
[13] Johnson and Williamson, *Whatta-Gal*, 142-144. Chandler was the medalist with a 79, Babe was second with an 85 on the River Oaks Country Club course in Houston. See "Mrs. Chandler of Dallas Medalist in Texas Women's Golf Association Tourney," *The Times* (Shreveport, LA), April 23, 1935, 12.
[14] Johnson and Williamson, *Whatta-Gal*, 145; Bill Parker, "Didrikson Beats Chandler 2 Up for Texas Title," *Abilene Morning Reporter-News* (TX), April 28, 1935, 5.
[15] Van Natta, *Wonder Girl*, 173; Gallico, *Farewell to Sport*, 241-242; Peggy Chandler to Connie Sullivan, January 7, 1936, in 1936 Curtis Cup files, USGA.
[16] Cayleff, *Babe*, 157; Rhonda Glenn, "A Friend Remembers Babe Zaharias," *Golf Journal*, July 1984, 30.
[17] Nancy Isenberg, *White Trash: The 400-Year Untold Story of Class in America* (New York: Viking, 2016), 225-227; Glenn, *The Illustrated History of Women's Golf*, 147; Van Natta, Jr., *Wonder Girl*, 36.
[18] Connie Sullivan (Mrs. Willard P. Sullivan) to John G. Jackson, April 24, 1935, Box 1, Folder 5, Connie Sullivan Papers (hereafter Sullivan Papers), USGA.
[19] Connie Sullivan to A.M. Reid, April 25, 1935, Sullivan Papers.
[20] Sullivan to Reid, April 25, 1935, Sullivan Papers; Parker, "Didrikson Beats Chandler 2 Up for Texas Title," 5.
[21] Van Natta, *Wonder Girl*, 173; Connie Sullivan to Mrs. George Thompson, Jr., April 30, 1935, Sullivan Papers.
[22] "Amateur Status Committee of USGA Begins Investigation of 'Babe' Didrikson's Career," *St. Louis Post-Dispatch*, April 30, 1935, 17; Connie Sullivan to A.M. Reid, May 8, 1935, Sullivan Papers.
[23] "USGA Bars Babe Didrikson from U.S. Meet," *St. Louis Post-Dispatch*, May 14, 1935, 13;

Van Natta, *Wonder Girl*, 176.

[24] Van Natta, *Wonder Girl*, 175.

[25] Van Natta, *Wonder Girl*, 176; Bill Parker, "Through with all Except Golf," *Longview News-Journal* (Longview, TX), April 23, 1935, 5.

[26] "Amateur Status Committee of USGA Begins Investigation of Babe Didrikson's Career," 17; Paul Gallico, "Ban on Didrikson Takes Excitement Out of Tournament," *Salt Lake Telegram*, May 15, 1935, 19.

[27] "Entry in Southern Championship Also Rejected," *The New York Times*, May 15, 1935, 29; Ralph Trost, "Mary K. Brown Case Recalls Reasoning of U.S, Governing Body," *The Brooklyn Daily Eagle*, May 15, 1935, 25; Gallico, "Ban on Didrikson Takes Excitement Out of Tournament," 19.

[28] Gallico, "Ban on Didrikson Takes Excitement Out of Tournament," 19; "Terms Action as 'Silly," *The Gazette* (Montreal, Canada), May 16, 1935, 17.

[29] Henry McClemore, "Today's Sport Parade," *The Tribune* (Coshocton, OH), May 18, 1935, 6; Bill Parker, "Texas Pro Golfers Hasten to Defend Babe Didrikson," *Star-Phoenix* (Saskatoon, Canada), May 16, 1935, 15.

[30] "Sentiment of Scribes with Babe Didrikson in Ruling of National Golf Officials," *The Times* (Shreveport, LA), May 16, 1935, 17; "Babe Didrikson Golf Ban Laid to 'Snootiness,'" *El Paso Herald-Post*, May 24, 1935, 1.

[31] "Babe Didrikson Asks Explanation of Ban," *The St. Louis Star and Times*, May 20, 1935, 16; "Babe Didrikson Takes her Latest Snub by USGA with Head Up," *The Brooklyn Citizen*, May 15, 1935, 6.

[32] Cayleff, *Babe*, 129; Johnson and Williamson, *Whatta-Gal*, 153.

[33] Gallico, *Farewell to Sport*, 240, 244; Jack Sher, "The Amazing Amazon," *Sport*, June 1948, 33.

[34] Marilynn Smith with Bob Cayne, *Have Clubs, Will Travel* (Goodyear, AZ: Ambassador Publishing, 2012), 6-7; Cayleff, *Babe*, 164.

[35] "When Ladies Compete," 9; Liz Kahn, *The LPGA: The Unauthorized Version, The History of the Ladies Professional Golf Association* (Menlo Park, CA: Group Fore Productions, Inc., 1996), ii.

[36] Carol Mann, interview by Alice Kendrick, July 8, 1992, USGA Oral History Collection, 69; Kahn, *The LPGA*, 148.

[37] Kathy Whitworth, interview by Alice Kendrick, January 23, 1993, USGA Oral History Collection, 5-6.

[38] Rhonda Glenn, "Betty Jameson Claimed Title at Del Monte Golf & C.C," August 3, 2010, http://www.usga.org/articles/2010/08/1940-womens-amateur-was-great-theater-2147489480.html, accessed October 28, 2019.

[39] Vivian Gornick, "Ladies of the Links," *Look*, May 18, 1971, 69; Bil Gilbert, "Can a Girl Find Happiness Under 80?" *Saturday Evening Post*, September 25, 1965, 35.

[40] Kahn, *The LPGA*, 36.

[41] Buddy Martin, "Lacking Sex Appeal," *The Daily Times* (Mamaroneck, NY), July 3, 1972.

[42] "1972 U.S. Women's Open Championship #3/3," You Tube.com, https://www.youtube.com/watch?v=eMJ_OTIipf8&list=PLfTXtdtH3b0POvD-vpHRDIjro-stPWEKt, accessed September 4, 2019.

[43] Roger Vaughan, *Golf: The Woman's Game* (New York: Stewart, Tabori & Chang, 2000), 102; May, "The Man Behind the Woman Pros," 46; "Orientation Rules" of the LPGA (c.1965) in Leonard Wirtz collection, USGA.

[44] Cahn, "From the 'Muscle Moll' to the 'Butch' Ballplayer," 356; Susan Brownmiller, *Femininity* (New York: Simon & Schuster, 1984), 235.

[45] Steve Goldstein, "Sex vs. Sock," *Golf Magazine*, June 1981, 65; Ray Volpe, preface to *Fairway* insert in *Golf Magazine*, February 1976, 99; Steve Cady, "Women Golfers Above Par in Dress," *The New York Times*, July 2, 1972, 4.

[46] Goldstein, "Sex vs. Sock," 65-66; Lisa D. Mickey, "Three LPGA Aces," *Golf Digest*, December 2000, 182.

[47] Goldstein, "Sex vs. Sock," 66-67; *Golf Digest*, September 1972, 17; Marlene Hagge, "Inside the LPGA Tour," *Golf Digest*, May 1977, 170.

[48] Carol Troy, "Total Immersion at the U.S. Open," *Women Sports*, December 1974, 35; "1972 U.S. Women's Open Championship #1/3," You Tube.com, https://www.youtube.com/watch?v=iyWj0I-4Nh0&list=PLfTXtdtH3b0POvD-vpHRDIjro-stPWEKt, accessed September 1, 2019.

[49] Luke Kerr-Dineen, "The Story of the Woman who Brought Sex to the LPGA Tour," *USA Today*, July 10, 2015, http://ftw.usatoday.com/2015/07/the-story-of-the-woman-who-brought-sex-to-the-lpga-tour, accessed October 29, 2019.

[50] Peter Kessler, "Golf Talk: Jan Stephenson," *Golf Magazine*, November 2003, 126; Kerr-Dineen, "The Story of the Woman who Brought Sex to the LPGA Tour."

[51] "The Colonel" [pseudonym], "Obiter Dicta," 401; "Humors of Golf as Played at Van Cortlandt Park," *The New York Times*, June 26, 1910, 32.

[52] George B. Kirsch, *Golf in America* (Chicago: University of Illinois Press, 2009), 29; "Mr. Webster's, 'Etc.,'" *Golfing*, May 1936, 21.

[53] Marshall Smith, "Please Lady, Get Off my Golf Course," *Life*, June 17, 1966, 106; Dick Miller, "No Dogs or Women Allowed," *Golf Magazine*, March 1969, 76-77.

[54] Marcia Chambers, "A Matter of Control," *Golf Digest*, May 2000, 203-204.

[55] David L. Hudson, Jr., *Women in Golf: The Players, the History, and the Future of the Sport* (Westport, CT: Praeger, 2008), 117.

[56] David Kligman, "Discrimination against Women Still Pervasive," *Golfweek*, September 9, 1995, 26. In 1990, the Olympic Club of San Francisco, founded in 1860, agreed to admit women, although several all male and all-female clubs endured in San Francisco despite a city ordinance that outlawed discrimination based on race or sex. See "Feminist Chronicles – 1990," http://www.feminist.org/research/chronicles/fc1990.html, accessed August 30, 2019.

[57] Marcia Chambers, *The Unplayable Lie: The Untold Story of Women and Discrimination in American Golf* (New York: Pocket Books, 1995), 93-94.

[58] Ann Gregory, interview by Rhonda Glenn, September 1988, USGA Oral History Collection, 4-5; M. Mikell Johnson, *The African American Woman Golfer: Her Legacy* (Westport, CT: Praeger, 2008), 41, 44, 46; Richard J. Moss, *The Kingdom of Golf in America* (Lincoln, Nebraska: University of Nebraska Press, 2013, 238-239. Gregory continued to win tournaments and when the Chicago Women's Golf Club became a member USGA club in 1956, she was eligible to play in USGA events.

[59] Rhonda Glenn, "Playing Through Racial Barriers," The Vault, *Sports Illustrated*, May 20, 1991, http://www.si.com/vault/1991/05/20/124241/playing-through-racial-barriers-ann-gregory-made-her-mark-in-amateur-golf-as-the-first-black-woman-to-play-on-the-national-level, accessed August 30, 2019. In 1971 Gregory nearly won the U.S. Senior Women's Amateur. In the final round of stroke play, her old rival and friend Carolyn Cudone parred the last hole to beat Gregory by a single stroke.

[60] Glenn, *The Illustrated History of Women's Golf*, 216; "Ann Gregory Nearly Pulls USGA Upset," *The Pittsburgh Courier*, September 29, 1956, 27.

[61] Gregory, interview by Rhonda Glenn, 6, 8; Bill Fields, "The Gospel According to Joe Dey," *Golf World*, June 7, 2002, 84, 86.

[62] JoAnne Carner, interview by Alice Kendrick, February 10, 1992, USGA Oral History Collection, 14.

[63] Peter Stevens, "The Natural," *Golf Journal*, September 1998, 53; Glenn, *The Illustrated History of Women's Golf*, 214; Interview transcript in the Box 2, Folder 14, Rhonda Glenn Collection, USGA.

[64] Glenn, *The Illustrated History of Women's Golf*, 213; Kahn, *The LPGA*, 125.

[65] Will Grimsley, "Althea Plans Golf Career," *The Bridgeport Post*, March 7, 1962; Kahn, *The LPGA*, 125-126; Renee Powell interview by Rhonda Glenn, USGA Oral History Collection, 2011, 83.

[66] Kahn, *The LPGA*, 126-127.

[67] "People of the USGA," *Golf Journal*, September 1995, 36.

[68] Pete McDaniel, "Powell's Legacy: He Persevered, For the Good of the Game," Golf Digest.com, August 13, 2009, https://www.golfdigest.com/story/powells-legacy-he-persevered-for-the-good-of-the-game, accessed October 2, 2019; Renee Powell biographical file, USGA.

[69] Powell interview by Rhonda Glenn, 107, 110.

[70] "IMG Speakers - Renee Powell Golf Champion," in Renee Powell biographical file, USGA.

Chapter 12: The Rest of the Story – "Honorable and Dishonorable Mention"

[1] Herb Graffis, "Hanging on the Lip," *Golfing*, April 1939, 5.

[2] "Excerpts from the 'War' Broadcast," *The New York Times*, November 1, 1938, 26; Internet Sacred Text Archive.com, https://www.sacred-texts.com/ufo/mars/wow.htm, accessed October 22, 2019.

[3] Graffis, "Hanging on the Lip," 5. Another account has Fred Corcoran being the passenger in the car. See Herbert Warren Wind, "World's Toughest Golf Course," *Holiday*, June 1954, 62.

[4] "Radio Listeners in Panic, Taking War Drama as Fact," *The New York Times*, October 31, 1938, 1.

[5] Bill Gaffney, "Golf Gossip," *The Morning Post* (Camden, NJ), November 2, 1938, 21; Ralph Trost, "Golf Season on into November," *The Brooklyn Daily Eagle*, November 1, 1938, 15.

[6] "The 'Attack from Mars,'" *The New York Times*, November 2, 1938, 22; James W. Finegan, *Pine Valley Golf Club: A Unique Haven of the Game* (Pine Valley Golf Club, 2000), 73.

[7] "The Campbells," *Golf World*, September 17, 1954, 16; Ray Kienzyl, "USGA President Calls Job 'Many-Splendored Thing,'" *Pittsburgh Press*, April 5, 1983.

[8] Bill Campbell to Ben Hogan, December 28, 1982 and Bill Campbell to Ben Hogan, February 4, 1983, both in 1983 U.S. Open file, USGA.

[9] "The One-Club Record," *Golf Digest*, October 1984, 31.

[10] Vartan Kupelian, *Forever Scratch: Chuck Kocsis – An Amateur for the Ages* (Ann Arbor, MI: Sports Media Group, 2007), 6.

[11] "A 76 With One Club," *Golf Digest*, April 1983, NE-12.

[12] Peter Andrews, "The Search for America's Worst Avid Golfer," *Golf Digest*, May 1985, 51; Scott Smith, "Still the Worst," *Golf Digest*, July 1999, 21.

[13] Lois Hains and John P. May, "Unusual Feats of 1985," *Golf Digest*, February 1986, 80; "36-56 – 92 and Why," *Golf World*, January 18, 1952, 3.

[14] *Golf World*, October 5, 1949, 10; David Kindred, "Establishing a New Low," *Golf Digest*, August 2012, 69-70; "Mr. 57," *Golf Digest*, September 1994, 14; "Record Setter," *Golf Digest*, March 1990, 14; "13-year-old Scores 58!" *Golf Digest*, September 1976, 29.

[15] Barry McDermott, "Hold up Your Head, Tom Doty," *Sports Illustrated*, January 17, 1972, 45.

[16] Ibid., 44.

[17] McDermott, "Hold up Your Head, Tom Doty," 45; "2 Double Eagles, 2 Eagles (and 2 Aces!) in 4 Consecutive Holes," *Golf Digest*, February 1972, 6.

[18] Will Gray, "Report: Virginia Golfer Makes 3 Aces, Shoots 57," June 26, 2015, Golf Channel.com, https://www.golfchannel.com/article/golf-central-blog/va-golfer-makes-three-aces-shoots-57, accessed November 30, 2019.

[19] Joe Horgan, "Early Days of American Golf: Chapter 1," *The Southern Golfer*, December 1925, 18; Joe Horgan, "Memoirs of an Ancient Caddie: Part 1," *Golfing*, March 1956, 28-29;

Joe Horgan, "Early Days of American Golf: Chapter 2," *The Metropolitan Golfer*, January 1926, 14. A partial list of champions Horgan caddied for and their wins:

Beatrix Hoyt, U.S. Women's Amateur (1897, 1898)

Findlay Douglas, U.S. Amateur (1898)

Jerome Travers, U.S. Amateur (1913) and U.S. Open (1915)

Harry Vardon, U.S. Open (1900 – also caddied for him in losses in 1913 and 1920)

Willie Anderson, U.S. Open (1901, 1905)

Laurie Auchterlonie, U.S. Open (1902)

Fred McLeod, U.S. Open (1908)

Genevieve Hecker, U.S. Women's Amateur (1902)

Edith Cummings, U.S. Women's Amateur (1923)

[20] Joe Horgan, "Memoirs of an Ancient Caddie: Part 1," *Golfing*, March 1956, 34; John Webster, "Sportscope," unidentified newspaper clipping in 1950 U.S. Open file, USGA.

[21] Luke Ross as told to Tom Place, "I Caddied for Jones when He Threw Clubs," *Golf Digest*, April 1969, 76.

[22] Ibid., 76, 78.

[23] Ross, "I Caddied for Jones when He Threw Clubs," 79; "Itinerant Caddy Under Ban in National Open," *Star Tribune* (Minneapolis, MN), April 25, 1926, 45.

[24] "Jones' Caddie at Merion," *Golf Digest*, June 1981, 33.

[25] Ibid., 33-34.

[26] Frank Finney, "Meet Doctor Buzzard," *The American Golfer*, March 1931, 37.

[27] Clifford Roberts, *The Story of the Augusta National Golf Club* (New York: Doubleday and Company, 1976), 45.

[28] Judy Frank, "Those Irreverent Caddies," *Golf Magazine*, May 1959, 37; Duke Hancock, "I Saw Better Golf in the '20s." *Golf Digest*, May 1958, 34. Hancock caddied for Sarazen when he won the U.S. Open in 1922 and 1932 and the PGA in 1922, 1923, and 1933.

[29] Hancock, "I Saw Better Golf in the '20s." *Golf Digest*, May 1958, 35; Frank, "Those Irreverent Caddies," 38.

[30] Don Wade, "People in Golf – Out of the Crowd and Onto Your Screen," *Golf Digest*, June 1982, TV12.

[31] "A Rollen Stone," *Golf Digest*, October 1983, 4; "Hair Freak Joins Hoopla," *Marion Star* (OH), January 21, 1979, 16; Wade, "People in Golf," TV12.

[32] Wade, "People in Golf," TV12; Guy Yocom, "Frank Chirkinian – My Shot," *Golf Digest*, September 2003, 111; Orley Hood, "There May be a Warning with Rockin' Rollen," *Clarion-Ledger* (Jackson, MS), July 18, 1993, 49.

[33] "Inconsiderate Gallery follows Bobby Jones," *The Brooklyn Daily Eagle*, July 9, 1926, 15.

[34] David Barrett, "Don't Fence In," *Golf World*, August 12, 2005, 26, 28; Bill Lee, "With Malice Toward None," *Harford Courant*, August 13, 1960, 31.

[35] Joe Williams, "English Golf Galleries Criticized for Behavior," *The Post Crescent* (Appleton, WI), July 6, 1937, 15.

[36] Barrett, "Don't Fence In," 26, 28.

[37] "Roping Off," *Golf World*, October 10, 1952, 8-9.

[38] Barrett, "Don't Fence In," 26; Will Grimsley, "Are the Galleries Getting Too Big?" *Golf Magazine*, November 1962, 61.

[39] "To Rope or not to Rope," *Golf World*, November 2, 1956, 16; Barrett, "Don't Fence In," 28.

[40] "To Rope or not to Rope," 16; "Ignorance of the Law," *Golf World*, August 24, 1956, 7.

[41] Frank Beard, "Golf's Crowds are a Show in Themselves," *Golf Digest*, May 1977, 159.

[42] Barrett, "Don't Fence In," 26; Will Grimsley, "Are the Galleries Getting Too Big?" 21.

[43] "What They Are Saying," *Golf Digest*, May 1968, 111; "Women's PGA Ex-President was on Plane," *The Palm Beach Post* (West Palm Beach, FL), February 22, 1968, 7.

[44] Women's PGA Ex-President was on Plane," 7; "Jet with 109 Back after Cuba Hijack," *The*

Boston Globe, February 22, 1968, 1; "What They Are Saying," 111.

[45] "Cupid Defeats Champion," *The Indianapolis Journal*, October 18, 1903, 8.

[46] John P. May, "Golf First, Marriage Next," *Golf Digest*, May 1957, 54; "Golf Champion Married," *The Herald* (Jasper, IN), November 6, 1903, 3; "Cupid Defeats Champion," 8.

[47] "Woman Golf Champion Dead," *Chicago Tribune*, November 23, 1912, 5.

[48] Charles Blair Macdonald was an American who came to St Andrews as a 16-year-old in 1872 to study. He brought the game back with him, founded the Chicago Golf Club in 1892, and won the 1895 U.S. Amateur.

[49] W. T. Linskill, "Random Rambling Recollections of St Andrews," *St Andrews Citizen*, November 19, 1927, on page labeled 52 of Scrapbook of W.T. Linskill (ms 380878/1), Special Collections Division, St Andrews University, St Andrews, Scotland (hereafter Linskill Scrapbook.) "Sonsie" means friendly, attractive, buxom, comely, or good-looking.

[50] W. T. Linskill, "More Rambling Recollections About St Andrews," *St Andrews Citizen*, December 3, 1927, on page labeled 53 of Linskill Scrapbook.

[51] Harry Cooper interview by J. Robert Windsor, USGA Oral History Collection, September 10 and 17, 1990, 140.

[52] "Didrikson Files Entry in U.S. Open," *Chicago Tribune*, March 6, 1948, 21.

[53] "Pro Golfers Pick Hogan to Win Open; Would Permit Babe Zaharias to Enter," *Hartford Courant*, April 4, 1948, 52; News Release, April 7, 1948, from 1948 U.S. Open file, USGA.

[54] "U.S.G.A. Bans Babe Zaharias from Open Golf," *The Decatur Herald* (Decatur, IL), 13; Robert L. Burnes, "The Bench Warmer," *St. Louis Globe-Democrat*, April 8, 1948, 21.